Holland House and Portugal

Holland House and Portugal

English Whiggery and the Constitutional Cause in Iberia

José Baptista de Sousa

ANTHEM PRESS

Anthem Press
An imprint of Wimbledon Publishing Company
www.anthempress.com

This edition first published in UK and USA 2018
by ANTHEM PRESS
75–76 Blackfriars Road, London SE1 8HA, UK
or PO Box 9779, London SW19 7ZG, UK
and
244 Madison Ave #116, New York, NY 10016, USA

British Library Cataloguing-in-Publication Data
A catalogue record for this book is available from the British Library.

ISBN-13: 978-1-78308-756-3 (Hbk)
ISBN-10: 1-78308-756-0 (Hbk)

This title is also available as an e-book.

To my grandmother, Mimi,

&

my mother, Maria Elvira

CONTENTS

Part 3. Aftermath

FOREWORD

The salon at Holland House, presided over by the formidable Lady Holland herself, is well known as a major institution in British political and cultural history. It is rightly regarded as at least as important as the rival salons of Dorothea Lieven and the Duchess of Dino. Anecdotes abound – for example, the occasion when Lady Holland sent a note to T. B. Macaulay asking him not to dominate the conversation. But the conversation then flagged and Lady Holland was forced to send another note to Macaulay which read 'Please *do* dominate the conversation Mr. Macaulay.' The salon was at its most influential in the 1820s and 1830s, with Lord and Lady Holland – Lord Holland was the nephew of Charles James Fox – seen as the guardians of the pure traditions of English Whiggery.

Perhaps the most important element in the Whig tradition was a belief in the importance of aristocracy, literally 'the rule of the best'. The role of a properly enlightened aristocracy was to place strict limits on the powers of absolutist-inclined monarchs and to provide leadership to the rest of society to protect it from the allure of demagogues and extreme radicals. The institutional embodiment of these principles was, of course, a parliament, but a parliament consisting of two chambers with the upper chamber largely composed of hereditary peers. In some respects, Whiggery was an ideology rooted in the England of the late seventeenth and eighteenth centuries. Long years of exclusion from office, coupled with a recognition that significant social and economic change was occurring, added a new dimension to the strategy – a readiness to enrol the new middle classes as junior partners in a sort of progressive coalition. Above all, this found expression in the Reform Bill of 1832. Whigs believed in religious toleration and were often somewhat sceptical about conventional religious beliefs; many were Freemasons. Within fairly broad limits, they believed in a free press and the rule of law. Although not completely identical, Whigs might be regarded as the precursors of later Liberals.

But Holland House stood for something more; it had a significant international dimension. In short, Lord and Lady Holland wanted to promote the development of societies and political systems based upon their own principles elsewhere in the world. Spain and Portugal – and to some extent South America – were of special interest to them. It is this that forms the main theme of José de Sousa's book. The Hollands could claim to be particularly well informed about Spain and Portugal, having made two extensive tours of the Peninsula. They made their journeys during the particularly interesting times of the Napoleonic Wars. On both occasions the Hollands kept diaries, works that provide a major source for this book.

In some respects at least, Portugal might appear an attractive possibility for the adoption of Whig/Liberal ideas. The links between England and Portugal were strong and long-standing. English crusaders had helped to expel the Moors from Lisbon and a treaty between the two countries dating to the fourteenth century was still valid. Symbols of the alliance were the marriages of Philippa of Lancaster into the Portuguese Royal House and later the marriage of Catherine of Braganza to Charles II of England. In some English circles, the drinking of port wine was seen as a patriotic duty. Above all, England and Portugal were seagoing countries that came to look outwards from Europe, to the Atlantic, to the Indian Ocean and beyond. Both were challenged by powerful neighbours – England by France and Portugal by Spain. It was always in the common interest of England and Portugal to prevent any close alliance or union between France and Spain.

But did a common interest mean that England and Portugal could develop on similar lines? It was true that, in common with many other European countries, both had developed early forms of parliaments in the Middle Ages – and the early Cortes was a major source of interest to Lord Holland. Yet divergences emerged and these seemed to increase over the years. England adopted Protestantism while Portugal committed itself to a particularly stifling version of the Counter-Reformation. Whereas the English Parliament grew from strength to strength, ultimately deciding who should be king and on what terms, the Portuguese Cortes withered and died. Perhaps the Portuguese were too successful; their empire brought so much wealth to the Crown that there was no need to go cap in hand to any representative body. With a few exceptions, the Portuguese nobility and clergy had little interest in constitutional issues, and a thriving commercial middle class – so important to the Whig model – was notably absent.

There had been attempts to modernize Portugal in the past, but these had been in the shape of reforms imposed from above upon a reluctant population. In other words, the main instrument of change had been Enlightened Despotism, embodied in the figure of Pombal. One of the phenomena that caused most intellectual difficulty for Whigs like Holland was to decide whether the merits of such a despotism outweighed their shortcomings. By and large they approved of the objectives of such despots but deplored their methods. They also noted that any improvements tended to be short-lived; when the despot fell, his reforms were quickly discarded.

The Hollands knew enough to appreciate that it would not be easy to sow the seeds of Liberalism on the somewhat stony ground of Portugal, but this did not deter them from trying. Lord Holland was ready to offer advice on constitutional matters to the Portuguese, the Spaniards and the Brazilians. His advice was essentially pragmatic; constitutional arrangements, ideally based on a bicameral system of representation, must take account of the traditions and realities of the countries concerned. This contrasted sharply with advice based on abstract principles, whether those of the French Revolution or those of Jeremy Bentham. It must be admitted that, by and large, Holland's advice was not listened to. Perhaps the story of constitutional government in Spain and Portugal and in South America might have been happier if his ideas had been more influential.

The Hollands' interest in Spain and Portugal did not end when they returned to England after their tours. In the 1820s and 1830s both countries experienced extreme political instability and civil war. Successive revolutions and counter-revolutions brought many refugees to England. Holland was active in raising funds to assist refugees and exiled politicians who supported the constitutional cause. In these years, Portuguese exiles were frequent guests at Holland House. In particular, Holland sought to arouse public opinion against the seizure of power by Dom Miguel, the absolutist claimant to the Portuguese throne. There was a real danger that Wellington's government would give formal recognition to Miguel's regime, a development Holland was determined to prevent.

Holland's influence increased when the Whigs under Charles Grey (1764–1845) came to power in November 1830. Although the new government was mainly preoccupied with drawing up and passing the Great Reform Bill, it also pursued a new line in foreign policy, aligning itself more clearly with the constitutional cause in both Spain and Portugal. Here again Holland's influence was significant, putting pressure on a sometimes reluctant Henry John Temple, 3rd Viscount Palmerston, to give clearer support to Dom Pedro. Pedro's victory in 1834 certainly owed a good deal to Lord Holland and the Holland House circle.

Throughout the 1820s and 1830s, Holland's main contact among the Portuguese Liberals was Duque D. Pedro de Palmela, whose thinking corresponded closely to his own. After the Liberal victory there were periods of estrangement, but Holland's underlying belief that Palmela was the best man to bring stability and moderate Liberalism to Portugal was undoubtedly correct.

This important study throws new light on political developments in both England and Portugal and on the complex relationship between the two countries. The author's knowledge of both Portuguese and English makes him ideally qualified to tackle an important and hitherto somewhat neglected topic.

John Clarke, MA, DPhil (Oxon)
Professor Emeritus
The University of Buckingham

FOREWORD

The nineteenth century started under the shadow of Napoleon, whose ambitions and course of life nobody could have foreseen at the time but, because of which, practically all European countries were to suffer long years of a ruthless war. Portugal, a small country with no political strength, had however a strategic relevance in the maritime trade between north Europe and the rest of the world. This was very important as far as England was concerned, because accessing Britain's naval and commercial might was Napoleon's most desired and ultimate goal. Between Portugal and the United Kingdom there was an alliance of mutual support in peace and war, still the oldest in the world, and the fulfilment of the implied duties was the real reason that made the Portuguese sea coast and politics particularly interesting for the emperor's projects.

The close connection between Portuguese, English and French ideologies during the four years the armies of the three countries coexisted in Portugal was perhaps the most direct cause of the spread of Liberal ideas that would change political and social life in Portugal, with the negative result of serious unrest, persecutions and a civil war that lasted for almost the entire first half of the nineteenth century.

The course of this period in Portugal is so entangled and difficult to follow, with the undecided diplomatic and actual positions taken by other countries, whose support was absolutely necessary to strengthen the small and unprepared Portuguese troops, that the general public has no clear idea about what really happened in Portugal at that time. Consequently, the development of the history of Portugal in the second half of the nineteenth century, both within Europe and overseas, particularly in Africa and Asia, deeply changed in a way never to return to the old order. That is why a detailed work like the one now presented is a fundamental contribution to the knowledge and understanding of what the nineteenth century really meant: the most agitated, devastating and bloody period in Portuguese history, changing the nation's course quickly and deeply. The same can be said about Spain, the Iberian country that Lord Holland preferred and whose history at that time ran parallel to that of Portugal.

In order to give us a complete picture of the time, J. Baptista de Sousa does not ignore other issues weighing heavily on the problems that arose between the two countries, one directly connected with the Liberal Wars, for example, the problem of the Portuguese émigrés in England, particularly the situation of those who stayed in Plymouth.

As Baptista de Sousa said – and I have witnessed – this book is the result of 20 years of intensive work, and is founded on an amazing array of sources, both manuscript and in print, and a bibliography which, I daresay, covers every publication on the subject up to the most recent ones.

The presentation of the men responsible for the course of political decisions and events, mostly derived from the aforementioned Anglo-Portuguese Alliance, gives this work an outstanding place in the bibliography published on this subject. In the case of the most representative Portuguese individuals, as the author in some way reminds us, their names are generally acquainted to the public because they were given to streets or squares of important towns, or due to their connection to one of the nineteenth-century great wars, the Peninsular War (better known in Portugal as the 'Invasões Francesas') or the Liberal Wars. But however complete the description of their character, their aims and their deeds may be, the readers must forcibly understand that, though this may not be the chief aim of the author, this book is also the study of the two men who in fact dominate the two sides of the acting on the European stage in the first half of the nineteenth century, sometimes even crossing beyond the Anglo-Portuguese borders: Lord Holland (Henry Richard Vassall-Fox, 1773–1840, third Baron Holland of Holland and third Baron Holland of Foxley, politician) and the Duque de Palmela (D. Pedro de Sousa e Holstein, 1781–1850, first Conde, Marquês and Duque de Palmela, diplomat and statesman). Indeed, together with the history of Portugal and the Anglo-Portuguese relations in most of the first half of the nineteenth century, sometimes leading even to the second, José Baptista de Sousa gives us the biography of these two prominent men, which the large number of footnotes in the original thesis underscores.

There is a note I would like to include, strangely enough, because it addresses the title of this work. The author himself felt the need for a justification, but I would like to add to the reasons why 'Holland House' is more appropriate than 'The Hollands' or 'Lord Holland': after the political turmoil in England in the seventeenth century, life ran smoothly in aristocratic circles, where social life, in a way parallel to that of the Court, developed around entertainment, literature, music and – most important in our case – politics. This allowed an improvement in the role of women who, beyond their duties as hostesses, could take part in the general conversation, and sometimes become important agents in the diffusion or even development of political affairs. Through this particular work, which is very interesting in that it focuses more strongly than we are used to on the social activities of what here becomes known as 'The Holland House Circle', we become acquainted with the importance of some women who definitely played a part in English history, not only because of their performances in their social and family environment, but also through a constant correspondence with their friends. This is the case foremost of Lady Holland, who also left an important diary, already translated and published in Portugal, but I think I should also mention Princess Lieven, the wife of Kristofers Heinrihs fon Līvens, the Russian ambassador to London, who was to become Lord Grey's confidant and to whom he regularly wrote about the political problems that surrounded him.

If we can fancy what a continuation of this work could lead to, there would be the political course of Europe in the nineteenth century, with the creation of new independent states and the advent of republican regimes over monarchies, and also the social revolutions that took place in the second half of the nineteenth century, not only in the conditions of the working class, but also in the activity of women in the defence of their rights. Freedom would be expressed in a way which the Liberal guests of Holland House and other similar circles would not have imagined.

On a final commentary on José Baptista de Sousa's book, I must say that it is a most interesting and thorough work, which tells and explains the history of an age, in the scope of a social activity fascinating in itself, and mainly because it was the staging of one of the most energetic and impressive periods of European life. It is also very important because it stresses the very meaning of Anglo-Portuguese relations, something that, the people of both countries are not aware of. After all, it is important to stress the fact that these relations are on their way to completing 700 years.

Maria Leonor Machado de Sousa
Professor Emerita
Universidade Nova de Lisboa

PREFACE

[...] this said honest gentleman, at his leisure hours,
which engrossed the greatest part of the year,
addicted himself to the reading of books of chivalry,
which he perused with such rapture and application,
that he not only forgot the pleasures of the chase,
but also utterly neglected the management of his estate.[1]

The present study – the edited version of my DPhil thesis submitted to the University of Buckingham in 2015 – is in the areas of political and diplomatic history, and focuses on the relations between Lord Holland and Portugal. It covers the period between 1793 and 1840 and traces the evolution of Holland's views on Portugal from the time of his first visit to Spain to his later contribution to the establishment of a constitutional regime in Portugal. Particular attention is given to the Hollands' visits to Portugal in 1804–5 and 1808–9. On their travels, they met a number of prominent Portuguese, notably Palmela, who were to remain in contact with Holland House – especially during periods of exile – for many years into the future. The Portuguese journeys and the continued contact with people like Palmela were to play an important part in the development of Lord Holland's views, not only on Portugal but also on broader political and constitutional issues.

Thus this study investigates Lord Holland's influence on the establishment of a constitutional regime in Spain in 1809–10 and – indirectly and unintentionally – in Portugal in 1820–23. It includes a study of Holland's contribution to the settlement of a government in Brazil in 1808 – that is, at the time the Braganças moved from Portugal to Rio de Janeiro – and his indirect influence on the establishment of the United Kingdom of Portugal, Brazil and the Algarves in 1815.

This book examines at some length Lord Holland's contribution to the establishment of a Liberal regime in Portugal in 1834. It includes a study of the extent of Holland's support for the Portuguese Liberal cause after Dom Miguel's usurpation of the throne in 1828 and of his subsequent role in the 'Liberal invasion' of Portugal. To this end, it investigates relations between Portuguese émigrés and the Holland House Circle, Holland's role in the triangular diplomacy between Lisbon, St James and South Audley Street in 1828 and later. Finally, it considers Holland's contribution to the end of the

1. Miguel de Cervantes, *The History and Adventures of the Renowned Don Quixote*, trans. T. Smollett. 2 vols (London: Printed for A. Millar, 1755), 1: 2.

Portuguese Civil War in 1834 and to the subsequent establishment of a constitutional regime in that country.

While the original plan was to investigate the Portuguese émigrés of 1828–34 in their association with Holland House, it soon became evident that the scope of the study had to be widened and the chronology extended. Work on the Holland House Papers, especially Lord and Lady Holland's journals of their travels in Portugal in 1804–5 and 1808–9, suggested that there was more to be said about the Hollands and Portugal than had been anticipated. The fact that much of the manuscript materials are related to Lord Holland – though, of course, not exclusively – led to further adaptation of the initial plan. The focus of the study, originally centred on Holland House, moved to Lord Holland, the main protagonist, thus giving the present study something of a biographical character.

The research supporting this study was formally initiated in 2001, when I first registered for a doctorate at the Universidade Nova de Lisboa, under the supervision of Maria Leonor Machado de Sousa, and continued at the University of Buckingham in 2007 under the supervision of John Clarke and co-supervised by the former. Yet, the process of collecting materials on relations between Holland House and Portugal began in 1995, while studying for my MA degree at the University of Buckingham. Since then I have been collecting documents and data that I thought would be useful for a later study – that is to say, the present work.

C. G. Jung said of himself, 'My life is the story of the self-realization of the unconscious.'[2] Jung was a conceited man, who claimed a place on Olympus, although, like Bellerophon, probably fell from Pegasus on his way there. Lord Holland, perhaps a man who never achieved his true potential, had none of Jung's conceit. But Holland too sought self-realization, even if this made him only too well aware of his frailties and limitations. In 1794, he wrote to Lady Caroline Fox, 'Do not, however, my dear little sister [...], indulge your ambition too much with regard to me.'[3] Yet, while it would be foolish to claim that Holland was as important as his uncle, Charles James Fox, his significance and good qualities should not be underestimated. Holland was remarkably consistent in his principles and was sincerely committed to improving the lot of humanity both in his own country and throughout the world. On occasion, Holland's good nature made him somewhat naïve and gullible; as Macaulay observed, Holland 'was now and then seduced [...] by a philanthropy so enlarged, that it took in all nations'.[4] In 1816, Sir Philip Francis, a frequent guest at Holland House, described him as an *homo cordatus*, the Latin expression meaning 'a wise man, in the sense of active zeal for the good of others'.[5] Perhaps

2. Carl Gustav Jung, *Memories, Dreams, Reflections* (New York: Vintage Books, 1965), 3.
3. Holland to Caroline Fox, quoted in 'Caroline Fox, 1767–1845: An Aristocratic Woman of Her Time', by Cynthia Parks Hamilton (PhD diss. University of Iowa, 1995), 261 (18 December 1784).
4. Thomas Babington Macaulay, 'The Late Lord Holland', *The Edinburgh Review: or Critical Journal* 148 (July 1841): 566.
5. Philip Francis, *A Letter Missive from Sir Philip Francis, K. B. to Lord Holland* (London: Printed for Ridgways, 1816), 2.

the best insight into Holland's character comes from Elizabeth Vassall, his mistress and future wife. While in Italy with Holland in 1794, she called him her '*sal volatile*', capable of enlivening her spirits when she felt melancholy.[6] While Paracelsus used *sal volatile* (i.e., ammonium carbonate and known in England as salt of hartshorn) to counter an excess of cold and phlegm, many eighteenth-century alchemists identified *sal volatile* as the germinative element in nature and man, linking the motions of microcosm and macrocosm, that is to say, an element of equilibrium and consensus.

Given a free choice, Holland might have opted for a career in diplomacy or devoted himself to serious scholarship. He could have been successful in either role, yet he succumbed to family tradition and pressure and became a politician. While his family had been intensely political, politics was not really to Holland's taste. As a result he became neither a consummate diplomat nor a brilliant writer, but a somewhat second-rate politician. With Holland it is impossible to escape the feeling of unfulfilled potential, even though his political career was not without achievement. He certainly did far more than his wastrel father, proving an effective speaker in the House of Lords. Of course, the fact that Holland succeeded to his barony while still an infant meant that, unlike his uncle, he had no direct experience of the House of Commons, already essential for serious politicians. There are hints of ambition in Holland but even then its direction seems determined by the preferences of others, not least those of Lady Holland. He explains in his memoirs, 'Lady Holland's predilection for foreign modes of living would make me prefer a diplomatick station to any other'.[7] He would have been delighted to be an ambassador in Paris, Berlin or Madrid, but this ambition always eluded him. Perhaps faced with his father's example, Henry Edward, later fourth Lord Holland, he decided to follow a diplomatic career rather than becoming an MP before taking his seat in the House of Lords.

Despite Lady Holland's influence, in both life and death, it was Charles James Fox who really controlled his nephew's career. Ultimately, Holland was the representative of the name and principles of Fox, in Leslie's words, 'the great high-priest of Whiggery'.[8] This seems a somewhat backhanded compliment. Holland occasionally 'rebelled'; he disappointed his friends and relations – and almost certainly the shade of Charles James Fox – when he left for Spain in 1808, effectively refusing to take the leadership of the Whig party, a role that would have been his for the asking as Fox's natural successor. But Holland never aspired to the premiership, preferring to remain in the background. Ironically, one of the factors that kept the Whigs in opposition for so long was the personal dislike George III and George IV felt for Grey. Neither had the same hostility to Holland and so, if Holland had accepted the leadership of the party after Fox's death, the Whigs might have been in government well before 1830. But Holland always turned away from positions of really major responsibility.

6. Elizabeth Vassall, 3rd Baroness of Holland, *The Journal of Elizabeth Lady Holland (1791–1811)*. 2 vols (London: Longmans, Green, 1908), 1: 125.
7. Henry Richard Vassall, 3rd Baron of Holland, *Memoirs of the Whig Party during My Time*. 2 vols (London: Longman, Brown, Green and Longmans, 1852–54), 1: 232–33.
8. Shane Leslie, *George the Fourth* (London: E. Benn, 1926), 70.

Lord Holland's allegedly weak character contrasted with the strong personality of his wife, Lady Elizabeth Holland, whose influence on her husband's personal and political life, though often exaggerated, was still significant. She once confessed to Lady Bessborough, 'women of a certain age and in a situation to achieve it should take to Politicks – to leading and influencing'.[9] Lady Holland's interest in politics, not uncommon in Whig circles, may have been partly responsible for her husband's failure to achieve the highest positions. In 1827, when she expressed surprise that Holland had not been offered the foreign office, John Russell, one of the few friends who never feared her temper, replied: 'Why, they say, Ma'am, that you open all Lord Holland's letters, and the Foreign Ministers might not like *that!*'[10] Perhaps owing to an underlying insecurity or simply because the ordinary business of government seemed too boring, Holland lived in the shadow of his uncle, his wife and Charles Grey. Yet, towards the end of a long and, perhaps, rewarding life, we find a man at peace with his own conscience and fully aware of his own limitations. In what amounted to a self-obituary, composed a few hours before his death, Holland wrote:

> Nephew of Fox, and friend of Grey,
> Enough my need of fame
> If those who deigned to observe me say
> I injured neither name.[11]

François Guizot once said: 'Not to be a republican at twenty is proof of want of heart; to be one at thirty is proof of want of head.' This maxim is certainly applicable to Holland. Although he never completely abandoned any of his uncle's progressive principles, the years – and probably the gout – softened much of his former revolutionary ardour. Age, however, gave him two important qualities, wisdom and respectability, which both proved useful when dealing with Portuguese Affairs during 1828–34. The mellowing – such as it was – came relatively late. When Holland embarked for Spain in 1808, he was already 35 years old, but still much of the same young man Lady Holland had met at Florence in 1794: 'His politics are warm in favour of the Revolution, and his principles are strongly tinctured with democracy.'[12] It was precisely this young man, full of hopes and with the image of his late uncle still fresh in his memory, who left for the Peninsula in 1808 to become the *chevalier andante* of the Liberal cause in Spain, thereby contributing, if unintentionally, to later political developments in Portugal.

---

9. Henrietta Ponsonby, 'Lady B. to G.L.G.', in *Lord Granville Leveson Gower (First Earl Granville): Private Correspondence 1781–1821*. 2 vols (London: John Murray, 1916), 2: 381.
10. John Russell, quoted in *The Croker Papers: The Correspondence and Diaries of the Late Right Honourable John Wilson Croker, LL.D, F.R.S., Secretary to the Admiralty from 1809 to 1830*, edited by Louis J. Jennings. 3 vols (London: John Murray, 1884), 1: 400.
11. Henry Richard Vassall Fox, 3rd Baron of Holland, last lines quoted in Marie Liechtenstein, *Holland House*. 2 vols (London: Macmillan, 1874), 1: 134.
12. Holland, *The Journal of Elizabeth Lady Holland*, 1: 121 (Florence, 10 June [1794]).

While probably unaware of the importance of his own contributions to political developments in the Peninsula, Holland's influence in the establishment of a constitutional regime in Spain in 1809 and – indirectly in Portugal – is now indisputable. His later commitment to the Portuguese Liberal cause in 1828–34 was probably the decisive factor that led to the final victory of the Liberals in 1834 – and that against formidable odds. He may well have satisfied his own 'need of fame', but Holland deserves a more prominent place in history than he has yet been accorded. Strikingly, despite many books on Holland House and several biographies of Charles James Fox, there is no comprehensive life of Lord Holland, nor a study of his relations with Portugal and his contribution to the establishment of a constitutional regime in that country. If the present work goes some way to rectifying this omission, then I will consider the time I have devoted to the life of this great man – now some 20 years – amply rewarded.

ACKNOWLEDGEMENTS

My first words go to my late father, José (1941–2002), to whom I owe most of my achievements and from whom I borrowed his love for England, his adoptive country, and to John Clarke, the supervisor of this and my former work, who honoured me with his friendship.

Second, a word of thanks to Maria Leonor Machado de Sousa, who kindly agreed to co-supervise my DPhil thesis, and Carlos Reis and Luís Costa Dias, with whom I had the honour to collaborate in the National Library, Portugal.

A word of affection and thanks is also due to those dear ones who have stood by me, sharing or indulging my anxiety, my beloved wife, Ксения, my children Ana Raquel, Маргарита, Constantino and Vicente, my uncle Henrique Smart, and especially to those remarkable women who raised me and shaped my personality, my late grandmother, Mimi, and my mother, Maria Elvira, to whom I dedicate this work.

Finally, I would like to record my gratitude to some other people and institutions who have contributed – directly or indirectly – to this work, namely my friends Teresa Almeida Lima, António Cruz, Irene Fialho, António Figueiredo, Luís de Bettencourt, Luís Garcez Palha and Alarcão Troni as well as Timothy Knox, John M. Prest and Lord Conrad Russell, and the following institutions: BNP – Biblioteca Nacional de Portugal; CETAPS – Centre for English, Translation and Anglo-Portuguese Studies; FCT – Fundação para a Ciência e a Tecnologia and the University of Buckingham.

ABBREVIATIONS

ANTT	Arquivo Nacional/Torre do Tombo [National Archives, Portugal]
BL	British Library
Cx.	Portuguese abbreviation for *Caixa* (box)
D.	Abbreviation for the titles of 'Dom' and 'Dona'
HGC	*História da Guerra Civil e do estabelecimento do governo parlamentar em Portugal comprehendendo a história diplomática militar e política d'este reino desde 1777 até 1834*, by Simão José da Luz Soriano
HHP	Holland House Papers [British Library, Department of Manuscripts]
Mç.	Portuguese abbreviation for *Maço* (pack)
MNE	Ministério dos Negócios Estrangeiros [Foreign Ministry, Portugal]
PALM	Arquivo da Casa de Palmela [House of Palmela Archives, Portugal]
Parl. Deb.	Cobbett's *The Parliamentary History of England* and Hansard's *The Parliamentary Debates*

Introduction

A LONG-LASTING RELATION

The treaty by which we were so bound was written in the hearts of Englishmen, – it was that love which they naturally bore to their own interests, and the generosity with which they looked upon those of an old and faithful ally.[*]

Lord Holland is often described as a Hispanophile, sometimes even as a Hispanist, yet his relationship with Portugal is less known.[1] A few nineteenth-century Portuguese works include rather vague references to Holland – mostly in connection with his role in opposing absolutism and in re-establishing the constitutional regime in the late 1820s and early 1830s. Later historiography, however, either ignores or seriously underestimates his contribution to developments in Portugal over a much longer time span. The most likely reason for this neglect is that Holland himself kept his interest in Portugal relatively quiet – in contrast with his much-publicized enthusiasm for Spain, a country he described as – 'mi segunda patria'.[2] Yet Holland's interest in Portugal was actually quite profound. Unlike his sudden, even violent passion for Spain, Holland's affection for Portugal was relatively milder and longer lasting, growing in an unobtrusive way. While Holland's relationship with Portugal begun with apparent disdain, it developed into a true sentiment of 'love' and 'affection', to quote his own words in a speech to the House of Lords in July 1828.[3] Indeed, while Holland may not qualify as a 'Lusophile', he was certainly a friend of Portugal, even if this long-lasting relationship is sometimes difficult to trace.

---

* Holland, address in the House of Lords on 'Foreign Affairs', *The Times*, 17, 1828, 6.

1. Henry Richard Vassall-Fox (1773–1840), 3rd Baron Holland of Holland and 3rd Baron Holland of Foxley, English Whig politician, statesman and Hispanist, son of Stephen Fox (1745–74), 2nd Lord Holland, by Mary Fitzpatrick (†1778), and grandson of Henry Fox (1705–74), 1st Lord Holland, and his wife Georgiana Caroline Fox, *née* Lennox (1723–74), the eldest daughter of Charles Lennox, 2nd Duke of Richmond, a grandson of Charles II. Holland was the nephew of Charles James Fox (1749–1806), the famous Whig politician, who was responsible for his education. In 1797, Holland married Elizabeth Vassall (1771–1845), whose marriage to Sir Godfrey Webster had just been dissolved; Elizabeth was the daughter of Richard Vassall (1732–95), the owner of extensive estates in Jamaica, by Mary Clarke (1747–1835), later known as Lady Affleck.
2. Holland to Jovellanos, in *Cartas de Jovellanos y Lord Vassall Holland sobre la guerra de la independencia (1808–1811)*. 2 vols (Madrid: Imprenta de los Hijos de Gómez Fuentenebro, 1911), 1: 166 (Cádiz, 15 Mayo 1809). In another letter, Holland described himself as 'Españolado', ibid., 2: 371 (6 September 1809); and again, 'medio español y españolado', ibid., 2: 375 (8 September 1809).
3. Holland, speech in the House of Lords on Foreign Affairs, *The Times*, 17 July, 1828, 6.

Lord Holland's initial – and indirect – encounter with Portugal probably occurred during his first visit to Spain in 1793. Fascinated with the character and costumes of the Spaniards, who 'gave such a warm reception to a 19 years old boy',[4] Holland dedicated himself to the study of the language, literature and history of their country. The dismissive tone in Holland's *Foreign Reminiscences* – 'I know little of Portugal or Portuguese that would have the interest of novelty to English readers' – suggests contamination with a widely held Spanish prejudice.[5] Holland's negative opinion also appears when, in a letter to Manuel Quintana,[6] a Spanish author he met in Madrid in 1803, he describes the Portuguese language as a 'patois'.[7] It was not until 1804, after his first direct contact with Portugal, that Holland begun to revise his opinions, announcing in a letter to his sister: 'I am safe on Portuguese territory (which by the way is very pretty territory too).'[8] Although Holland was to say unflattering things about Portugal in the future, this favourable first impression never completely left him.

It was in the political sphere that Lord Holland's relationship with Portugal was most significant. Holland's contribution to the political developments in Portugal in the first half of the nineteenth century is remarkable and far more significant than one might suppose at first glance. However, unlike Spain, in whose internal politics Holland was directly involved from 1808–9, his involvement in the affairs of Portugal was generally indirect and thus less obvious. In part, this explains why historians have never appreciated Holland's role in the establishment of Liberalism in Portugal. Yet, apart from John of Gaunt or George Canning, there is probably no other example in the long history of relations between the two countries of an English politician who devoted himself to Portugal as Holland did.

Although there is no record of meetings with Portuguese leaders during Holland's first visit to Portugal from 1804–5, he was able to collect information about the country and to identify the political dilemmas it faced. This knowledge proved useful when, during the Ministry of All the Talents, Charles James Fox ordered a squadron, under Earl St Vincent, to the Tagus to negotiate the terms of British military assistance to Portugal to prevent or repulse a combined invasion of France and Spain. The offer was rejected

4. BL, HHP, MSS Add. 51618, G. M. Jovellanos: 1808–9, Lord Holland to Jovellanos, f. 3r (12 September 1808); 'con tanto agasajo a un muchacho de 19 años'. (My translation).
5. Henry Richard Vassall Fox, 3rd Baron of Holland, *Foreign Reminiscences* (London: Longman, Brown, Green, and Longmans, 1850), 161.
6. Manuel José Quintana y Lorenzo (1772–1857), Castilian poet, playwright, journalist and ultra-liberal politician verging on radicalism.
7. Quintana to Lord Holland, in 'Principios políticos y razones personales para la reforma del estado en España (1805–40): (De la correspondencia inédita de M. J. Quintana con Lord Holland)', by Manuel Moreno Alonso, *Revista de estudios políticos* 70 (Oct.–Dic. 1990): 317 (Madrid, 7 Febrero 1805); 'Yo no puedo leer libro ninguno suyo, sino las obras de Camoens'. (My translation). Although the whereabouts of Lord Holland's letter are not known, Quintana's reply reproduces the expression 'patois' used by Holland: 'No wonder that the Portuguese language seems to you a *patois*.'; 'No extraño que la lengua portuguesa le parezca a V. un *patois*.' (My translation).
8. BL, HHP, MSS Add. 51737, Lord Holland to Caroline Fox, f. 133r (2 December [1804]).

because of fears that British aid would jeopardize Portugal's safety by raising French and Spanish suspicions that it had abandoned its neutrality.

Faced with Portugal's hesitation about joining the Continental System, Napoleon invaded in November 1807. But the emperor wanted more than Portugal and planned to become master of the whole Peninsula. Hence, during the first months of 1808, French armies occupied Portugal and most of Spain, except Andalusia. Lured to France by Napoleon, the Bourbons where forced to abdicate and were made prisoners, while Joseph Bonaparte was placed on the Spanish throne. Here, at least, Portugal was better placed than Spain, in that the Braganças had been successfully removed to Rio de Janeiro on 27 November 1807, just before the first French troops arrived in Lisbon.

The Hollands' second and last journey to the Peninsula – Lord Holland's third – included two periods in Portugal, the first from 16 December 1808 to 26 January 1809, the second from 5 to 19 July 1809, when they embarked from Lisbon for England. Although the original plan was to reach Madrid by land – where a patriotic junta had been established on 25 September 1808 – when the Hollands were at Oporto on 20 December, they learned that the Spanish capital had capitulated to the French on 4 December and that the junta had been transferred to Seville. Unable to travel to Andalusia by land and with no suitable British ship to take them to Cadiz, the Hollands were forced to cross Portugal and reach Spain through Badajoz and later to use the same route back to Lisbon.

The bad roads Holland encountered in his last journeys through Portugal must have been physically challenging, but he was also engaged on something of a spiritual quest, where his Whig principles were tested. The contrast between the ignorance and superstition of the population, now dominated by equally ignorant authorities, and the traces of the benefits of Pombal's enlightenment, seems to haunt him. Parliamentary institutions had appeared in Portugal even earlier than in England, yet while England had developed a parliamentary system of government, Portugal had moved towards despotism.[9] Although Holland did not put the question directly, there must have been times when he doubted whether the type of parliamentary regimes, which he hoped that Spain and Portugal would adopt in 1808, would prove viable in the long run.

Two more decades were to elapse before Holland attempted an answer – and then only a partial one. At the end of a speech to the House of Lords in 1828 he declared: 'When we were told that the people of Spain and Portugal hated the constitutional form of government, we should consider the conditions in which those countries were placed.'[10] Holland's admission suggests that, while there may have been no fundamental reason that prevented the countries of southern Europe from sustaining constitutional governments,

9. The first Portuguese *Cortes* in the modern meaning of the word – where members were allowed the right to address petitions and put questions to the monarch – met at Leiria in 1254, in the reign of Dom Afonso III (titles of 'Dom' and 'Dona' will be henceforward abbreviated to 'D.'). These *Cortes* were also the first where the Third Estate was represented by town procurators, similar to the arrangements made in England in 1265 on the initiative of the Earl of Leicester.
10. Holland, speech in the House of Lords on 'Foreign Affairs', *The Times*, 17 July 1828, 6.

the problems they experienced with these systems of government, whether external or internal in origin, had deep roots in the past.

On the surface at least, Holland was not much involved with Portuguese matters between 1814 and 1828. His role in the establishment of a constitutional regime in Portugal in 1820 was apparently confined to a speech supporting a toast to the 'Prosperity and durability to the new representative governments of Spain, Portugal, and Naples', proposed by Lord Albemarle at a dinner held in Norwich on 19 January 1821 to commemorate the anniversary of the death of Charles James Fox.[11] Thus, whereas Holland played a significant role in the establishment of constitutional government in Spain in 1808–9, his direct involvement in the establishment of a similar system in Portugal appears minimal. Upon closer observation, however, it emerges that Holland's apparent lack of interest owes more to the succession of extraordinary events affecting Europe as a whole in the aftermath of the Napoleonic wars than to any serious antipathy to Portugal. The years 1814–20 correspond to a period of adaptation to the new *status quo* emerging from the Congress of Vienna. Napoleon's fall forced the Whigs – Holland in particular – to re-interpret political reality and accommodate their doctrines to a Europe in which France neither presented a threat nor provided a model, a Continent where Metternich's legitimist Austria was now playing a determinant role. And if the Foxite Whigs wanted to survive politically, they would have both to overcome the trauma they experienced on the fall of Napoleon – once the symbol of the 'civilizational conquests' of the French Revolution – and to adapt themselves to the new *Leviathan*. This was probably what John Russell hinted in *A Letter to Lord Holland on Foreign Politics*, when declaring 'the old system of the balance of power which governed the wars and treaties of Europe from the fifteenth century to the year 1818, has now been exchanged for another, which may be called the system of the Holy Alliance'.[12] These circumstances, together with several private and family issues, meant there were few opportunities for involvement in developments in the Peninsula, and in particular those in Portugal. This explains Holland's apparent lack of enthusiasm for the liberal revolutions in southern Europe in 1820, particularly in the Peninsula, which in other circumstances might have been expected to rekindle his eagerness to play the roles of crusader against tyranny and patron of liberties.

The period 1822–27 was dominated by George Canning, whose policies Holland did not totally reject. It also corresponded with Metternich's struggle to dominate Continental Europe, including the Iberian Peninsula. Luckily for Portugal, Canning proved a staunch ally, probably the country's greatest English friend since John of Gaunt, and certainly the most Lusophile of all English ministers. While foreign secretary, Canning devoted himself to the affairs of Portugal in a way that no other British minister has done either before or since. Knowing that Portugal was in such good hands, it is not surprising that Holland paid little attention to Portuguese affairs during these years, even though they represented one of the most disturbing and confused periods

11. 'Norwich Fox Dinner', *The Times*, 22 January 1821, 3.
12. John Russell, *A Letter to Lord Holland on Foreign Politics* (London: James Ridgway, 1819), 44.

in the history of that country. It is striking that Holland's interest in Portugal 'revived' sharply after Canning's death.

Despite Holland's apparent lack of interest in Portugal during Canning's ministry, he did not lose contact completely. Significantly, Palmela,[13] the Portuguese minister in London and a close friend of the Hollands since 1813, or – during his absences in Portugal – his brother-in-law, the Conde de Vila Real, were regular guests at Holland House.[14] Yet it was only after Canning's death and, more clearly following the resignation of Dudley and Aberdeen's appointment as foreign secretary on 30 May 1828, that Holland's concern for Portugal became acute. Dudley resigned while the Three Estates of the Realm in Lisbon were acclaiming the Infante D. Miguel as absolute King of Portugal, a sham conceived by his supporters to give some semblance of legality to the usurpation.[15]

D. Miguel had arrived in Lisbon on 22 February 1828 to take the regency, after almost four years in exile in Austria. He soon began to persecute leading Liberals and freemasons, forcing many to seek refuge abroad, mostly in Britain. By 22 July, there were already 300 Portuguese exiles of high rank living in London. Some of these émigrés

---

13. D. Pedro de Sousa e Holstein (1781–1850), conti di Sanfré in the Piedmontese peerage, 1st Conde, Marquês and Duque de Palmela, Portuguese diplomat and statesman, was the only son of D. Alexandre de Sousa e Holstein (1751–1803), also a diplomat, and his first wife, D. Isabel Juliana Sousa Coutinho Monteiro Paim (1753–93). Pedro was born in Sanfré, Piedmont, on 8 May 1781. His grandfather was D. Manuel de Sousa (1703–59), Lord of Calhariz, who was persecuted by Pombal and died in prison. His grandmother was Maria Anna Leopoldine (1717–89), Princess von Schleswig-Holstein-Sonderburg-Beck, daughter of Friedrich Ludwig von Holstein-Sonderburg-Beck (1653–1728), Herzog (Duke) von Schleswig-Holstein-Sonderburg-Beck, and his wife Maria Antonia Isnardi di Castello (1692–1762), contessa di Sanfré. On 4 June 1810, Pedro married D. Eugénia Francisca Xavier Teles da Gama (1798–1848), a descendant of Vasco da Gama, who bore him several children. Palmela was undoubtedly one of Holland's closest Portuguese friends, even if relations cooled after 1834 when Palmela took office in the Portuguese government. It was largely through Palmela that Holland derived his knowledge of Portugal, in turn the basis of his growing affection for that country. Palmela and his family became frequent guests at Holland House: between 21 March 1813, the date of his first reported appearance at Kensington, and 1 July 1838, when he was in Britain to attend Queen Victoria's coronation, Palmela's name appears 49 times in the dinner books and *Holland House Diaries*, while his relations– his wife, two sons, Alexandre de Sousa e Holstein (1812–32), 1st Conde do Calhariz, and Domingos de Sousa e Holstein (1818–64), 2nd Conde do Calhariz, 1st Marquês do Faial and 2nd Duque de Palmela, and a Miss Sousa, probably one of his sisters – are mentioned 15 times.
14. D. José Luís de Sousa Botelho Mourão e Vasconcelos (1785–1855), 1st Conde de Vila Real, Portuguese diplomat and statesman, the son of D. José Maria do Carmo de Sousa Botelho Mourão e Vasconcelos (1758–1825), 5th *Morgado* de Mateus, and his first wife, D. Maria Teresa Soares de Noronha (1760–85). He married D. Teresa Frederica Cristina de Sousa e Holstein (1786–1841), Palmela's sister, in 1811.
15. D. Miguel Maria do Patrocínio João Carlos Francisco de Assis Xavier de Paula Pedro de Alcântara António Rafael Gabriel Joaquim José Gonzaga Evaristo de Bragança e Bourbon (1802–66), the youngest son of D. João VI and D. Carlota Joaquina. He ruled Portugal as D. Miguel I from 11 July 1828 to 26 May 1834.

were entertained at Holland House in 1828–29, accompanied by Palmela. Towards the end of August and beginning of September 1828, the émigrés were joined by thousands of their countrymen, who had fled from Oporto following an attempted revolution against D. Miguel's regime. A depot of refugees was established in Plymouth, where they lived in extremely difficult conditions for several months. On 27 September, D. Maria da Glória, the legitimate young queen of Portugal, now herself an exile, arrived in Falmouth.[16] D. Maria had been sent to Europe to be educated in Vienna until she reached the age to marry her uncle D. Miguel, but when the events in Portugal became known during the journey, she was immediately diverted to England, where she lived for almost a year.

The difficult situation of the young queen and of thousands of Portuguese refugees inspired the sympathy of the British public, partly due to Palmela's efforts, who skilfully used the press to promote the case. Holland and other members of the Whig Party, then in opposition, responded to Palmela's campaign and eventually gave their full support to D. Maria. When the affairs of Portugal were discussed in Parliament in June 1829, Sir James Mackintosh and Lord Palmerston spoke in the Commons in favour of D. Maria, while Holland defended her rights in the Lords. Their speeches were printed in both English and Portuguese and circulated in Europe by Palmela. Wellington, prime minister from January 1828, did everything in his power to favour D. Miguel and to thwart Palmela. But the prince's inflexibility and tactlessness made it impossible for the British government to recognize him as the legitimate King of Portugal.

Wellington's resignation on 16 November 1829 opened the way to Grey to form a cabinet, in which Holland became Chancellor of the Duchy of Lancaster. With Holland in the government, Palmela expected nothing less than the full recognition from Britain of D. Maria, carrying the tacit acknowledgement that D. Miguel had usurped her throne. But Palmerston, the new foreign secretary, was reluctant to give his support to a party of refugees without a proper army or sufficient financial resources to attempt an invasion of Portugal. Holland, who disagreed with Palmerston, joined Palmela in a campaign to win over other members of the Cabinet in London and also the French authorities in Paris. For a while Holland became a sort of 'rival foreign secretary' to Palmerston.

D. Pedro's abdication of the Brazilian throne on 7 April 1831 and his arrival in Europe to lead the fight for his daughter's rights gave credibility to the cause and filled the Liberals with a new enthusiasm.[17] Holland, who admired Pedro and recognized in him the archetypal *chevalier andante* of liberty, did all he could to promote his image

16. D. Maria da Glória Joana Carlota Leopoldina da Cruz Francisca Xavier de Paula Isidora Micaela Gabriela Rafaela Gonzaga (1819–53), the eldest daughter of D. Pedro de Bragança, later Pedro I of Brazil and IV of Portugal, by his first wife Maria Leopoldina, Archduchess of Austria, a daughter of Francis II. She ruled Portugal as D. Maria II from 26 May 1834 to 15 November 1853.

17. D. Pedro de Alcântara Francisco António João Carlos Xavier de Paula Miguel Rafael Joaquim José Gonzaga Pascoal Cipriano Serafim de Bragança e Borbón (1798–1834), the eldest surviving son of D. João VI and D. Carlota Joaquina. He ruled as D. Pedro I of Brazil (1822–31) and D. Pedro IV of Portugal (1826), later adopting the title of Duque de Bragança (1831–34).

and facilitate his access to William IV, who at first showed little sympathy for the ex-emperor. The following months were employed in raising funds for an expedition to Portugal, while Palmela resumed diplomatic contacts with both British and French ministers to obtain a formal support to D. Maria with the more or less open assistance of Holland.

Finally, on 10 February 1832, the expedition left Belle-Île, France, for the Azores, the only territory of Portugal loyal to D. Maria. On 27 June, it left São Miguel for Portugal and on 8 July about 7,500 Liberal troops, including foreign mercenaries, disembarked at Arnosa de Pampelido, on the north coast of Portugal. On the following day, D. Pedro made a triumphal entrance at Oporto, while the Absolutist troops, who had hurriedly abandoned the town, repositioned in the south bank of the Douro. Despite the numerical disproportion between the two armies – the absolutists had about 80,000 men – the Liberals repulsed several attacks on Oporto and held the town until 18 August 1833, when the enemy finally withdrew.

Palmela, who had joined Pedro's expedition, visited Britain in July and November 1832 to raise funds and collect levies. While in London, Palmela persuaded Holland to act as an intermediary with the other members of the Cabinet. Faced with the partial success of the Liberals at Oporto, Palmerston became less sceptical about the possibility of a victory and thus more flexible. During his second stay in London, Palmela succeeded in organizing a fleet of steam vessels to reinforce the Liberal fleet. On 21 June 1833, the fleet left Oporto for the Algarve, where the absolutist squadron was defeated on 5 July at the Battle of Cape St Vincent. The capture of Lisbon by the Liberals on 24 July represented the culmination of the Portuguese Civil War, which ended up on 26 May 1834 with D. Miguel's capitulation at Evoramonte and subsequent exile.

The transition to Liberalism proved difficult, sometimes even confused, especially for foreigners like Holland, who found it hard to decide who was the hero or the villain of the new regime. Taking advantage of martial law and temporary suspension of constitutional rights, Pedro implemented a number of political and administrative reforms, which would not have been passed under normal circumstances. They included the suppression of monastic orders and confiscation of monastic property, the abolition of tithes and manorial privileges, separation of judicial and administrative roles and the reorganization of courts of justice, and so forth. Of course, the reforms involved the removal of institutions and arrangements typical of an *Ancien Régime* society, which Holland had criticized during his time in Portugal in 1808–9. Holland now made it clear that he would not oppose Pedro's reforms, even if they were being achieved by essentially despotic means. Palmela, a conservative Liberal and leader of the so-called Aristocratic Party – a Portuguese version of the British Whiggism – became the chief opponent of Pedro's policies. Differences over Pedro's reforms led to a deterioration in relations between Palmela and Holland, who went so far as to question his former friend's liberalism. The rift between Holland and Palmela widened in September 1834, when Palmela became chief minister, apparently against the wishes of Holland's new hero, D. Pedro, who was then close to death. Although Palmela later returned as a guest to Holland House, the friendship – once the main link between British and Portuguese Liberalism – never fully recovered.

Lord Holland's last significant contribution to the affairs of Portugal was in 1835, during the negotiations between Portuguese diplomats and Palmerston for choosing a suitable husband for D. Maria II. Maria had married August, duc de Leuchtenberg, a grandson of Josephine de Beauharnais, on 1 December 1834, but August died on 28 March 1835 from crupal angina.[18] Leuchtenberg's premature death made finding another husband for the young queen urgent, in order to guarantee the succession. The name of Ferdinand August Saxe-Coburg Gotha,[19] a cousin of Princess Victoria, emerged on 22 July 1835 during a meeting between Palmerston and the Portuguese representatives.[20] The fact that almost the same party had assembled at Kensington on 1 March and on 16 June, together with the references to the royal bride in Holland's diaries, suggests that the issue had already been extensively discussed within the Holland House circle.

Lord Holland's relationship with Portugal was deeply influenced by individual Portuguese, especially by those who became his close friends. The total of 165 visits by Portuguese guests to Holland House is remarkable, even if it is exceeded by their Spanish, Italian and French counterparts. Adding the three visits the Hollands paid to the Portuguese Embassy at South Audley Street in 1808, 1810 and 1817, and the 10 guests they entertained while at Paris, the number rises to 177. Dinner books and the Hollands' diaries identify 21 Portuguese who visited Holland House between 11 February 1802 and 1 July 1838. A further 29 visited or were visited by the Hollands – mainly during their second journey to Portugal of 1808–9 (there are no records of meetings during their first stay from 1804–5) – making a total of 50 names, family members included. Overall, the number of references to Portuguese amounts to 217. Some will be a constant presence throughout the following chapters, while others appear only occasionally.

While the application of statistical methods to the study of political and cultural history is questionable, relating the number of Portuguese names with the dates of their appearance in the Holland House Circle may assist understanding of the development of Holland's relationship with Portugal. The following graph – based on information derived from correspondence, diaries and dinner books – charts social contacts with Portuguese between 1795 and 1838, whether as guests, hosts, or accompanying family members.

---

18. August Charles Eugène Napoléon de Beauharnais (1810–35), 2nd duc de Leuchtenberg, Prince Consort of D. Maria II of Portugal, the eldest son of Eugène de Beauharnais, Napoleon's stepson, and Princess Augusta of Bavaria.
19. D. Fernando II of Portugal, *née*Ferdinand August Franz Anton von Sachsen-Coburg-Gotha-Koháry (1816–85), Prince of Saxe-Coburg and Gotha and King Consort of Portugal, eldest son of Prince Ferdinand of Saxe-Coburg-Saalfeld-Koháry (1785–1851) and the Princess Maria Antonia Koháry de Csábrág. On 10 June 1869, long after Maria's death, Ferdinand married the Swiss-born actress Elisa Hensler (1836–1929), created Gräfin von Edla.
20. Palmerston, quoted in *The Foreign Policy of Palmerston 1830–1841: Britain, the Liberal Movement and the Eastern Question*, by Charles Webster. 2 vols (London: G. Bell, 1951), 1: 483; Eugène Goblet d'Alviella to M. Vander Weyer, in *L'établissement des Cobourg en Portugal: études sur les débuts d'une monarchie constitutionnelle* (Paris: Librairie Internationale, 1869), 38.

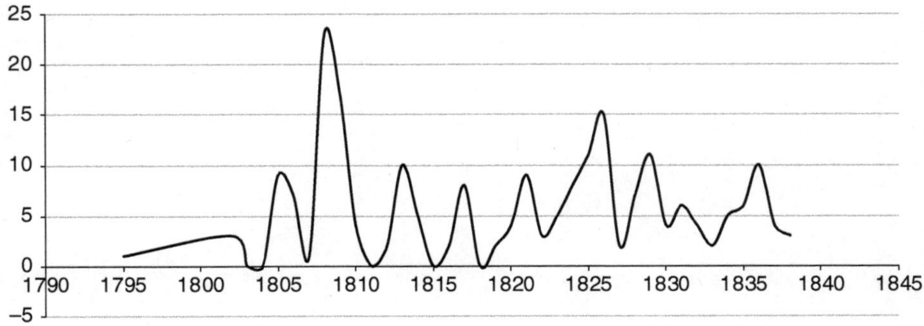

There are clearly peaks of attendance in 1808–9, 1825–26 and 1828–29. The 1808–9 peak corresponds to the Hollands' journey in Portugal; that in 1825–26 is related to Palmela's return to London after his dismissal as foreign minister; while that of 1828–29 corresponds to the arrival of Portuguese émigrés following Miguel's usurpation. This preliminary conclusion will be developed further in the following chapters.

Part 1

CHAMPION OF LIBERTIES

Chapter One
FIRST IMPRESSIONS

I am safe on Portuguese territory (which by the way is very pretty territory too).[*]

Lord Holland's standing in British political life, his close family relationship with Charles James Fox, his command of Spanish and his direct experience of Spain and Portugal meant that he was well placed to comment on developments in these countries and their overseas possessions. The combined assault of the ideas of the French Revolution and those of humanitarianism, coupled with French conquests and local reactions to it, were testing traditional institutions to breaking point. There were many different notions of what the future could or should be like. Holland clearly felt that he had a right and a duty to contribute to this debate. Sometimes he was optimistic, sometimes pessimistic. In England – as a Whig and hence for most of the time out of office – Holland was in favour of moderate reform. Despite his reservations on particular aspects of the British system, Holland certainly believed that it was superior to others. Indeed the central – though by no means only – question posed in Holland's speeches, memoranda, diary entries and correspondence is whether it is possible for other countries to develop political systems that more or less follow the British model.

Holland first became interested in Portugal – if only slightly – during the brief conflict in 1801 later known as *Guerra das Laranjas* (the War of the Oranges).[1] A Franco–Spanish invasion of Portugal had already been envisaged under the terms of the Treaty of San Ildefonso of 1796. In 1800, France had presented Portugal with a series of demands, including repudiation of the alliance with Britain. The Portuguese had refused and, on 29 January 1801, France and Spain agreed to invade if Portugal still refused to close her ports to British ships. On 20 May 1801, following a formal declaration of war in early March, a Spanish force under Prince of Peace Manuel Godoy occupied Olivença and proceeded to take over the province of Alto Alentejo. On 6 June, Portugal was forced to conclude a truce at Badajoz, agreeing to close its ports to British ships and to pay 20 million francs to the French republic.

---

* BL, HHP, MSS Add. 51737, Lord Holland to Caroline Fox, f. 133[r] (Dec.[r] 2.[d] [1804]).

1. The name 'War of Oranges' was given after Godoy presented the Queen María Luisa de Borbón a branch or orange tree taken from Elvas. Olivença, conquered from the Moors by Afonso Henriques in 1170 – though lost in 1189 – had been formally annexed to Portugal in 1297 under the terms of the Treaty of Alcañices. According to article 105 of the *Final Act of the Congress of Vienna*, Spain agreed upon the immediate return of the town to Portugal, a promise never fulfilled. Olivença is still disputed between Spain and Portugal.

Although Napoleon wished to impose even harsher terms, Spain – guarantor of the Franco–Portuguese Treaty – was satisfied with the annexation of Olivença and so matters were concluded for the time being. A new Franco–Portuguese Treaty was signed at Madrid on 29 September 1801 whereby Portugal agreed to close its ports to Britain. However, the Treaty of Amiens of 25 March 1802, meant to be a definitive peace agreement between Britain and France, saved Portugal from having to take this dangerous step.

These events had major implications for Britain. Reponses to Portuguese requests for assistance were disappointing. Lord Grenville, and later Lord Hawkesbury, merely promised not to oppose a bilateral Franco-Portuguese treaty 'except on the condition of excluding from the ports of Portugal the ships of war of his majesty, and even merchant vessels of his subjects'.[2] The issue was discussed in Parliament on 18 May 1801, when approval was given to Hawkesbury's proposal for a subsidy of £300,000 to enable Portugal to maintain an army of 20,000 men. Holland opposed the subsidy; while professing himself ready to assist 'our most ancient and faithful Ally', he considered the subsidy too small to have any military impact.[3] It would only encourage the French to invade and then take the money as reparations. In reality Hawkesbury's proposal would simply vote subsidies 'into the pockets of General Bonaparte'.[4] Holland implies that Hawkesbury is guilty of ineffective half-measures, a line he was to repeat many times in the course of the Peninsular War.

Holland spoke in similar terms when Portuguese affairs were debated on 10 May 1802. He noted that, under pressure from Britain, Portugal had not ratified a number of previous agreements with France – notably the convention of Campo Formio of 1797. In other words, Britain had forced the Portuguese to stand up to the French when a more accommodating stance might have been wiser, but then, by failing to provide sufficient assistance, effectively abandoned its old ally to the vengeance of an angry France. Significantly, António de Araújo,[5] the Portuguese plenipotentiary who negotiated with

2. Hawkesbury, dispatch to João de Almeida, in *Historia da Guerra Civil e do estabelecimento do governo parlamentar em Portugal comprehendendo a historia diplomatica militar e política d'este reino desde 1777 até 1834*, by Simão José da Luz Soriano. 19 vols (Lisboa: Imprensa Nacional, 1866–90), 1.ª época, t. III [3]: 432 ([June 1801]), henceforward abbreviated to 'Soriano, *HGC*'; see also Grenville, dispatch to the Portuguese minister plenipotentiary to London, José Luís de Vasconcelos e Sousa, quoted in *HGC*, 1.ª época, t. II [2]: 322–23 (18 January 1801). This work in 19 physical volumes is organized by 'épocas' ('periods'), then by 'tomos' ('volumes') and finally by parts (e.g. '3.ª época, t. III, pt. 2 [15]'); the number in square brackets corresponds to the physical volume, though with no relation to the work's internal organization.

3. Holland, answer to Lord Hobart's address at the House of Lords upon His Majesty's message respecting the defence of Portugal (20 May 1801), *The European Magazine and London Review* 39 (June 1801): 451.

4. Ibid.

5. D. António de Araújo e Azevedo (1754–1817), 1st and only Conde da Barca, Portuguese diplomat and statesman, the son of António Pereira Pinto de Araújo e Azevedo and Maria Francisca de Araújo e Azevedo. Araújo was Envoy Extraordinary and Minister Plenipotentiary to The Hague (1787, 1801–2), Minister Plenipotentiary to the French Republic (1795, 1797 and 1801) and Minister to Russia (1802–3). He was recalled in 1804 to take the foreign

France in 1797, is the first reported Portuguese visitor to Holland House, appearing on 11 and 16 February 1802, and again on 12 June 1802.[6] Of course in May 1802, Britain and France were officially at peace. Indeed if Britain could be at peace with France, Portugal certainly could. It may be that in 1801 and 1802, Holland really thought – although he did not make himself entirely clear – that Portugal should come to terms with France.

Lannes, the French minister in Lisbon,[7] displayed a hard, even contemptuous, attitude to the regent, later D. João VI.[8] Lannes wanted to force Portugal to take the French side in the renewed war with Britain. The regent attempted to be conciliatory and managed to secure an agreement that Portugal should remain neutral in return for a payment of 16 million francs. The regent's policies had to reflect the fact that Britain was no more supportive than it had been in 1801 and 1802. Replying to a memorandum of 1 June 1803, addressed to the British government by Domingos de Sousa Coutinho, Minister Plenipotentiary to London and future Conde do Funchal, Hawkesbury promised to respect Portuguese neutrality in the renewed war with France, but offered no guarantee of military assistance if the French invaded, at least not until Britain could secure its own dominions.[9] Lack of British support forced Portugal to make further concessions to France. A pro-French party

---

ministry, a position he accumulated with that of Kingdom Minister (Home Secretary) from 1806, and which he held until the transference of the Portuguese Court to Rio de Janeiro in November 1807. While in Brazil Araújo was Foreign Secretary (1815–17), Home Secretary (1817) and Minister of Navy and Ultramar (1814–17). Araújo was created Conde da Barca on 17 December 1815 and died in Rio de Janeiro 21 June 1817.

6. BL, HHP, MSS Add. 51950, Dinner Books: 1799–1806, ff. 80^r–80^v, 98^r (11, 16 February, 12 June 1802).
7. Jean Lannes (1769–1809), 1st duc de Montebello, French Marshal and diplomat, the son of Jean Lannes, a merchant, and Cécile Fouraignan. One of Napoleon's true friends, Lannes was appointed Envoy Extraordinary and Minister Plenipotentiary to Lisbon on 14 November 1801, where he arrived from Madrid in March 1802. He remained in Portugal until July 1804, when he left for Paris to attend Napoleon's coronation, never to return.
8. D. João Maria José Francisco Xavier de Paula Luís António Domingos Rafael de Bragança (1767–1826), later D. João VI of Portugal (r. 1816–26), second son of Queen D. Maria I and D. Pedro III. Following the premature death of his eldest brother, the Infante D. José in 1788, João became the heir of the Portuguese throne. When his mother was impeded to rule in 1792 after having been declared mentally incompetent by her physicians, João became the de facto Regent of Portugal, although rejecting the idea of a formal regency until 1799. D. João was King of the United Kingdom of Portugal, Brazil and the Algarves from 1816 to 1822, and, although the de facto United Kingdom ceased to exist after the independence of Brazil in 1822, he remained as a de jure king until 1825. After there cognition of Brazilian independence under the 1825 Treaty of Rio de Janeiro, João continued as King of Portugal and the Algarves until his death in 1826.
9. D. Domingos António de Sousa Coutinho (1760–1833), 1st Conde and Marquês do Funchal, Portuguese diplomatist, the son of D. Francisco Inocêncio de Sousa Coutinho (1726–1780), Governor of Angola (1761–72), and his wife, D. Ana Luísa Joaquina da Silva Teixeira de Andrade Barbosa. Coutinho was appointed Minister to Copenhagen in 1788 and replaced his brother, D. Rodrigo, at Turin in 1796. On 13 May 1803, Coutinho was appointed Minister Plenipotentiary to London, remaining there until 1814, when he was replaced by the Conde de Palmela. He was created Conde do Funchal on 17 December 1808 and Marquês do Funchal on 9 April 1833. Coutinho returned to Britain as D. Pedro's Plenipotentiary on 24 February

appeared at the court, and Lannes was able to persuade the regent to dismiss supposedly pro-British ministers and replace them with men more sympathetic to France.[10] Lannes left for Paris in July 1804 to attend Napoleon's coronation as emperor.

Later in the same year – during a time when there was no French minister in Lisbon – Holland made his first visit to Portugal. The visit began on 30 November when Holland and his party crossed the eastern border at Elvas on their way back from Madrid. Over two years earlier, Dr Vaughan had recommended that the Hollands take their eldest son, Charles Richard,[11] to a warmer climate – advice they readily accepted.[12] Anxious to meet his Spanish friends and collect further material for his account of the life of sixteenth-century Spanish dramatist Félix Lope de Vega y Carpio (1562–1635), Holland planned an extended tour of the Peninsula.[13] Preparations included the appointment of a physician to replace Dr Drew, whose own health was failing. The choice fell on Dr John Allen (1771–1843), a young Scottish physician recommended by Sydney Smith and Lord Lauderdale, who joined the group setting off for the Continent. Allen soon became part of the family, first as resident physician, private secretary and archivist, and then as devoted friend and inseparable companion. Apart from Allen, the party included the Hollands' two children, Charles and the newborn Henry Edward,[14] William Howard[15] and Rev. Matthew Marsh.[16] They left

---

1832 and died unmarried on 1 December 1833, aged 73, in a hotel room in Brighton arranged for him by Lord Holland.

10. In August 1803, the prince regent accepted Lannes's demands for the removal of several ministers thought to be pro-British, including João de Almeida de Melo e Castro (1756–1814), 5th Conde das Galveias, and Rodrigo de Sousa Coutinho, 1st Conde de Linhares, Foreign Minister and President of the Royal Treasury. They were replaced by Luís Pinto de Sousa Coutinho (1735–1804), 1st Visconde de Balsemão, and Luís de Vasconcelos e Sousa (1742–1809), 4th Conde de Figueiró, considered more compliant to France.
11. Charles Richard Fox (1796–1873), army officer and archaeologist, was the natural son of Lady and Lord Holland born before their marriage. Charles married in 1824 to Lady Mary Fitz Clarence, a daughter of William IV by his mistress Dorothy Jordan.
12. Holland, *The Journal of Elizabeth Lady Holland*, 2: 149.
13. The book, published as *Some Account of the Life and Writings of Lope Felix de Vega Carpio* (London: 1806), was dedicated to Manuel Quintana, who had assisted Holland in collecting material. It was a success and its 500 initial copies sold in the first months, requiring a second printing. In 1814 Holland began a second edition, now including a biography of Guillén de Castro y Bellvis (1569–1631), published in 1817 in two volumes as *Some Account of the Lives and Writings of L. F. de Vega Carpio, and G. de Castro.*
14. Henry Edward Fox (1802–1859), afterwards 4th Lord Holland, the son of Henry Richard Vassall Fox and his wife Elizabeth Vassall. He was born at Holland House on 7 March 1802 and died at Naples on 8 December 1859. Henry Edward married Mary Augusta Coventry (1812–1889), the daughter of George William Coventry, 8th Earl of Coventry, and Lady Mary Beauclerk, on 9 May 1833. The couple had no issue and the barony became extinct.
15. William Howard (1781–1843), the son of Frederick Howard (1748–1825), 5th Earl of Carlisle, and his wife, Lady Caroline Leveson-Gower (1753–1824).
16. Matthew Marsh (†1840), chancellor and canon residentiary of Salisbury, son of Rev. Philemon Marsh and his wife, Mary Hornsey. Married 8 September 1808 Margaret, daughter of Rev. Peter Billinger Brodie.

Kensington on 8 July 1802, spending the summer in Paris, where they were introduced to Napoleon himself.[17] The party entered Spain on 7 November and remained there for two years. On 14 November 1804, the Hollands left Madrid for Portugal, which they reached on 30 November, before embarking for England on 14 March 1805.

The visit began badly. On arriving at Estremoz on 2 December, Charlotte, Elizabeth's *femme de chambre*, fell ill. After a few days' delay, the party resumed the journey to Lisbon, leaving Allen behind to care for Charlotte.[18] By the time they reached Aldeia Galega on the south bank of the Tagus, on 7 December, almost everyone was ill.[19] On 10 December, still at Aldeia Galega, Holland reported to his sister that 'Charles & Harry E. are both ill & Lady H.^{d} very much out of spirits & ill too.'[20] On 11 December, after a twenty-four-hour quarantine in an open boat, they finally arrived in Lisbon, 'still unsettled, tho' in an excellent house'[21] – in the Parish of Santa Isabel, close to the church and the British cemetery – arranged for them by Chamberlain, British consul at Lisbon.[22]

Lady Holland was so ill that she 'had no courage to keep her notes of anything that occurred' for a month and a half, although Holland maintained a regular correspondence with his sister.[23] Holland's letters to Caroline Fox refer to a dinner with Lord and Lady Robert Fitzgerald[24] on 11 December, but – unusually for the Hollands – no other engagements are mentioned.[25] The letters suggest anxiety and depression. On 28 December Holland criticizes the Lisbon climate which 'has fallen very low of its reputation in judging either by its appearance & by its effects. It has rained incessantly & all the houses humid &c. &c'[26] so that '[o]ur servants as well as ourselves have been all ill.'[27] Complaints follow about 'dirty streets, bad pavements, inconvenient carriages & dangerous roads & above all enormous distances'.[28] But the mood lifts when, in the New Year, the weather finally improves. On 3 January 1805, Holland is pleased to note that 'Henry E. begins to walk a little & is in all respects a charming child.'[29] By 16 January, he

17. BL, HHP, MSS Add. 51950, Dinner Books: 1799–1806, f. 97^{r} (Thursday, 8 July 1802).
18. BL, HHP, MSS Add. 51737, Lord Holland to Caroline Fox, f. 133^{r} (2 December 1804); ibid., f. 137^{v} (10 December 1804).
19. Elizabeth Vassall, 3rd Baroness of Holland, *The Spanish Journal of Elizabeth Lady Holland* (London: Longmans, Green, 1910), 183.
20. BL, HHP, MSS Add. 51737, Lord Holland to Caroline Fox, f. 137^{v} (10 December 1804).
21. Ibid., f. 141^{r} (11 December 1804).
22. Sir Henry Chamberlain (1773–1829), Consul General and Chargé d'Affaires at Lisbon and Rio de Janeiro.
23. Holland, *The Spanish Journal*, 183.
24. Lord Robert Stephen Fitzgerald (1765–1833), British diplomat, one of the many children of Lieut.-General James Fitzgerald, 1st Duke of Leinster, and his wife, Lady Emilia Mary Lennox (1731–1814), one of the daughters of the Duke of Richmond. Robert married Lady Sophia Charlotte Feilding, the daughter of the Commodore Charles Feilding and Sophia Finch.
25. BL, HHP, MSS Add. 51737, Lord Holland to Caroline Fox, f. 141^{v} (11 December 1804).
26. Ibid., f. 152^{r} (28 December 1804).
27. Ibid., ff. 152^{r}–152^{v} (28 December 1804).
28. Ibid., f. 152^{v} (28 December 1804).
29. Ibid., f. 158^{r} (3 January 1805). Henry Edward suffered from leg trouble from the time of his birth.

announces that Lady Holland is better and Charles 'occasionally in good looks [*sic*].'[30] His own gout has improved, though he can 'hardly venture to walk in these ill paved streets so that I am likely to get it from want of exercise'.[31] A new reference to the Fitzgeralds and their kindness suggests that social life had recommenced.[32]

On 20 February 1805, the Hollands left for 'a short excursion into the country',[33] visiting Batalha, Alcobaça, Marinha Grande, Leiria and the famous baths at Caldas da Rainha, 'which has improved Lady H's health & induced me to try restoring Baby's strength & my own'.[34] On 14 March, after collecting their children at Lisbon, the Hollands were back to Caldas, where they remained for about three weeks. On 8 April, they returned to Lisbon and, a few days later, embarked for England on the *Walsingham* packet.

Lady Holland's illness and that of other members of the party in December 1804 curtailed the family's normally busy social life and gave Lord Holland plenty of time to read, think and write about Portugal.[35] The result was an impressive piece of political analysis, a manuscript dated 8 January 1805, where Holland identifies the terrible choice that Portugal must make.[36] If Portugal stays true to its old alliance with Britain, it will face war with France and likely French invasion. If Portugal achieves some kind of accommodation with France, the British will probably seize its colonies.

Holland wonders, whether in the face of French pressure, Portugal will find 'the means of resisting these demands? Or will she avail herself of them?'[37] Holland thinks Portugal will do neither. The choice between Britain and France is so difficult that, in reality, Portugal has no choice but to resort to evasion and equivocation. Much depends on the abilities of Portugal's rulers. Holland's estimate of the Portuguese ruling class was never entirely favourable and, over the years, ranged from qualified approval to something approaching contempt. Perhaps the best summary is to be found in Holland's *Foreign Reminiscences*: 'the leading men in Portugal are not deficient in character or knowledge […] but they are full of little jealousies and artifices, and more cunning in their negotiations with powerful states than wise in the management of their own'.[38]

---

30. Ibid., f. 165^{r} (16 January 1805).
31. Ibid.
32. Ibid., f. 166^{r} (16 January 1805).
33. Ibid., f. 181^{r} (9 March 1805).
34. Ibid.
35. Ibid., f. 163^{v} (10 January 1805); ibid., f. 165^{r} (16 January 1805).
36. Holland's political memorandum, consisting in six manuscript loose folios, truncated, is preserved among other documents relating to Portugal in the Holland House Papers (Add. 51633). Based on the calligraphy and subject it is reasonable to argue that it is a continuation of Lord Holland's Journal for 1802 (Add. 51860). This valuable document may explain the hiatus in his journals between the period 1802 and 1808–9. John Clarke's and my own edition of Holland's memorandum was published as 'Lord Holland's Portuguese Journal (1805): Extract', *Revista de estudos anglo-portugueses* 23 (2014): 260–63.
37. Ibid., f. 9^{r}.
38. Holland, *Foreign Reminiscences*, 162.

While Holland is unimpressed with 'the present disorganized and dispirited [Portuguese] army', he believes that, if the French do invade, they will not make an easy conquest.[39] Provided the government does not fall into 'sudden and incurable panics'[40] – sadly a serious possibility – Lisbon should remain fairly safe, largely because the invaders would have to contend with 'the natural defences of a barren frontier, a burning sun and a savage peasantry'.[41] But Holland never suggests that the Portuguese can defeat the French on their own; some foreign military assistance will be needed – although not very much. At the end of 1804 and beginning of 1805, Holland thinks in terms of 'a very trifling additional force of English or Russian troops',[42] noting that 'Russia & England were cordially united'.[43]

One of the features of Holland's analysis, now and later, is his readiness, perhaps natural in an essentially 'opposition' politician, to blame the British government for some of the problems facing Portugal. It must be said that Holland is not entirely consistent; sometimes he criticizes the British government for too much involvement in Portuguese affairs and sometimes for too little. It is important first to consider this memorandum in the light of Holland's previous dealings with Portugal and then to compare it to the subsequent course of events in that country.

The period between the end of Holland's first visit to Portugal and the fall of Lisbon to the French on 30 November, 1807 was important for Holland's own career. Following the death of William Pitt in January 1806, Holland's uncle, Charles Fox, so long in the political wilderness, became foreign secretary in the 'Ministry of All the Talents'. Holland's relationship with his uncle was close, and Fox had developed a habit of discussing all political matters with his 'dear young one.' Fox certainly seems to have given more attention to the Peninsula than his predecessors had done. It is tempting to attribute this change to Holland, although there is little direct evidence of his influence. The surviving correspondence between Holland and Fox for this period is sparse and, as Lord John Russell later remarked, their 'letters are more literary than political'.[44] In his memoirs, Holland refers to conversations with Fox about the peace negotiations with France, but there is no specific mention of Portugal.[45] Yet Holland's Lisbon notes could have been useful to Fox and, while Holland's presence in Portugal had been largely fortuitous, he probably had more direct knowledge of the situation there than any other member of Fox's circle.

Fox, a man who had welcomed the French Revolution and admired Napoleon, believed that he could achieve a lasting peace with France.[46] Yet, once the negotiations

---

39. BL, HHP, MSS Add. 51633, Papers relative to Portugal: 1831–1830: Lord Holland's Political Notes, f. 9^{r}.
40. Ibid.
41. Ibid.
42. Ibid.
43. Ibid., f. 14^{v}.
44. John Russell, preface to *Memorials and Correspondence of Charles James Fox*. 4 vols (London: Richard Bentley, 1853–1857), 1: viii–ix.
45. Holland, *Memoirs of the Whig Party*, 1: 256.
46. Holland, 'Negotiations for Peace between England and France', *Annual Register for the Year 1806* 47 (1806): 173.

began, it soon became clear that the French terms would be unacceptable. Fox's position hardened – and Holland's probably did too. On receiving dispatches from Paris, Fox admitted to Holland that the French were 'playing a false game' and concluded that the negotiations would fail.[47] Whereas in the past, Holland appears to have believed that the question of the wisdom of an alliance with Britain or an alliance with France was finally balanced, his position seems to have changed over the course of 1806 and 1807. Now there can be no question that an alliance with Britain was to be preferred and – despite continuing good will for Portugal – there was more thought about how that alliance could be used to Britain's advantage.

In the course of the negotiations in Paris, Talleyrand threatened that if a peace treaty with Britain was not concluded, France would invade Portugal with a force of 30,000 men. Fox responded vigorously by ordering Earl St Vincent to take a squadron to the Tagus.[48] On 25 August Lieut.-General Simcoe, Lord Rosslyn and Henry Brougham joined St Vincent at Lisbon, bringing with them Fox's instructions on terms of British aid.[49] Although Brougham was officially the secretary to the British negotiators, he later claimed to have been a de facto commissioner.[50] Fox had outlined three possible courses of action:

1. To assist Portugal in preventing or repulsing a combined invasion of France and Spain by putting all the necessary military, naval and pecuniary resources at the disposal of the Portuguese government;
2. To escort the Portuguese royal family on their retreat to Brazil if Portugal found itself unable or unwilling to resist an invasion;
3. To confiscate Portugal's resources, including its fleet, thus preventing it from falling into enemy hands if the Prince Regent chose to stay in Lisbon and 'be voluntarily swallowed by the enemy'.[51]

While the first plan entails the prospect of a much more substantial British commitment to Portugal than envisaged in the past, the second and, even more, the third reveal a

47. Ibid., 1: 257.
48. John Jervis (1735–1823), 1st Earl of St Vincent, British Admiral of the Fleet and an MP, the second son of Swynfen and Elizabeth Jervis. He served in the Seven Years' War, the American War of Independence, the French Revolutionary War and the Napoleonic Wars. His victory at the Battle of Cape St Vincent in 1797 earned him the title of Earl of St Vincent.
49. John Graves Simcoe (1752–1806), British army officer and first Lieutenant Governor of Upper Canada (1791–96), the only surviving son of General John Simcoe and his wife, Katherine. During the outward voyage to Lisbon, Simcoe had fallen ill and stayed in Portugal for only one month before returning to England; he died a few hours after landing at Plymouth. The negotiations with the Portuguese authorities were therefore conducted by Rosslyn and St Vincent alone.
50. Henry Brougham, *The Life and Times of Henry Brougham written by himself.* 2nd edn. 3 vols (Edinburgh; London: William Blackwood, 1871), 1: 327.
51. Fox, 'Dispatch from Mr. Secretary Fox to the Earls of Rosslyn and St. Vincent, and lieut. gen. Simcoe, dated Downing Street 9th Aug. 1806', in *Parl. Deb.*, 10 (1808): cc. 537–43.

ruthless determination to protect British interests, regardless of the implications for Portugal.

From the Portuguese perspective, the most alarming possibility was that the British might attempt to seize Brazil.[52] The British might not be able to prevent the French from overrunning most of Europe but if European states occupied by the French had overseas empires, the British had no intention of allowing these empires to be controlled by France's allies. In this case the British could do something about it. Yet, if the British were to take Brazil there could be no certainty that it would be returned when hostilities ceased.

Hence, on 30 August, during a conference at the Royal Palace of Mafra, Araújo rejected Rosslyn's offers of military, naval and financial aid. The next day St Vincent informed Howick that 'the government of Portugal will be either openly or tacitly adverse [*sic*] to landing the troops, much more so to giving them possession of the three most important forts'.[53] Araújo claimed that the vaunted French army of 30,000 at Bayonne was a fiction and, hence – although grateful for Britain's concern – declined Fox's offer of assistance. He went on to complain that Britain's 'excessive zeal' had already jeopardized Portugal's safety by raising suspicions in both France and Spain that it had abandoned its neutrality. St Vincent received orders to return home, leaving the Tagus on 28 September 1806.

Fox died on 13 September 1806 and the peace negotiations with France ended without result on 9 October. The new foreign secretary was Howick, the very man who had blocked Holland's appointment as a peace commissioner. Holland's influence on policy towards Spain and Portugal – likely though difficult to prove in Fox's time – was now substantially diminished, although his interest remained strong.

In 1805 Holland had predicted that some time would elapse before France applied serious pressure on Portugal. In this he was proved right – although for rather different reasons than those advanced in Holland's memorandum. Again, Portugal's fate was affected by developments on the other side of Europe. Prussian preparations for war forced Napoleon to postpone his plans for Spain and Portugal and to recall troops on their way to Bayonne. But Portugal's respite was short lived. Prussia was rapidly defeated and, since any hopes of defeating Britain at sea had ended at Trafalgar, Napoleon determined on economic warfare. On 21 November 1806, the emperor issued the Berlin Decree, intended to bring Britain to its knees by closing all of Europe to its exports. Russia agreed to join what became known as the Continental System under the terms of the Treaty of Tilsit of 7 July 1807, thus removing the possibility of Anglo-Russian collaboration in defence of Portugal envisaged in Holland's memorandum. Only three European states, Denmark, Sweden and Portugal, now remained outside the System. If Napoleon's

52. During preparations for the expeditions to the Cape of Good Hope and Buenos Ayres, rumours began to circulate that Britain was about to attack Portugal's South American possessions. Suspicions became so strong that Sousa Coutinho was forced to ask the British government whether there was any truth to them. Howick responded with a flat denial (Soriano, *HGC*, 1.ª época, t. II [2], 627).

53. St Vincent, 'To Viscount Howick', *Life and Correspondence of John, Earl of St. Vincent.* 2 vols (London: Henry Colburn, 1838), 2: 306 (1 September 1806).

plans were to have any chance of success these powers had to be persuaded, or if necessary, forced to join. Of course, the construction of the Continental System meant that Britain would seek to find other outlets for its exports – and Brazil was perhaps the most attractive target. In other words Portugal faced one of the most acute crises in her history, a crisis remarkably similar to the one predicted in Holland's memorandum.

On 12 August 1807, the French Chargé d'Affaires, Maximilien de Rayneval,[54] demanded that Portugal close its ports to British ships by 1 September, detain all British residents and seize their property and agree to the transfer of the Portuguese navy to Spain and France. As Holland had foreseen in 1805, Portugal attempted to follow an evasive policy. Thus when Portugal accepted the French ultimatum and declared war on Britain on 20 October 1807, this was followed by a secret treaty with Britain agreeing to transfer the Portuguese capital to Brazil and to British temporary occupation of Madeira (22 October). But Napoleon had already decided on an invasion of Portugal and on 27 October the Franco-Spanish Treaty of Fontainebleau was concluded to that end.

Even before the treaty was signed, a French force in Spain, commanded by Jean-Andoche Junot (1771–1813), was making its way to the frontier, crossing into Portugal on 19 November with 25,000 troops. Thereafter events moved with remarkable speed and Junot was able to take Lisbon – with a force of only 1,500 men – on 30 November 1807. Junot had made such haste in his advance on Lisbon – so much so that his men were exhausted and almost starving – because he wished to prevent the escape of the prince regent and his court.[55] In this he failed, though by a slender margin. On 29 November, the day before Junot's arrival, the regent, accompanied by as many as 15,000 followers, had completed his departure – with British assistance – and was now on his way to Brazil.

The departure of the Portuguese court for Brazil prompted Holland to produce another memorandum – perhaps even more important than that of 1805 – this time intended for the attention of his friend Domingos de Sousa Coutinho. This fascinating piece of political writing, perhaps one of Holland's finest of the kind, was originally written in English or in French – the languages used in their correspondence – although it survived only indirectly through a Portuguese translation by Soriano.[56] Holland concentrates on Brazil and is clearly excited at the prospect of the creation of 'an independent and sovereign monarchy'. He trusts that this is also the real objective of the

54. Maximilien Gérard (1778–1836), comte de Rayneval, French diplomat, was entrusted with the mission of communicating to the Portuguese government the French ultimatum demanding that Portugal join the Continental System.

55. Although the French invading force was 25,000–30,000 strong, Junot decided to take a detachment of 3,000–4,000 men ahead, hoping to reach the capital before the prince regent could escape. This explains why the first French to reach Lisbon were completely exhausted. The severe winter and desolate country with no passable roads had delayed the main body of Junot's army.

56. Henry Richard Vassall, 3rd Baron of Holland, 'Carta ou memoria de lord Holland dirigida ao conde do Funchal relativamente á saida da côrte portugueza para o Brazil', in *HGC*, 2.ª época, t. V, pt. 1 [9]: 249–56.

Regent, who should 'look forward to the loss of his Lisbon palaces with the same indifference that his ancestors witnessed the confiscation of their goods in Spain'.[57]

As far as Holland is concerned, the most serious danger is that the regent and his advisors will regard Brazil merely as a place of temporary refuge, whose only purpose is 'the avoidance of Bonaparte's resentment'.[58] One of the characteristic features of Holland's thinking is his ability to draw comparisons between Spain and Portugal on the one hand and other somewhat similar societies, notably those in southern Italy. Thus he warns that the court in Brazil must not repeat the example of 'the two escapes [to Sicily] of the King of Naples [Ferdinand IV in 1799 and 1806] from his capital'.[59] If the regent behaved like Ferdinand, 'we may look for the same result, viz.; the dismemberment of the kingdom, the degradation of some of the people and the discontent of the other'.[60] Fortunately Holland has a higher expectation of 'the reputation of the House of Braganza' than that of the Neapolitan Bourbons.

But Holland was too much of a Whig to suppose that the success of the project would depend entirely on the regent and his court. It was essential to involve the inhabitants of Brazil, to encourage them to identify with the idea of a Brazilian monarchy both for reasons of self-esteem and interest. Holland hoped that without formally renouncing the Portuguese throne, the prince would be proclaimed emperor of Brazil, a title with 'the double advantage of being, I dare say, *very fashionable*, and would give preference to Brazil without offending the self-esteem of the Portuguese'.[61]

Holland recommends the speedy establishment of 'a system of external commerce', especially in respect of trade with Britain. Holland talks of the laws that 'an enlightened ministry' would enact 'to animate the commerce of their country'. He suggests that new arrangements would be in the interests of both Britain and Brazil, but his language is curiously guarded: 'Discretion prevents me from stressing my ideas, although I trust, and actually believe, that every Englishman, especially every minister, thinks as I have stated above'.[62] It is reasonably clear, however, that Holland is urging the prince to abolish the colonial laws that – at least in theory – permitted Brazil to maintain direct commercial relations with Portugal only. But Holland had to be careful. If Brazil were to open its trade, the chief beneficiary would likely be Britain. Only a few months earlier, some in the British government had been contemplating a takeover of Brazil, and there must have been some who suspected that support for the establishment of 'an independent and sovereign monarchy' in Brazil was merely a cover to advance British interests – in other words 'Informal Empire' *avant la lettre*.

Holland insisted that it was vital to appoint Brazilians to ministerial positions and not to restrict them to subordinate positions. The exclusion of locals from positions of authority had been the great mistake of the King of Naples when he moved to Palermo, a policy that 'will soon reap the malign fruit of its odious partiality and misplaced

57. Holland, 'Carta ou memoria', 250.
58. Ibid.
59. Ibid.
60. Ibid.
61. Ibid., 251.
62. Ibid., 252.

mistrust'.[63] It is true that Holland seems to harbour doubts as to whether any Brazilians have the talents necessary to make an outstanding contribution to the ministry, but finds consolation in the thought that 'there should at least be someone of sufficient stature in terms of birth, fortune and probity not to dishonour it'.[64]

Perhaps the most distinctive feature of Whig political thinking is the stress placed on the role of the aristocracy and landowners. Thus Holland argues that 'the great Brazilian proprietors must enjoy all consideration that would enable them to keep their dignities, titles, orders and benefits from the Court'.[65] Indeed there should be a law that guarantees the nobility 'due consideration from the state'.[66]

Holland proposes a meeting of deputies but argues that it should be held with the least possible formality. He is even reluctant to give it a name, anything like *Cortes* 'could give rise to excitement in a manner inconvenient to circumstances'.[67] Holland wishes to avoid 'the inconvenience of an extraordinary election',[68] suggesting that it would probably be better simply to summon men who already held office as 'chief or mayor of each municipality'.[69] He does stress that great care must be taken in choosing a minister who can liaise with the deputies and encourage them to draw up lists of desirable measures that can then be presented to the prince. It is especially important to listen to their advice on everything relating to taxes. But the powers of the prince remain remarkably large: 'it will be entirely up to the Prince to indicate the subject of their deliberations, and after learning the result, he should have the exclusive privilege of drawing up laws and arranging their promulgation'.[70] In England attempts by the Crown to confine parliamentary debates to topics designated by the monarch had failed in the 1590s.

Although some of Holland's proposals were ignored, others were reflected in the arrangements made in 1815 when the United Kingdom of Portugal, Brazil and Algarves was set up.[71] Holland's memorandum may be seen as the first in a series of similar attempts to influence the nature of constitutional governments in Spain, Naples and, indirectly, in Portugal. Thus many of Holland's 'Brazilian' recommendations reappear in the advice he gave to the Spanish authorities in 1809 and again in his sketch for a Neapolitan Constitution in 1815.

Perhaps for a while, Lord Holland took emotional refuge in contemplating Brazil's bright future, because prospects in Spain and Portugal seemed so bleak. But there were soon to be signs of vitality and a yearning for national and political freedom in those countries, developments that inspired Holland to take a third and final visit to the Peninsula and to further constitutional analysis.

---

63. Ibid.
64. Ibid.
65. Ibid.
66. Ibid.
67. Ibid., 253.
68. Ibid.
69. Ibid.
70. Ibid., 254.
71. By decree of 16 December 1815, Brazil was officially elevated to the category of kingdom as part of the United Kingdom of Portugal, Brazil and Algarves.

Chapter Two

RENEWED ACQUAINTANCE

It must be confessed that Portugal appears to great advantage when one enters it by this road leaving behind the dreary plains of Spanish Estremadura.[*]

A few hours before embarking for Brazil, on 27 November 1807, D. João issued a declaration to his 'faithful and beloved subjects', explaining the reasons for his departure and announcing the appointment of a council of regency. The council was to prove totally ineffective, not least because D. João had expressly forbidden it from resisting the French invaders. Unlike Spain, however, Portugal had preserved its monarchy and hence Napoleon could not claim the Portuguese crown for himself or for one of his brothers. While Carlos IV and his son Fernando VII resigned the Spanish throne into Napoleon's hands during their confinement in France in 1808, the House of Bragança never renounced its rights. Although Junot declared the authority of House of Bragança extinguished on 5 February 1808, this unilateral proclamation was unlikely to be recognized by other European powers.[1]

For a while it seemed that the French would encounter little opposition in either Spain or Portugal. But, as Holland had always appreciated, the peoples of the Peninsula were fiercely independent; the real question was whether, in the event of a rising, leaders of sufficient quality would emerge or foreign powers, especially Britain, would provide effective support. Madrid was the first town to rise on 2 May 1808. Although the rebellion was quickly suppressed and ended with the execution of at least one hundred people, it encouraged risings elsewhere. Within two months, patriotic juntas had been established throughout the Peninsula. Influenced by developments in Galicia, the first Portuguese risings broke out in the north, in Chaves and Oporto, on 6 June 1808. The first Oporto rising collapsed after three days owing to the cowardice of the military governor, Brigadier Luís Osório.[2] Two weeks later, however, on 18 June, a new rebellion led

---

* BL, HHP, MSS Add. 51861, Lord Holland's Travel Journals: 1809, f. 3^v (4 July 1809).

1. Junot, declaration to the 'Habitantes de Portugal', *Gazeta de Lisboa*, suppl. extra. Fevereiro 5, 1808, [1]. The plan to remove the dynasties of Borbón and Bragança from the Peninsula had been decided in a secret Russian–French convention signed by Prince Kurakin and Talleyrand on 7 July 1807 as part of the Tilsit compacts.
2. Luís de Oliveira da Costa de Almeida Osório (1753–1809), governor of Oporto at the beginning of the French invasions and imprisoned on 17 September – immediately after the French's withdrawal. In 1809, Osório and 14 other prisoners were murdered by a mob which forced its way into the dungeons. A subsequent court decision (28 March 1817), declared Osório innocent and his honour restored.

to the establishment of a patriotic junta headed by the bishop of Oporto.[3] There were further risings, at Leiria on 30 June and Évora on 20 July, though both were suppressed. Most crucially, however, the remaining French troops left Lisbon on 15 September, though with British protection and under the terms of the controversial Anglo-French Convention of Sintra (30 August 1808).

The British certainly made a significant contribution to ending the first French occupation of Portugal. The affairs of Spain were debated in the Commons on 15 June 1808, and for once government and opposition were in agreement, a fact reflected in the king's speech of 4 July.[4] The Spaniards, who had been instructed by their provincial juntas to decline any offer of direct military assistance, asked for money, arms and stores – requests promptly granted. The British government was prepared to send an expeditionary force to Portugal, which would tie down Junot and prevent his forces being used against General Blake's army in Spain. Domingos de Sousa Coutinho, understandably eager to see the French expelled from his country, agreed.

Hence, in July 1808, Secretary for War Viscount Castlereagh dispatched a modest force of 8,743 men from Cork to Portugal.[5] The command was given to young but experienced Lieut.-General Arthur Wellesley. The first action, on 17 August, was at Roliça and Columbeira, when the Anglo-Portuguese army forced the French, under Delaborde, to retreat but without any great loss. On 15 August Junot took a small force to meet Wellesley; fearing that Lisbon would be vulnerable to attack from the British fleet under Sir Charles Cotton, he left 6,500 men behind.[6] A few days later, after joining Delaborde and Loison, Junot advanced to the Vimeiro heights, where Wellesley had concentrated his forces.[7] Joined by Anstruther's Ramsgate Brigade and Acland's Harwich Brigade, which had disembarked on 19 and 20 August, Wellesley now had a force of 16,778 men plus 2,000 Portuguese provided by Bernardim Freire de Andrade.[8] The French, with about 13,000 men, attacked on the morning of 21 August but were routed and retired in confusion. If Sir Harry Burrard, who had arrived before the end

3. D. António de São José de Castro (1745–1814), a Carthusian friar and a natural son of the Conde de Resende, appointed Bishop of Oporto in 1798. On 19 June 1808, after Oporto rose against the French, Castro was elected President of the *Junta Provisional do Supremo Governo do Reino*. Following the French withdrawal, he was appointed to the Council of Regency although he did not move to Lisbon until the beginning of 1809. He was then elected Cardinal Patriarch of Lisbon, but the pope refused to confirm him because of his illegitimacy.

4. *Parl. Deb.*, 11: 886–8.

5. Misled by inaccurate intelligence furnished by the Spanish deputies, suggesting that Junot had no more than 15,000 men, Castlereagh, agreed to send a force of 8,743 men to Portugal. The British force, previously intended for Mexico, was clearly insufficient for the task ahead of it in Portugal.

6. Sir Charles Cotton (1753–1812), 5th Baronet, a senior Royal Navy Officer of the French Revolutionary and Napoleonic Wars.

7. Louis-Henri Loison (1771–1816), French general, son of François Loison, a lawyer, and of Marie-Thérèse Charlotte Patusset, from Saint-Germain.

8. Bernardim Freire de Andrade e Castro (1759–1809), Portuguese army officer, son of D. Fernando Martins Freire de Andrade e Castro, *Morgado* (Lord of the Manor) of Ribeira do Sado and Bom Despacho, by his second wife, D. Joana Isabel de Lencastre Forjaz.

of the battle with orders to take command, had not prevented the pursuit and destruction of the remnants of Junot's army, the Battle of Vimeiro could have ended the first French occupation of Portugal.[9] But Burrard, fearing that Junot might still have a large reserve, decided to wait for the arrival of John Moore's division from the Baltic.

Burrard commanded the British army in Portugal for only 24 hours. On the morning of 22 August, Sir Hew Dalrymple (1750–1830), an elderly general with little field experience, landed at Porto Novo (Maceira Bay) with orders to replace Burrard. That afternoon, the new British commander received a visit from François-Étienne Kellermann (1770–1835), a French general who had been given full powers to negotiate an armistice. Kellerman soon realized that Dalrymple was ready to conclude a convention on terms favourable to the French. Although Kellerman had been prepared to accept almost any terms, he now became self-confident and spoke of the possible resumption of hostilities; his bluff gave the French a far better result than they could have reasonably expected. The armistice, later known as the Convention of Sintra, was signed at Lisbon on 30 August 1808, despite Wellesley's objections and the strong protests of the Portuguese leaders. Under its terms, Junot's army was 'to be transported with its arms, ammunition, and plunder, at the expense of Great Britain, in British vessels', back to France.[10]

After the French left Portugal, the country descended into violence, and several people accused of collaboration with the invader were murdered. The *Gazeta de Lisboa*, last published under French control on 24 August, reappeared on 16 September and contained a proclamation from Lieut.-General John Hope appealing for peace and order.[11] The appointment of a government whose members were untarnished with French links appeared essential. Significantly, the establishment of a new council of regency, effectively under British supervision, was announced by Dalrymple in a proclamation dated 11 September.[12] With the French gone and the court in Brazil, Portugal seemed incapable of governing itself. What were the options? To some at least, Portugal had passed from an independent kingdom to a French protectorate and from that to something resembling a British protectorate.

The dramatic events in Spain and Portugal were bound to be of interest to Lord Holland, who was much concerned with them in the summer of 1808. In addition to his visits to the Spanish Club,[13] Holland received several Spaniards, who had been sent to England

9. Sir Harry Burrard (1755–1813), British officer, a veteran of many campaigns in America, Flanders and Denmark.
10. William Wordsworth, *Concerning the Relations of Great Britain, Spain and Portugal to Each Other and to the Common Enemy, at the Crisis and Specifically as Affected by the Convention of Cintra* (London: Longman, Hurst, Rees, and Orme, 1809), 50.
11. 'Proclamação do Tenente General Hope, e Commandante das tropas Britanicas, para a immediata segurança de Lisboa', *Gazeta de Lisboa*, 1.° suppl Setembro 16, 1808, [3].
12. 'Proclamação do General Dalrymple aos Portuguezes (Praias, 11 September 1808)', in *Supplemento á collecção dos tratados, convenções, contratos e actos publicos celebrados entre a Corôa de Portugal e as mais potencias desde 1640 até ao presente.* 22 vols (Lisboa: Imprensa Nacional, 1872–80), 16: [105]–7.
13. BL, HHP, MSS Add. 51951, Dinner Books: 1806–12, ff. 71^{v}–78^{r}. The president of the Spanish Club in London was Alexander Munro (1731–1809), one of its founders in 1780. Holland was the vice president.

by their provincial Juntas to seek assistance against the French. Agustín de Argüelles and Sousa Coutinho, Chargé d'Affaires of both Spain and Portugal, were also regular guests.[14]

The guests hoped that Lord Holland would persuade George Canning, now foreign secretary, to support their cause. Impressed with the enthusiasm of the Spanish deputies, Holland decided to go to the Peninsula to play, in Keppel's words, 'the part of impresario to the epic performance about to begin in Spain'.[15] Holland was determined to take an active part in the revolutionary events in Spain that had followed the Madrid uprising of 2 May 1808. In particular, he hoped to assist the *Junta Suprema Central Gubernativa del Reino* – created on 25 September to govern in the absence of Fernando VII and Carlos IV – to establish a viable constitutional regime in Spain. Perhaps his social status, political influence and knowledge of Spanish could contribute to the liberation of the country and to the establishment of a liberal regime. By acting as an intermediary between the Spanish leaders and the British authorities, Holland might influence political developments and even change the course of history.

Holland's decision to leave for Spain at the beginning of the war and at a time when the Whig Party faced serious problems puzzled many of his friends. Some tried to dissuade him, yet Holland seemed determined to abandon his political career to embark upon an adventure with highly unpredictable consequences. The strongest protest against Holland's apparent irresponsibility came from Lady Caroline Fox, to whom he wrote on the eve of departure: 'You must not my Dear little Sister consider this as a serious *going abroad* but merely as an excursion. […] you may depend on our being back at the very utmost in Spring April or May & Lady H thinks most probably in February.'[16] Early in January 1809, he wrote to his sister: 'you suppose that I am such a Quixote as to put myself in the slightest degree of danger'.[17] But attempts to calm Lady Caroline's anxiety as to the safety of her 'little brother' and nephews probably produced little effect. Holland himself was conscious of the risks, as indicated in a letter to his Spanish friend Jovellanos: 'I beg you to let me know your opinion if I may travel with my wife and family in security'.[18] But was the risk worthwhile? Perhaps it was. Holland's apparent indifference to the claims of immediate duty arguably produced his greatest contribution to humanity. His influence on Spanish and, indirectly, Portuguese constitutionalism, now seems indisputable and will be investigated in more detail in the following chapters.

14. Don Agustín de Argüelles Álvarez Gonzáles (1776–1844), Asturian lawyer, politician and diplomat, he was later called 'el divino' owing to his eloquent speeches during the *Cortes* of Cádiz. Lord Holland had met him in 1793 at Oviedo.
15. Sonia Keppel, *The Sovereign Lady: A Life of Elizabeth Vassall, Third Lady Holland, with Her Family* (London: Hamish Hamilton, 1974), 147.
16. BL, HHP, MSS Add. 51738, Lord Holland to Caroline Fox: 1805–8, ff. 90^{r}–93^{r} (*c.* 7 October 1808).
17. Ibid., f. 142^{v} (Lisbon, 10 January 1809).
18. BL, HHP, MSS Add. 51618, G. M. Jovellanos: 1808–9, Holland to Jovellanos, f. 7^{r} (12 September 1808); 'Le suplico me diga su parecer si pudiese yo viajar con mi muger [sic] y familia con toda seguridad.' (My translation).

The Hollands' second and final visit to the Peninsula – Lord Holland's third – began on 9 October 1808, when they left Kensington for Falmouth, and ended on 12 August 1809, when they arrived back at Holland House.[19] According to Lady Holland, the 'party consisted of ourselves Mr A.[llen] Charles & Ld John Russell (who overtook us near Andover) 2 maids & five men two carriages only being resolved to take as few persons & incumbrances as possible'.[20] The excursion included two periods in Portugal, the first from 16 December 1808 to 26 January 1809, the second from 5 to 19 July 1809, when they embarked from Lisbon for England on the *Lively*.

The second Portuguese journey was largely accidental and resulted from factors beyond the travellers' control. Russell later admitted 'our journey to Portugal was a wild scheme'.[21] The initial plan had been to go to Madrid but, to Lord Holland's regret, the increasingly dangerous situation in Spain made this impossible.[22] Seville, capital of revolutionary Spain after the fall of Madrid in May 1808, seemed the only possible destination, but even then the French advance made a direct journey across Spain hazardous. There were only two reasonably safe ways of reaching Seville – either on a British ship around the coast to Cadiz or a land journey over Portugal's notoriously bad roads. It was only when no suitable ship could be found that the Hollands reluctantly decided on the Portuguese route.[23]

While there is little information about the first journey in 1804–5, the final visit to Portugal in 1808–9 is well documented with the travel journals of Lord Holland, Lady Holland and John Allen, of which my own Portuguese translation was published as *Três diários de viagem em Portugal em 1808–1809*. From a political point of view, Lord Holland's journals are the most interesting. They remind us of Dante's account of the passage through the dark and obscure wood, 'where the straightway was lost'.[24] The crossing of the Lima on 16 December 1808 – identified by the Romans as the Lethe, the mythological river of oblivion – symbolizes the entry into another dimension. But like Junius Brutus before them, the Hollands never forget their own identities.[25] However, subsequent experiences made a decisive impression, especially on

19. Holland, *The Journal of Elizabeth Lady Holland*, 2: 247.
20. BL, HHP, MSS Add. 51933, Lady Holland's Journals: 1806–8, f. 72^{r} (9 October 1808).
21. John Russell, Journal, in *The Life of Lord John Russell*, edited by Spencer Walpole. 2 vols (London: Longmans, Green, 1891), 1: 42 (Lisbon, 7 January 1809).
22. Holland to Jovellanos, in *Cartas de Jovellanos y Lord Vassall Holland*, 1: 97 (La Coruña, Diciembre 4 de 1808); see also Manuel Moreno Alonso, *La forja del liberalismo en España: (Los amigos españoles de Lord Holland 1793–1840)* (Madrid: Congreso de los Diputados, 1997), 135.
23. By mid-November, faced with further French advance, a general retreat of the British forces appeared imminent. Although Admiral de Courcy had put two ships at the Hollands' disposal, first *The Tonnant* and then *The Champion*, they decided to attempt an overland journey to Portugal.
24. 'El mezzo del cammin di nostra vita / Mi ritrovai per una selva oscura, / Che la diritta via era smarrita.' Dante, *Della commedia di Dante Alighieri: transportata in verso latino Eroico da Carlo d'Aquino*. 3 vols (In Napoli: per Felice Mosca, 1728), 1.1: 16.
25. Decimus Junius Brutus Callaicus (180–113 BC), Roman politician and general, the son of the consul Marcus Junius Brutus, led the Roman legions in the conquest of western Iberia.

Lord Holland, whose belief in the possibility of adopting a Whig solution for Portugal was deeply shaken.

The journals seem dominated by the ghost of the Marquês de Pombal. Here we encounter one of the central dilemmas of Whiggery: should one disapprove of enlightened despots because they are despotic or approve of them because they are enlightened? Holland found it difficult to decide. The sight of Pombal's coffin lying unburied and waiting for better days, gave rise to the reflection that 'much of the good he [Pombal] had effected at the expense of every honest & humane feeling was done away at the death of his master & all the improvement he had set on foot arrested in their progress'.[26] Holland disapproves of Pombal's means – 'effected at the expense of every honest and humane feeling' – while acknowledging that real good had been achieved. The comment that this good had been done away with once Pombal's master died is intriguing: is it a simple statement of regret or does it imply that progress achieved through compulsion is inherently precarious and likely to vanish once those who impose it disappear from the scene? Yet, however read, Holland's comment suggests that his usual commitment to the principles of liberty was shaken when faced with the reality of Portugal. He may not have particularly wanted to visit Portugal at all, but there can be no doubt that the experience changed him, notably by increasing his appreciation of the importance of history. The experience is reflected in a statement contained in *Letter to a Neapolitan from an Englishman*, a remarkable piece of political analysis written in conjunction with John Allen and addressed to Murat: 'Constitutions, Sir, cannot be given, – they must be the growth of time.'[27] This seems a tacit acknowledgement that 'freedom' cannot be artificially imposed from above, but must be fought for and deserved.

Holland's doubts about the universality of the Whig solution were clearly beginning to trouble him. Despite the many crimes imputed to Pombal, 'Not less than 17,000 persons were imprisoned by this Minister', Holland recognized that he had left some signs of progress.[28] In the short run Holland could resolve the problem with an axiom, that it was 'Another among the many proofs of the very *short lived* benefits which it is in the power of Despotism to confer on a Country', but he must have felt that the Whig model of society and political system did not fit the Portuguese case.[29] Holland found it impossible to decide whether to emphasize the monstrosity of Pombal's acts or the 'Great courage firmness & sagacity he certainly possessed'.[30] As Clarke suggests, Holland 'must have wondered whether the short-lived benefits of Enlightened Despotism would prove any more enduring if the despot were Napoleon rather than Pombal.'[31] Unable to resolve his dilemma, Holland found comfort in Corneille's famous strophes on Richelieu:

26. BL, HHP, MSS Add. 51862, Lord Holland's Travel Journals: 1808–9, f. 14^{v} (29 December 1809).
27. Henry Richard Vassall, 3rd Baron of Holland, 'To the Reader', in *Letter to a Neapolitan from an Englishman, 1815* (London: Printed by Thomas Davison, 1818), iv.
28. BL, HHP, MSS Add. 51862, Lord Holland's Travel Journals: 1808–9, f. 14^{v} (29 December 1809).
29. Ibid., f. 14^{v} (29 December 1808).
30. Ibid., f. 15^{r} (29 December 1808).
31. John Clarke, preface to *Três diários de viagem em Portugal em 1808–1809* (Lisboa: Caleidoscópio/CETAPS, 2011), 14.

Il a fait trop du bien pour en dire du mal
Il a fait trop de mal pour en dire du bien[32]

It is significant that the Hollands' time in Portugal corresponded to the period between the departure of the French troops following the Convention of Sintra and the beginning of the second French invasion. This confused and sometimes violent period may well have induced Lord Holland to take a pessimistic view of Portugal, a view to be expressed in speeches in the House of Lords in 1810. An almost tangible sense of the threat of a new French invasion, together with anxiety about Portugal's future, permeates all journals. These concerns, sometimes suppressed, can suddenly burst out of the pages. The anxiety of the British officers and panic of English merchants together with the frustration and nervousness of the Portuguese authorities, are particularly evident in Lady Holland's journal. From time to time, there are dramatic expressions such, 'God forbid affairs should be in such a desperate state',[33] or 'all matters very bleak'.[34] At times, the Hollands claimed that Portugal was as backward as Turkey. Of course, the country was divided and devastated, with the wounds of the recent French invasion still fresh and national identity in crisis after the transference of the royal family to Brazil. In Holland's words, the Portuguese nation was 'dispirited' and 'discontent'.[35] The economy had been dreadfully damaged and public finances, deteriorating since Pombal's fall in 1777, were now totally exhausted. Much agricultural land and rudimentary industry had been abandoned or destroyed, and there was an obvious lack of *main d'ouvre*.

The government had been entrusted to a council of regency, described by Holland as 'a helpless timid & unwilling government',[36] where there 'does not seem to be one man of consequence, character or abilities'.[37] An ignorant, fanatic and superstitious population coexisted with an arrogant and arbitrary authority considered by most foreign observers to be as corrupt and equally ignorant. As Allen observed on 29 December, on the road from Condeixa to Pombal, 'In no country have I ever seen the lower orders in such complete & habitual subjection to the Agents of govert as in this. – In our former journey in Portugal as well as in our present we have had daily instances of it.'[38]

With a few exceptions, the elite had accompanied the royal family to Rio, leaving Portugal in the hands of unscrupulous and ignorant politicians. It was these kinds of people that Holland had in mind when he wrote: 'the leading men in Portugal are not

32. BL, HHP, MSS Add. 51862, Lord Holland's Travel Journals: 1808–9, f. 15r (29 December 1809); 'Qu'on parle mal ou bien du fameux Cardinal, / Ma prose ni mes vers n'en diront jamais rien / Il m'a fait trop de bien pour en dire du mal, / Il m'a fait trop de mal pour en dire du bien.' (Pierre Corneille, 'XXVIII. Vers sur le cardinal de Richelieu', in *Oeuvres de P. Corneille*. Nouvelle ed. (Paris: L. Hachette, 1862), X: 86).
33. BL, HHP, MSS Add. 51935, Lady Holland's Journals: 1809, f. 13v (19 January 1809).
34. Ibid., f. 11r (18 January 1809); see also *The Spanish Journal*, 253.
35. BL, HHP, MSS Add. 51862, Lord Holland's Travel Journals: 1808–9, f. 21v (January 3 [1809]).
36. Ibid.
37. Ibid.
38. BL, HHP, MSS Add. 52200, John Allen's Journal of a Tour to Spain in 1808–9, f. 78v (28 December 1808).

deficient in character or knowledge [...] but they are full of little jealousies and artifices, and more cunning in their negotiations with powerful states than wise in the management of their own.'[39] About 15,000 people – the most important carefully selected but also including servants, merchants and crew – had left for Brazil in December 1807. Most never returned and found their purpose in building a new country.

39. Holland, *Foreign Reminiscences*, 162.

Chapter Three

LA GRANDE AFFAIRE: THE HOLLANDS' INFLUENCE ON SPANISH LIBERALISM

Lord Holland, a name which no Spaniard can pronounce without strong feelings of affection and respect, as that of a zealous and steadfast friend of their country.[*]

Traditional historiography focuses on French influence in the Peninsula in the early nineteenth century – first through the spread of revolutionary doctrines, and then through the impact of invasion. Only recently have historians recognized there was at least some English influence on the origins of Iberian Liberalism. There are various reasons for this neglect: there were few contemporary signs of such influence and, above all, it was the French version of Liberalism and its constitutional ramifications that prevailed. Yet Manuel Alonso rightly argues that English influence was present. Indeed, it seems clear that Lord and Lady Holland were its chief protagonists. While Lord Holland's plans for Spain were overtaken by events, many of the friends he made during his Spanish and Portuguese journeys later became major figures in the government and politics of their countries. It is probably through them, rather than through constitutional minutiae, that the significance of Holland's contribution should be traced. In Spain, the Hollands were directly involved in politics, whereas in Portugal their influence is harder to trace. Hence, while Spanish historians now acknowledge the Hollands' involvement in the constitutional cause, Portuguese still virtually ignore it.[1]

The histories of Spain and Portugal display many similarities. At the time of the Renaissance, the Peninsula made an enormous contribution to European culture and enterprise. Thereafter, as Antero de Quental observed in 1871, it sank to become a 'dark, motionless, poor, unintelligent and half unknown world'.[2] In Alonso's metaphor, Lord Holland sought to sow this barren land with the seeds of English Liberalism.[3] Spain and

---

* Antonio Alcala-Galiano, *An Introductory Lecture Delivered in the University of London, on Saturday, November 15, 1828*, 2nd edn (London: John Taylor, 1829), 18.

1. The Hollands' influence on Portuguese society was considered only in somewhat general terms in my article with John Clarke, 'Critics to Enthusiasts: The Hollands Discover Portugal', *Portuguese Studies* 21 (2005): 70–89.
2. Antero de Quental, *Conferencias democraticas: Causas da decadencia dos povos peninsulares nos ultimos tres seculos. Discurso pronunciado na noite de 27 de Maio, na sala do Casino Lisbonense* (Porto: Na Typographia Commercial, 1871), 13; 'mundo escuro, inerte, pobre, inintelligente e meio desconhecido.' (My translation).
3. Alonso, *La forja del liberalismo en España*, 18.

Portugal were Catholic countries, despotically governed for centuries and ruling large but declining empires. To a limited extent, both had been exposed to the ideas of the Enlightenment and to those of the French Revolution. Then, both experienced French invasion. The crucial question was whether to welcome the French as liberators from an oppressive past or to resist them as tyrants and conquerors. For those who favoured resistance, there was difficult choice: either they could oppose the French on the basis of tradition and Absolutism or they could combine an appeal to patriotism with a programme of liberty and modernization. Holland's Whig principles inevitably inclined him to this last option.

From 1807–8, under the pretext of sending reinforcements to Portugal, Napoleon had invaded and occupied several Spanish towns. On 22 November 1807, an army of 25,000 men under Dupont crossed the Spanish frontier. But rather than moving towards Portugal, as previously agreed with Spain, Dupont occupied the Spanish towns of Burgos and Valladolid. Dupont's invading army was followed by a second force of 30,000 men under Moncey, which entered Spain on 8 January 1809 to occupy Navarre and Biscay. Soon there were up to 100,000 French troops spread throughout Spain. On 15 June 1808, Napoleon summoned a puppet junta at Bayonne to acknowledge his brother Joseph as King of Spain and to take oaths to what Karl Marx aptly described as 'one of his ready-made constitutions'.[4] Joseph was proclaimed Don José I on 25 June.

It is true that few of the provisions of what came to be known as the Bayonne Statute were ever implemented – because Don José's reign was a period of continuous conventional and guerrilla warfare and hence the statute was effectively suspended by the military authorities. Yet its provisions need to be considered, not least because these issues could sometimes cross the lines of battle and national animosity. In theory, the Bayonne Statute placed many limits on royal power, established an independent judiciary and recognized some individual liberties. But these did not extend to freedom of religion; Catholicism remained the state religion and other religions were banned. In the Spanish tradition the statute was promulgated 'En el nombre de Dios Todopoderoso'.[5] Other measures undertaken by the Bonapartist regime included the abolition of internal customs barriers, feudalism, the Inquisition, and the Council of Castile. Numerous convents and monasteries were suppressed as were all the military orders. The country was divided into French style departments, and steps taken to introduce the Code of Napoleon into the legal system. At least on paper this represented a progressive agenda and some Spaniards were undoubtedly attracted to it.

There were risings against the French throughout Spain and Portugal in the summer of 1808. While most, including the one in Madrid, were suppressed, some Spanish Juntas survived and came together on 25 September 1808 to form the *Junta Suprema Central Gubernativa del Reino*, a body that would govern the country in the absence of the

4. Karl Marx, 'Revolutionary Spain', in *Collected Works* (Moscow: Progress Publishers, 1980), 13: 399.

5. Preamble to the *Constitucion política de la Monarquia Española: Promulgada en Cádiz á 19 de Marzo de 1812* (Cadiz: en la Imprenta Real, dicho año [1812]), [1].

Bourbons and to coordinate efforts against the French. Of course, the authority of the junta was confined to areas outside French control – at times only a small part of Spain.

But the fundamental question was what kind of Spain those who had risen against the French really wanted. Lord Holland's contacts in London in the summer of 1808 suggested that there were many in Spain who, though committed to the expulsion of the French, wanted a liberal and constitutional government. Holland embraced this aspiration and believed that he could use his knowledge of English history and politics to help the Spaniards achieve something comparable to the Glorious Revolution of 1688. When the *Ancien Régime* began to crumble in 1788, Fox and others, mindful of the centenary of 1688, hoped that the same process was about to begin on the other side of the Channel. Sadly the French had taken things too far but, perhaps with Holland's help, the story would be different in Spain. In order to have any chance of influencing events, it was clear that Holland would have to be physically present in Spain.

Holland's 'mission' seems all the more remarkable when we remember that, at the time of his visit, the military situation appeared so unfavourable, and was to deteriorate further after he left. The Spanish defeat at Somosierra on 30 November 1808 removed the last obstacle to Napoleon's march on Madrid, which – although recovered by the Spanish on 5 September – was retaken on 4 December, with King José making a triumphal entrance on 22 January 1809. The Supreme Junta appeared to be in headlong retreat. Its members had left Aranjuez on 1–2 December on their way to Badajoz, where they hoped to establish their new headquarters. While at Mérida, they decided to go to Seville instead, arriving on 17 December.

It is important to stress that in both their first and second visits to the Peninsula, the Hollands spent considerably more time in Spain than in Portugal. Spain was their real destination and their forays into Portugal were essentially the result of the exigencies of war. For much of their second visit, they were in Seville or Cadiz, the two towns most closely associated with the Supreme Junta. They were in Seville from 30 January to 7 April 1809, when they left for Cadiz, intending to proceed to Gibraltar and from thence to England. However, unable to find a suitable ship, the Hollands decided to 'proceed again to Lisbon by the way of Seville'.[6] After an excursion to Puerto de Santa María and Jerez, they reached Seville on 24 June, staying until 30 June, when they set out for Portugal.

As far as Holland was concerned, although other institutions mattered, the most important was parliament. But was there a traditional Spanish institution comparable to the English Parliament? There clearly was – in the shape of the *Cortes*, a body to whose composition, function and relationship with other institutions Holland and Allen now devoted much attention. Obviously, Holland's allies would be those, despite the unfavourable military situation, planning to summon a *Cortes*, somewhere in 'free' Spain, as soon as possible. Holland was soon to discover, however, that many of the leading figures in the Supreme Junta did not want to summon a *Cortes* and even those who did were divided about its proper constitution and role. Apart from the Conde de Floridablanca,[7]

6. BL, HHP, MSS Add. 51937, Lady Holland's Journals: 1809, f. 23^{v} (18 June 1809).
7. Don José Moniño y Redondo (1728–1808), Conde de Floridablanca, Spanish statesman.

Antonio Valdes[8] and Gaspar de Jovellanos,[9] the members of the junta were little-known figures, unrelated to the former regime. From this perspective, the Supreme Junta was a revolutionary body compared to its Portuguese counterparts. Both the Council of Regency appointed by the regent and the government imposed by the British after the Convention of Sintra were formed by men associated with the old regime. Thus while the Portuguese regencies had a claim to legitimate authority, the Supreme Junta was established by a revolutionary act.

While at Seville, the Hollands established themselves at *Las Dueñas*, 'a Palace belonging to the Duke of Berwick inherited from the family of Alba', where they recreated something of the style of Holland House.[10] Apart from a few English people, there is an impressive list of Spanish guests, most of them refugees who had come to Seville, now effectively capital of free Spain, following the fall of Madrid on 4 December 1808. Of all the Hollands' guests, Jovellanos was the most frequent and if for some reason they could not meet, Holland took it as 'a day lost'.[11] Jovellanos, whom Lord Holland had met during his first visit to Spain in 1793 was 'my philosophical and patriotic friend',[12] 'whom I knew more intimately and respected most sincerely'[13] and whose 'intellectual endowments' and 'moral qualities' were most admired.[14]

This relationship, traceable through the diaries and correspondence, was central to the Hollands' role in Spanish constitutionalism. It was mainly through Jovellanos, who acted as an intermediary between the Hollands' political doctrines and the Spanish leaders, that their influence was exerted. According to Jovellanos, contact had begun in 1808 before the Hollands left England. Holland had written to Floridablanca urging him to re-establish the *Cortes*. Jovellanos replied that while Holland's letter 'to our Nestor F.[lorida] B.[lanca] was received with the greatest satisfaction', he suspected that Floridablanca was 'not inclined to the summoning of a Cortes', a reluctance due either to attitudes carried over from the old system of government or to fears of disturbances.[15] In the same letter Jovellanos insisted that while every Spaniard had an interest in the future of the Constitution, differences as to the best way to achieve it might jeopardize the whole project.

8. Don Antonio Valdés y Fernández-Bazán (1744–1816), Spanish admiral and statesman, descended from a noble family; his mother was the daughter of one of the wealthiest landlords of Fuenmayor.
9. Don Baltasar Melchor Gaspar María de Jovellanos y Ramirez (1744–1811), Spanish neoclassical author and politician, descended from an impoverished noble family of Gijón, the son of Don Francisco Gregorio de Jovellanos and Doña Francisca Apolinaria Jove Ramírez.
10. BL, HHP, MSS Add. 51935, Lady Holland's Journals: 1809, f. 38v (1 February 1809).
11. Holland to Jovellanos, in: *Cartas de Jovellanos y Lord Vassall Holland*, 1: 117 (Sevilla: n.d.); 'un dia perdido'. (My translation).
12. Holland to Jovellanos, ibid., 1: 155–56 (Cádiz: 5 May 1809); 'mi filosófico y patriotico amigo'. (My translation).
13. Holland, *Foreign Reminiscences*, 90.
14. Ibid.
15. Jovellanos to Holland, ibid., 1: 93 (2 November 1808); 'lacarta de V. E. á nuestro Nestor F. B. sé que fué recibida com el más alto aprecio', Jovellanos suspected that Floridablanca was 'poco inclinado á la convocacion de las Córtes'. (My translation).

Thereafter, especially during their time in Spain, Holland and John Allen collaborated closely with Jovellanos in the task of preparing for the *Cortes*. This '*la grande affaire*',[16] as both Lord Holland and Jovellanos called it, proved complicated, not least because, while England had centuries of almost unbroken experience of parliaments, the last effective *Cortes* had met in Toledo from 1538–39. In any case, as Marx observed 'neither the French States General, nor the British Parliaments of the Middle Ages are to be compared with the Spanish Cortes'.[17] Unfortunately, many leading Spaniards remained implacably opposed to any kind of parliament and would do anything to prevent it. Jovellanos wrote, 'this assembly does not please some people who did not want to restore to it the authority they are now enjoying'.[18]

While at Cadiz, Holland and Jovellanos conducted an almost daily correspondence, later collected and edited by Julio Somoza García-Sala in the impressive two-volume *Cartas de Jovellanos y Lord Vassall Holland sobre la Guerra de la Independencia (1808–1811)*.[19] After his return to England – and hence unable to discuss the *grande affaire* in person – Holland used the written word to guide his Spanish friends towards constitutionalism. These letters are of great biographical and historical importance, revealing interesting aspects of Holland's personality and political thought as well as his ideas about constitutions. Although Holland and Jovellanos did not always agree, they certainly engaged in a dialogue unique in Anglo-Spanish relations.

Faced with delays in summoning the *Cortes* and unable to hide his anxiety, Holland wrote to Jovellanos on 17 May: 'Dear friend, why such delay with *la grande affaire*? *Bis dat qui cito dat*'.[20] Two days later, he asked: 'Why are you moving so slowly in *la grande affaire*? [...] The Cortes, the Cortes, as you will see is the only solution; and if it does not come soon it will be insufficient, and either a civil war or a series of usurpations will break out in Spain'.[21] The next day he kept up the pressure: '*La grande affaire* was indeed great and

16. Holland to Jovellanos, ibid., 1: 177 (Cádiz: 17 May 1809).
17. Marx, 'Revolutionary Spain', 393.
18. Jovellanos to Holland, in: *Cartas de Jovellanos y Lord Vassall Holland*, 1: 92 (2 November 1808); 'esta reunion no agrada á algunos que no quisieran restituir á ellas la autoridad que disfrutan.' (My translation).
19. While the original letters from Jovellanos are preserved at the British Library, Lord Holland's letters were owned by Doña Purificación Alvargonzález, the widow of Don Victoriano Sánchez Cifuentes, when García-Sala transcribed them in the early twentieth century. In his political memoirs, Holland explained 'I forwarded their respective letters [Floridablanca's and Jovellanos's], with a translation to the Secretary of State's office, and a copy of my answers, in which I pointedly disclaimed all connection or influence with any Ministry, but expressed my private conviction that every Englishman in or out of our Councils would be forward in assisting Spain in so arduous and so honourable a struggle.' (*Further Memoirs of the Whig Party 1807–1821: with some miscellaneous reminiscences* (London: John Murray, 1905), 13–14).
20. Holland to Jovellanos, in: *Cartas de Jovellanos y Lord Vassall Holland*, 1: 177 (Cádiz: 17 Mayo 1809); 'Querido amigo mío: ¿Cómo tanta tardanza *dans la grande affaire? Bis dat qui cito dat.*' (My translation).
21. Ibid., 1: 182 (Cádiz: 19 May 1809); '¿Por qué van Vms. tan poco á poco dans la *grande affaire*? [...] Las Córtes, las Córtes, mientras tendrán opinión es la única prevención: y si no vengan [vienen] luego, aún ellas no serán suficientes, y sucederá en España, ó guerra civil, ó una serie de usurpaciones.' (My translation).

I deeply regret you have not hastened with it. [...] and without hopes to see it established very soon, I fear that many disagreements and very difficult situations will arise'.[22]

Finally, on 20 May, Holland learned that the Supreme Junta had decided to summon a *Cortes* for the following year, if not earlier, and to appoint a commission to make appropriate recommendations and arrangements. Holland hastened to congratulate Jovellanos on the great victory: 'Congratulations and many thanks, my esteemed and dearest friend. Things have now a much better prospect; but, for God's sake, do not delay the announcement of the Cortes; and if possible, hasten its establishment.'[23] The next day, Jovellanos effusively announced: '*Signor vinciemo i geli di trioni... La grande affaire* concluded. It [the *Cortes*] has been decreed for next year, or earlier, if circumstances will allow. [...] Do you want more? Enough for today.'[24] A few days later, Jovellanos asked for Holland's assistance on constitutional matters. He also returned notes on the proceedings of the British Parliament that Holland had kindly sent to him, asking him to transcribe them in 'buena letra' (clear handwriting) so that he and his friends could read them easily.[25]

Holland, to whom the Spanish *Cortes* had become a '*Hobby-horse*', sent several suggestions.[26] At the outset, he argued that, after the *Cortes* itself, complete freedom of the press was the most essential attribute of a constitutional regime. In a letter of April, he questioned:

> How it is possible to distinguish what is public opinion or not? Without popular representation and a great liberty to speak and write, *je reviens toujours à mes moutons*, convinced that it will be impossible to rule a great nation in time of revolution [...].[27]

Faced with resistance from the Supreme Junta, if not from Jovellanos himself – who feared the consequences of opening the Pandora's box of a freepress – Holland adopted a less radical definition of 'free press' 'in which I do not include more than the suppression of censorship in advance, that is to say, what we call a *imprimatur*'.[28]

---

22. Ibid., 1: 184 (Cádiz: 20 May 1809); 'Largo en efecto ha sido el de *la grande affaire* y siento muchísimo que no la apresuran. [...] y si esperanzas de verlas celebradas *muy luego*, recelo habrán muchísimas desavenencias, y especies muy dificultosas.' (My translation).
23. Ibid., 1: 186 (Domingo, Cádiz: 21 May 1809); 'Parabienes y gracias, mi estimadísimo y queridísimo amigo. Las cosas tienen muy buen semblante; pero por el amor de Dios, no tarden Vms. á anunciar las Córtes; y si es todavía posible, apresuren [aceleren] la celebración de ellas.' (My translation).
24. Jovellanos to Holland, ibid., 1: 188 (Sevilla, 22 May 1809); '*Signor vinciemo i geli di trioni... La grande affaire* concluido. Decretadas para el año próximo, ó antes, si las circunstancias lo permitieren. [...] ¿Quiere Vm. más? Basta hoy.' (My translation).
25. Ibid., 1: 208 (Sevilla: 29 May 1809).
26. Ibid., 1: 155 (Cádiz: 5 May 1809).
27. Holland to Jovellanos, ibid., 1: 121 (April 1809); 'Cómo se puede averiguar qué es opinion pública ó qué no lo es? Sin representacion popular, y grande libertad de hablar y de escribir, *je reviens toujours à mes moutons*, muy persuadido que no se ha de gobernar una grande nacion en tiempo de revolucion [...].' (My translation).
28. Jovellanos to Holland, ibid., 1: 156 (Cádiz: 5 May 1809); 'la libertad de la imprenta, en la cual no incluyo mas que la supresion de cesura por anticipacion, esto es, lo que llamamos nosotros un *imprimatur*.' (My translation).

Holland argued that ultimate purpose of the *Cortes* was 'to give the people their legitimate share in the management of things which, one cannot forget, *belongs to them*'.[29] Jovellanos replied that, while agreeing with the principle, he could not see how they could put it into practice, except, perhaps, through 'convocation of *Cortes*'.[30] He observed, 'I very much distrust political theories, especially abstract ones', a point of view that Holland shared.[31] Jovellanos agreed with Holland that 'Each country, as you have said, has its own ways and customs, and Spain above all'.[32] On 17 April, Lord Holland had warned that the summoning of the *Cortes* – if adapted to *las luces del siglo* and to the many laws made in Spain from the sixteenth century – was the only way to rescue the country.[33] The essential point, later précised by Allen, was that the presence of ancient forms in constitutional systems was 'at once the best check on the rashness of innovation', and a protection against demagogic measures.[34] Thus, the Hollands and Jovellanos wanted a parliamentary system based on a compromise between modern constitutions and the traditional Spanish system. Hence Holland's ideal was close to that of Aristotle's 'good constitution' or 'Polity', a compromise between democracy and Aristocracy or between *las luces del siglo* and the traditional laws of the Kingdom.[35]

In an undated letter probably written on 25 May as a continuation of that of 21, Holland explained to Jovellanos that, the convocation of *Cortes* was good news. He added, 'However, your task is not yet completed; one must now reflect at length about the way to elect and hold it'.[36] Thus, Holland proceeded with a battery of questions: what towns, provinces and districts would have the right of vote? Would deputies represent towns or provinces? And how many deputies would each province elect? How would the votes of citizens be recorded? How would the nobility, clergy and Castilian counsellors be represented? Would they have the right to vote? How many chambers would there be? Once these questions had been settled, it would be necessary to proceed to other matters – 'Once the substance is settled, the form needs as much attention':[37] how would bills be introduced, amended and passed and how would debates be conducted? Holland

29. Holland to Jovellanos, ibid., 1: 137 (Cádiz:12 April 1809); 'dar al pueblo su porcion legítima en el manejo de cosas que nunca se debe olvidar *son suyas*.' (My translation).
30. Jovellanos to Holland, *Cartas de Jovellanos y Lord Vassall Holland*, 1: 145 (Sevilla: 16 April 1809); 'la convocación de las Córtes'. (My translation).
31. Ibid., 1: 188 (Sevilla: 22 May 1809); 'Desconfio mucho de las teorías políticas, y más, de las abstractas.' (My translation).
32. Ibid., 1: 156 (Cádiz: 5 May 1809); 'Cada país como dice Vm., tiene sus usos y sus costumbres, y más que todos, España'. (My translation).
33. Holland to Jovellanos, ibid., 1: 153 (Jerez de la Frontera: 17 April 1809).
34. John Allen, *Suggestions on the Cortes* (London: [Printed for the author by] E. Blackader, 1809), 20.
35. See Henry William Carless Davis, 'Analysis' to *Aristotle's Politics* (Oxford: Clarendon Press, 1916), 12, 15.
36. Holland to Jovellanos, in: *Cartas de Jovellanos y Lord Vassall Holland*, 1: 200–1 (25 May 1809?); 'Con todo, no se acabó su trabajo, se ha de reflexionar muy despacio sobre el modo de elegir y tenerlas'. (My translation).
37. Ibid., 1: 201 (25 May 1809?); 'Ya acabada la sustancia, no poco esmero pide la forma.' (My translation).

concludes by explaining that he has arranged for a copy of the rules of the House of Commons to be sent to Isnardy, who he hopes will translate them into Spanish.[38]

Towards the end of May, the Supreme Junta set up a commission to study ways of convoking and summoning the *Cortes*. Although Jovellanos was chairman of this commission, he was unhappy with some of the other members, complaining to Holland that the junta had voted for 'El amigo Caro, Castañedo el Arzobispo, y Riquelme', adding '*Sunt bona, sunt mala, quædam, sunt mediocria multa*'.[39] But although Jovellanos anticipated obstacles, he believed, rather naïvely, that the process was already irreversible. Though not Spanish and half Jovellanos's age, Holland was more pessimistic: ' there is no excuse for devolving the management of a business to someone who is declaredly its enemy. – It would be the same as trusting the lamb to the wolf, and I cannot see what kind of politic that might be'.[40] The commission first assembled on 8 June and decided to meet thereafter every Monday and Thursday.[41]

Throughout the following months, John Allen was employed on the *grande affaire*, sometimes obsessively, contributing valuable notes or '*apuntaciones*', which Jovellanos enjoyed reading while taking his meals.[42] Allen's reflections on the *Cortes*, though similar to Holland's, are more systematic and include a comprehensive study of ancient Spanish laws and the traditional *Cortes*. Although most of Allen's notes have been lost, a few manuscript drafts are preserved at the British Library and included under 'Account books & Journal Spain-Portugal'.[43] Lady Holland also transcribed a few of Allen's notes on the ancient *Cortes* and laws into her journal.[44] Fortunately, the extensive correspondence between Holland and Jovellanos provides detailed information about Allen's researches and writings.

Allen's '*apuntaciones*' raised many doubts in Jovellanos, who returned them with new questions and his own reflections. In a letter dated 5 June, Jovellanos commented with humour: 'very tasty lunch which you, my dear Lord, served me with the reading of our Mr. Allen's notes',[45] which he would not only eat but also ruminate to better digest it.[46] The result of this interesting and unusual interchange was a paper printed for private circulation entitled *Suggestions on the Cortes*. Allen explains that the text had been 'drawn up some months ago, at the desire of the Supreme Junta soon after the

38. Don Francisco de Isnardi (1750–1841), Italian merchant, politician and journalist, born in Turin, was involved in the independence of Venezuela.
39. Jovellanos to Holland, ibid., 1: 209 (Sevilla: 29 May 1809); also BL, HHP, MSS Add. 51936, Lady Holland's Journals: 1809, f. 72^{v} (30 May 1809).
40. Holland to Jovellanos, ibid., 1: 221 (Cádiz: 31 May 1809); 'no hay disculpa de haber entregado el arreglo de un negocio á uno que es su enemigo declarado. – Es fiar el cordero al lobo, y no veo qué política haya en eso'. (My translation).
41. Jovellanos to Holland, ibid., 1: 253 (Sevilla: 9 June 1809).
42. Ibid., 1: 232 (Sevilla: 5 June 1809).
43. BL, HHP, MSS Add. 52199, John Allen's Account Books & Journal Spain-Portugal.
44. BL, HHP, MSS Add. 51936, Lady Holland's Journals: 1809, ff. 1–7.
45. Jovellanos to Holland, in: *Cartas de Jovellanos y Lord Vassall Holland*, 1: 232 (Sevilla: 5 June 1809); 'muy sabroso el almuerzo que Vm., mi querido Lord, me ha proporcionado con la lectura de los apuntamientos de nuestro Mr. Allen'. (My translation).
46. Ibid., 1: 232–33 (Sevilla: 5 June 1809).

promulgation of the decree of the 22d of May'.[47] The questions that Holland had put to Jovellanos were now fully answered. Many of the ideas contained in *Suggestions on the Cortes* were later included in the *Letter to a Neapolitan from an Englishman*, which, although signed by Lord Holland alone, may have well been largely written by Allen.

Allen's *Suggestions on the Cortes* begins by defining its powers, which he believes should be almost absolute, thus effectively rejecting the separation of powers theory originally proposed by Montesquieu and later adopted as an essential principle of the US Constitution. Apart from its legislative role, the *Cortes* should have ultimate control over all aspects of the state including the judicial and the executive: 'The Cortes will then consist of the king represented by the Central Junta'.[48] Logically, the *Cortes* will be the state itself. But how can a single body judge its own actions, who will supervise and control its powers? The answer is a bicameral system, where 'Two houses are also mutual checks on each other's conduct'.[49] Alluding to the French Congress, Allen notes that 'Reason and experience declare equally against a single legislative assembly' and 'such an assembly has been found inattentive to forms in its proceedings, and regardless of justice in its decisions, precipitate and changeable in its determinations, and governed entirely by the popular clamour, and temporary interests of the day'.[50] He concludes that 'a single legislative assembly would be unsuitable to the circumstances of Spain' as well as 'the other extreme, and divide the Cortes into three chambers', as in Sicily.[51]

Another important issue is the number of members in each chamber, considered by Holland as 'the main point, *sine qua non* of a free Government'.[52] Holland argues that 'it does not require a great deal of knowledge to guess that neither is it possible to stifle debate in a large assembly, nor to hide what is happening there'.[53] Allen agrees, arguing that 'in a large assembly, there will always be some members whom it will be impossible to reduce to silence'.[54] Allen thinks that 'a house of 500 country gentlemen is better able to conduct business, than without them an assembly of 100 clerks of office, or veterans of diplomacy'.[55] But while Holland argues that the Spanish *Cortes* should contain between 400 and 500 deputies, Allen's 'Sketch of a Plan for the Cortes' included in the *Suggestions*, proposes about 144 members in the Upper Chamber and 300 deputies in the Lower Chamber. Each province should be represented according to its population, 'one deputy being allowed for every 40,000 souls, according to the Census of 1797'.[56] Although Jovellanos supports the calling of a parliament, provided that the number of deputies to

---

47. Allen, *Suggestions on the Cortes*, [3].
48. Ibid., 11–12.
49. Ibid., 14.
50. Ibid., 12.
51. Ibid.
52. Holland to Jovellanos, in: *Cartas de Jovellanos y Lord Vassall Holland*, 1: 221 (Cádiz: 31 May 1809); 'el punto principal, el sine quâ non de un Gobierno libre.' (My translation).
53. Ibid., 1: 221 (Cádiz: 31 May 1809); 'no pide mucho conocimiento adivinar, que en una asamblea *numerosa* no se puede ahogar la discusion, ni disimular lo que pasa en ella.' (My translation).
54. Allen, *Suggestions on the Cortes*, 19.
55. Ibid., p. 21.
56. Allen, *Suggestions on the Cortes*, 42.

the Lower Chamber does not exceed 300, he doubts the possibility of bringing so many to the first *Cortes*.

As in most Continental countries, the Spanish nobility was too numerous for all noblemen to sit in an Upper Chamber. Allen proposes two alternatives: either to apply the traditional formula adopted at the *Cortes* of Toledo of 1539, where only the '*Ricos Omes*, the *Infanzones*, the masters and knights of the military orders, and other descriptions of inferior nobility'[57] had seats, or simply to consider the Grandees of Spain as 'the only legitimate representatives of these ancient nobles'.[58] Yet, if the Castilian titles of nobility were also to be taken into consideration, then 'as they are too numerous to have seats individually in that assembly, it will be necessary for them to elect a certain number of delegates as their representatives'.[59] In respect to the clergy, Allen suggests they could be represented by the archbishops, the bishops of León and Oviedo and twelve of the oldest bishops, 'to which might perhaps be added the generals of some of the monastic orders, and a few of the principal mitred abbots'.[60]

On 11 June, while acknowledging the receipt of further suggestions, Jovellanos asks Holland for Allen's opinion on the ratio between the two houses. Jovellanos then poses more questions about parliamentary procedures: will each chamber discuss and vote separately on its own proposals? Will bills pass from one chamber to the other? Will votes be absolute or proportional? Is it not to be expected that deputies will reject proposals from the Upper Chamber, knowing that the role of the peers is to limit and counterbalance their own powers? Finally, in a cry of despair Jovellanos exclaims: 'Oh, My Mr. Allen and you, my dear Lord! Help! Enlighten me, I beg you, in this perplexity: enlighten me especially about the advantages with which this assembly may give to the upper classes yet not antagonize the people.'[61]

Instead of investing so much time and energy over minutiae, Holland concludes that the leaders should simply adapt the ancient practices of Spain to the needs of the modern *Cortes*. Although written regulations and constitutions are interesting in peacetime, they are unnecessary and even dangerous in wartime and could jeopardize the summoning of the *Cortes*. Although Holland does not completely reject the idea of a written constitution, he believes it is more important to call assemblies together and then let them decide. Holland's position seems quite close to Wellington's belief that republican constitutions were 'too regularly constructed ever to answer any practical good effect'.[62] The same line is taken in the

57. Ibid., 15.
58. Ibid.
59. Ibid., 15–16.
60. Ibid., 15.
61. Jovellanos to Holland, in: *Cartas de Jovellanos y Lord Vassall Holland*, 1: 259 (Sevilla, Domingo: 11 June 1809); 'Ah ¡mi Mr. Allen, y Vm. mi querido Lord! ¡Socorro! Alúmbrenme, les pido, en esta perplejidad: alúmbrenme sobre todo, en cuanto á las ventajas con que esta reunión se puede presentar á las clases privilegiadas, y aquellas que tendrá el pueblo para no temerla.' (My translation).
62. Arthur Wellesley, 'Memorandum' (8 February 1808), in *Supplementary Despatches, Correspondence, and Memoranda of Field Marshal Arthur Duke of Wellington, K.G.* 15 vols (London: John Murray, 1858–72), 6: 65.

Letter to a Neapolitan from an Englishman, which argues that an over-precise definition of the roles of the various branches of the state will lead those invested with some share of power seeking to use it as often as they can, 'like children with their playthings, to try the new weapon with which they have been entrusted'.[63]

After the first meetings of the commission, Jovellanos began to doubt the practicality of the Hollands' ideas. Although widely acknowledged as a moderate and wise man, Jovellanos was more conservative than his English friends, even though, in reality, the Hollands were hardly 'advanced'. As Blanco White explained, Jovellanos 'wished to restore the Cortes: but more like a piece of antiquity, in the full costume of the fifteenth Century, than as an effectual depositary of power', that is to say, without the novelties Allen was proposing.[64] Yet Jovellanos's position was difficult; he was between the Hollands on one side and his fellow commissioners and members of the Supreme Junta on the other. Perhaps faced with the opposition of some of the commissioners to the Hollands' alien plans for the *Cortes*, Jovellanos was forced to restrain the enthusiasm of his British friends.

The first signs that things were not developing as Holland anticipated came on 3 June 1809, when Jovellanos notes that, while Allen's plan for the *Cortes* is interesting and well conceived, it might not be possible to adapt it to 'the ideas of *mes confrères*'.[65] Despite his later insistence that 'My wish was to prepare through our plan a Constitution modelled upon the English, and improved as much as possible', Jovellanos believed that such matters should be first submitted to the Supreme Junta by the *Cortes* and not vice versa.[66] When Holland criticized changes to the original plan, Jovellanos felt he had to explain. On 7 June, he notes that although 'We have approved the plan and reflections of our Mr. Allen, because, in general and in the end, I approve it', he could not imagine that it could be imposed without the approval of the *Cortes* itself.[67] Indeed although Jovellanos was convinced that the *Cortes* would consider Allens's plan and vote on it, he was now uncertain as to the outcome.[68]

Holland understood that if he wanted the *grande affaire* to succeed, a sincere commitment to the cause was not enough. He had to build bridges between the enthusiastic and young liberals, including Quintana's group with whom he was deeply involved, but who wanted to replicate the French system, moderate conservatives like Jovellanos, who wanted to re-establish the medieval *Cortes* and then introduce gradual reforms, and those who, more or less openly, rejected the idea of a *Cortes* of any sort. In short, Holland had to achieve the impossible, a dialogue between the *Ancien Régime* and Liberalism. Holland's approach was

63. Holland, *Letter to a Neapolitan*, 15.
64. José Maria Blanco y Crespo (after Joseph Blanco White), *The Life of the Rev. Joseph Blanco White: Written by Himself with Portions of His Correspondence*. 3 vols (London: John Chapman, 1845), 1: 150.
65. Jovellanos to Holland, in: *Cartas de Jovellanos y Lord Vassall Holland*, 1: 226 (Sevilla: 3 June 1809); 'las ideas de *mes confrères*.' (My translation).
66. Ibid., 2: 525 (Muros: 5 December 1810); 'Mi deseo, era preparar por medio de nuestro plan, una Constitucion modelada por la Inglesa, y mejorada en cuanto se pudiese.' (My translation).
67. Ibid., 1: 244 (Sevilla: 7 June 1809); 'El *plan y reflecciones* de nuestro Mr. Allen, démosle por aprobado, pues que en general, y en el fondo, yo le apruebo.' (My translation).
68. Ibid., 1: 244 (Sevilla: 7 June 1809).

sensible, yet he seems to have forgotten that, except for Andalusia, Spain was under French occupation, and even Andalusia was experiencing a revolution. Holland's solution might have succeeded in the context of a reasonably stable social and political environment, but it is harder to see how it could have worked in the middle of a revolution. Revolutions usually produce various kinds of extremism and are rarely conducive to concessions or consensus. Those nostalgic for the *Ancien Régime* were prepared to do anything to obstruct the cause of progress and – on the perverse notion that better is worse – some actually argued for a French-style constitution. Nor would radical liberals like Manuel Quintana or Blanco White give up their chance to establish a completely new order in Spain.[69] Between the two extremes moderates like Jovellanos had few cards to play.

Jovellanos was showing signs of fatigue, admitting to Holland on 4 June that despite his commitment to the *grande affaire*, he does not wish to take part in the executive activities of the Supreme Junta, where he would be useless and a waste of time.[70] One month later, on 8 July, he confesses to Lady Holland that he is 'very much discontented with their Colleagues in regard to the Asturias, & other things' and 'thinks for the sake of decoro & his own feelings he shall ask leave to go to the Baths. No progress about the affair of the Cortès'.[71] The correspondence breaks suddenly on 20 June 1809, when Holland writes to Jovellanos from Puerto de Santa María announcing that his party is on its way to Jerez, and when the correspondence resumes on 4 July, the Hollands are already at Badajoz and about to enter Portugal. Thereafter the correspondence continues intermittently until 28 August 1811 when, three months before his death, Jovellanos, then at Gijon, wrote his last known letter to Holland. Inevitably, the Hollands' departure from Seville for Portugal limited their capacity to influence the progress of the *grande affaire*. The letters become less frequent, leading Jovellanos to complain on 6 December 1809: 'Another post has arrived bringing several letters from London, but I did not receive a single one.'[72]

In the same letter, Jovellanos explains that, although the commission had voted for a bicameral system, a majority of others who had been consulted had opposed it. One week later, Jovellanos informs Holland that everything is ready for the calling of the *Cortes*. The Lower Chamber would have 300 deputies, the number suggested by Allen, one for each 50,000 inhabitants (increased to 70,000 by decree of 23 May 1812), one for each town, one for each Superior Junta and another one for the Spanish Americas. A few days later, on 27 December, Jovellanos announces that the prospect of introducing the English system of parliament has been abandoned, because the Supreme Junta has rejected the Constitutional Commission's proposal for a bicameral system.

69. José María Blanco Crespo (1775–1841), afterwards known as Joseph Blanco White, Spanish theologian and journalist of Irish Catholic ancestry, the son of Guillermo Blanco (alias William White), a merchant whose father had settled in Seville in the early eighteenth century.

70. Jovellanos to Holland, in: *Cartas de Jovellanos y Lord Vassall Holland*, 1: 229 (Sevilla: 4 June [1809]).

71. BL, HHP, MSS Add. 51937, Lady Holland's Journals: 1809–10, f. 68v (16 July 1809).

72. Jovellanos to Holland, in *Cartas de Jovellanos y Lord Vassall Holland*, 2: 427 (Sevilla: 6 December 1809); 'Otro correo ha llegado, y en él, varias cartas de Lóndres, sin que yo haya recibido una sola letra.' (My translation).

Perhaps Holland was partly to blame for this outcome; his close relations with the Spanish radicals like Quintana and White raised the suspicions of conservative elements. Although he did not tell Holland directly, the defeat of the *grande affaire* at the hands of the Absolutists was a devastating blow to Jovellanos, both politically and personally. Following the dissolution of the Supreme Junta, here turned to the Asturias, refusing to take part in the first Spanish *Cortes Generales*. During his voluntary exile, Jovellanos sought to regain his health and to restore his reputation – the latter through a memoir of the Supreme Junta printed at Coruña in 1811 as *D. Gaspar de Jovellanos a sus compatriotas: memoria en que se rebaten las calumnias divulgadas contra los individuos de la junta central*, regarded as his political testament.

One year later, in a letter dated from Muros on 5 December 1810, Jovellanos complains to his English friend about political developments in Spain, which 'Afflicts me and leaves me in a state of alarm'.[73] Jovellanos regrets the arrangements adopted for the *Cortes*, especially the form 'free and confused as to how it was established'.[74] The one-chamber system had prevented any kind of double deliberation or second thoughts and many resolutions were now taken precipitately after a single discussion and without any kind of previous preparation.[75] A few years later, Holland himself concluded that the adoption of a single chamber system – instead of the English or American bicameral model – had been a major reason for the failure of the parliamentary regime in Spain.[76]

Jovellanos also criticized the negative influence of the French Congress in the *Cortes Generales*, considering the adoption of demagogic concepts like '*soberania de la nacion*' or the *avant la lettre* acknowledgement of a future constitution, highly dangerous. Indeed if there was to be such a constitution, all citizens should have the right to approve it or not. Jovellanos fears that political theories alone, with which only a few are acquainted, are not enough to create a good constitution. The works of Rousseau, the Abbé de Mably, Locke, Harrington or Sidney, which fill the minds of the very few young Spaniards who read at all, are not sufficient to make a constitution. From his point of view, the freedom of press, another of Holland's hobbyhorses that had meanwhile been approved by the *Cortes*, was now being perversely used by the French against Spain. Jovellanos concludes directly, even brutally: 'Do you still hope this benefit [an English constitution] to be established in Spain?'[77]

Although the Hollands may have failed in their main objective – the establishment of an 'English Constitution' in Spain – their presence at Seville in the first months of 1809

73. Ibid., 2: 525 (Muros: 5 December 1810); 'Me llena de aflicción y me tiene en sobresalto.' (My translation).
74. Ibid., 2: 524 (Muros: 5 December 1810); 'libre y confusa en que se constituyeron.' (My translation).
75. Ibid., 2: 524 (Muros: 5 December 1810); 'at a stroke and after minimum discussion, not previously prepared or meditated.' (My translation).
76. Holland, *Letter to a Neapolitan*, 22.
77. Jovellanos to Holland, in *Cartas de Jovellanos y Lord Vassall Holland*, 2: 525 (Muros: 5 December 1810); '¿Podrá Vm. esperar ya este bién [an English constitution] para la España?' (My translation).

and their commitment to the *grande affaire* had contributed to the Supreme Junta's vote to re-establish the *Cortes*. As Toreno notes, the decree of 22 May 1809, though 'late and vague', launched the foundations for the *Cortes* of Cadiz.[78] Despite all the obstacles and shortcomings, it is undeniable that this decree opened the way to the establishment of the *Cortes Generales*. In Jovellanos's words: 'But what matters? The step has been taken and nothing will be able to undo it without breaking its spine.'[79] As Quintana acknowledged in his obituary of Lord Holland first published in the *Gaceta de Madrid* for 23 January 1841,

> The resolution of the Supreme Junta to re-establish our ancient *Cortes* owes in great measure to his impulse. The decree of 22 May 1809 opened the way to the political reformation of the State, which two years earlier would have seemed a criminal dream springing from a sick imagination [...].[80]

After the Hollands' return to England, the military situation deteriorated further. On 23–24 January 1810, anticipating a French attack, the junta announced that it would move to the Isla de León, now San Fernando, Cadiz. A week later, when the French were already at the gates of Seville, the junta – now facing popular protest – abolished itself and set up the *Consejo de Regencia de España e Indias,* a five-member regency to rule on behalf of Fernando VII. On the afternoon of 1 February, Seville capitulated and five days later, the French began the Siege of Cadiz, the last redoubt of 'Free' Spain.[81] The siege was to last for two and a half years. Remarkably, Cadiz did not fall and in August 1812, the French were forced to abandon the siege and retreat from Andalusia following their defeat at Salamanca on 22 July. The Siege of Cadiz marked a crucial turning point in the transition from *Ancien Régime* to modernity. Almost within range of the French cannons, the first constitutional *Cortes Generales* assembled on the Isla de León on 24 September 1810, a date Toreno calls 'the real beginning of the Spanish revolution'.[82] Its greatest achievement, on 19 March 1812, was the promulgation of the *Constitucion política de la Monarquia Española,* widely regarded as the most liberal of its time.

Holland must have viewed these developments with mixed feelings. While he may have regretted that the Constitution did not reflect his ideas, there was surely now reason to hope that his overall vision of a constitutional Spain might be realized. In the short run any such hopes were dashed. Once more the course of events in Spain and Portugal

78. José María Queipo de Llano Ruiz de Saravia, Conde de Toreno, *Historia del Levantamiento, Guerra y Revolucion de España.* 5 vols (Madrid: Imprenta de Don Tomas de Jordán, 1835–37), 3: 16.
79. Jovellanos to Holland, in *Cartas de Jovellanos y Lord Vassall Holland*, 1: 206 (Sevilla: 28 May de 1809); 'Pero, ¿Qué importa? El paso está dado, y nadie ya será capáz de volverle atrás sin riesgo de romperse la cabeza.' (My translation).
80. Manuel José Quintana, 'Necrologia: Lord Holland', *Gaceta de Madrid*, 23 enero 1841, 3; 'A su impulso se debió en gran parte la resolución tomada por la Junta Central de restablecer la institución de nuestras antiguas Cortes. En el decreto de 22 de Mayo de 1809 se abrió el camino a la reforma política del Estado, que dos años antes habría parecido sueño criminal de una imaginacion lisiada [...].' (My translation).
81. Toreno, *Historia del Levantamiento*, 3: 197.
82. Ibid., 3: 387; 'verdadero comienzo de la revolución española.' (My translation).

followed a similar course. In May 1814 the returning Bourbons issued the decree of Valencia, abolishing the Constitution and reinstating absolute monarchy, while Portugal turned into something closely resembling a British colony run by the autocratic Beresford. But the vision that Holland had helped to form surfaced again with the uprising in Spain that established the *Trienio Liberal* (1820–23) which reinstated the Cadiz Constitution. Six months later, Portugal created its own version of the Spanish system. Thereafter, Spain and Portugal oscillated between Liberalism and Absolutism, with the Cadiz Constitution reintroduced in 1836 while the Spanish progressive Constitution of 1837 was being prepared. Indeed the 1812 Constitution became a 'sacred code' of nineteenth-century Liberalism, serving as a model for several Latin American constitutions but above all for the *Constituição política da Monarquia Portuguesa* of 1822. Holland followed these developments with interest, and, when possible, did his best to assist the Liberal cause. Not only was this consistent with his principles but clearly reflected a sense of personal involvement and commitment going back to his time in the Peninsula and maintained through his continued contact with prominent Spaniards and Portuguese, most of whom were firmly in the Liberal or Constitutional camp.

While some of the results of Holland's commitment to the *grande affaire* may have been disappointing, his time in Seville and Cadiz had been a valuable political experience that greatly increased his knowledge of constitutional matters. His *Letter to a Neapolitan from an Englishman* clearly reveals a more mature approach to constitutional issues. Furthermore, many years later, between 1828 and 1834, first in opposition and then in government, Holland's role in the re-establishment of Portuguese constitutionalism reflects the wisdom and experience derived from his time in Spain. Above all, by influencing the decision of the Supreme Junta of 22 May 1809 to re-establish the *Cortes*, leading to its summoning at Cadiz in 1810, the Hollands had indirectly and unintentionally contributed to the origin of Portuguese constitutionalism.

Chapter Four

GLIMPSES OF LIBERTY

*Prosperity and durability to the new representative governments of Spain, Portugal, and Naples, and may the arms of any power who dares to invade their rising liberties be turned against itself.**

Under the terms of the Convention of Sintra, French forces were withdrawn from Portugal in September 1808. But the British remained, not only for the rest of the Peninsular War, but actually retained virtual control of Portugal for many years after the war was over. It was not until August 1820, in the aftermath of the Liberal Revolution in Oporto, that the British 'occupation' came to an end. Early in 1809, the Prince Regent had ordered Sousa Coutinho, now Conde do Funchal, to request the British government to recommend a general capable of reorganizing the Portuguese army and restoring its discipline. As Holland noted on arrival in Lisbon in January 1809, 'The Portuguese army which was in a deplorable state before the arrival of the French was entirely disorganized by them & there seems neither General nor officers capable of forming or conducting them'.[1] João was given the names of Sir Arthur Wellesley and Sir William Beresford.[2] Wellesley declined, probably unwilling to serve under Portuguese orders, but recommended Beresford, who accepted.

By a decree of 7 March 1809, Beresford was appointed commander in chief of the Portuguese Army, which he reorganized and disciplined with acknowledged efficacy. Given the ineffectiveness of the regency, Beresford became the de facto ruler of Portugal. The prince regent's absence in Brazil made it impossible to operate the normal machinery of government, not least because measures requiring the regent's approval took months to reach Brazil and even longer to return to Portugal. Thus day-to-day matters had to be left to the *Governadores*, aided by the armed branch of the state – and that meant Beresford.

Holland strongly disapproved of these arrangements. In the House of Lords, alongside Lord Grenville, he denounced the waste of a 'glorious opportunity for raising the

* 'Norwich Fox Dinner', *The Times*, 22 January 1821, 3.

1. BL, HHP, MSS Add. 51862, Lord Holland's Travel Journals: 1808–9, ff. 21^r–22^r (3 January 1809).
2. William Carr Beresford (1768–1854), Baron Beresford of Albuera and Dungarvan, Waterford, Viscount Beresford of Beresford, Staffordshire, Conde de Trancoso, Marquês de Campo Maior and Duque de Elvas in the Portuguese peerage, Grand Cross of the Tower and Sword (Port.) and of San Fernando (Spain). British army officer and Tory MP, illegitimate son of George de la Poer Beresford, Earl of Tyrone, and later first Marquess of Waterford in the Irish peerage (1735–1800), with an unidentified mother.

Portuguese nation from that wretched and degraded condition, to which a lengthened succession of mental ignorance, civil oppression, and political tyranny and prostitution, had reduced it'.[3] In his journals, Holland had already blamed Dalrymple for accepting the appointment of the new Council of Regency, even though he had known that its proposed members were regarded as corrupt and incompetent. According to Holland, the British should have either taken over Portugal completely or given its people real liberty:

> If England interfered at all in regulating the Government she ought to have established one either entirely subservient to her own objects or calculated to call forth the energies of the country. By a paltry endeavour to avoid the appearance of interference & a dread of leaving the people rely to themselves she has drawn on herself the double inconvenience of a helpless timid & unwilling government & a dispirited discontented people.[4]

It seems that Holland was attracted to 'all or nothing' types of argument. Yet, while intellectually logical, neither of Holland's alternatives looks practical. Britain had so many calls on its military resources that it probably did not have enough manpower to take over Portugal in its entirety. In any case, any such attempt would surely have provoked resistance and made the British seem as bad as the French. The opposite course, 'calculated to call forth the energies of the country' can only be a euphemism for British withdrawal and, especially in the light of Holland's own observations about the state of the Portuguese army, would have greatly increased the risk of a successful French invasion. It also flew in the face of Holland's earlier assertion that, if the Portuguese were to defeat the French, they would need at least some foreign help.

Despite the failure of the first French invasion of Portugal, Napoleon still intended to take over the entire Peninsula and probably saw Portugal as easier prey than before. A second invasion began on 9 March 1809, when Marshal Jean-de-Dieu Soult (1769–1851) crossed the northeastern frontier of Trás-os-Montes, and lasted until 18 May, when the French were forced to retreat to Galicia by Anglo-Portuguese forces under Wellesley. With Soult out of the way, Wellesley could concentrate on Victor's army, a force of 30,000 French gathered in the Spanish Extremadura waiting for an opportunity to invade Portugal through Alentejo. Wellesley moved back to Coimbra and from thence to Abrantes, where he arrived on 17 June. Ten days later, he crossed into Spain where he defeated the French at the battle of Talavera (27–28 July 1809).

Despite signs of improvement in Portugal, when Holland returned to England in August 1809, the French controlled virtually the whole of Spain. It still seemed likely that Napoleon would destroy the British forces in the Peninsula and then reduce Portugal to complete subjection. A third invasion appeared imminent, yet the finances of the Portuguese government, always precarious, had been completely exhausted by the

3. Grenville, speech on the 'King's Message respecting Portugal', in *Parl. Deb.*, 15 (22 February 1810): c. 516.
4. BL, HHP, MSS Add. 51862, Lord Holland's Travel Journals: 1808–9, ff. 21^{r}–22^{r} (3 January 1809).

previous invasions. Hence, the King's Speech on 23 January 1810 proposed 'pecuniary advances to be made to Portugal, in support of its military exertions' and that a force not exceeding 30,000 men should be maintained there.[5] Apart from the time when Fox was foreign secretary, Holland had usually been critical of British policy to Portugal. Sometimes he had argued that Britain had not committed itself enough, sometimes that it had become too much involved. But there had always been an element of equivocation. Now, however, it seemed that Holland had finally made up his mind; he wanted Britain to leave Portugal to fend for itself. Marquis Wellesley, who spoke for the ministry, insisted that, although the situation in Spain seemed desperate, to abandon Iberia to its fate would waste all the blood and treasure hitherto expended on its behalf. Other speakers, however, agreed with Holland; Lord Grenville believed that Portugal was 'the least defensible of any country in Europe',[6] while, on the basis of his military experience, Lord Moira dismissed the government's plan for Portugal as impracticable.[7]

Holland argued that the Portuguese government was not worth saving, even if such a thing were possible. To have any chance of success, 'A great plan was necessary: nothing neutral or narrow, nothing minute, nothing temporary',[8] but no plan would work unless the Portuguese government possessed qualities 'which no man could hope for in the present ministry'.[9] The government's proposals would harm those they were supposed to benefit: 'if we were to embark in the cause of that sinking people, we were not to load them with our imbecility, in addition to their own weakness'.[10] Thus, 'It would be criminal to force a nation to a defence which might draw down ruin on them',[11] so Britain should

> leave the country of our ally with the spirit of friendship and the purity of honour. It was of great moment to us, in even that meanest and lowest view in policy, to leave the people of the peninsula our friends, but we must be actuated by a higher principle, and be regretted and revered by those whom we were forced to abandon.[12]

Despite Holland's talk of honour and principle, his speech lacks substance. Perhaps he was simply taking the opposition line, even against his own personal inclination. Unfortunately, his political memoirs are silent on the episode and we can only speculate about his real position. Holland may have been suffering from the depression that

5. Robert Southey, *History of the Peninsular War*. 3 vols (London: John Murray, 1823–32), 2: 640; see also 'The Lords Commissioners' Speech: [on Opening the Fourth Session of the Fourth Parliament]', in *Parl. Deb.*, 15 (23 January 1810): c. 3.
6. Grenville, speech on the 'King's Message respecting Portugal', in *Parl. Deb.*, 15 (22 February 1810): c. 523.
7. Earl Moira, speech on the 'King's Message respecting Portugal', in *Parl. Deb.*, 15 (22 February 1810): c. 530.
8. Holland, speech on the 'King's Message respecting Portugal', in *Parl. Deb.*, 15 (22 February 1810): c. 535.
9. Ibid.
10. Ibid.
11. Ibid.
12. Ibid., c. 536.

afflicted him from time to time. He had been ill – confined to bed by gout – and the political outlook appeared bleak. His advice on constitutional matters in Spain had been ignored and events at home were disappointing. Holland had hoped that, once the Prince of Wales became regent, he would eject his father's ministers and install his old friends, the Whigs, in power. But the prince intended no such thing and Holland's disappointment was unassuaged even when the regent came to his sick-bed to explain why he had changed his mind. Thus Holland may have felt especially bitter about the ministry, leading him to attack proposals he might have supported in other circumstances.

Holland's position on Portugal is probably an instance of 'politics' in the worse sense of the word, an episode when principles are sacrificed to tactics or, in Holland's words, to the 'meanest and lowest view in policy'.[13] Holland contends that while there may be a case for supporting a democratic government capable of energizing heroic resistance against the French, since that is impossible, there is no alternative to withdrawal and abandonment. Of course, Holland has a low opinion of Portuguese politicians, rating their Spanish counterparts more highly, not to mention the fact that the real ruler of Portugal was the ultra-conservative Beresford. Yet he ignores the fact that if the British abandon Portugal, French occupation is a certainty. Perhaps he believes that if defeat and occupation are inevitable, the Portuguese might secure better treatment if they surrender at once rather than put up a doomed fight. Yet, given that Holland's Spanish and Portuguese journals are full of accounts of French atrocities, he should have had few illusions about what French occupation would involve. Under the circumstances, suggestions that the Portuguese might thank the British for leaving them in the lurch seem absurd. But perhaps Holland was naïve. Despite irrefutable evidence of French atrocities, part of him was still more attracted to the principles of the French Revolution – even to Bonaparte himself – than to the characteristic features of what was still an essentially *Ancien Régime* society.

Holland's pessimism about the prospects of resisting another French invasion of Portugal was not borne out by events. The expected third invasion began in July 1810, when the French besieged the Portuguese eastern town of Almeida, which eventually capitulated on 28 August. On 15 September, a force of nearly 62,000 men under the great André Masséna (1758–1817), the 'Son of Victory', began to march on Lisbon. On 27 September, the French were defeated at the battle of Buçaco by the Anglo-Portuguese Army under Wellesley. Despite this reverse, Masséna decided to press on to the Portuguese capital. On approaching Torres Vedras, however, he encountered the maze of trenches and palisades made on Wellesley's orders, which effectively blocked all roads to Lisbon. The French remained in the lines of Torres Vedras for five months; drenched by winter rains and short of food, they were finally forced to retreat to Santarém (14 November) and Guarda (6 March 1811). Following Wellesley's attack near Sabugal on 3 April, the French were finally expelled from Portugal.

However misguidedly, Holland's opposition to further British military involvement in Portugal may have sprung from a desire to spare its people from suffering. Now that the

13. Ibid.

war had come to an end, he was quick to recognize the need for humanitarian assistance. Early in 1811, Holland joined a group – headed by the Duke of York and including the Dukes of Grafton and Montrose and the Earls Spencer and Buckinghamshire – which raised funds to help the victims of the war in Portugal. The second meeting, held in Willis's (Almack's) Rooms on 1 May, set up a commission, including Holland, to coordinate the collection of funds. The initiative, supported by Funchal, the Portuguese minister in London, could be seen as a response to the Prince Regent's message to the House of Lords on 8 April 1811, drawing attention to 'the distresses which in a part of the inhabitants of Portugal were plunged by the savage barbarities exercised against them by the French army in retreat' and expressing his desire to 'afford the sufferers speedy and effectual relief'.[14] The issue was discussed in the House of Commons on 10 April and a grant of £100,000 was agreed unanimously.[15]

Following the withdrawal of the French troops in April 1811 – marking the end of the third and last invasion of Portugal – the remaining battles of the Peninsular War were decided in Spain. Towards the end of July 1814, with the war apparently over, the first Portuguese troops began to return from Spain, followed by their commander, Marshal Beresford, who arrived in Lisbon on 16 August after a short stay in Britain. Although the war was ending, Portugal remained important to Britain, an importance indicated by the appointment of the former – and future – foreign secretary, George Canning, as ambassador to Lisbon in 1814. It is striking that Holland and Canning – both of whom had first-hand experience of Portugal – were to be strong supporters of the constitutional cause there in the 1820s.

The continued absence of the royal family at Rio de Janeiro and the reduction of Portugal to the condition of a mere Brazilian colony in 1815 and ultimately to a British protectorate, led to widespread discontent. Anti-British propaganda, fomented within Masonic circles, circulated in coffeeshops and elsewhere, and was linked to growing interest in ideas of constitutional government. The situation was aggravated when, on 18 October 1817, Gomes Freire de Andrade, a retired general and grandmaster of the Portuguese Freemasons, was executed. Andrade and several other officers had been found guilty of high treason for an alleged conspiracy with Spanish agitators to overthrow the regency and expel Beresford. The Marshal believed that Andrade had been used by others – dismissing him as 'a weak, vain and light-headed person' – but supposed that he would prevent further trouble by making an example of this well-known figure.[16] But Beresford miscalculated; far from silencing discontent in the army and in society as a whole, Andrade's 'martyrdom' became a rallying point for anti-British feeling and for those Portuguese who sought to regain what they saw as their lost independence. Although Andrade's execution is usually attributed to Beresford alone, some

14. 'Prince Regent's Message relating to Portugal', in *Parl. Deb.*, 19 (8 April 1811): 736.
15. 'Relief to the Inhabitants of Portugal', in *Parl. Deb.*, 19 (10 April 1811): 755–57.
16. Beresford, quoted in 'Lord Beresford and the Gomes Freire conspiracy', by Malyn Newitt, in *Lord Beresford and British Intervention in Portugal 1807–1820* (Lisboa: Imprensa de Ciências Sociais, 2004), 99.

authors claim that members of the Council of Regency, especially Miguel Forjaz[17] and the principal Sousa, were also involved, putting on a show of ruthlessness to hide their own incompetence.[18] But whoever was responsible, the execution damaged Beresford's reputation and helped to turn Portuguese public opinion against the British presence.

To prevent the spread of subversive propaganda, an edict forbidding secret associations and threatening members with severe penalties was issued in Rio de Janeiro on 30 March 1818. Among these associations was the *Sinédrio*, a society linked to Spanish Freemasonry and founded on 22 January 1818 by Manuel Fernandes Tomás (1771–1821), an Oporto magistrate later seen as the father of Portuguese Liberalism. Tomás was to be one of the authors of the Constitution of 1822, though he did not live to see it introduced. The *Sinédrio*, which met once a month at São João da Foz, Oporto, sought to monitor political developments and changes in public opinion, keep up with the news coming from Spain and ultimately prepare for revolution. But the repressive measures of the Portuguese authorities could not prevent the inevitable explosion; events in Spain and Naples provided the necessary spark.

Encouraged by revolutionary successes in Spain in January 1820 and Naples in July, the Portuguese Colonels Bernardo Sepúlveda (1791–1833) and Sebastião Cabreira (1763–1833) began a military revolt in Oporto on 24 August and established a junta.[19] The Liberal Revolution broke out almost spontaneously and encountered little resistance, spreading quickly to other Portuguese towns. Lisbon adhered to the revolutionary movement on 15 September, when an interim government replaced the Council of Regency. On 28 September, the provisional juntas of Lisbon and Oporto combined

17. D. Miguel Pereira Forjaz Coutinho Barreto de Sá e Resende (1769–1827), 9th Conde da Feira, Portuguese army officer and politician, the son of D. Diogo Pereira Forjaz Coutinho Barreto de Sá e Resende by D. Luísa Teresa Antónia da Câmara Meneses.
18. D. José António de Meneses de Sousa Coutinho (1757–1817), better known as Principal Sousa, Principal Deacon of the Lisbon Patriarchate (1811–17), appointed member of the regency by Royal Decree of 24 May 1810. Son of D. Francisco Inocêncio de Sousa Coutinho and D. Ana Luisa da Silva Teixeira de Andrade, and brother of D. Domingos and D. Rodrigo de Sousa Coutinho.
19. On 1 January 1820, Rafael del Riego (1784–1823) led a rebellion against the Absolutist regime in Spain. The Cadiz Constitution of 1812, abolished by Fernando VII on his return from exile in 1814, was proclaimed in Andalusia. Riego's example was followed at Coruña, where the Constitution was proclaimed on 21 February; in the space of a few days the revolutionary ferment spread to other Galician towns and elsewhere in Spain. On 7 March, incapable of containing the rebellion, Fernando VII was forced to take the oath to the Constitution and to issue a proclamation to the 'Espanõles', announcing his full adherence to the new constitutional regime and inviting his countrymen to follow his example: 'Let us follow openly, myself first, the path of the Constitution'. ('Manifesto of the King of Spain to the Nation' (Madrid, 10 March 1820), in *British and Foreign State Papers: 1819–1820*, 281). Inevitably, events in Spain affected places elsewhere. Trouble began in Naples in early days of July, when Guglielmo Pepe (1783–1855), a Sicilian general who had served under Murat, led a liberal revolt and forced Ferdinand I to accept a constitution based on the Spanish one. Following the invasion of Naples by Austrian troops on 23 March 1821, as agreed at the congress of Laibach (1821), Pepe was forced into exile in Britain, where he published *A Narrative of the Political and Military Events which Took Place at Naples, in 1820 and 1821…* (London: 1821).

to form the *Junta Provisional do Supremo Governo do Reino*. On 22 November 1820, after much hesitation and disagreement, the new government announced the convocation of a parliament that would draw up a constitution. The progressive *Constituição política da Monarquia Portuguesa*, mainly modelled on the Cadiz Constitution, was published on 23 September 1822. The *Cortes Gerais* were held from 26 January 1821 to 3 June 1823, when it was abolished after the *Vilafrancada*, a coup led by Infante D. Miguel that ended the first Portuguese constitutional regime, commonly known as *Vintismo*.[20]

It was not until 17 October 1820 that news of the Portuguese rebellion reached Brazil. Although Beresford had previously warned D. João VI that something like the recent Spanish revolution might be replicated in Portugal, the king's ministers in Rio did not know how to react. If the king refused to recognize the new regime, then a separation between Brazil and Portugal would be inevitable; but if the new authorities in Portugal were recognized in Rio de Janeiro, then Brazil itself would necessarily revert to a mere Portuguese colony. While the Brazilians favoured the first option, arguing that the royal family should remain in Rio, the Portuguese were inclined to the second, suggesting that either João or his eldest son, Pedro, should hasten to Portugal and take control over the situation. Britain, which had secured free access to the Brazilian commerce under the terms of the Alliance of 1810, wanted the Portuguese out of Brazil and thus wished the royal family to return to Europe. As Holland had noted in 1808, 'the interests of both countries [Britain and Brazil] are the same; that any of one or another party will represent a loss for both; and finally that there are nothing but advantages for either party'.[21] The question was how to negotiate with the Portuguese 'rebels' without compromising the king's authority. Palmela, the Portuguese minister in London, who arrived in Rio on 23 December 1820 to take the foreign ministry, vacant since António de Araújo's death in 1817, had his own ideas.

Palmela left England in June or July 1820 and arrived in Portugal shortly before the rising at Oporto. He had been at the Head of the Portuguese Legation in London since 1813, and was a frequent guest at Holland House. Although avoiding any direct interference in politics, Palmela now advised the regency to summon a *Cortes* as the only possible way to prevent the growing signs of discontent from developing into a serious 'revolution'. However, the rising at Lisbon on 15 September and the establishment of a junta frustrated Palmela's plans. He left for Brazil on 6 October, thus enabling him to avoid having to take an oath to the revolutionary junta, a requirement that came into force one week after his departure.

While in Rio de Janeiro, Palmela advised D. João that if he wanted to keep Brazil, he must also be King of Portugal. Palmela argued that the only way to regain control of the situation in Portugal would be to issue a Charter, apparently willingly. It would be better to follow the example of Louis XVIII of France in 1814 than to have a constitution imposed in humiliating circumstances as happened recently to Fernando VII of Spain. Palmela recommended that João's son Pedro move to Portugal to preside over

20. The last session of the *Cortes Gerais* was held on 21 May 1823, when a bill to regulate the public finances was discussed (see *Diario das Cortes Geraes*, 2.ª Legisl., 3 [10] (21 May 1823): 48–65).
21. Holland, 'Carta ou memoria', 251.

the *Cortes* and make sure the charter was respected. Palmela's proposals were embodied in a 'Project for a Manifesto to the Portuguese Nation', presented to the king on 27 January, setting out the principles of a constitution, including the separation of powers, the establishment of a parliament, equality before the law, freedom of press, and so on.[22] It is not known whether Palmela was in contact with Lord Holland during this period, but Holland may well have had some influence on these proposals. It is certainly undeniable that Palmela's overall approach to politics owed much to the traditions of English Whiggery, traditions that Palmela literally imbibed during his many visits to Holland House between 1813 and 1814 and again between 1816 and 1820.

Palmela's proposals were discussed at meetings of the King's Council in January 1821. Strong opposition came from António Tomás Vila Nova Portugal, the king's chief minister.[23] Tomás was a self-confessed Absolutist, who maintained that any mistaken negotiations with the rebels would constitute a betrayal of the principles of royalism; the slightest compromise could be fatal. He added: If [the king] surrenders the slightest parcel of regal power to the aristocrats, then he must lose it all to the people; the more effective way to preserve the aristocracy is to preserve the traditions of the realm, and it is for the Sovereign to defend it.'[24] Tomás also opposed the idea of sending Pedro to Lisbon, at least until order was fully restored there.

Palmela's position was strengthened by news of a rising in São Salvador da Baía on 10 February 1821, involving the establishment of a junta and oaths of loyalty to the future Portuguese constitution at the Governor's Palace. Eventually, during the King's Council on 18 February, D. João agreed to send Pedro to Portugal to re-establish order, as well as to publish the outline of a constitution, asking Palmela to prepare a draft. On 21 February, Palmela sent D. João a draft for a manifesto to the Portuguese nation, accompanied by ideas about the bases of a constitution, which António Tomás contemptuously dismissed as 'an English constitution'.[25] But while keeping the first part of the promise, some of the chief principles of 'Palmela's constitution' were dropped. Thus, the royal decree of 18 February (published on 24), mentioned two different constitutions: one for Portugal, which Pedro was to collect in Lisbon and convey to Rio de Janeiro for royal approval and the other for Brazil. The Brazilian constitution should include some modifications suggested by a junta appointed by the king. Strikingly, this constitution whose centrepiece would be a *Cortes* in Brazil – to be made up of the representatives of the main cities and

22. Palmela, 'Projecto de Manifesto', in *Despachos e Correspondencia do Duque de Palmela*. 4 vols (Lisboa: Imprensa Nacional, 1851), 1: 161–64; see also *Memórias do Duque de Palmela* (Lisboa: Dom Quixote, 2010), 159–61; João Manuel Pereira da Silva, *História da fundação do imperio brazileiro*. 7 vols (Rio de Janeiro: B. L. Garnier, 1864–1868), 5: 63–65.
23. Tomás António de Vila Nova Portugal (1755–1839), Portuguese magistrate and politician, chief minister (1817–21). Tomás died in Portugal in misery.
24. António Tomás de Vila Nova Portugal to D. João VI (14 January 1821), quoted in *História da independência do Brasil*, by Francisco Adolfo de Varnhagen (Rio de Janeiro: Imprensa Nacional, 1917), 51; 'Si cede, para repartir com a nobreza, virá a perder-se toda, tirando o povo tudo: o meio de conservar-se a nobreza, é conservar-se os usos do reino; e o soberano é que a defende.' (My translation).
25. Varnhagen, *História da independência do Brasil*, 58–60.

towns in Brazil, Açores, Madeira and Cabo Verde – seems to have been adapted from Lord Holland's Memorandum of 1808, suggesting 'it would be wise to summon deputies to the assembly individuals with specific roles such as the chief or mayor of each municipality'. The major difference was that Holland had advised that the actual words *Cortes*, Assembly, Parliament or even estates, should be avoided because they might 'give rise to excitement in a manner inconvenient to circumstances'.[26]

Furious with what he regarded as treachery, Palmela resigned, although he agreed to remain in post until the king could find a suitable successor. But Palmela's departure from office probably came sooner than he expected, and it was not the appointment of a successor but rather the consequence of a rebellion, led by Brigadier Francisco Joaquim Carretti, that broke out in Rio de Janeiro on 26 February. Pedro himself seems to have been implicated, perhaps with his father's knowledge. João was forced to dismiss all his ministers and to appoint others imposed by the rebels, including Silvestre Pinheiro Ferreira (1769–1846), a radical theorist who took the foreign ministry. The king's decree of 18 February was revoked and replaced by another dated 24 and published on 28 February, containing an *avant la lettre* approval of the constitution being prepared at the Portuguese *Cortes* and a promise to adopt it in Brazil.[27] As Palmela had predicted, by obstructing the grant of a moderate constitutional charter, D. João VI had actually been responsible for the eventual proclamation of a much more radical constitution. This was almost exactly the same course that Fernando VII of Spain had taken in 1820.

Unable to postpone his return to Portugal any longer, D. João VI left Rio de Janeiro on 26 April 1821, leaving Pedro as regent, and disembarking in Lisbon on 4 July. On the same day, he visited the *Cortes* and was forced to take the *avant la lettre* oath to the principles of the future constitution. But Parliament took the opportunity to subject the king to a series of humiliations; contrary to his wishes, it delayed his landing by requiring him to remain on board ship overnight. This was followed by other minor slights. No doubt they were intended to show that Parliament was really in charge of the country, but they were probably counterproductive. Despite all that had happened, the royal family still commanded the respect and loyalty of the bulk of the population and so, rather than making the revolution more secure, slights on the king weakened the Liberal regime and hence prepared the way for the partial re-establishment of Absolutism in 1823.

Perhaps the main obstacle to the establishment and consolidation of a Liberal regime in Portugal after 1820 – as in Spain in 1808 and 1820 – was the apparent incompatibility between ideals and social and economic reality. Lord Porchester, who lived in Portugal for many years, later concluded,

> The first Portuguese Constitution was wholly opposed to the feelings of the country, and could only have maintained itself by effecting a revolution, not solely in the general disposition of property, but in the habits and opinions of all classes of society.[28]

26. Holland, 'Carta ou memoria', 253.
27. *Gazeta do Rio de Janeiro*, 28 February, 1821, [2–3].
28. Porchester, Henry George Herbert, 2nd Earl of Carnarvon, Lord, *The Last Days of the Portuguese Constitution* (London: Henry Colburn and Richard Bentley, 1830), [1].

This fundamental weakness had already been identified by Count Giuseppe Pecchio (1785–1835), an Italian Liberal who visited Portugal in 1822:

> But what could I say, since I have traversed the Kingdom without remarking a single proof of political regeneration? The old edifice is still entire. It is announced, and solemnly sworn that a Constitutional structure will be erected, but as yet, nothing more than the façade of the building exists, that is to say, the political code.[29]

In other words, both Spanish and Portuguese constitutionalists failed to appreciate that their countries lacked the necessary economic and social capital to sustain the 'pure' form of Liberalism aspired to by the idealists of 1820. In Continental terms, a weakening of the *Ancien Régime* – a process that had occurred to some extent in Spain and Portugal – could be identified as a precondition for the emergence of Liberalism. But this weakening needed to be accompanied by the rise of a successful and self-confident middle class that would take the lead in urbanization and industrialization – and of that there was little sign. But Liberalism could have emerged in a different way. In Britain, the *Ancien Régime* did not visibly disintegrate; rather, its outward features were preserved, cloaking a more modern reality. Although the British middle class played a part in this process, commercially minded landowners were probably even more crucial to it. Unfortunately, Portugal had neither a flourishing bourgeoisie nor a commercially minded aristocracy. Indeed, despite Pombal's modest attempts at modernization and a considerable trade with Brazil, in most essentials Portugal was still distressingly backward in the 1820s.

But while Portugal seemed unable to regenerate herself and thus appeared condemned to decay, her main colony, Brazil, could move towards 'order and progress' – the motto of the present Brazilian flag – so that by the beginning of the twenty-first century it was among the most rapidly expanding nations in the world. As Holland had suggested in 1808, 'if the aim proposed by the aforementioned [Portuguese] Court is to raise Brazil to an independent and sovereign monarchy, then the project seems to me as grand and worthy of a great prince, and the means to achieve its execution are certain and simple'.[30] However, 'the great prince', the prince who would rise to the challenge of establishing a new and great empire on the other side of the Atlantic, was not to be D. João VI. Rather, this was to be the role of João's son, Pedro, who proclaimed the independence of Brazil on 7 September 1822.

Unlike his parents and grandmother, the old Queen D. Maria I, who had been so traumatized by their forced emigration to Brazil, Pedro had adapted to his new home with ease. And unlike other members of his family who spent much of their time complaining about the roughness of Brazilian society, the extremely hot and humid climate, or the disgusting bugs and other revolting creatures, Pedro was thrilled by almost every aspect of what he saw as an earthly paradise. The extreme wideness, the bright and polychromatic landscapes, the variety of the fauna and flora, the wildness of the virgin forests, the

29. Giuseppe Pecchio, *Anecdotes of the Spanish and Portuguese Revolutions* (London: G. and W. B. Whittaker, 1823), 126.
30. Holland, 'Carta ou memoria', 250.

easiness of the populations – everything conspired to excite the imagination of a nine year old boy. Above all, rather than spending most of his time indoors or confined to the gardens of the Lisbon and Queluz palaces, Pedro was now free to explore a brand new world that must have seemed infinite.

It would be wrong to dismiss such a response as mere childish naïvety. Perhaps the true spirit of Portugal and the glorious achievements of its past survived not in the country itself, but rather through its prodigal child, Brazil. This was probably what António Vieira, a seventeenth-century Brazilian-born Jesuit, had foreseen when alluding to the 'Fifth Empire' in his visionary and polemical *Historia do futuro*(1718), viz. the mythical time when Portugal would rise and rule over a spiritual and temporal empire that would replace the European hegemony.

Part 2

THE PORTUGUESE QUESTION

Chapter Five

ROAD TO ABSOLUTISM

*The House ought to pause before they acknowledged abloody usurper as the tyrant of a country so essential to England.**

The 'Portuguese Question', as it may be defined *stricto sensu*, corresponds to the dynastic crisis following the death of D. João VI in 1826. More broadly, it covers the political, legal and theoretical issues surrounding the contest between D. Pedro, Duque de Bragança, and his brother, Infante D. Miguel, for the throne of Portugal. It may even extend to the final battle between the *Ancien Régime* and the new Liberal order, that is to say, between the old and contemporary Portugal. In 1834, under the terms of the Convention of Evoramonte, the 'Portuguese Question' was eventually decided in favour of Pedro's daughter, D. Maria, while D. Miguel was banished from Portugal *ad æternum* and his descendants excluded from the succession. In its earlier stages the 'Portuguese Question' was regarded as an essentially internal affair – despite the secret interference of Britain, Austria and Spain – but, following D. Miguel's usurpation in 1828, it developed into an international diplomatic conflict. Finally the 'Portuguese Question' became part of a much bigger conflict, the battle between the forces and principles of Absolutism and Liberalism. In the end it was the Liberals who won and their victory marked the end of what Lord Holland described in 1828 as the 'associations called by the name of Holy Alliances […] which sat like an *incubus* upon the liberties of the world'.[1] But while Canning had 'shaken off the trammels and the shackles of the Holy Alliance',[2] as Holland also admitted, the final *coup de grâce* for Metternich's system came only with the perpetual banishment of his two chief agents in the Peninsula, infantes Don Carlos of Spain and D. Miguel of Portugal.

Liberal historiography usually present the years between 1826 and 1828 as dominated by a conspiracy to overthrow representative government in Portugal and to replace it by an authoritarian regime. The title of this chapter, 'Road to Absolutism', seems an appropriate description of the extraordinary events that led to Miguel's accession to the throne in 1828. At least in retrospect, the story resembles a Greek tragedy, in which history follows its course whatever the characters may want or seek to achieve. Thus Portuguese constitutionalism seems doomed, no matter what mortals may have done to

---

* Holland, '[debates on 4 Feb. 1828 upon] The Royal Speech', in *The New Monthly Magazine and Literary Journal*, 30: 111 (1 March 1830): 91.

1. Holland, speech in the House of Lords on 'Foreign Affairs', *The Times*, 17 July 1828, 6.
2. Holland, quoted in Lord Aberdeen's speech on 'Foreign Affairs', *The Times*, 17 July 1828, 6; see also, *A Brief Exposition of the Foreign Policy of Mr. Canning: as Contrasted with That of the Existing Administration* (London: J. Hatchard and Son, 1830), 24.

save it. As noted in *A Brief Exposition of the Foreign Policy of Mr. Canning*, the revolution of 1826 was already 'pregnant with a most disastrous future to the country'.[3] Even wise and perceptive politicians like Palmela, who could foresee what was going to happen next, seemed impotent or unwilling to stop the inevitable outcome. In a letter to Cândido José Xavier,[4] referring to the alarming signs that, at least in retrospect, seem to point to eventual usurpation, he still insists that it will not happen; he is sure that God will answer his prayers and not allow the terrible omens to be fulfilled. Perhaps Palmela refused to see what was staring him in the face or, like Antigone, half realized that he could not do anything to change the inevitable course of events. The sense of helplessness may have been increased by the knowledge that, in the last resort, the political and social crisis that racked Portugal in the years following the death of João VI would not be settled by the Portuguese themselves. Its outcome would actually be determined by the complex and often self-seeking manoeuvres of the Great Powers, in what Garrett appropriately called the 'labyrinth of diplomacy'.[5] Of course, powerful nations often interfere in the affairs of weaker countries but, short of outright invasion, interference by outside powers in the affairs of Portugal between 1822 and 1834 must constitute one of the most blatant and unseemly examples.

Despite British objections, a French invasion of Spain as a way to overturn the 'devilish' Constitution of Cadiz and to restore a 'legitimate' Absolute government had been decided at the Congress of Verona in October 1822. On 22 April 1823, fearing that French intervention in Spain would extend to Portugal, Holland 'moved for extracts from the correspondence of government respecting Portugal in case of an invasion of Spain by France', but withdrew his motion when Lord Liverpool gave assurances that Britain would assist Portugal if she were to suffer an unprovoked attack.[6] Two days later, however, relevant documents were laid on the table, including a despatch to Canning – now foreign secretary again – from Charles Stuart, dated from Paris on 7 April, stating that Chateaubriand had assured him that the French government had no intention of intervening in Portugal.[7] This was followed by a speech from Lord Ellenborough arguing that war had been made more likely by the government's indecisive policies of refusal to accept the Spanish people's right to decide their own future – coupled with a readiness to leave them to the mercy of the French. Ellenborough's address was rejected with 142 votes to 46.[8] Holland, who had supported the address, entered a protest in the *Journals* of the House, which was signed by several other peers who agreed with Ellenborough. According to Holland, not only was the government to blame for the decline of Britain's

---

3. Anon., *A Brief Exposition*, 6.
4. Cândido José Xavier Dias da Silva (1769–1833), Portuguese army officer, statesman and D. Pedro's private secretary.
5. [Almeida Garrett], 'Parte politica: introdução, ou razão d'ordem da chronica da primeira semana', *O chronista: semanario de politica, litteratura, sciências e artes* 9 (March–May 1827): [1].
6. *The New Monthly Magazine* 9: 30 (1 June 1823): 241.
7. Charles Stuart (1799–1845), 1st Baron Stuart of Rothesay, British diplomat.
8. *The New Monthly Magazine* 9: 30 (1 June 1823): 241.

influence on the Continent, but it had also unnecessarily exposed 'Portugal to menace, invasion, and subjugation'.[9]

On 27 May 1823, three days after the Duke d'Angoulême entered Madrid, Infante Miguel, instigated by his mother, Queen Carlota Joaquina, launched a coup d'état against the constitutional regime from Vila Franca, a town about twenty miles north of Lisbon.[10] This episode, later known as *Vilafrancada*, re-established a mild Absolutism. On 31 May, forced by events, the king announced his intention to replace the Constitution, the work of 'corrupt Men in exalted stations', with a new charter – a promise never fulfilled.[11] Miguel received the title of *Generalíssimo* (Supreme Commander of the King's Armies) while the queen, who had been banished to Queluz for refusing to take the oaths to the Constitution, returned to Lisbon, her political and civil rights restored. Freemasons and ultra-Liberals were persecuted and forced into exile, while Absolutist émigrés were rehabilitated and allowed to return.[12] Beresford, who had been impeded from landing in Lisbon after the Liberal Revolution of 1820, also returned to Portugal and regained much of his former influence.

Unsatisfied with the 'incomplete' achievements of the counter-revolutionary coup, Queen Carlota Joaquina continued to conspire against her husband. On the night of 29 to 30 April 1824, while Sir Edward Thornton, the British minister, was giving a ball in his house, a plan to remove the king was launched by the queen and her son Miguel, later known as *Abrilada*.[13] Under the pretext of foiling a supposed plot to assassinate the King, orchestrated by what Miguel called the 'pestilential sect of Freemasons', troops loyal to the infante besieged the Royal Palace of Bemposta.[14] The king was placed in custody while more than three hundred people were arrested, including Palmela, foreign minister and himself a Freemason, who was taken from his house to the Tower of Belém in the middle of the night.

When the ultra-royalist movement seemed to be succeeding, the situation was transformed by the concerted intervention of the whole diplomatic body, especially by the

9. 'Holland's Protest', *The Times*, 28 April 1823, 3; see also *The Opinions of Lord Holland, as Recorded in the Journals of the House of Lords, from 1797 to 1841* (London: J. Ridgway, 1841), 105, 110.
10. D. Carlota Joaquina Teresa de Borbón y Borbón-Parma (1775–1830), Infanta of Spain and Queen of Portugal. She was the eldest daughter of King Carlos IV of Spain and his wife María Luisa de Parma, and sister of Fernando VII.
11. 'Proclamation of the King of Portugal, on the Dissolution of the Constitution of the Cortes', translation of the 'Proclamação de Vila Franca' (3 June 1823), in *British and Foreign State Papers: 1822–1823*, 1031.
12. Secret societies, viz. Freemasonry, were prohibited by Royal Decree of 20 June 1823.
13. Sir Edward Thornton (1766–1852), Conde de Cacilhas in the Portuguese nobility, British diplomat, third son of William Thornton, a Yorkshireman settled in London as an innkeeper, and brother of Thomas Thornton. Envoy Extraordinary and Minister Plenipotentiary to Lisbon (1823–24), with temporary rank of Ambassador Extraordinary (1823). Thornton arrived in Lisbon on 31 August 1823, a sign that Canning was taking events in Portugal seriously. Thornton remained in Portugal until 29 September 1824 when he was replaced by Sir William A'Court.
14. 'Proclamação dirigida à tropa pelo infante D. Miguel em 30 de abril de 1824', quoted in *HGC*, 3.ª época, t. VI [18], p. 504; 'pestilenta cáfila dos pedreiros livres' (translation in *The Times*, 19 May 1824, 3).

French ambassador, Hyde de Neuville, who played a crucial role in the whole affair.[15] Evading Miguel's guards, Neuville managed to reach the king's apartments, where he found João in discussion with Beresford, which naturally raised suspicions that he had been involved in the plot. Arrests continued during the following days until 9 May when, at the suggestion of Neuville, Thornton and Palmela (who had already been released), the king went secretly aboard the *Windsor-Castle* anchored in the Tagus, and remained on the ship until 14 May. Under the protection of the British flag, the king could exert some semblance of independent authority, ordering the liberation of all political prisoners and the banishment of his rebellious son from Portugal to Austria, where Miguel remained until the end of 1827.

D. João VI died on 10 March 1826. Four days earlier, he had signed a document appointing his daughter, Infanta D. Isabel Maria, head of a regency, to rule during his illness.[16] He further declared that, if he should die, Isabel Maria was to await instructions from the legitimate heir.[17] For some unknown reason, however, the king did not name his heir, thus leaving the door open for all kinds of speculation. João had confirmed his eldest son Pedro as his heir in his *Carta Patente* of 13 May 1825, but Pedro had rebelled against his father by proclaiming the independence of Brazil on 7 September 1822, and was thus seen as a traitor by many Portuguese.[18] Miguel, who was still in Vienna, was also open to serious objection. In such circumstances, the late king's failure to provide unambiguous identification of his successor was bound to deepen divisions within Portuguese society, in turn leading to political crisis and ultimately to a civil war.

On hereditary grounds, Pedro had the strongest claim. Even Metternich admitted to Resende,[19] the Brazilian minister in Vienna, that

> a declaration of recognition to the sovereignty of a legitimate successor, being an entirely new act in diplomacy, could make one believe that there are some doubts, which do not exist, on the de facto and de jure succession of your master to the crown of Portugal.[20]

---

15. Jean-Guillaume Hyde de Neuville (1776–1857), baron Hyde de Neuville, Conde and Marquês da Bemposta in the Portuguese nobility, French politician and diplomat. He was the son of Guillaume Hyde, a gentleman belonging to an English family who had emigrated with the Stuarts after the rebellion of 1745. Neuville was possibly a descendant of Edward Hyde (1609–1674), 1st Earl of Clarendon, Chief Minister of Charles II from 1660 to 1667.
16. D. Isabel Maria de Bragança (1801–1876), Infanta of Portugal, fourth daughter of D. João VI and D. Carlota Joaquina. Her complete name: Isabel Maria da Conceição Joana Gualberta Ana Francisca de Assis Xavier de Paula de Alcântara Antónia Rafaela Micaela Gabriela Joaquina Gonzaga de Bragança e Bourbon.
17. *Gazeta de Lisboa*, suppl. 7 Março 1826, 225.
18. *Collecção dos tratados, convenções, contratos e actos publicos celebrados entre a Corôa de Portugal e as mais potencias desde 1640 até ao presente.* 8 vols (Lisboa: Imprensa Nacional, 1856–58), 5: 503–5.
19. António Teles da Silva Caminha e Meneses (1790–1875), 1st and only Visconde and Marquês de Resende in the Brazilian nobility, Brazilian diplomat of Portuguese origin, the son of D. Fernando Teles da Silva Caminha e Meneses, 3rd Marquês de Penalva and 7th Conde de Tarouca, and D. Joana de Almeida, daughter of the 2nd Marquês de Lavradio. Resende was one of many Portuguese nobles who supported the Brazilian revolution and made a career at the court of Rio de Janeiro. He married Fanny Hélèbe Le Roi in 1800.
20. Metternich, quoted in *Éclaircissements historiques sur mes négociations relatives aux affaires de Portugal*, by the Marquês de Resende. 2nd edn (Paris: Paulin, 1832), 24; 'Une déclaration de la

Hence, on 20 March 1826, Pedro was unanimously acknowledged as the de facto and de jure King of Portugal. However, this was regarded as a formality, as it was clear that the emperor intended to remain in Brazil. But Pedro was preparing a surprise; on 29 April, five days after the news of his father's death reached Rio de Janeiro, Pedro issued a Constitutional Charter for Portugal and, on 2 May, abdicated the throne of Portugal in favour of his daughter, the eight-year-old Infanta Maria da Glória. Pedro further stipulated that Maria should marry her uncle Miguel in the course of the following year. After taking the oaths to the Charter, Miguel was to become regent when he reached the age of 25.[21] Sadly, this arrangement, intended to reconcile conflicting factions in Portugal and elsewhere, was to produce the opposite effect. A few days later (11 May), Sir Charles Stuart sailed for Lisbon on the frigate *Diamond*, not as an English envoy but as a Portuguese plenipotentiary to convey the original of the *Carta Constitucional*.

Canning, who distrusted Pedro, seems to have been displeased when he learned of the Charter. But England possessed the oldest constitution in the world and would do nothing to injure Pedro's Charter. Canning was less worried by the Charter itself than by the possible reactions to Pedro's surprise in Spain – perhaps going as far as a Spanish invasion of Portugal. Fernando VII, now ruling as an Absolute monarch, refused to acknowledge either the Constitution or Isabel Maria's regency. Hence Canning warned Spain to abstain from any hostile action against Portugal, which would be regarded as an aggression against Britain herself. At the same time, Canning also warned Portugal against any agitation or propaganda 'attempt to carry their new constitution out of their country and to stir up commotions in Spain.'[22]

Metternich proved less tolerant of the 'deplorable work of Don Pedro',[23] believing that the Emperor of Brazil had introduced in Portugal 'not a Constitution, but a system of anarchy'.[24] Yet amidst all the alarm, there was one consolation. Unlike the former Spanish and Portuguese Constitutions, which had been imposed by revolutionary acts, the Charter had been granted by a rightful sovereign, something that made it more tolerable from a legitimist point of view. Moreover, the death of Alexander of Russia on 19 November 1825 represented a serious blow to the Holy Alliance and to legitimist doctrine, thus contributing to the weakening of Austria.

In many ways, the situation in Portugal was the mirror image of the European norm. Elsewhere, the causes of Absolutism and Legitimatism appeared natural allies, whereas Constitutionalism was linked to insurrection. In Portugal, however, Legitimatism was

---

reconnaissance de la souveraineté d'un successeur légitime étant un acte tout-à-fait nouveau dans la diplomatie, pourrait faire croire qu'il y a quelques doutes, qui n'existent pas, sur la succession de droit et de fait de votre maître à la couronne de Portugal.' (My translation).

21. According to Article 92 of the Charter, in case of the sovereign's minority (i.e., until the age of 18), Portugal was to be ruled by the closest relative in the line of succession, who must be at least 25.
22. Canning, Dispatch to A'Court, quoted in *Life of Canning*, by Harold Temperley (London: James Finch, 1905), 371 (F.O., 11 August 1826).
23. 'Metternich to Count Bombelles', in *Memoirs of Prince Metternich 1815–1829*. 4 vols (London: Richard Bentley, 1880–81), 4: 330 (St. Petersburg, 7 September 1826).
24. Ibid., 4: 329.

linked to Constitutionalism. The question was whether Absolutism would ally itself with insurrection. To do so would violate some of the core values of Legitimatism, but not to do so would assist the growth of everything else most Legitimatists deplored. Much depended on Metternich, who possessed a potential means of overthrowing the 'abominable' Charter, in the shape of Miguel, still in exile in Vienna. But Metternich faced a dilemma and his immediate reaction was cautious. He advised Miguel not to hasten to Lisbon – as the Queen Mother and her circle probably wanted – but to wait for instructions from either the regency or from Pedro. Pedro himself had urged Miguel to wait in Vienna for further instructions, and for the time being Miguel did as he was told. Given Miguel's notorious impatience, the wait must have been difficult to endure. Metternich now tried to persuade Pedro that Miguel was a changed man who would genuinely accept the Charter and hence could be trusted with the regency. Finally, on 4 October 1826, Miguel took the oaths to the Charter, both verbally and in writing, while an application for a Consanguinity Dispensation was sent to Rome so that he could marry his niece. The royal marriage was celebrated by proxy and *per verba futuri* in Vienna on 29 October in the presence of Emperor Francis and Metternich.

In Portugal reactions to Pedro's Charter were mixed. While Liberals celebrated, the ultra-royalists instigated by Carlota Joaquina sought to discredit the new regime by engaging in manoeuvres intended to disturb public order and precipitate civil war. For the time being the Liberals seemed in the ascendant, especially after General Saldanha – the Liberals' main leader – became Minister of War, but the Absolutists were unlikely to acquiesce.[25] Towards the end of July 1826, mutinies were reported in several Portuguese towns close to the Spanish frontier. Officers sympathetic to Miguel, including the Marquês de Chaves[26] and the Visconde de Montalegre,[27] encouraged troops to desert

---

25. D. João Carlos Gregório Domingos Vicente Francisco de Saldanha Oliveira e Daun (1790–1876), 1st Conde, Marquês and Duque de Saldanha, Portuguese army officer, diplomat, politician and statesman. Son of D. João Vicente de Saldanha Oliveira e Sousa Juzarte Figueira (1746–1804), 1st Conde de Rio Maior, by his wife, D. Maria Amália de Carvalho Daun (1756–1812), daughter of the Marquês de Pombal by his second wife, Eleanore Ernestine, Gräfin von Daun. Saldanha married twice: first, on 5 October 1814 to D. Maria Theresa Horan FitzGerald (1796–1835), daughter of Thomas Horan, Esq., an Irish resident in Lisbon, and his wife Isabella FitzGerald; second, in 1856 to Charlotte Elisabeth Mary Smith-Athelstane (b. 1808), daughter of Michael Athelstane-Smith (1762–1831) and his wife, Sarah Walton (1767–1849); her brother was John Smith-Athelstane (1813–1886), 1st Conde da Carnota in the Portuguese nobility. Although Saldanha was hardly a radical, his penchant for the melodramatic – probably more a reflection of his flamboyant and egocentric personality than of any particular political inclination – led many people to think of him as a progressive. In the course of his long and active life, Saldanha was implicated in several *coups*; the last, known as *Saldanhada*, took place in 1870, when he was already 80 years old. Following the failure of this last attempt to interfere in politics, King D. Luís sent Saldanha to London as a minister to get rid of him. He remained there until his death in 1876 aged 86.
26. Manuel da Silveira Pinto da Fonseca Teixeira (1784–1830), 2nd Conde de Amarante and 1st Marquês de Chaves, Portuguese army officer, the son of Francisco da Silveira Pinto da Fonseca Teixeira. Amarante was one of Miguel's most effective supporters.
27. Luís Vaz Pereira Pinto Guedes (1770–1841), 2nd Visconde de Montalegre.

and move into Spain – with the objective of forming an army to invade Portugal.[28] Obviously they had the assistance or, at least, the connivance of the Spanish authorities.[29] Despite Saldanha's attempts to re-establish order and to prevent the rebellion from spreading, desertions and mutinies continued.[30] On the night of 19 November, a group of rebels gathered in La Mezquita, Galicia, crossed the Portuguese border at Trás-os-Montes and entered the town of Moimenta, while a guerrilla group of approximately 60 deserters attacked Vinhais to plunder and steal horses. Although the official *Gazeta de Lisboa* concluded its report by insisting, 'Despite these events, peace rules everywhere', these were merely the first episodes in a campaign that lasted until the beginning of February 1827, when forces loyal to the government finally defeated the rebels and forced them to retreat into Spain.[31]

Had it not been for the disorganization of the rebel forces – whose leaders were unable to establish a common strategy or line of action – the government would have found it difficult to re-establish order. The rebels consisted of several independent guerrilla groups, each with its own egocentric leader, preoccupied with his own interests and unwilling to accept a single command or even to contribute to a common cause. But the most decisive factor was probably the arrival in the Tagus in December of a fleet with 5,000 British troops under General Clinton dispatched under the terms of the Anglo-Portuguese Alliance.[32] Holland had given strong support when, on 11 December 1826, the Lords approved assistance to Portugal: 'he would not hesitate to say, that with a pure mind, a steady purpose, and a clear conscience, he gave his unqualified support to the

28. The first significant mutiny took place in Chaves on the night of 21–22 July 1826, although this was quickly suppressed. It was followed by several mutinies in Bragança (27 July) – headed by the Visconde de Montalegre – Estremoz and Vila Viçosa (31 July), ending with the escape of the insurgents to Spain. According to official figures from the Ministry of War, published in the *Gazeta de Lisboa* on 4 August, the mutineers on 31 July included 80 men from the 2nd Regiment of Cavalry (Vila Viçosa), 211 from the 17th Regiment of Infantry (Estremoz) and 211 from the 24th Regiment of Infantry (Bragança), making a total of 502 men.
29. Despite Fernando VII's assurances that Spain would never permit its territory to be used as a springboard for aggression against Portugal, the deserters were welcomed by the Spanish authorities, who went as far as to pay their wages. Indeed, although the rebels appeared to be under Portuguese command, in reality their leaders reported to Spanish General Francisco de Longa.
30. The measures adopted by Saldanha included a general curfew (*Gazeta de Lisboa*, 13 Setembro 1826, 874), the interdiction of public meetings in the streets of Lisbon and other towns (*Gazeta de Lisboa*, 13 Dezembro 1826, 1317), the temporary suspension of freedom of the press and reestablishment of censorship (*Gazeta de Lisboa*, 21 Agosto 1826, 784). Yet, orders given for the dismissal of magistrates suspected of collusion with the rebels were ineffective, as magistrates and civil servants ignored or sabotaged government orders (*Gazeta de Lisboa*, 6 Setembro 1826, 843–45; 7 Setembro 1826, 847–48; 8 Setembro 1826, 854).
31. *Gazeta de Lisboa*, 29 Novembro 1826, 1248; 'Apezar destes acontecimentos continuava o secêgo em toda a parte.' (My translation).
32. The first British troops arrived in Lisbon on 24 December 1826 (*Gazeta de Lisboa*, suppl. 24 Dezembro 1826, 1380).

address now moved by the noble earl'.[33] In accordance with the terms of the alliance, the British forces did not intervene directly in the fighting – something later deplored by the Liberals – but their presence itself seemed to discourage the rebels.

On 6 December 1826, Saldanha fell seriously ill and was replaced in the Cabinet by the Marquês de Valença, leaving the Constitutional Party temporarily without its main leader.[34] This fact, together with the gravity of the symptoms, led Althelstane to suggest that Saldanha had been poisoned. Saldanha's sudden illness was undoubtedly a boon to the ultra-royalists, in that the only man capable of opposing their plans was removed from the scene for some time.[35] On his returning to office on 28 April 1827, Saldanha tried to frustrate the ultra-conservative party, by measures such as the abolition of censorship and reorganization of the army. But Saldanha could not regain his former influence. On 8 June, several ministers accused of conspiring against the Constitutional Charter were acquitted, including the ultra-conservative Bishop of Viseu.[36] Disagreements with Isabel Maria led Saldanha to resign on 24 July, another serious blow to the Liberal Party, which lost the only man capable of overawing the Ultras.

News of Saldanha's resignation caused uproar in Lisbon with crowds assembled on the Praça do Comércio on the evening of 25 July, shouting 'vivas!' to the Constitutional Charter, to D. Pedro and to General Saldanha. As the demonstrators were carrying torch lights, the protest became known as *Archotadas*– the protests of the 'archotes' (torch lights). The demonstrations, which peaked on 26 July, continued until the evening of 28, when the cavalry, led by the Conde de Vila Flor, dispersed the remaining demonstrators.[37] Although one year had still to elapse before the re-establishment of Absolutism, the suppression of the *Archotadas* marked the real end of representative government. The following months saw persecutions of Liberals, with house searches and several detentions without trial. About 150 people were arrested at Oporto following a repeat of the Lisbon

33. 'Parliamentary Intelligence: Spain and Portugal', *The Times*, 13 December 1826, 1; see also Leslie Mitchell, *Holland House* (London: Duckworth, 1980), 202.

34. José Bernardino de Portugal e Castro (1780–1840), 12th Conde de Vimioso and 5th Marquês de Valença, Portuguese officer and politician, Peer of the Realm, Minister of War (6 December 1826–9 January 1827) and prime minister for one day (4–5 November 1836).

35. On his way back from Algarve to Lisbon, Saldanha had decided to spend the night in Beja, at the Palace of the Bishop, when 'Strange symptoms declared themselves the following morning.' (Saldanha and Carnota, *Memoirs of Field-Marshal The Duke de Saldanha with Selections from His Correspondence*. 2 vols (London: John Murray, 1880), 1: 119).

36. D. Francisco Alexandre Lobo (1763–1844), Portuguese clerical, erudite writer and ultra-conservative politician, Minister of the Kingdom Affairs (16 December 1826–5 September 1827). Lobo was appointed minister in replacement of Pedro de Melo Breyner (1751–1830), who was dismissed after criticizing some of his colleagues whose loyalty to the constitutional regime was doubtful.

37. *Gazeta de Lisboa*, 27–28 Julho 1827, 1011, 1017. According to Soriano and Gomes de Amorim, the police had placed several *agents provocateurs* among the demonstrators with instructions to shout 'Viva a República' with the purpose of creating disorder, which was avoided due to the prompt and skilful intervention of Vila Flor (Soriano, *HGC*, 3.ª época, t. II, pt. 2 [13]: 143; Francisco Gomes de Amorim, *Garrett: memorias biographicas*. 3 vols [Lisboa: Imprensa Nacional, 1881–84], 1: 427).

protests on 28–30 July. Fearing for their safety, Saldanha and his family fled to England on 21 October 1827.

Pedro's abdication in favour of his daughter had been subject to two conditions: Miguel should take the oaths to the Charter and D. Maria II, whom he should also marry. Although the first condition had been fulfilled, the second had not, as the marriage had not been consummated. Arguably, therefore, Pedro's abdication became effective only when both conditions had been fulfilled and, since they had not been, he was still King of Portugal. In their different ways – and indicative of their attempts to turn the situation in Portugal to their own advantage – both Canning and Metternich chose to ignore these legal and constitutional niceties.

In November 1826, Metternich had dispatched Neumann to Rio de Janeiro to persuade Pedro to send his daughter to Europe as soon as possible, so that the young queen could receive a proper education and be prepared to rule. Neumann had also been instructed to persuade the emperor to issue a public declaration promising that Miguel would become Regent of Portugal as soon as he reached the age of 25 (i.e. on 26 October 1827). Despite Neumann's diplomatic skills, the most he could obtain from Pedro was a refusal to comment on the British and Austrian proposals – virtually identical – until Miguel appeared in person in Rio de Janeiro. But Miguel had other plans. Metternich had advised him to remain in Vienna and to ignore his brother's summons to Rio, a position to which Britain did not object or, at least, overlooked. Metternich claimed that Miguel had an unquestioned right to the regency and that this had been confirmed by Pedro himself – a point of view apparently accepted by Britain.

Pressured by Austria, Dudley, now British foreign secretary, agreed to send a deputation to Rio de Janeiro to urge Pedro to complete the process of abdication, a decision that pleased both Metternich and Czar Nicholas. Palmela, the Portuguese minister in London, wrote to Pedro on 10 July 1827, warning the emperor that he needed to clarify his position on the future of Portugal as soon as possible. But Palmela could not have guessed that Pedro had already reached a decision one week earlier. Faced with Britain's unwillingness to support a different policy, the emperor had little choice but to comply with Austria's demands and, on 3 July, appointed Miguel his lieutenant-general and Regent of Portugal.

On 12 September, Dudley informed Palmela that his government and Austria agreed about Portugal's future. Miguel should return to Lisbon as soon as possible to become regent, although in the course of his journey he should pay a short visit to Britain – an arrangement intended to pacify the Liberals and please the British authorities. On 18, 20 and 23 October, three meetings were held at Metternich's house in Vienna to discuss the affairs of Portugal. At the first, Miguel promised to 'maintain religiously its institutions, to bury what had passed in entire oblivion, but to restrain at the same time, with energy and firmness, the spirit of party and of faction which has too long agitated Portugal',[38] words that gained the approval of everyone present.[39] At the second meeting, the parties agreed

38. 'Protoc. – Vienna, October 18th 1827', in *Journals of the House of Commons: Sess. 1829*, 84, app. D (19 June 1827): 777.

39. The meetings were attended by Miguel, the Barão de Vila Seca and the Conde de Vila Real for Portugal, Metternich, the Graf von Lebzeltern, Neuman and Henri de Bombelles, comte de

that Pedro should complete 'his act of abdication, the sending of the Queen Maria da Gloria to Portugal, and the total and definitive separation of the two crowns'.[40]

On 6 December 1827, Miguel left Vienna for Paris, where he arrived on 13 December escorted by the Conde de Vila Real. He then moved to Calais, embarking on the royal yacht to Greenwich, where he landed on 30 December. Miguel was met by Palmela and by the Duke of Clarence, commissioned to convey the prince and his suite to Lord Dudley's house, and by Wellington, soon to be appointed prime minister – with the possible exception of Metternich, his strongest foreign supporter. On 12 January, the infante attended a conference with Dudley, Prince Esterhazy, Comte Henri de Bombelles, Palmela and Vila Real, where the British and Austrian representatives stressed that the abdication of Pedro IV in favour of his daughter Maria II should be concluded as soon as possible. It was also agreed that Britain would provide the Portuguese government with a loan of £200,000, through the Rothschild Bank, so that Miguel's regency could start without embarrassments resulting from lack of funds. During the conference, Dudley announced that the British government hoped to withdraw its troops from Portugal in the near future.[41]

Miguel remained in London until 13 January 1828 when, after taking leave of George IV at Windsor, he went to Strathfieldsaye, Wellington's seat in Hampshire, where he and Palmela remained for two days. According to Greville's *Memoirs*, when they were in the Duke's library trying to agree on the wording of the oath to be taken by Miguel on arrival in Portugal, the prince took no interest in the discussion but rather 'sat flirting with the Princess Therese Esterhazy'.[42] One wonders whether Miguel realized that he must go through the charade of taking an oath to the Constitution but, since he had no intention of keeping it, simply did not care about its terms. Wellington quickly became irritated by Miguel's behaviour, commenting to Palmela: 'This will never do, he must settle the terms of the oath, and if he is so careless in an affair of such moment, he will never do his duty',[43] to which Palmela replied 'Oh, leave him to us, we will manage him.'[44] As Princess Lieven acutely observed, 'Don Miguel tries to make himself out in all things a thoroughgoing Constitutionalist. Is not the part somewhat suspicious in one who has so recently

---

La Motte-Saint-Lié, for Austria, while Britain was represented by Henry Wellesley, the Minister at Vienna ('Prince Metternich to Sir Henry Wellesley', in *Journals of the House of Commons: Sess. 1829*, 84, app. D [19 June 1827], 776 [29 October 1827]).

40. Act of Vienna (20 October 1827), quoted in *Observations on the Papers Lately Submitted to Parliament upon the Subject of the Affairs of Portugal*, by Frederick Lamb, later Lord Melbourne (London: Edward Bull, 1830), 25.

41. 'Protocole de la Conférence tenues à Londres, ce 12 Janvier, 1828', in *British and Foreign State Papers: 1828–1829*, 493–94; Resende, *Elogio historico do Senhor Rei D. Pedro IV: recitado na Academia Real das Sciencias de Lisboa em sessão ordinaria de 13 de Julho de 1836* (Lisboa: Typographia da Academia, 1867), 165.

42. Charles Cavendish Fulke Greville, *The Greville Memoirs: A Journal of the Reigns of King George IV. and King William IV.* 3 vols (London: Longmans, Green, 1874), 3: 26 (24 August 1833).

43. Wellington quoted in Greville's *Memoirs*, 3: 26 (24 August 1833).

44. Palmela quoted in Greville's *Memoirs*, 3: 26 (24 August 1833).

left Metternich's workshop?'[45] Miguel arrived at Plymouth on 17 January to embark on the Portuguese frigate *Pérola*, but poor weather prevented him from sailing until 9 February.[46] In his journey, Miguel was accompanied by Vila Real and Frederick Lamb,[47] who had been chosen to succeed A'Court as British minister to Portugal.[48]

Miguel landed in Lisbon on 22 February 1828, where he was enthusiastically received by a huge crowd shouting 'Long live Dom Miguel the First'.[49] This and subsequent demonstrations in favour of the infante and the re-establishment of Absolutism, reveals the presence of a strong anti-Liberal sentiment in Portugal, especially among the lower classes. Since the constitutional regime appeared to have brought the country to the edge of bankruptcy and civil war, many people looked for a strong leader to solve Portugal's problems. The inability of representative institutions to respond to the needs of ordinary people often leads to their replacement by authoritarian or even dictatorial regimes. But the hope that Miguel's resolute character would save Portugal was based on an illusion. In reality Miguel was not resolute at all and soon revealed that he was little better in coping with pressures than his father and sister had been, especially when those pressures came from Queen Dowager and her party.

On 26 February, at the Royal Palace of Ajuda, Miguel solemnly took the oath to the Constitutional Charter, to his brother and niece, D. Maria II, on whom he promised to devolve the government as soon as she attained her majority. On the same day, a new government headed by the Duque do Cadaval was appointed. The inclusion in the Cabinet of the Condes de Basto, da Lousã and de Vila Real, all members of the ultra-conservative party – although the latter subsequently joined the Liberals – boded ill for the constitutional cause. At his first appointment with Miguel, on 5 March, Lamb urged the regent to include at least one moderate in his government, but Miguel disregarded this advice. Rather than seek to reconcile the various different factions and traditions – as had been hoped – Miguel's government acted in a provocative way, thus leading to further

45. Princess Lieven 'To Earl Grey', in *Correspondence of Princess Lieven and Earl Grey*. 3 vols (London: Richard Bentley, 1890), 1: 76 (27 November 1827).
46. 'Don Miguel: (from the Plymouth Herald)', *The Times*, 22 January 1828, 3.
47. Frederick James Lamb (1782–1853), 3rd Viscount Melbourne, known as Lord Beauvale from 1839 to 1848, British diplomat. Younger son of Peniston Lamb, 1st Viscount Melbourne, and his wife Elizabeth Milbanke, and the younger brother of Prime Minister William Lamb, 2nd Viscount Melbourne. Frederick Lamb accompanied D. Miguel from London to Lisbon in 1828, where he landed on 22 February. He remained in Portugal until 5 July 1828, when he went back home in consequence of Miguel's usurpation of the Portuguese throne.
48. Sir William A'Court, or À Court (1779–1860), 1st Baron Heytesbury, British diplomat, the son of Sir William Pierce Ashe A'Court, 1st Baronet (1747–1817), MP for Aylesbury, and his second wife, Letitia (†1821), daughter of Henry Wyndham of Salisbury. A'Court was appointed Envoy Extraordinary and Minister Plenipotentiary to Madrid in August 1822, where he remained until September 1824, when he replaced Sir William Thornton as Minister to Lisbon.
49. 'No. 16 – Sir Frederick Lamb to the Earl of Dudley' (1 March 1828), in *British and Foreign State Papers: 1828–1829*, 396; Porchester, *The Last Days of the Portuguese Constitution*, 72.

divisions. As Lamb explained in a dispatch to Lord Dudley on 22 March, although 'at Dom Miguel's arrival, all Parties were disposed to receive him with open arms' his 'subsequent conduct, has been the total destruction of all confidence in him'.[50]

On 13 March, Miguel decreed the dissolution of the Lower Chamber and the appointment of a junta to prepare new elections. In consequence, the Conde de Vila Real, the only moderate in the Cabinet, resigned and left the country. He was replaced at the Ministry of War by the Conde de Rio Pardo, a protégé of Queen Dowager, and at the Foreign Ministry by the Visconde de Santarém, a convinced ultra-royalist. With Vila Real out of the way and with no one else left to prevent the usurpation, the situation became critical. Repressive measures were applied in an arbitrary and ferocious way; while the Liberal press was systematically attacked, Absolutist newspapers were treated favourably and allowed to publish calumnies and threats against the constitutionalists. On 2 April, the British force under Clinton began to withdraw, leaving the Constitutionalists at the mercy of their tormentors. Persecutions, detentions and confiscations were conducted on a large scale, leading several Liberals to emigrate to France or England – including Thomas Stubbs,[51] Saldanha's right-hand man, the Condes de Vila Flor, da Taipa and de Lumiares, among many others.[52] These departures, together with the general purge in the army and the dismissal of magistrates and civil servants associated with the constitutional regime, left the Liberal party without capable leaders, leaving the way open for those who wanted Miguel to become king.

On 25 April 1828 – Queen Dowager's birthday and regarded by some as the beginning of the usurpation – several petitions were addressed to the infante begging him 'to assume the Crown' as Absolute King of Portugal.[53] They included a *Representação da cidade de Lisboa* by the Senate of the Lisbon Municipality and an address from members of the aristocracy signed at the house of the Duque de Lafões. Although it is clear that many of the signatures had been obtained under duress, Miguel described the petitions as 'demonstrations of affection' to which he could not remain indifferent. Although the only 'legal channel' that could authorize such a dramatic change was Pedro IV himself – or, at least, the Chambers of the Parliament – it was decided to summon the traditional *Cortes*. No doubt it was calculated that such a course would confer a measure of legality on Miguel's usurpation and hence make it more acceptable to public opinion at home and abroad. It was probably also safer than putting the matter to the existing Parliament, where rejection, even if unlikely, would have a distinct possibility. Foreign

50. 'No. 23 – Sir Frederick Lamb to the Earl of Dudley' (22 March 1828), in *British and Foreign State Papers: 1828–1829*, 398.
51. Thomas Williams Stubbs (1776–1844), knighted by the Prince Regent on 10 October 1817 and later 1st Visconde de Vila Nova de Gaia in the Portuguese nobility, was a British officer in the Portuguese service. Stubbs was one of few British officers who were allowed to remain in Portugal after the Liberal Revolution of 24 August 1820.
52. See Chapter Six.
53. 'No. 26 – Sir Frederick Lamb to the Earl of Dudley', in *British and Foreign State Papers: 1828–1829*, 403 (26 April 1828); 'Manifesto dos direitos de Sua Magestade Fidelissima a Senhora D. Maria II e exposição da questão portugueza' (16 September 1829), in *Supplemento á collecção dos tratados*, 25: 280.

diplomats quickly saw through the scheme and on 7 May Lamb reported to London: 'I could not but feel the voice of the Cortes, though illegally convoked, would yet have the effect of giving to the usurpation a character of conformity to the views of the Nation, and of consequent legality, which it would otherwise want.'[54] According to Francisco Lobo, the Duque de Cadaval's biographer, the decision to summon the *Cortes* was taken unanimously at a meeting held in secret in Lisbon on 2 May, although, as Soriano noted, all those who attended supported the strategy.[55]

'The mock Cortes, or the sham Assembly of the Three States of the Realm', as *The Times* called it, met from 23 June to 11 July 1828, when the final act was concluded.[56] Miguel was acknowledged as the only legitimate successor of João VI, while Pedro was divested of any rights to the Portuguese throne following his recognition of Brazilian independence in 1825.[57] On 30 June 1828, Miguel had already signed a decree declaring his accession to the Portuguese throne and, on 7 July, took the oath as King of Portugal in a solemn ceremony attended by the Three Estates of the Realm. The usurpation had been completed.

The news of the events in Portugal was received in the European courts with astonishment and anxiety, especially in London and Vienna. On 19 March, when news of Vila Real's resignation had not reached Britain, Palmela had reported to Lisbon that Wellington and his colleagues were following the political developments in Portugal with understandable concern. In reply, the Visconde de Santarém, the new foreign minister, instructed Palmela to assure the British Cabinet that the infante was acting according to the decisions of the Vienna Conferences. On 22 March, Santarém had sent a circular to all Portuguese diplomatic missions, justifying Miguel's actions and preparing the ground for the usurpation. Although Palmela was already becoming alarmed at the course of events and irritated by the arrogant tone of Santarém, he obeyed his instructions by taking the official line in a note to Dudley dated 8 April. The reply came in an extensive dispatch dated 22 April, explaining the British position on the developments in Portugal. Although the paper was signed by Dudley, Palmela recognized Wellington's style, which seems to indicate that the Duke was becoming anxious. While acknowledging 'the desire of His Royal Highness the Infante Don Miguel to cultivate the friendship and acquire the confidence of His Majesty', the British government could not avoid declaring the 'sentiments of uneasiness and disappointment' regarding 'the many events which have marked the outset of His Royal Highness's Regency'.[58] The paper also admitted, 'this anxiety has not been removed

54. 'No. 29 – Sir Frederick Lamb to the Earl of Dudley', in *British and Foreign State Papers: 1828–1829*, 410 (7 May 1828).

55. Francisco Alexandre Lobo, *Rezumida noticia da vida de D. Nuno Caetano Alvares Pereira de Mello, sexto Duque de Cadaval* (Paris: Na Typographia de Casimir, 1837), 56; Soriano, *HGC*, 3.ª época, t. II, pt. 2 [13]: 230.

56. *The Times*, 7 July 1828, 6.

57. *Assento dos Três Estados do Reino juntos em cortes na cidade de Lisboa, feito a onze de Julho de mil oitocentos e vinte e oito* (Lisboa: Na Impressão Regia, 1828), 4; *Gazeta de Lisboa*, 182 (2 Agosto 1828): 984.

58. 'No. 3 – The Earl of Dudley to the Marquis de Palmela. Foreign Office, 22nd April, 1828', in *British and Foreign State Papers: 1828–1829*, 495.

from the minds of His Majesty's Servants, by the Extract of the letter from the Vicomte de Santarem'[59] and concluded by stating that, 'Under these circumstances, His Majesty waits for the result of the events now passing in Portugal, though without impatience, yet with an anxiety proportioned to the interest which he has invariably felt for the happiness and tranquillity of that Kingdom'.[60]

Lamb was recalled, embarking for England on 5 July, refusing to pay Miguel £50,000, the last tranche of the £200,000 loan agreed at the Vienna Assemblies in October 1820, hoping to force the infante to abandon his wild scheme. Lamb had also tried to persuade his colleagues to adopt joint measures to pressure Miguel and his ministers to change their policy. As a result, the ministers of Rome, Austria, Prussia, France, Spain, Netherlands, Sweden, Sardinia and Naples suspended their diplomatic activities at the Portuguese Court – but Miguel was unmoved. Metternich, who had already lost control over Miguel and his collaborators, instructed his minister at Lisbon, de Bombelles, to warn the Portuguese authorities that neither Austria nor Britain could assist the infante if Pedro's took action against Miguel for breaching the Constitutional Charter and the Vienna proceedings. Austria and Britain had guaranteed that the Portuguese Constitutional institutions would be respected after the infante's return to Portugal and Metternich could not accept a revolutionary act, even in the name of legitimist principles. Identical reactions came from Paris and St Petersburg, with the Comte de Ferronays, the French foreign minister, declaring that France would not agree to any changes to Pedro's Charter, a position shared by the Russian minister Pozzo di Borgo.

But despite the general condemnation of Miguel's conduct, when the Visconde de Itabaiana[61] and the Marquês de Resende, the Brazilian ministers to London and Vienna, requested the British and Austrian governments to intervene, they were met with evasive answers. In a memorandum on the affairs of Portugal dated 30 June 1828, Wellington declared that 'It is my opinion that Monsieur de Itabayana is not accredited as minister from Don Pedro, *King of Portugal*; but that he is so from Don Pedro, *Emperor of Brazil*.'[62] Although Wellington and Metternich were displeased by Miguel's behaviour that did not mean that they were ready to take drastic measures to re-establish a Liberal regime, a system and set of principles that both detested. This new direction in British foreign policy became more evident after Dudley, the last 'Canningite' in Wellington's Cabinet, resigned on 30 May. Dudley was succeeded by Lord Aberdeen, described as 'the known

59. Ibid.

60. Ibid.; see also Palmela, *Despachos*, 3: 486–92 (22 April 1828).

61. Manuel Rodrigues Gameiro Pessoa (†1846), 1st Barão and Visconde de Itabaiana (or Itabayana), Brazilian diplomat born in Portugal. His only daughter and heir, D. Camila Leonor Júlia Gameiro, was the 1st Viscondessa de Gameiro, in the Portuguese Peerage, by decree of 20 August 1851.

62. Wellington 'Memorandum – State of Affairs in Portugal', in *Despatches, Correspondence, and Memoranda of Field Marshal Arthur Duke of Wellington, K.G.* 8 vols (London: John Murray, 1867–1880), 4: 504 (30 June 1828).

admirer of Metternich', and whose political views were more consentaneous with those of Wellington.[63] In one of his last actions at the Foreign Office, Dudley had refused to acknowledge the Visconde de Asseca – Miguel's representative in London – as an accredited diplomat, but Asseca remained in London in a semi-official capacity.[64]

When Palmela learned of Miguel's decree of 3 May summoning the *Cortes*, through a circular of Santarém dated 6 May, he decided that things had gone too far.[65] On 24 May, he wrote to Lisbon announcing that he was unable to continue representing Miguel. Of course Palmela was in London as a representative of Pedro IV and he decided to remain there until he received instructions to the contrary. Palmela proceeded to address a circular to the ministers of other states resident in Britain explaining the situation in Portugal and giving reasons for his decision to serve no sovereign other than Pedro. Palmela's example was followed by several other Portuguese diplomats, including Funchal (Rome), Abreu Lima[66] (The Hague and Brussels) and Cristovão de Morais Sarmento (Copenhagen) – all guests of Holland House at one time or another.[67] In response, Miguel appointed his own representatives including the Visconde de Asseca (London), the Conde da Ponte (Paris), the Conde da Figueira (Madrid), the Conde de Oriola (Berlin) and the Barão de Vila Seca (Vienna) – though Vila Seca resigned soon. It was the beginning of the parallel or triangular diplomacy between Lisbon, St James and South Audley Street, the Portuguese Legation in London, that lasted until August 1831, when Asseca resigned and returned to Portugal.

Unaware of all that was happening in Europe, Pedro had signed a decree on 3 March completing his abdication in favour of his daughter Maria and renouncing his rights to

63. Anon., *A Brief Exposition*, 24.
64. António Maria Correia de Sá Benevides Velasco da Câmara (1786–1844), 6th Visconde de Asseca.
65. Santarém, 'Circular do ministro dos negocios estrangeiros ao Corpo Diplomatico', in *Correspondência do 2.° Visconde de Santarém*. 8 vols (Lisboa: Alfredo Lamas, Motta & C.ª L.da, 1918–19), 1: 149 (6 May 1828).
66. Luís António de Abreu e Lima (1785–1871), 1st Visconde and Conde da Carreira, Portuguese army officer and diplomat, was the son of João Gomes de Abreu e Lima (1741–1788) and his wife Maria Josefa de Queirós y Gayozo e Montenegro (1746–1803), a Galician. While in Paris, in 1847, Luís António married Ana Luísa Dannemarck (†1875), of German origin, but the couple had no issue. Lima was an attaché to the Portuguese Legation during the Congress of Vienna, seven years Chargé d'Affaires at St Petersburg (1817–24), Minister Plenipotentiary to The Hague (1824–30), London (1830–34), Paris (1833–40) and the Holy See (1840–41).
67. Cristóvão Pedro de Morais Sarmento (1788–1851), 1st Barão da Torre de Moncorvo, son of Tomás Inácio de Morais Sarmento (b. 1750) and brother of Alexandre de Morais Sarmento (1786–1840), also a diplomat. He was born in Bahia (Brazil) on 13 May 1788 and studied law at the University of Coimbra. Sarmento served as Chargé d'Affaires in London in 1822 in succession to João Francisco de Oliveira Álvares (1761–1829). He was an '1820' ultra-Liberal and probably a Freemason. On 21 December 1833, he was ordered to London to request Palmerston to send an expedition to Portugal under the terms of the Anglo-Portuguese Alliance. Sarmento was created Barão de Torre de Moncorvo on 23 May 1835 and Visconde on 13 July 1847. He was twice married: first on 1 December 1838, at Copenhagen, to Amalia Jordan (1806–1842), and then on 23 May 1843 in London, to Carolina Guilhermina Jordan, his sister-in-law (b. 1809). Sarmento died in London on 11 January 1851.

the Portuguese crown. By abdicating, Pedro deprived himself of any right to act against his brother; legally he could not revoke the decree appointing the infante as his lieutenant. Pedro's act was known in London two months later, through a Rio de Janeiro gazette, and officially on 18 May. On 5 July, when the recent events in Portugal were still unknown at Rio de Janeiro, the young Queen Maria was sent to Austria aboard the Brazilian frigate *Imperatriz*, where she was to remain under the protection of her grandfather, Emperor Francis, until she reached the age to consummate her marriage with her uncle.[68] On 2 September, the Marquês de Barbacena, who had been commissioned to escort the young queen to Lisbon, was informed of the events in Portugal when the ship put into Gibraltar.[69] The Marquês immediately diverted the *Imperatriz* to Falmouth, where she arrived on the morning of 24 September.

68. *Gazeta de Lisboa*, Outubro 6, 1828, 1240.

69. Felisberto Caldeira Brant Pontes de Oliveira Horta (1772–1842), 1st Visconde and Marquês de Barbacena, Brazilian officer, diplomat and politician born in Portugal but left for Brazil in 1807 with the royal family.

Chapter Six

SUPER FLUMINA BABYLONIS

Those individuals attempted at Oporto once more to raise the standard of Donna Maria, and failed in the attempt. [. . .] [Holland] had in his pocket a list of the names of four-and-twenty or thirty of them, and there were not individuals more distinguished for rank, wealth, talent, and principle.[*]

While Lisbon appeared relatively acquiescent towards the trend to absolutism and usurpation, the mood in Oporto was very different. On 17 May 1828, following an uprising at Aveiro, a military council established at Oporto issued a manifesto promising to restore the legitimate monarch, dethroned by a rebellious faction.[1] On 20 May, the military council was replaced by a provisional junta, whose members consisted of 'educated, God-fearing men, respectful to the King, loyal to the Charter, trusted by the people and chosen from the different Classes of Society'.[2] Despite this promising start, divisions in the junta between moderate and radical Liberals made it hesitant and ineffective – in contrast to the determination shown by the *Miguelistas*.

Yet the rebellion spread to other northern towns and, within a few days, demonstrations in favour of Pedro and the charter had been held throughout Portugal, except in Lisbon, where, despite some initial alarm, the authorities managed to maintain order. On 25 May, Marshal Póvoas left Lisbon with a force loyal to Miguel and headed north.[3] On 2 June, when the *Miguelistas* were already at Leiria, General Saraiva left Coimbra, where the Liberal forces were concentrated, to meet the enemy before reinforcements could arrive from Lisbon.[4] Yet Saraiva hesitated and Póvoas took the initiative. Although Saraiva was intelligent and well-educated, he had little military experience and, according to Hugh Owen, 'very modestly, constantly declared his own deficiencies'.[5] Saraiva had actually

---

* Holland, speech in the House of Lords on the 'Affair at Terceira', in *Parl. Deb.*, 23 (23 March 1830): c. 756.

1. *Diario do Porto*, Maio 18, 1828, [1].
2. *Diario do Porto*, Maio 21, 1828, [2]; 'Forão convidadas pessoas doutas, tementes a Deos, respeitosa ao Rei, fieis á Carta, e de confiança pública, escolhidas das differentes Classes da Sociedade.' (My translation).
3. Álvaro Xavier da Fonseca Coutinho e Póvoas (1773–1852), Portuguese officer, served under D. Miguel during the Civil War.
4. Francisco Saraiva da Costa de Refóios (1779–1842), 1st and only Barão de Ruivós, Portuguese officer, son of Pedro Saraiva da Costa Pereira de Refóios, *Morgado* of Refóios, and Maria Antónia de Almeida Amado e Meneses. He was military governor of Oporto in 1828 when Miguel usurped the Portuguese throne.
5. Hugh Owen, *The Civil War in Portugal and the Siege of Oporto* (London: Edward Moxon, 1836), 42–43.

asked to be replaced as commander of the Liberal forces, but the junta seemed unable to find a suitable successor. On 25 June, Miguel's forces attacked the Liberal positions at Cruz de Marouços. Despite their numerical inferiority the Liberal forces repulsed the attack. This action was known as *Acção dos Capitães* (the Captains' Action), as all senior officers were absent at Coimbra, attending an extraordinary council of war called by the provisional junta.

This council decided to pull the Liberal forces back to Oporto, although several officers, including Major Bernardo de Sá Nogueira, the future Marquês de Sá da Bandeira, opposed the retreat.[6] News of victory in the Captains' Action did little to change the mood of pessimism; several members of the junta were clearly afraid of what would happen to them if Miguel won the war. Prospects appeared even less promising when it was learned that the British government had refused to acknowledge the junta – thus implicitly recognizing Miguel's legitimacy.[7] The hesitation of the Liberal leaders proved fatal in that it was regarded as a confession of weakness, lowering the morale of their own forces and giving the enemy the confidence to advance on Oporto. The retreat turned out to be clumsy and chaotic with Miguel's forces hard on the Liberals' heels.

The junta hoped that the arrival of several generals, including Saldanha and Vila Flor, who had fled to Britain, would give the Liberal army a better chance of success. According to Owen, 'The Oporto government had written to all the general officers of the country, who were living in England, inviting their co-operation' – although most proved reluctant to return.[8] News of the rebellion of Oporto had reached Palmela in London in the beginning of June, through a packet from Portugal. Palmela immediately acknowledged the legitimacy of the junta – at least so long as Pedro's orders remained unknown – putting himself at the service of this heroic enterprise.

On 7 June, Palmela informed the junta that Itabaiana had agreed to finance the Portuguese Liberal cause. Under the terms of an additional Act to the Treaty of Recognition of the Independence of Brazil of 29 August 1825, the emperor had agreed to pay Portugal £2,000,000 in compensation for its losses. It was agreed however that the compensation should not be transferred directly to the Portuguese government; instead Brazil would take over responsibility for a loan raised in London by Portugal in October 1823. To this end, every six months, the Brazilian minister in London would pay £350,000 to his Portuguese counterpart – who would then transfer the money to the original English lender. However, when news of Miguel's decree of 13 March dissolving

6. Bernardo de Sá Nogueira de Figueiredo (1795–1876), 1st Barão, Visconde and Marquês de Sá da Bandeira, Portuguese army officer and politician, five times Prime Minister of Portugal, son of Faustino José Lopes Nogueira de Figueiredo e Silva and his wife D. Francisca Xavier de Sá Mendonça Cabral da Cunha Godinho.
7. Wellington had instructed his minister in Lisbon that 'As long as Don Miguel's government exists *de facto*, Sir Frederick Lamb ought to avoid to communicate [*sic*] with the Junta of Oporto, excepting through the Consul of Oporto', even if they 'have had or will have some success'. (Wellington 'Memorandum upon the Portuguese case', in *Despatches, Correspondence, and Memoranda*, 4: 498 (23 June 1828)).
8. Owen, *The Civil War in Portugal*, 44.

Temporary Suspension Exemplified: [Palmela suspended] / A. Sharpshooter. London: G. Humphrey, 1829. BM Satires 15893. © The Trustees of the British Museum.

the Parliament reached London, Itabaiana suspended the payments. Despite Palmela's efforts to persuade his colleague to reconsider, the Brazilian minister was unmoved. Yet, once Palmela declared his loyalty to Pedro and announced his readiness to fight against the usurper, Itabaiana did not hesitate to support the Liberal cause with a loan.

Saldanha, who probably saw the Liberal rising as an opportunity to regain his former influence, decided to organize an expedition to Portugal and take the leadership of the movement. According to Saldanha's own version of events, as soon as news of the rebellion in Portugal reached England, he hastened 'to demand aid of the Viscount of Itabayana, in order to convey myself to Oporto, and for which purpose he immediately offered me a fast sailing Schooner, ready in Plymouth'.[9] But when Palmela learned of Saldanha's intentions through Itabaiana, he decided to take command of the expedition himself. It may be that Palmela was carried away by enthusiasm or that he had a low opinion of Saldanha's abilities – or perhaps a combination of the two. Soon after his interview with Itabaiana, Saldanha was invited to a meeting at the Brazilian Legation on 5 June; there he found Palmela, the Condes de Sampaio, de Vila Flor and da Taipa,

9. Saldanha, *Observations of Count de Saldanha to a Letter which the Members of the Oporto Junta Addressed to His Imperial Majesty the Emperor of Brazil… Translated from the Portuguese* (London: A. Redford and W. Robins, 1830), 6; see also *A perfidia desmascarada: ou a carta da Junta do Porto a sua Magestade o Imperador do Brazil… pelo Conde de Saldanha e por outro emigrado* (Paris: [n. pub.], 1830), 12.

Thomas Stubbs, Francisco de Paula Azeredo and Cândido José Xavier already assembled. After a formal acknowledgment of the legitimacy of the Provisional Junta by all those present, the Conde da Taipa proposed that Palmela go to Oporto; his very presence would give credibility to the cause. Before Saldanha's arrival it had been agreed that he should not be given command of the expedition. Saldanha protested but Palmela's opinion prevailed.

On 9 June, Palmela told Aberdeen that he had decided to leave Britain for a while in order to serve the Liberal cause in Portugal. During his absence, Itabaiana would be in charge of the Portuguese Legation. On 11 and 12 June, Palmela met Wellington to discuss the affairs of Portugal.[10] Maia, who accused Palmela of being a friend of the Holy Alliance, suggested that these meetings might have been part of a plot to betray the Liberal cause.[11] In his memoirs, however, Palmela claimed that the duke had simply warned him not to embark on such a dangerous adventure, advice he later wished he had heeded.[12] Besides, as Croker told Wellington on 21 June, 'The case of Palmella, if fallen in with, may become very serious.'[13] Furthermore, the fact that Palmela was at Holland House on 8 June, just prior to his meeting with Wellington, makes it even less likely that he was involved in some complicated *Miguelist* conspiracy.[14]

According to a letter from Itabaiana to Mouzinho da Silveira,[15] a former minister and deputy who fled to Paris in April 1828, the plan was to send the liberal leaders ahead, while the remaining émigrés would follow.[16] Instead of the Brazilian schooner *Isabel* promised to Saldanha, Itabaiana chartered the *Belfast*, an old steamer in poor condition, for the daily sum of £47, with a discount of £15 for each day in the destination harbour. The expedition, composed of 29 people including a few women, left Falmouth on 18 June and arrived at Matosinhos, near Oporto, on 26 June. After an enthusiastic reception in Oporto, the junta proceeded to distribute appointments among the returning exiles – supposedly corresponding to their rank and influence. Palmela, who now emerged as the leading figure of the moderate Liberals – and perhaps the closest approximation to a Holland-style Whig – became president of the provisional government, assisted by Filipe de Sousa Holstein, his half-brother, the Conde de Sampaio and Cândido Xavier. Palmela became overall commander of the Liberal armed forces – a

10. 'Court Circular', *The Times*, 12 June 1828, 6; 'Court Circular', *The Times*, June 13, 1828, 3; see also *London Public Ledger and Daily Advertiser*, 12 June 1828, 2.

11. Joaquim José da Silva Maia, *Memorias historicas, politicas e filosoficas da Revolução do Porto em Maio de 1828, e dos emigrados portuguezes pela Hespanha, Inglaterra, França e Belgica* (Rio de Janeiro: Typographia de Laemmert, 1841), 85.

12. Palmela, *Memórias*, 192.

13. 'The Right Honourable J. Wilson Croker to Field Marshal the Duke of Wellington', in *Despatches, Correspondence, and Memoranda*, 4: 494 (21 June 1828).

14. BL, HHP, MSS Add. 51954, Dinner Books: 1825–31, f. 86v; see also Soriano, *HGC*, 3.ª época, t. II, pt. 2 [13], p. 394.

15. José Xavier Mouzinho da Silveira (1780–1849), jurist, politician and statesman, one of the major figures of Portuguese Liberalism.

16. The Visconde de Itabaiana to José Xavier Mouzinho da Silveira, in *Obras de Mouzinho da Silveira*. 2 vols (Lisboa: Fundação Calouste Gulbenkian, 1989), 1: 362 (22 June 1828).

position for which he was clearly unprepared, while Stubbs was given the command of the Northern Army. Significantly, Saldanha, acknowledged as the leader of the progressive party, was given a more modest position in the army and had little influence over military decisions. Whatever his faults, it was unwise to humiliate Saldanha, exacerbating divisions in Liberal ranks and ultimately contributing to the failure of the whole enterprise.

The *Belfastada*, the name by which this ludicrous episode became known, culminated a few days later in the clumsy retreat of the liberals before the advancing Absolutists. Despite Palmela's political and diplomatic skills, his appointment as commander in chief proved a dreadful mistake. Although in 1809 Palmela had served in the Academic Corps under Lieut.-Colonel Trant, a British officer in the Portuguese service, he had no experience of command. It was not long after that Palmela himself realized he was unsuitable, and on 30 June he offered the command to Saldanha; the offer was declined. Saldanha's pride would never allow him to be a second choice and, in any case, the signs of fear and despair in the army were already only too obvious.

On 2 July, with the enemy approaching Oporto, the Liberal leaders rushed back to the *Belfast*, leaving their soldiers behind and abandoning the population to the mercy of the Absolutists. During an emergency meeting attended by the members of the junta and the military leaders, Saldanha had been asked to stay behind and lead the retreat of the troops into Galicia, an offer he accepted reluctantly. Yet, when the *Belfast* was ready to depart, Saldanha presented himself aboard, claiming that the corps commanders had refused to follow his orders. Despite Saldanha's later complaint that he had been used as a scapegoat to cover the cowardice of his comrades, Sá Nogueira suggested in his memoirs that Saldanha had been as cowardly as everyone else; seized with panic, he had simply abandoned his troops to join his fellow officers on the *Belfast*.[17]

But whatever really happened, none of the leaders of the attempted revolution emerged with credit; they had clearly put their own safety above their obligations to their supporters, both military and civilian. It is extraordinary that Palmela, on other counts one of the most skilful and respected Portuguese politicians in the whole of the nineteenth century, should have even taken part in one of the most bizarre episodes in the history of his country let alone bear most responsibility for its deplorable outcome. To make things worse, in a report sent to Pedro on 4 August, Palmela tried to absolve himself from any responsibility for the fiasco by blaming the junta and the military commanders.[18] It was this version of events that appeared in *The Times*, a newspaper often used by Palmela to promote his own views and to influence increasingly important public opinion.[19] Yet, while the *Belfastada* remains a black mark on Palmela's reputation, it is surely more than balanced by the patriotism and commitment to the Liberal cause he displayed at other times. In some ways indeed, the enormity of Palmela's behaviour pales in comparison to

17. Sá da Bandeira, *Diário da Guerra Civil (1826–1832)*. 2 vols (Lisboa: Seara Nova, 1975), 1: 28–29.
18. Palmela, *Despachos*, 4: 63–68.
19. *The Times*, 22 July 1828, 2.

Saldanha's. Astonishingly, when reinstated as military commander of Oporto in 1835, Saldanha accepted arrears of payment – from July 1828 onwards – allegedly due to him as commander in chief of the forces.

When all the experienced and charismatic generals were safely on the *Belfast*, Brigadier Joaquim Pizarro, an unknown retired naval officer, modestly agreed to lead the retreat of the Liberal soldiers to Galicia and from thence to England.[20] At dawn on 3 June, while the *Belfast* was leaving the Douro, Pizarro began a hazardous retreat through the Gerês Mountains, avoiding the main roads, a passage never before attempted by an army. Pizarro was assisted by Sá Nogueira, at the time a mere major of engineers trained in Britain, who distinguished himself by his courage and military skills. A few hours before his embarkation, Palmela had offered Nogueira a place on the *Belfast*, which he had gallantly refused.[21]

Fearing for their lives, thousands of people of all ages and social status, many ill-clad and without money, abandoned their homes and belongings at Oporto to join the troops, estimated by Soriano at 5,000 men.[22] Despite desertions from the army and civilians who abandoned the convoy during the retreat, the total number of people who reached the Portuguese frontier on the evening of 6 June was so impressive that Maia, one of refugees, compared the episode to the exodus of the Hebrews from Egypt.[23] From the initial 8,000 people who had left Oporto on 3 July, only one-fifth, the more resilient, managed to reach their destination and leave for England. According to the figures provided by Maia and generally accepted by historians, the total number of troops and civilians who arrived at Ferrol and Coruña towards the end of July 1828 amounted to 2,383. The first 200 refugees left Coruña on 13 August on the Neapolitan brigs *S.to Antonio* and *Fortuna*, followed a few days later by other Spanish and Swedish ships.[24] These refugees, together with those from Galicia and others either already in Britain or arrived later, were assembled in Plymouth, where they remained for several months, living in overcrowded barracks.

---

20. Joaquim de Sousa Quevedo Pizarro (1777–1838), 1st Visconde de Bóbeda, Portuguese navy officer and politician.
21. Sá da Bandeira, *Diário*, 1: 26.
22. Silva Maia estimated the total number who left Oporto for Galicia, including troops, at about 12,000. This number, probably exaggerated, was later reduced to 8,000–10,000 by Soriano, who reckoned the total number of forces at about 5,000. Hence, it is possible to argue that the total number of civilians who initially accompanied the troops was between 3,000 and 4,000 (Soriano, *HGC*, 3.ª época, t. II, pt. 2 [13]: 424; ibid., 3.ª época, t. III, pt. 1 [14]: 13–14, 17; cf. Maia, *Memorias*, 104, 108).
23. Maia, *Memorias*, 108.
24. ANTT, MNE, Legação Portuguesa em Londres, MSS Cx. 161, Mç. 34, Relação nominal dos Emigrados Portuguezes, que embarcão no Navio Napolitano = Fortuna = para Portsmouth [Ago. 1828]; Rellação nominal dos Emigrados Portuguezes que embárcão no Brigue Napolitano S.to Antonio, de que he Cappitão Nicoláo Martinho para Portsmouth (15 Ago. 1828); Relação dos Portuguezes emigrados, que tendo embarcado na galera Sueca Onterpreis, Cap.am Backman com direção ao Porto de Falmouth por impocivelidade [*sic*] de seguir viagem para alli vierão arribadar [*sic*] a Oeste no dia 29 do Corrente [September 1828]; see also *Documentos para a historia das Cortes Geraes da Nação Portugueza*. 8 vols (Lisboa: Imprensa Nacional, 1883–91), 3: 116.

Although there is no entirely reliable figure for the number of refugees during Miguel's usurpation, the total exceeded 10,000. Victor de Sá, probably following Oliveira Martins, estimated 13,000, which appears realistic.[25] Lists of refugees in Plymouth in 1828 and 1829 preserved at Torre do Tombo (National Archives) suggest at least 2,500 exiles. Richard Worth estimated the number at 3,000, a figure probably taken from *The Portuguese Emigrant*, a bilingual newspaper published in Plymouth under Palmela's sponsorship.[26] In mid-November, according to a summary list enclosed with a dispatch from Wellington to Palmela, this had already increased to 3,250 plus officers.[27] This figure is close to the 3,738 Portuguese nationals who, according to William Walton, were living in Plymouth on 5 January 1829.[28] If we add a few hundred for those based in London, the total number of Portuguese exiles in England comes to about 4,000, very close to Freire de Carvalho's estimate.[29]

Among the first exiles in this period were actually Saldanha and his family, who embarked for England on 21 October 1827 aboard *The Falmouth* packet and, in November, settled in London at the home of a Portuguese friend. The next on the list were the Marquês de Loulé[30] and his wife D. Ana de Jesus de Bragança, youngest daughter of João VI, who left Portugal in February 1828.[31] The marriage had been precipitated by the princess's unexpected pregnancy and celebrated in secrecy at the Palace of Queluz on 5 December 1827 under the protection of Queen Dowager. As Isabel Maria and Miguel were against their union, Carlota Joaquina thought it prudent to send them abroad, a measure that did not prevent the confiscation of Loulé's properties as soon as Miguel

25. Victor de Sá, *A crise do liberalismo e as primeiras manifestações das ideias socialistas em Portugal 1820–1852* (Lisboa: Seara Nova, 1969), 97–98; cf. the *Courrier* for 31 July 1829, quoted in *Portugal contemporâneo*, by Oliveira Martins. 3.ª ed. 2 vols (Lisboa: Livraria de Antonio Maria Pereira, 1895), 1: 145.
26. *O portuguez emigrado: ou realista constitucional = The Portuguese Emigrant: or constitutional royalist*, 18 Novembro 1828, 53.
27. 'The Duke of Wellington to the Marquis de Palmella: Third Enclosure B in No. 37', in *Papers Respecting the Relations between Great Britain and Portugal* (London: Printed by J. Harrison, 1829), 81 (20 Nov. 1828); see also *Annual Register*, 71 (1829): 450); 'Le Duc de Wellington au Marquis de Palmella', in *Despachos*, 4: 244 (20 November 1828).
28. William Walton, *Dom Pedro's Expedition: or Neutrality in Disguise* (London: Hatchard, J. Richardson, and Booth, 1832), 47.
29. José Liberato Freire de Carvalho, *Memorias com o titulo de annaes, para a historia do tempo que durou a usurpação de D. Miguel.* 4 vols (Lisboa: Na Imprensa Nevesiana, 1841), 1: 103.
30. D. Nuno José Severo de Mendonça Rolim de Moura Barreto (1804–1875), 9th Conde de Vale de Reis and 2nd Marquês de Loulé, afterwards 1st Duque de Loulé, several times Chief Minister of Portugal. Son of D. Agostinho Domingos José de Mendonça Rolim de Moura Barreto, 1st Marquês de Loulé, whose murder at Salvaterra on 28 February 1824 has been attributed to Miguel and his collaborators. The Loulés descended from Don Lopo Sarraciniz (fl. 871), Lord of Biscay, and are the ancestors of D. Pedro José Folque de Mendonça Rolim de Moura Barreto, the present 6th Duque de Loulé, who claims the right to the Portuguese throne against the official claimant, D. Duarte Pio de Bragança, D. Miguel's descendant.
31. D. Ana de Jesus Maria Luís Gonzaga Joaquina Micaela Francisca Xavier de Paula de Bragança e Bourbon (1806–1857), the youngest daughter of D. João VI and his wife, Queen D. Carlota Joaquina.

arrived in Lisbon. On 3 February the royal exiles embarked at Gibraltar for Falmouth, to arrive at the British capital on the night of 25 February. The couple remained in London, at Mivart's Hotel, Mayfair, until the 13 April, when they moved to Paris. From thence, at Pedro's invitation, they passed to Rio de Janeiro, where they were received and lived according to their rank.

The Loulés were followed by many other distinguished exiles, who began to arrive during the early months of 1828. On 19 March, Palmela told Vila Real that he had been astonished to see the Conde da Taipa[32] arriving in London.[33] One week later, now beyond surprise, Palmela reported to Vila Real that 'The packet from Lisbon arrived after a passage of seven days of journey, carrying aboard many passengers whose names it is pointless to list, as Your Excellency is already acquainted with them.'[34] These refugees included the Marquês de Fronteira accompanied by his wife and daughter,[35] who moved to Paris soon afterwards, the Conde de Vila Flor and his wife,[36] the Conde de Sampaio,[37] Filipe de Sousa Holstein and a brother of the late Manuel Fernandes Tomás.

This first group of exiles was enlarged with the arrival of a new batch of famous refugees in May, including Fronteira's brother, Carlos Mascarenhas,[38] the Marquês de Valença,[39] the Conde da Cunha[40] with his daughter, the Conde de Alva accompanied

32. D. Gastão da Câmara Coutinho Pereira de Sande (1794–1866), 1st Conde da Taipa. He married D. Francisca de Almeida Portugal.
33. 'O Marquez de Palmella ao Conde de Villa Real', in *Despachos*, 3: 449 (19 March 1828).
34. Ibid., 3: 460 (26 March 1828); 'Chegou um paquete de Lisboa com sete dias de viagem, a bordo do qual vieram muitos passageiros, cujos nomes escuso indicar, por serem notorios a V. Ex.ª' (My translation).
35. D. José Trazimundo Mascarenhas Barreto Palha (1802–1881), 7th Marquês de Fronteira, Portuguese army officer and a convinced constitutionalist, the son of D. João Mascarenhas Barreto Palha (1777–1806), 6th Marquês de Fronteira, by D. Leonor Benedicta de Oyenhausen e Almeida (1779–1850), daughter of D. Leonor de Lencanstre, Marquesa de Alorna. On 14 February 1821, he married D. Maria Constança da Câmara (1808–1860), daughter of D. Luís Gonçalves da Câmara Coutinho Pereira de Sande by D. Maria de Noronha. The daughter here mentioned is D. Maria Mascarenhas Barreto (1822–1914), afterwards 8th Marquesa de Fronteira.
36. D. António José de Sousa Manuel de Meneses Severim de Noronha (1792–1860), 7th Conde de Vila Flor and later 1st Marquês de Vila Flor and Duque da Terceira, Portuguese army officer and statesman, the son of D. António de Populo Manuel de Sousa e Meneses Severim de Noronha (1765–1795), 6th Conde de Vila Flor, and his wife, D. Maria José de Mendonça (1773–1824). António de Noronha married twice: first, on 5 August 1811, D. Maria José do Livramento e Melo (1793–1818), daughter of Marquês de Sabugosa; and secondly, on 23 April 1821, D. Maria Ana Luísa Filomena de Mendonça (1808–1866), daughter of the 1st Marquês de Loulé and sister of the 1st Duque de Loulé.
37. Manuel António de Sampaio Melo e Castro Moniz e Torres de Lusignano (1762–1841), 2nd Conde and 1st Marquês de Sampaio.
38. D. Carlos Mascarenhas (1803–1861).
39. D. José Bernardino de Portugal e Castro (1780–1840), 5th Marquês de Valença.
40. D. José Maria Vasques Álvares da Cunha (1793–1867), 4th Conde da Cunha.

by his wife,[41] his son and daughter in law,[42] the Conde de Lumiares[43] with his sons José Félix and Francisco da Cunha Meneses, Field-Marshal Francisco de Paula Azeredo and many others. Francisco de Almeida, the second Conde de Lavradio, arrived in Falmouth on 21 June and joined his father in London four days later, although he moved to Rome on 9 August.[44] On 22 July 1828, four days after the *Belfast's* arrival at Plymouth, Palmela announced that the number of Portuguese exiles living in London had already reached 300, and included 'the flower of the Portuguese Nation, either for their merit, loyalty, patriotism, and for their birth and consideration that makes them conspicuous'.[45] These exiles concentrated near the Portuguese Legation, in South Audley Street, the usual place of assembly. According to Esterhazy, quoted in Greville's memoirs, 'Palmela entertains from twenty to thirty of his countrymen at dinner every day, of whom there are several hundreds in London, of the best families, totally destitute.'[46]

In addition to these émigrés, most of them aristocrats associated with Portuguese Freemasonry, other less distinguished exiles began to arrive. Some were on their second exile – like Almeida Garrett, the reputed founder of Portuguese Romanticism, who left Portugal for Britain via Ferrol, to land in Falmouth on 19 June 1828.[47] On 16 April 1829, Palmela appointed Garrett as cultural attaché to the Portuguese Legation to assist him writing texts and articles, a position he held at least until 11 March 1831, when he tendered his resignation.[48] Garrett might have been invited to Holland House, but there

41. D. Luís Roque de Sousa Coutinho Paim (1783–1850), 3rd Conde de Alva, afterwards 1st Marquês de Santa Iria, and his wife D. Mariana Vicência de Sousa Holstein, Palmela's elder sister.
42. D. Vicente de Sousa Coutinho Monteiro Paim (1805–1841), afterwards 4th Conde de Alva, and his wife, D. Juliana Luísa Mascarenhas (1804–1841), Fronteira's sister.
43. José Manuel Inácio da Cunha e Meneses da Gama Vasconcelos Carneiro de Sousa Portugal e Faro (1788–1849), 4th Conde de Lumiares, Portuguese army officer, politician and Freemason, Chief Minister in 1836.
44. D. Francisco de Almeida Portugal (1796–1870), 2nd Conde de Lavradio, Portuguese diplomat and statesman, was the son of D. António Máximo de Almeida Portugal Soares Alarcão Melo Castro Ataíde Eça Mascarenhas Silva e Lencastre (1756–1833), 3rd Marquês de Lavradio, and D. Ana Teles da Silva (1762–1821). His eldest brother, D. António de Almeida Portugal Soares Alarcão Melo Castro Ataíde Eça Mascarenhas Silva e Lencastre (1794–1874), was a convinced *Miguelista*.
45. 'O Marquez de Palmella a S. M. o Imperador do Brazil', in *Despachos*, 4: 36–37 (22 July 1828); 'parte da flor da nação portugueza, tanto pelo merecimento, lealdade, patriotismo, quanto pelo nascimento e consideração que os torna conspicuos.' (My translation).
46. Greville, *The Greville Memoirs: A Journal of the Reigns of King George IV and King William IV*, 1: 138 (16 August 1828).
47. João Baptista da Silva Leitão de Almeida Garrett (1799–1854), 1st and only Visconde de Almeida Garrett, Portuguese poet, playwright, novelist, essayist, deputy and politician, son of António Bernardo da Silva (1740–1834) by Ana Augusta de Almeida Leitão.
48. ANTT, MNE, Legação Portuguesa em Londres, MSS Cx. 164, Mç. 40, Garrett's Petition to D. Maria II (11 March 1831).

is no conclusive evidence.[49] An 'M. d'Almeida' figures among the Hollands' guests for 3 August 1828, but it is unclear whether this was Almeida Garrett or someone with a similar name, for example, Francisco de Almeida.[50]

Towards the end of August and beginning of September 1828, the first refugees from Galicia began to arrive in Portsmouth, Falmouth and St Ives. From thence they were conveyed in steamers chartered by Palmela to Plymouth, where two warehouses at Coxside had been converted into barracks to receive them. The refugees, who had travelled in overcrowded ships in conditions not much better than those experienced by African slaves on the Middle Crossing, had very poor accommodation in Plymouth. According to *The Times*, quoting the *Hampshire Telegraph*, 'The Portuguese refugees: the principal part consists of non-commissioned officers and privates, who are in the most destitute condition, many having been compelled to dispose even of their clothes, for the purpose of relieving their pressing necessities'.[51] Except for the few who could afford paying 'lodgings' or hotel rooms,[52] most of the refugees lived in the overcrowded barracks or aboard four ships, the Russian *Delphin* and the British *Susannah*, *Miverva* and *Lyra*, the latter reserved for officers.[53]

When the refugees from Galicia begun to arrive on 26 August, a line of command was established in Plymouth, under the direction of Cândido Xavier, the son of a blacksmith who had served in the Peninsular War, and described by Nemésio as an obscure individual and by Soriano, who knew him well, as one of those people who never look others in the eye.[54] Xavier answered directly to Palmela and was assisted by Paulo Midosi, Garrett's brother in law, who had been appointed his secretary. A system of administration was introduced, which divided the refugees into six classes according to their profession and rank, each receiving financial support according to their status:

1st	War Department general staff
2nd	First line officers
3rd	Second line officers, volunteers and orderlies
4th	Civil servants (e.g. magistrates, treasury and justice officers)
5th	Priests, merchants, landlords, physicians, and other liberal professions
6th	First and Second lines enlisted soldiers, volunteers, servants, etc.[55]

This application of the Portuguese administration system to the community of exiles in England seems a rather strange arrangement, one certainly characterized by excessive

49. José Baptista de Sousa, *Almeida Garrett (1799–1854) the Founder of Portuguese Romanticism: A Study in Anglo-Portuguese Cultural Interaction* (Lewiston: Edwin Mellen, 2011), 124.
50. BL, HHP, MSS Add. 51954, Dinner Books: 1825–31, f. 91^{v} (3 August 1828).
51. *The Times*, 15 September 1828, 2.
52. Soriano, *Revelações da minha vida e memorias de alguns factos e homens meus contemporaneos* (Lisboa: Typographia Universal, 1860), 397.
53. ANTT, MNE, Legação Portuguesa em Londres, MSS Cx. 161, Mç. 34, Depozito de Caçadores. Relação das praças deste Depozito abordo do Transporte Delfim (8 September 1828); MSS Cx. 161, Mç. 33, Ordem do Dia N.° 2 (Plymouth, 28 August 1828).
54. Vitorino Nemésio, *Exilados, 1828–1832: história sentimental e política do liberalismo na emigração* (Lisboa: Livraria Bertrand, [n.d.]), 51; Soriano, *HGC*, 3.ª época, t. III, pt. 1 [14]: 170.
55. Maia, *Memorias*, 163–64.

bureaucracy, nepotism and corruption – in short by features only too likely to exacerbate social divisions. The establishment of a Portuguese micro-society on English soil, where the injustices and weaknesses of the original model were imported – sometimes even amplified – may even provide a clue as to the nature and reasons for the decadence of Portuguese society which appears to be such a striking feature of the early nineteenth century. It is hardly surprising that people like Soriano, a student who had enlisted as a volunteer and who now lived in Plymouth in very straitened circumstances, became critical of the grandees who lived in London 'supported as gentlemen, many of them better than they would be in their own houses in Portugal'.[56] Despite Garrett's literary abilities and his later contributions to his country, it is undeniable that while his countrymen were suffering and fighting for the cause of liberty, he was playing the dandy in London with Palmela's assistance.

In addition to a daily meal valued at 6*d* to be served indiscriminately to all refugees, a first Order of the Day decreed that 'All military staff will continue receiving their wages' as in Portugal, which, as a result of the conversion from reis to pounds, corresponded to an increase of 35 per cent.[57] A captain, for example, received the monthly payment of £7.15*s*. But if those at the top of the hierarchy were better off, further down there was real hardship and privation. Thus those in the fifth class were paid £3 per month and those in the sixth class a miserable 14 shillings, clearly insufficient to guarantee minimum living conditions. As a result, many refugees failed to pay their rent, while others begged in the streets, thus risking the hostility of the English population. A report attached to the Order of the Day No. 27, of 24 September, referred to problems with the locals because the Portuguese refused to pay their rent weekly in accordance with English custom. The report mentioned cases of begging, a practice also against the laws and customs of England. Strikingly, these episodes surprised Cândido Xavier, to whom 'assistance and food enough to secure livelihood were generally provided'.[58] Finally, the Portuguese women were advised not to wash their clothes in the reservoirs that supplied Plymouth's drinking water.

These stories soon reached the press, with several local and national newspapers including *John Bull*, the *Morning Post* and the *Devonport Telegraph* denouncing the refugees, with the *Devonport Telegraph* suggesting that in Plymouth only merchants, innkeepers and prostitutes sympathized with the Portuguese.[59] In an attempt to improve the image of the refugees, *The Portuguese Emigrant* rebutted the accusations made by the British and French press:

> One of the London prints called the Portuguese Emigrants, *conspirators*. We have witnessed the contempt such an accusation excited in the English public. The inhabitants of this town in particular felt and expressed the greatest indignation at the virulent attack. Far from paying

---

56. Soriano, *Revelações*, 397; 'sustentados á cavalheira, e muitos delles melhor do que seriam nas suas proprias casas em Portugal.' (My translation).
57. ANTT, MNE, Legação Portuguesa em Londres, MSS Cx. 161, Mç. 33, Ordem do Dia N.° 1 (Plymouth, 26 August 1828).
58. ANTT, MNE, Legação Portuguesa em Londres, MSS Cx. 161, Mç. 33, Ordem do Dia N.° 27 (24 September 1828); 'pois que a todos geralmente se ministrão socorros e alimentos suficientes para a sustentação da vida'. (My translation).
59. Maia, *Memorias*, 158–59.

> the least attention to these absurd insinuations, they have continued to show the same hospitality, the same urbanity, and the same marked kindness that they previously had shown to the Emigrants; who will ever feel the most heart-felt gratitude for their benevolent attentions, and will never cease to offer to heaven their ardent prayers for their prosperity and for that of the British Nation in general.[60]

Parts of this article were reproduced in *The Times*, probably at Palmela's request and in return for payment.[61] As he admitted in a dispatch to Pedro, dated 18 September 1828, 'I continue inserting in the English public papers, especially in *The Times* and *Courier*, articles aiming to support the cause and the interests of Y. M.'.[62] Yet, Palmela's counter-attack proved insufficient to change the British public's negative impression of the Portuguese refugees. In December, when the situation was getting out of control, Richard Freeman, the mayor of Plymouth (1828–29), called a town assembly at which local people were invited to express their views. According to Maia, several speakers defended the Portuguese, arguing that they gave the people of Plymouth all the money they possessed, buying food, paying for accommodation and so forth.[63] Eventually, as Sir James Mackintosh later acknowledged,

> the inhabitants of that town, at a public meeting, unanimously passed a resolution, expressive of their sense of the unimpeached integrity of the loyal subjects of the Queen of Portugal, whom they further petitioned His Majesty not to remove from Plymouth.[64]

Perhaps as a consequence of these events – or under its pretence – Wellington decided that the depot at Plymouth should be broken up and that ordinary soldiers should be separated from their officers – an order Palmela refused to obey.

As noted earlier, Queen D. Maria had landed in Falmouth on the morning of 24 September 1828, after a long journey from Rio de Janeiro to Gibraltar and from thence to Britain. The arrival of the young queen, herself an émigré, filled the refugees with enthusiasm and aroused the sympathy of the British public. The local authorities received her with appropriate civic and military honours, in accordance with instructions from King George IV, who sent Lord Clinton and Sir William Freemantle to receive D. Maria.[65] It was announced that the queen would proceed to Plymouth 'where she will be presented to the Portuguese refugees, the unfortunate sufferers by adherence to her cause, collected

60. *O portuguez emigrado*, 18 November 1828, 53.
61. 'Plymouth Emigrant Depot', *The Times*, 21 November 1828, 3.
62. 'O Marquez de Palmella a S. M. O Imperador do Brazil', in *Despachos*, 4: 175 (18 September 1828); 'Continuo a inserir nos papeis publicos inglezes, e principalmente no Times e no Courier, artigos conducentes a sustentar a causa e os interesses de V.M.'. (My translation).
63. Maia, *Memorias*, 158–59.
64. Mackintosh, speech on 'Portugal', *The Times*, 2 June 1829, 2.
65. *The Times*, 27 September 1828, 2; 'Journey of the Queen of Portugal', *The Times*, 30 September 1828, 2; 'O Conde de Aberdeen ao Marquez de Palmella', in *Despachos*, 4: 178 (20 September 1828).

at that place'.[66] Maria's first night in England was spent in Truro, at Pearce's Royal Hotel, from whence she was escorted by the fourth corps of Royal Irish Dragoon Guard to Exeter, 'where dinner was ordered at six o'clock on that evening at the New London Inn'.[67] The next morning, rather than proceeding to Plymouth as initially advertised, the queen took the Bath road to London.[68] On 5 October, she visited Bristol, returning to York House, Bath, to dinner, where she was met by the Duke of Wellington, who had been authorized by the king to welcome her. According to *The Times*, 'She was dressed quite in the English fashion, with white silk hat, and acknowledged, by the constant motion of her head and hand, the marks of respect which were invariably paid her by all ranks through whom she passed.'[69] In the morning of 6 October, Maria left Bath for Bristol to embark in a frigate to London where she arrived in the evening. This somewhat puzzling itinerary was chosen to delay Maria's arrival so as to give Barbacena enough time to make appropriate arrangements with the British authorities for her accommodation in London. Maria stayed at Grillon's Hotel until 26 October, when she moved to Laleham House, Surrey, the seat of the Earl of Lucan, where she remained until her departure to Rio de Janeiro in August 1829.

When it was learned that D. Maria would not visit Plymouth, it was decided to send a deputation, including Cândido Xavier, Brigadier Joaquim Pizarro and Colonel Henrique da Silva Fonseca, to welcome her at Exeter. A few days earlier, Xavier had instructed the refugees not go to Falmouth to greet the young queen, an order widely ignored. The refugees then decided to celebrate the occasion with a theatrical performance at the barracks. According to Maia, 'Despite the lack of means, they organized a collection among themselves and some friends and built a stage in the barracks'.[70] There they performed the comedy *Elvira* by João de Matos, followed by recitals of music and poetry.[71] The performance was so successful that it was repeated the following evenings, until Cândido Xavier 'was foolish enough to ban the play and close the theatre on the third day' to punish the refugees for crossing the limit when satirizing him and Palmela.[72] Xavier's report of the events makes only oblique reference to this episode:

> The volunteers asked my permission to perform an elegy and a play at the barracks, where they arranged everything with their own skills. This will be the last of the three evenings

66. *The Times*, 27 September 1828, 2.
67. 'Journey of the Queen of Portugal', *The Times*, 30 September 1828, 2; see also *A Hand-Book for Travellers in Devon & Cornwall* (London: John Murray, 1851), 141.
68. 'Journey of the Queen of Portugal', *The Times*, 30 September 1828, 2.
69. 'The Queen of Portugal', *The Times*, 6 October 1828, 2.
70. Maia, *Memorias*, 176; 'Apesar da sua falta de meios, abrirão huma subscrição entre si, e alguns amigos; construiram no barracão hum scenario'. (My translation).
71. João Xavier de Matos (*c.* 1730–1789), Arcadian poet, known by the literary pseudonym of 'Albano Eritreu', was the author of the eclogue *Albado e Damiana* (1758).
72. Maia, *Memorias*, 176; 'teve a fraqueza, no terceiro dia, de prohibir a peça, e fechar o theatro'. (My translation).

> I allow them this entertainment. So far, all has been going in the most tranquil and satisfactory way.[73]

Encouraged by the success of the recitals, Paulo Midosi suggested the performance of Garrett's *Catão* in Plymouth to a more select audience. The tragedy was first performed on 29 September 1821 at the Bairro Alto Theatre, Lisbon. Anticipating that the play would have a positive impact on the British public, Palmela agreed to Midosi's proposal. Unlike the earlier performances, involving amateurs from among the refugees and a few locals, the idea now was to use Garrett's play as a means to impress public opinion and to create a more favourable image of the refugees. Garrett's *Catão* seemed the perfect choice: it had been written by one of Palmela's followers and – better still – had been inspired by Addison's *Cato*, giving it a better chance of being accepted, even of being understood by the English public. Furthermore, as Paulo Midosi (Junior) suggested in an article published many years later in the *Diário de notícias*, Garrett's *Catão* 'is associated with a great national epic whose objective is to bring back memories of the death-throws of one of the strongest republics of Antiquity'.[74]

Catão was performed on 24 October and 1 and 23 December 1828 at Royal Hotel and Theatre, Plymouth. Although there were three performances of *Catão*, only the second seems to have attracted the attention of the local press. According to *The Devonport Telegraph*, the play was attended by a 'very brilliant and crowded audience',[75] including Mayor Freeman, a few locals, 'the Tikenesses, the Heydens, and many others', as well as several distinguished Portuguese.[76] A manuscript note by Garrett about the performance of *Catão* carries the names – 'Lord Holland – Palmerston – Mackintosh – Palmela' – and it is just possible that one or more of these august figures attended, although it is more likely that they were invited.[77] Among other distinguished Englishmen who may have been also present, was Earl Morley, owner of the Royal Hotel and Theatre.[78]

---

73. ANTT, MNE, Legação Portuguesa em Londres, MSS Cx. 164, Cândido José Xavier to Palmela (15 October 1828); 'Os voluntarios pedirão-me licença para representarem hum elogio e huma pessa, no Quartel, onde, pela sua industria, arranjárão elles mesmos tudo. Hoje acabarão as tres noutes, e[m] que lhes permitti esse divertimento. Tudo, ate aqui, se tem passado na maior satisfação, e tranquilidade.' (My translation).
74. Paulo Midosi [Junior], 'Os ensaios do Catão', *Diario de noticias*, 11 Outubro 1828, [1]; 'associa-se a uma grande epopeia nacional, e tem por fim recordar as ultimas agonias de uma das republicas da antiguidade mais solidamente constituidas'. (My translation).
75. *The Royal Devonport Telegraph & Plymouth Chronicle*, 6 December 1828, 3.
76. *Descripsam das trez cidades unidas [Poem]: Plymouth, Ston Hause, e Devenport. Mostra-se a sua grandeza, Industria, Religião, Commercio, Policia, e Costumes, &c.* (Angra: Impressam do Governo, 1829), 13; 'os Tikenesses, Heydens, e outros muitos'. (My translation).
77. Almeida Garrett, MS notes entitled 'Literatura Anglo-Portuguesa' included in the Garrett Papers at University of Coimbra, *Espólio Literário de Garrett*, quoted in Ofélia Paiva Monteiro, *A formação de Almeida Garrett: experiência e criação*. 2 vols (Coimbra: Centro de Estudos Românicos, 1972), 2: 57, note 146.
78. A more detailed study on these performances is available in my article '*Catão* em Plymouth', *Revista de estudos anglo-portugueses* 10 (2001): 23–41.

But despite the positive effect of Maria's arrival and Palmela's steps, including the performance of *Catão*, to counteract the negative impression of the refugees, the improvement was only partial. The biggest problem facing Palmela and the refugee community was lack of effective political support. Things began to change only in March 1829 when it became known that in January the British government had used force to prevent several ships loaded with refugees from landing in Terceira. This action caused outrage in Liberal circles throughout Europe and some politicians in Britain and France began to take up the refugees' cause.

The Plymouth depot was closed on 25 April 1829, when, on Palmela's instructions, the remaining 450 refugees were transferred to Ostend, where they arrived on 10 May. A large majority, about 2,000 in all, had already been transferred to the Azores, Brazil or France early in 1829, in compliance with the British government's instructions. The refugees who stayed in England and those who joined them later remained in Plymouth or in London at least until the end of 1831, when Pedro's army left France for Terceira, and from thence to Portugal, where the famous disembarkation of Mindelo – alias Arnosa de Pampelino, near Oporto – was effected on 8 July 1832.

Chapter Seven
THE AFFAIR OF TERCEIRA

Last night news came that Villa Flor had routed Miguel's expedition against Terceira, and at the same time the little Queen is embarking with the Empress for the Brazils. This probably comes too late; some time ago it might have been of some use.[*]

After the *Belfastada*, Palmela was determined to launch a new expedition, not least to restore his own reputation. In Plymouth, he formed the Battalion of Volunteers of the Queen, which he planned to send to Terceira, an island in the Azores and the only Portuguese territory still loyal to Pedro. In a dispatch dated 15 October, Palmela informed Itabaiana: 'I wrote today to the Commander of the Plymouth Depot urging him to have the three transports to convey the battalion ready to sail [...] within the next forty-eight hours'.[1] On board there were already several crates of guns and ammunition, some destined for Madeira, others for the Azores, and others for the use of the Plymouth battalion. However, the less than cooperative attitude of the British government was to cause serious delays to the project, which, in the end, only went ahead after complicated manoeuvres involving a good deal of deception and half truth.

On 15 September, Barbacena, the accredited Brazilian plenipotentiary, requested Wellington to agree to the departure for the Azores of 'a part of the faithful Portuguese Troops, which are now in England, and whose presence in the above mentioned Islands would ensure its defence as well as its tranquillity'.[2] Three days later, Wellington replied: 'We know of no Portuguese Troops in this country. If there be any they must quit the Country without loss of time.'[3] Wellington's response seems ambiguous although it could be construed as accepting Barbacena's request. But Wellington was becoming concerned. Less than two weeks later, he admitted to Aberdeen,

> I can have no confidence in Palmella, Rezende, Barbacena, and Itabayana; and four thousand soldiers, with their officers, who with money can get arms and ammunition in this

---

* Greville, *Memoirs*, 1: 230 (31 August 1829).

1. 'O Marquez de Palmella ao Visconde de Itabayana', in *Despachos*, 4: 196 (15 October 1828); 'escrevi hoje ao commandante do deposito de Plymouth, prevenindo-o para que os tres transportes que devem levar o batalhão, estejam promptos a fazer-se á vela [...], dentro de quarenta e oito horas.' (My translation).
2. 'The Marquis de Barbacena to the Duke of Wellington', in *Papers Respecting the Relations between Great Britain and Portugal*, 78 (15 October 1828).
3. 'The Duke of Wellington to the Marquis de Barbacena', ibid., 79 (18 October 1828).

> country when they please, without our knowledge, are in Plymouth, a little too near our naval arsenals.[4]

That too might suggest that Wellington would be glad to be rid of the Portuguese force, but at virtually the same time he warned Barbacena:

> If those Portuguese subjects desire to make war at the Azores, instead of doing so in Portugal, of which they have the choice, let them go there as Individuals if they please. But I must candidly tell you, Monsieur le Marquis, that it cannot be permitted that Individuals, of whatever character they may be, should prepare warlike expeditions in the Ports and Arsenals of this Country in order to make attacks upon others.[5]

In other words, Wellington might be willing to countenance the departure of a group of civilians but not that of embodied military force: unless the Battalion was disbanded, Wellington would have to prevent its members leaving British territory. As Palmela admitted in a dispatch to Gomes da Silva, Pedro's closest collaborator, Wellington's position was difficult because the Cabinet was divided over the issue. On the one hand, Palmela had some credibility among the statesmen of Europe, while the cause he defended was beginning to gain public sympathy in Britain – partly as a result of his own astute manipulation of the British press. On the other hand, Wellington was annoyed with Palmela for causing him serious political discomfort.[6] But if the British government wanted to pursue a policy of non-interference – as it seemed now inclined to do at least officially – it could not simply deport the exiles back to Portugal, where prison or even death awaited them, without incurring the wrath of public opinion at home. Many of the Portuguese leaders had already been arrested or condemned to death *in absentia*, including Palmela, Saldanha, Stubbs, Rendufe, etc.[7] Equally, however, Wellington could not openly allow the refugees to prepare an assault on Portugal, without being accused of connivance by Miguel's government and, even worse, by Austria.

To resolve this dilemma, Wellington decided to disband the depot at Plymouth, separating the soldiers from their officers and dispersing them throughout several towns and villages in the southwest of England, namely Truro, Bodmin, Launceston, Oakhampton, Exeter and so forth.[8] On 20 November, Wellington communicated his decision to Palmela

4. Wellington, 'To the Earl of Aberdeen', in *Despatches, Correspondence, and Memoranda*, 5: 144 (29 October 1828).
5. 'The Duke of Wellington to the Marquis de Barbacena', in *Papers Respecting the Relations between Great Britain and Portugal*, 79 (18 October 1828).
6. 'O Marquez de Palmella a Francisco Gomes da Silva', in *Despachos*, 4: 215 (29 October 1828).
7. Palmela was sentenced to hang on 21 August 1828. His head was to be cut off, stuck on a pole and exposed until it rotted. His other remains were to be burned and the ashes thrown into the sea and his property confiscated. Although Palmela's son Alexandre received the same penalty, this was commuted to life transportation to India because he was still a minor (BL, HHP, MSS Add. 51633, Papers Relative to Portugal: 1801–30: List of Condemns to be Executed (21 August 1828); Soriano, *HGC*, 3.ª época, t. III, pt. 1 [14]: 152–53).
8. 'The Duke of Wellington to the Marquis de Palmella', in *Papers Respecting the Relations between Great Britain and Portugal*, 81 (20 November 1828).

both verbally and in writing. It was a devastating blow to the Liberal cause. Palmela lamented in a dispatch to Barbosa de Figueiredo, 'No one could imagine that the British government would dare to reveal such a formal partiality towards the usurpation'.[9] As Palmela also observed, by preventing the refugees from embarking, even if in Brazilian vessels, and by forcing their separation, the British government appeared to want to render ineffective any future resistance to the usurpation. From this point, diplomatic relations between the Portuguese Liberals and the British authorities were overshadowed by a mutual mistrust, which prevailed until Wellington's fall in 1830.

This mistrust is evident in the fascinating correspondence between Wellington and Palmela from November 1828 to January 1829. When writing to Wellington, Palmela was assisted by Brougham and Thomas Denman,[10] an 'ardent "Foxite"',[11] probably recommended by Holland and whom Palmela described as the most eminent jurist in England.[12] The respective strategies were subtle. Palmela was trying to win time in the hope of preventing the separation of the troops from their officers and attempting to lure Wellington into indiscretions that could be used against him subsequently. Wellington sought to use the correspondence to provide evidence that Palmela was engaging in various devious manoeuvres to frustrate a clear command issued in the name of the King of England. He also hoped to use material gained in this way to persuade the British public to accept the harsh measures the prime minister intended to employ against the refugees. In the end, it was Palmela who emerged as the real victor, with Wellington making one of the biggest mistakes of his political career when he instructed the Royal Navy to attack Portuguese refugees on the high seas in order to prevent their landing at Terceira. This mistake turned opinion throughout Europe against Wellington and may have been more important than generally appreciated in destroying his premiership. In other words it played some part in bringing the Whigs – far more sympathetic to the Portuguese Liberals – back to power after twenty years in the political wilderness.

In the course of his meeting with Wellington on 20 November 1828 – with Aberdeen also present – Palmela announced his intention to send the refugees to Rio de Janeiro rather than allow them to be spread around Cornwall and neighbouring counties, thus 'avoiding the ignominy of being treated as prisoners of war'.[13] On 3 December, Wellington sent a terse note to Palmela:

> I beg you to be so kind as to let me know when the Vessels, having on board the Portuguese Troops, destined to be sent to the Brazils, will be ready to sail, in order that I may have

9. 'O Marquez de Palmella a Nuno Barbosa de Figueiredo', in *Despachos*, 4: 253 (26 November 1828); 'Ninguem suppunha que o governo britannico se atrevesse a mostrar pela usurpação uma parcialidade tão formal'. (My translation).
10. Thomas Denman (1779–1754), 1st Baron Denman, appointed in 1832 as Lord Chief Justice of England by Grey.
11. Joseph Arnould, *Memoir of Thomas, First Lord Denman: formerly Lord Chief Justice of England*. 2 vols (London: Longmans, Green, 1873), 1: 24.
12. 'O Marquez de Palmella ao Conde de Sabugal', in *Despachos*, 4: 267 (6 December 1828).
13. 'O Marquez de Palmella a Nuno Barbosa de Figueiredo', in *Despachos*, 4: 253 (26 November 1828); 'evitar a ignominia de sermos aqui tratados como prisioneiros de guerra'. (My translation).

> directions given for the Officer commanding His Majesty's Ships at Plymouth, to send Convoy with them.[14]

In other words, Wellington would be prepared to provide 'assistance' to the refugees but this 'assistance' could also be used to make sure they went to Brazil (now a separate country from Portugal) rather than to one or more of the Atlantic islands – which were still part of the territories of the Portuguese Crown and on which the Miguelite regime had forces. It seems clear, however, that Palmela always intended that the bulk of the refugees should go to the Azores. His task was twofold: he had to try to deceive Wellington about the real destination of the ships assembling in Plymouth but, if that proved impossible and Wellington used the Royal Navy to frustrate his scheme, Palmela would still be able to use the episode to discredit Wellington and thus bring his plans closer to fruition.

On 7 December, on Palmela's instructions, Thomas Stubbs – who had replaced Cândido Xavier as director of the depot at Plymouth – published an Order of the Day declaring that

> Given the impossibility of remaining longer in this Depot, because the Government of H. Britannic M. do not allow, it is necessary for the Portuguese Emigrants to leave this Country [...] they must be prepared to embark within few days to that destination [Rio de Janeiro], according to the present orders.[15]

On 20 December, Palmela wrote a further letter in an attempt to persuade Wellington to agree to the refugees going to the Azores. Recent information suggested that Terceira 'remains tranquil, and entirely under the Legitimate Government [...] and that the Expedition which the Government *de facto* [i.e., the Miguel regime] had sent with the design of invading it, has entirely disappeared from the latitude of the Azores'.[16] Under the circumstances Palmela could 'see no obstacle in directing the refugees to that Island rather than to Brazil'. He concluded 'having come to England freely, no opposition can be made to their leaving it in the same manner, unarmed, and not for the purpose of committing any act of aggression, or attacking any territory'.[17] It is unlikely that Palmela expected that he could convince Wellington and, in any event, the prime minister's answer, dated 23 December, insists that 'His Majesty's Government could not allow these troops to proceed from England, in a hostile character, to Portugal, or to the Portuguese

14. 'The Duke of Wellington to the Marquis de Palmella', in *Papers Respecting the Relations between Great Britain and Portugal*, 83 (3 December 1828).
15. ANTT, MNE, Legação Portuguesa em Londres, MSS Cx. 161, Mç. 33, Ordem do Dia N.° 102 (7 December 1828); 'Não sendo possivel que os Emigrados Portuguezes se conservem por mais tempo, neste Depozito, por que o Governo de S. M. Britannica o não consente é forçozo que elles saião deste Paiz [...] devem achar-se prevenidos, para embarcar, dentro em poucos dias, para aquelle destino [Rio de Janeiro], segundo as ordens que acabão de receber.' (My translation).
16. 'The Marquis de Palmella to the Duke of Wellington', in *Papers Respecting the Relations between Great Britain and Portugal*, 89 (20 December 1828).
17. 'The Marquis de Palmella to the Duke of Wellington', ibid., 90 (20 December 1828).

Dominions or Colonies', while also reminding Palmela 'that above a month has now elapsed since I desired, in the name of His Majesty's Government, that the Portuguese Officers and Troops should be removed from Plymouth'.[18]

In a dispatch to the British prime minister dated 28 December, Palmela explained his views at length:

> I had hoped that you would have taken into consideration the distinction I had drawn in my Letter of the 20th of this month, namely, the essential difference which exists between the intention entertained by the Portuguese Refugees of proceeding to the Island of Terceira, and that which you attribute to them of going to attack some part of the Portuguese Territory. I do not find, however, in your Excellency's Answer, a single word relative to this distinction, although it appears to me evident.[19]

On 30 December, Wellington, while claiming to write 'in the true spirit of a Friend', specifically warned Palmela that the Portuguese troops could not be allowed to land in the Azores.[20] Since there appeared to be a danger that British neutrality might be compromised, Palmela's equivocal conduct had now, 'imposed upon me, personally, a most painful duty in obliging me to inform you, that you will be responsible for all the consequences which will follow your omission to obey His Majesty's commands, as conveyed to you by me'.[21]

On 2 January 1829, Palmela responded to Wellington's dispatch by regretting the British government's insistence on the immediate removal of the Portuguese exiles from Plymouth. However, he was pleased to announce 'that *at the moment at which I write*, four Transports, with Persons on board, which for the last fortnight have been ready to take their departure with the first fair wind, will have set sail.'[22] These transports, including the Danish *Fortuna*, conveying 266 German mercenaries to Rio de Janeiro under the command of Schwalbach,[23] left Plymouth in December 1828.[24] Other vessels were preparing to sail, but Palmela could not give the precise date for their departure 'on the account of the continuance of contrary winds; an obstacle which neither the orders of the British Government, nor all the good will on my part, can enable them to surmount.'[25] On a defiant note, Palmela added that, owing to adverse weather conditions, he believed it would be impossible to order the vessels to change their course to Brazil. Palmela further declared that they

> do no more than avail themselves of the right which it is impossible to deny them without injustice, and that, far from violating the neutrality of His Britannic Majesty, they respect it

18. 'The Duke of Wellington to the Marquis de Palmella', ibid., 92 (23 December 1828).
19. 'The Marquis de Palmella to the Duke of Wellington', ibid., 97 (28 December 1828).
20. 'The Duke of Wellington to the Marquis de Palmella', ibid., 101 (30 December 1828).
21. Ibid.
22. 'The Marquis de Palmella to the Duke of Wellington', ibid., 104 (2 January 1829).
23. Johann Schwalbach (1774–1874), 1st and only Barão de Setúbal, a German officer in the Portuguese service.
24. 'The Marquis de Palmella to the Duke of Wellington', in *Papers Respecting the Relations between Great Britain and Portugal*, 90 (20 December 1828).
25. Ibid., 104 (2 January 1829).

> as they ought, in quitting, without arms, and on board Merchant Vessels, the Territory of His Britannic Majesty, in order to proceed to an Island, of which Her Majesty the Queen of Portugal is Sovereign *de facto* as well as *de jure*.[26]

It must be acknowledged that, in his dealings with Wellington, Palmela had not been entirely frank. Only when he thought it was too late to do anything about it did he reveal that the real destination of the ships was Terceira – in direct defiance of Wellington's orders. Throughout, he had been careful not to reveal that a major operation in which some 2,000 refugees would land in the Azores was in an advanced stage of preparation. The plan involved the English merchant ships *Edward*, *Hope*, *Blanche* and *Trusty*, which had been chartered to convey about 150 refugees to Terceira, to be followed by an expedition led by Saldanha, which was to leave Plymouth on 6 January with 652 troops and officers aboard the *Susannah*, *Lyra*, *Minerva* and *Delphin*.[27] This convoy was followed by further departures, including the Portuguese brig *Industrioso*, which left Plymouth on 11 January for Le Havre and from thence to Terceira with 145 passengers, the schooner *Santa Lucia*, which sailed on the same day with 46 refugees, the *True Briton* and the *Countess of Liverpool* carrying guns and ammunition, the American *James Cropper* that left Falmouth on 30 January with 304 volunteers, two large vessels, the *Bolivar* and the *Hayden*, which left from Plymouth on 24 February with 607 men, the Danish *Cecrops*, which sailed in March with 186 men and the Portuguese brig *Filinto* with 127 men, the last intended to sail directly to Brazil.

Palmela may have calculated that Wellington would be furious when he discovered that he had been misled. This may have been Palmela's intention all along. Politicians who are angry are liable to overreact, to the detriment of their own reputations. If Palmela concluded that Wellington was an enemy, whose removal from office was essential to the ultimate success of the Liberal cause in Portugal, it would make sense to lure an angry Wellington into a step that would damage his reputation in Britain. Whether intentionally or not, Palmela's letters to Wellington led the prime minister into a trap from which he could not escape unscathed. In other words, through skilful political manoeuvres, Palmela achieved something that Napoleon had failed to accomplish on the battlefield. On 12 December, anticipating Palmela's move, Wellington had instructed Commodore William Walpole to proceed immediately to the Azores and prevent 'an attack on Terceira or other of the Western islands'.[28] Crucially, as Lord Ellenborough commented in his journal on 20 January,

> At Hatfield in the evening H. de Ros told me Lord Holland had got hold of the idea that the sealed orders given to the captain of the ship which accompanied the Portuguese when they left Plymouth, were to the effect that he should prevent their going to Terceira, and that he intended to inveigh against this as a breach of neutrality.[29]

---

26. Ibid.
27. *The Times*, 6 January 1829, 2.
28. 'No. 38 – Instructions to Captain Walpole, December 12th, 1828', in *Papers Respecting the Relations between Great Britain and Portugal*, 106; see also *The Times*, 10 January 1829, 2.
29. Ellenborough, Edward Law, Earl of, *A Political Diary 1828–1830*. 2 vols (London: Richard Bentley, 1881), 1: 306 (20 January 1829).

The Abstruse Joke: A Scene off Terceira / John Doyle. London: S. Gans, [1829]. Biblioteca Nacional de Portugal E-1421-V.

This unwise step, understandable only in the light of Wellington's military background, cast a shadow over his political career and contributed to his fall two years later. As Holland remarked sometime later in a speech in the House of Lords, 'The noble Duke at the head of his Majesty's Government sometimes shewed that he understood the tactics of debate as well as he did those of the field.'[30] Indeed, after this episode, Wellington's popularity would never fully recover.

Stubbs had instructed Saldanha that the four ships under his command should leave Plymouth separately rather than in a convoy to avoid raising the suspicions of the British authorities. But the general ignored the order and left the harbour in grandstyle. When Saldanha arrived off Terceira, he discovered that Walpole, who had arrived two days earlier, was waiting for him. Stubbs had also warned Saldanha that 'in case of meeting some English warship that, against the rights of the People, will try to force the Ships to take other course, he must protest and employ all means at his disposal to

30. Holland, Speech in the House of Lords on the 'Affair at Terceira', in *Parl. Deb.*, 23 (23 March 1830), c. 753; see also *The Times*, 24 March 1830, 4.

accomplish the landing.'[31] Hence, ignoring Walpole, Saldanha pushed into the harbour with the *Susannah*, forcing *The Ranger* frigate to open fire on her, killing one Portuguese and wounding another two.[32] On 24 January, after an exchange of letters between Walpole and Saldanha – in which Saldanha accused Walpole of using 'over me the discretion of a Conqueror',[33] the Portuguese commander finally agreed to be escorted 'as far as Latitude 43° 51' 0" N. and Longitude 14° 37' 0" W', viz. off Cape Finisterre.[34] In a note dated 16 January, on board the *Susannah*, Saldanha had declared 'I consider myself your Prisoner, and will follow your Vessels wherever you will lead us'.[35]

Although Saldanha's 'fleet' had been turned away, there remained the question of the other Portuguese ships that had sailed separately. Walpole was able to deal with some of these – such as the *Trusty* with 40 Portuguese officers – which was prevented from landing on 14 February.[36] Yet Walpole's mission was more of a failure than a success. In particular, he was unable to stop several vessels, including the *James Cropper*, the *Edward*, the *Hope*, the *Blanche*, the *Bolivar* and the *Hayden*, from landing safely in Terceira. During the first three months of 1829, Palmela succeeded in disembarking approximately 1,000 refugees in Terceira, as well as 4,000 guns, powder, swords and about 50 cannons.

Once free of his British 'captors', Saldanha sailed for Brest, where he landed on 29 January to be met with a warm reception from the local authorities. The refugees were transferred to depots at l'Ille-et-Vilaine and la Mayenne, where they remained until 25 October 1829, when they were transferred to Ostend and Bruges to join a further 460 comrades who had come directly from Plymouth. According to a report from a lieutenant of Gendarmerie, 'The officers were well received by all the Liberals at Fougères, who assembled to collect money for them and they seemed touched by their painful situation; they sought a thousand honest ways to make them forget.'[37]

When Palmela learned of the establishment of a provisional government in Terceira he dispatched seven trusted officers to the Azores to secure the island. They included

31. ANTT, MNE, Legação Portuguesa em Londres, MSS Cx. 161, Mç. 34, Officios dos Commandantes do Depozito de Plymouth: Despatch N.° 14 from William Stubbs to Palmela (Plymouth, 29 December 1828); 'no cazo de ir encontrar Embarcação de guerra Ingleza, que contra o direito das Gentes, queira obrigar os Navios a tomar outro rumo, deve protestar, e empregar todos os meios ao seu alcance, a fim de realizar o desembarque.' (My translation).
32. 'No. 39 – Report of Captain Walpole. His Majesty's Ship, *Ranger*, Off Terceira, 14th February, 1829', in *Papers Respecting the Relations between Great Britain and Portugal*, 107.
33. 'Count Saldanha to Captain Walpole', ibid., 112 (24 January 1829).
34. 'No. 39 – Report of Captain Walpole. His Majesty's Ship, *Ranger*, Off Terceira, 14th February, 1829', ibid., 107.
35. 'Count Saldanha to Captain Walpole', ibid., 110 (16 January 1829).
36. 'No. 39 – Report of Captain Walpole. His Majesty's Ship, *Ranger*, Off Terceira, 14th February, 1829', ibid., 107.
37. Arch. dép. d'Ille-et-Vilaine, 4 M 433, Lieutenant of Gendarmerie of Fougères to His Commander of Company, 17 mai 1829, quoted in 'Les réfugiés portugais dans l'Ouest de 1829 à 1834', by Jean-François Tanguy, *Annales de Bretagne et des Pays de l'Ouest* 4 (2002): 60; 'L'État applique à leur soulagement un fonds de secours pour trois mois, durée présumée de leur séjour dans le Royaume.' (My translation).

Colonel José Torres[38] and Brigadier Cabreira, who left Falmouth on 21 August 1828 aboard the Brazilian frigate *Isabel.*[39] On their arrival at Terceira on 8 September, Cabreira was immediately appointed governor and, on 5 October, elected president of a new provisional junta with wider powers than the former one. On 21 June 1829, Vila Flor landed in Terceira bearing Palmela's instructions to replace Cabreira as governor and president of the junta, together with Sá Nogueira's appointment as chief of the War Department. This measure conferred enhanced credibility on the Terceira government, not only internally, but also internationally.[40]

Palmela was right in thinking that the island of Terceira would be ideal as a base for a Liberal government and as a point of departure for the invasion of other islands and ultimately of metropolitan Portugal. The island had the double advantage of being the only territory of Portugal still loyal to Pedro and the Charter, while carrying the symbolic meaning of having resisted Spanish rule from 1580 to 1583.[41] Like Felipe II in the sixteenth century, Miguel quickly appreciated that continued existence of a separate government in Terceira constituted a significant obstacle to his claim to be the undisputed and legitimate king of Portugal. Both Felipe and Miguel took steps to crush what they regarded as rebellion. In Miguel's case, a large fleet under the Vice Admiral Henrique Prego arrived off Terceira on 29 July 1829.[42] In all, the force amounted to 6,000 men, including crew, against Vila Flor's 2,386 troops. The attack began on the foggy morning of 11 August, with the ships' cannons bombarding the Terceira fortresses for four hours, followed by the landing of 1,100 troops at Praia. Despite the numerical superiority of the invaders, they were defeated after a fierce fight that lasted until five o'clock. A second landing was attempted but boats carrying the soldiers from the ships were driven back by fire from land. Miguel's force then sailed away, having lost an estimated 400–600 men and 388 prisoners, against 12 dead and 27 wounded from the Liberals. The unexpected success of Terceira gave a psychological boost to the Liberals and also, from a political and diplomatic perspective, strengthened the legitimacy of their cause.

On 15 June 1829, Pedro had decreed the establishment of a provisional government headed by Palmela, which would rule from Terceira on behalf of Maria II. Five days

38. José António da Silva Torres (1782–1848), 1st and only Barão do Pico do Seleiro and Visconde da Serra do Pilar.

39. Diocleciano Leão de Brito Cabreira (1772–1839), 1st Barão de Faro.

40. Sá Nogueira sailed from England on 4 May aboard the brig *Briton* and arrived at Terceira on 3 June, after a hazardous journey during which he was in danger of being captured by the *Miguelistas* at S. Miguel, while Vila Flor embarked at Le Havre on 5 June on *The Countess of Liverpool,* landing in Terceira on 21 June.

41. After the death of the childless Cardinal-King D. Henrique in 1580, D. António Prior do Crato (1531–1595), the natural son of Infante D. Luís and a grandchild of D. Manuel I, emerged as a claimant to the throne. After his defeat by a Spanish force under Don Fernando Álvarez de Toledo y Pimentel (1507–1582), 3rd Duque de Alba, at the battle of Alcântara on 25 August 1580, D. António established a government at Terceira, which resisted the Spaniards until 27 July 1583, when the island was finally subdued by Don Álvaro de Bazán (1526–1588), Marqués de Santa Cruz.

42. Henrique da Fonseca de Sousa Prego (1768–1847), Portuguese Commodore.

later, Palmela informed the emperor that the three appointed members – José António Guerreiro, the Marquês de Valença (although the latter was afterwards replaced by Vila Flor) and himself – were already in London, and the council of regency 'virtually established', yet waiting for further instructions from Rio de Janeiro. It was important to make appropriate financial arrangements since, at the beginning of 1829, the emperor had instructed Itabaiana to cease payments to Palmela as stipulated under the terms of the Treaty of 1825. Of course, Pedro's decree of 15 June 1829 was issued in Brazil and so it should have been impossible for Palmela – in London – to know its contents only five days later. It seems likely therefore that Palmela was given advance information about the decree – probably through Guerreiro – before its official release. No doubt this was intended to hasten the establishment of an effective Liberal government in the Azores but, in any event, little time was gained. Due to lack of funds, however, the plan was adjourned. As Princess Lieven commented in a letter to Grey in February 1830: 'The Emperor Don Pedro has sent him [Palmela] peremptory orders to betake himself forthwith to Terceira, and inaugurate the Regency there, of which he was named President. But he gives him neither a ship nor money'.[43] It was not until 15 March 1830 that Palmela landed in Terceira to formally establish the new government.

43. Lieven 'To Earl Grey', in *Correspondence*, 1: 448 (20 February 1830).

Chapter Eight

THE AFFAIRS OF PORTUGAL

*A work which (great as the regeneration of Portugal would be) was, for the happiness, prosperity, and peace of this country, the very greatest in which any government could possibly be engaged.**

Wellington's devious conduct over the Portuguese question did not show the iron duke at his best. While never going so far as to withdraw recognition of Maria as legitimate Queen of Portugal, in practice he did everything in his power to assist Miguel. In the dying days of his government – in October 1830 – he actually offered the Lisbon Embassy to Beresford. At that time Wellington believed that Miguel could be recognized as King of Portugal in the near future; all that was needed was the proclamation of a General Amnesty for his opponents. Wellington was thus on the brink of abandoning the policy announced in George IV's message (of course really Wellington's) when Parliament rose on 28 July 1828:

> The just Expectations of his Majesty have been disappointed; and Measures have been adopted in Portugal, in disregard of the earnest Advice and repeated Remonstrances of His Majesty, which have compelled His Majesty, and the other Powers of Europe acting in concert with His Majesty, to withdraw their Representatives from Lisbon.[1]

Thereafter the official line was that Britain would follow a policy of non-interference, but the effect of Aberdeen's measures – clearly taken with Wellington's approval and probably on his instructions – was to favour the Absolutist cause and weaken the Liberal one.

On 25 August 1828, Lord Strangford left for Rio de Janeiro aboard the *Galatea*, with instructions to persuade Pedro not to waver in his decision to abdicate the Portuguese throne and to send his daughter to Vienna as quickly as possible, so that she could marry her uncle as previously agreed. The emperor refused. As Lafayette noted in a speech to the *Chambre des Députés* on 9 July 1829, Strangford had no chance of succeeding because he was seeking to reconcile two irreconcilable principles: 'the alleged sovereignty of Miguel's Cortes, with the institutions that a British Ambassador, by the way, had brought from Brazil'.[2] In fact neither the Absolutists nor the Liberals now wanted the marriage;

* Holland, address in the House of Lords on the 'Affairs of Portugal', *The Times*, 10 February 1829, 2.

1. 'The King's Speech at the Close of the Session', in *Parl. Deb.*, 19 (28 July 1828), cc. 1781–82.
2. Lafayette, speech to the Chambre des Députés (9 July 1829), in *Mémoires, correspondance et manuscrits du général Lafayette*. 6 vols (Bruxelles: Société Belge de Librairie, 1837–1838), 2: 425; 'la prétendue souveraineté des cortès miguélistes avec les institutions qu'un ambassadeur britannique, soit dit en passant, avait apportées du Brésil.' (My translation).

the Absolutists wanted Miguel to rule as king, not as regent for his wife, while the Liberals now regarded Miguel with complete loathing. As Palmela remarked to Princess Lieven, 'the rightful Queen is not to be married to a usurper, and that the victim shall not freely be given to a Minotaur'.[3] However, the British government still favoured the marriage, seeing it as a *sine qua non* condition for recognition of the Miguelite regime and, indeed, as the only decent exit from the imbroglio.

Palmela had initially interpreted Maria's cordial reception in England as indicating tacit official support for the Liberal cause. Palmela's optimism rose further when Maria visited Windsor Castle on 22 December 1828; George IV proposed a toast 'to my young friend and ally, the Queen of Portugal',[4] and 'in addressing her (in French), his Majesty is said to have used the word "Majesty" and not "Royal Highness"'.[5] Yet, the fact that George IV took so long to receive Maria – in contrast to his solicitous behaviour towards Miguel – suggested that Palmela's optimism might be misplaced. While it was given out that the delay in receiving Maria was caused by the king's illhealth – an attack of gout – George could probably have received Maria earlier had he (or Wellington) really wanted. As Palmela admitted in a dispatch to Nuno de Figueiredo, 'The acts of the English Government are, as everyone knows, distinct and independent from the Sovereign's will; it may be said that they are often opposite to that will'.[6] It must be also noted, moreover, that Maria was the daughter of the emperor of Brazil, where Britain had its own interests.

While in England, Maria was certainly the centre of attention. At least two children's balls were organized for her, one by the Duchess of Clarence on 19 January 1829, and the other by the king himself on 28 May – the first attended by the future Queen Victoria. At Laleham Maria was visited by several distinguished people, including the arch anti-Liberal Beresford, who, according to Lady Holland, eccentrically presented himself to the young Queen 'in full Portuguese Marshal's uniform' and 'on his knees kissed her hand, & asked if there was anything for her services he could execute, a complete offer of duty & obedience to her commands'.[7]

Despite all the civilities addressed to the young queen, Wellington never intended to withdraw his tacit support for Miguel. As he admitted in a memorandum to Aberdeen on 19 September 1828, 'The arrival of this young Queen in England is the work of an intrigue, and is intended to give and will give us a good deal of trouble'.[8] In a conversation with Zea Bermudéz, the Spanish minister at London, Wellington declared:

3. Palmela, quoted in a letter from Lieven 'To Earl Grey', in *Correspondence*, 1: 161 (8 October 1828).
4. Soriano, *HGC*, 3.ª época, t. III, pt. 1 [14]: 208.
5. *The Globe*, quoted in *The Spectator*, 27 December 1828, 2.
6. 'O Marquez de Palmella a Nuno Barbosa de Figueiredo', in *Despachos*, 4: 363 (11 February 1829); 'Os actos do governo inglez são, como todos sabem, distinctos e independentes da vontade do Soberano; muitas vezes póde dizer-se que são contrarios a essa vontade'. (My translation).
7. *Lady Holland to Her Son 1821–1845* (London: John Murray, 1946), 104 (1 June [1829]).
8. Wellington, 'Memorandum for the Earl of Aberdeen', in *Despatches, Correspondence, and Memoranda*, 5: 63 (19 September 1828).

> What do I care if the King D. Miguel, D. Maria da Glória or someone else rules in Portugal? England has enough strength to sustain in Portugal whoever may be her King or her Government; the reason why I have been declaring so much in favour of the King D. Miguel is because I have a natural affection for him [...].[9]

In fact, even before Maria's cordial reception at Windsor, there were signs that any gestures of friendship would mean little. Thus, in October 1828, Wellington had refused to acknowledge Palmela's credentials as Pedro's ambassador in London with special powers to defend Maria's interests in Europe. According to the British government, a tutor invested with political powers was not a common diplomatic practice and thus unacceptable. Strikingly, while Palmela was snubbed at the diplomatic level, he was 'admirably' received by George IV, who called 'him twice to his side and naming him his "friend" '.[10] As a result, Palmela remained in London in a semi-official capacity, retaining the honours of an ambassador but without formal status or power. In its treatment of Palmela, the British government was tacitly admitting – though not openly – its non-recognition of Maria as legitimate Queen of Portugal.

On 25 November, Barbacena launched a diplomatic counter-attack, demanding Britain's assistance in upholding Maria's rights. The communication, actually written by Palmela, sought 'effectual assistance in placing Her Most Faithful Majesty upon the Throne belonging to her, as well as in securing to Her the possessions of Her Kingdom'.[11] To support his claim, Barbacena, alias Palmela, alluded to former Anglo-Portuguese alliances and to the Vienna and London Protocols of 1827–28. But Barbacena's request was rejected with Aberdeen insisting that

> It is then, either for the purpose of resisting successful Rebellion, or for that of deciding, by force, a question of doubtful Succession, that Great Britain has now been called upon to act. But it is impossible to imagine that any Independent State could ever intend thus to commit the direction and control of the internal affairs to the hands of another Power.[12]

Apart from some moral support from Russia as a way to annoy Wellington, it was in France that the Portuguese Liberals found their strongest political allies, especially from ministers such as Hyde de Neuville and the comte de la Ferronnays.[13] In March 1829,

---

9. Wellington to Zea Bermudes, quoted by the Conde da Ponte, in Santarém's *Correspondencia*, 2: 292; 'Pois que me importa a mim que em Portugal reine El-Rey D. Miguel, D. Maria da Gloria ou outro qualquer? A Inglaterra tem suficiente força para sustentar em Portugal sua influencia qualquer que seja seu Rey ou seu Governo; A razão porem porque eu me tenho declarado tanto a favour de El-Rey D. Miguel, hé por lhe ser naturalmente affeiçoado [...].' (My translation).
10. Lieven 'To Earl Grey', in: *Correspondence*, 1: 210 (24 December 1828).
11. 'The Marquis de Barbacena to the Earl of Aberdeen (Translation)', in *Papers Respecting the Relations between Great Britain and Portugal*, 64 (25 November 1828); see also Palmela, *Memórias*, 206.
12. 'The Earl of Aberdeen to the Marquis de Barbacena', in *Papers Respecting the Relations between Great Britain and Portugal*, 71–72 (13 January 1828).
13. August-Pierre-Marie Ferron (1777–1842), comte de la Ferronays, French army officer, diplomat and statesman, Foreign Minister of Charles X.

it was announced that 'The [French] State provides an emergency fund to their relief for three months, the estimated duration of their stay in this kingdom'.[14] French support was based upon a mixture of political calculation and sentiment. Ferronnays, himself an exile in 1790, was proud of fighting for the cause of legitimacy for more than 20 years. Ferronnay was supported by Hyde de Neuville, former French ambassador to Portugal and now Minister of Marine. Neuville had long advocated French support for the Liberal cause in Portugal, hoping that this would ultimately allow France to replace Britain as the dominant influence in Lisbon.

The conduct of the British government towards the Portuguese refugees at Terceira had astonished many in Europe, not least in France, where the incident was used as a propaganda weapon. As Mackintosh noted in his speech of 1 June 1829, the attack by the Royal Navy on the vessels of its most ancient ally had the perverse effect of compelling the Portuguese refugees 'to expose the wounds we inflicted on them to the Court of France'.[15] The issue was taken up by leading French Liberals, including Benjamin Constant, Sébastiani, Lamarque and Lafayette, who remonstrated strongly against the arrogance of the British government.

In England, the episode also made considerable impact, leading Wellington to admit in a private conversation, 'Well, Croker, here we are in another mess!'[16] Although the king's speech at the opening of the Parliament on 5 February 1829 avoided the subject – confining itself to the brief declaration that 'His Majesty laments that His diplomatic relations with Portugal are still necessarily suspended'[17] – it seemed likely that the Whigs might use the issue as a political weapon. Greville noted:

> The affair of the Portuguese at Terceira (which certainly, unless it can be explained, seems a gross outrage) they all fell upon very severely, and Lord Harrowby told me afterwards he could not understand it, and thought for the honour of the country it should be explained forthwith.[18]

Although Wellington was yet to appreciate the full significance of Terceira, he could already see that it had made him vulnerable, telling Croker:

> If the Opposition (I mean the old Opposition, the Whigs) had moved an amendment on any topic of the address – for instance, Portugal – the Government would have been in a minority, for a great body of our usual supporters would have voted with them. The Whigs themselves saw this, and Holland afterwards told Aberdeen that this was the reason that he did not push on the Portuguese question.[19]

---

14. Arch. dép. d'Ille-et-Vilaine, 4 M 430, 26 mars 1829, quoted in 'Les réfugiés portugais dans l'Ouest de 1829 à 1834', 60; 'L'État applique à leur soulagement un fonds de secours pour trois mois, durée présumée de leur séjour dans le Royaume.' (My translation).
15. Mackintosh, Speech on 'Portugal', *The Times*, 2 June 1829, 2.
16. Croker, *The Croker Papers*, 2: 10 (Tuesday, 10 February 1829).
17. King's Speech at the Opening of the Parliamentary Session (5 February 1829), in *Journals of the House of Commons: Sess. 1829*, 84: 4; 'Parliamentary Intelligence', *The Times*, 6 February 1829, 1.
18. Greville, *Memoirs*, 1: 169–70 (8 February 1829).
19. Croker, *The Croker Papers*, 2: 10 (Tuesday, 10 February 1829).

For a while the old Whig reticence remained and, according to Croker, Holland told Aberdeen that it was precisely this reason that he had decided not to 'push' on the Portuguese question. Whatever the strength of feeling about Portugal, the Whigs were not yet ready to try to bring down the government on an issue upon which – in the country as a whole – there was still comparatively little interest. But in the absence of satisfactory explanations from the Ministry, not even the Whigs would wait forever.

On 8 February, Lord Ellenborough admitted in his journal that he had been reading the correspondence between Aberdeen and Barbacena and between Wellington and Palmela, 'both referring to the Portuguese question, upon which we shall, I dare say, have a question this week. We have a good case'.[20] Ellenborough's expectation proved correct and, on the following day, Holland raised the subject in the Lords, 'in consequence of some occurrences reported to have taken place recently, in which he conceived that the national honour and the interests of Portugal were alike interested'.[21] Holland expected Aberdeen 'to lay the fullest and most satisfactory information before the house with regard to the policy pursued by this country towards Portugal'.[22] But Aberdeen refused to provide the information Holland demanded, claiming that this could compromise ongoing negotiations and, pointing out that the government still awaited the official report of the events in the Azores. Holland now threatened Aberdeen with 'an inquiry with regard to the affairs of Portugal, and our relations with that country',[23] although admitting that

> He felt great diffidence and disinclination to commit himself in hostilities with His Majesty's Ministers, at a time when they were engaged in a work which (great as the regeneration of Portugal would be) was, for the happiness, prosperity, and peace of this country, the very greatest in which any government could possibly be engaged.[24]

Holland said that he knew 'some one better able than himself to accomplish the end he had in view', viz. the inquiry.[25] He was clearly referring to Mackintosh, who, on the same day, raised the subject in the Commons. Although claiming that 'He [Mackintosh] had been anxious, in the first instance, to suffer a longer period to elapse, with a view not to embarrass His Majesty's ministers', recent events in the Azores had induced him 'to move for copies or extracts of the various despatches or communications concerning the relations which subsisted between our Government and that of Her Majesty Donna Maria II, Queen of Portugal and Algarve'.[26] Mackintosh kept his promise and, on 16 February, put down a motion concerning relations between Britain and Portugal.[27]

---

20. Ellenborough, *A Political Diary*, 1: 339–40 (8 February 1829).
21. 'Parliamentary Intelligence: Affairs of Portugal', *The Times*, 10 February 1829, 2.
22. Ibid.
23. Ibid.
24. Ibid.
25. Ibid.
26. Ibid.
27. Ibid.

On 1 June 1829, the day scheduled for the discussion in the Commons, Lady Holland wrote to her son:

> The debate will be upon Sir J. Mackintosh's motion upon Terceira, which will bring in all the question of Portugal. Some persons are in hopes that there is a more favorable [feeling] towards that unfortunate nation, but of *this*, nothing I noticed has transpired.[28]

During the debates, the Opposition adopted the traditional Whig approach to foreign affairs, placing more stress on ideological criteria than upon considerations of national interest. Mackintosh made this clear at the beginning of his long and, in Peel's words, 'able and eloquent speech',[29] declaring that 'In dealing with the subject, he relied more on topics which related to the general welfare and dignity of mankind, than on particular cases or instances'.[30] 'The absolutists [...]' he declared, 'were our enemies from instinct – were our sworn foes from principle'.[31] Although the principle of mutual non-interference in internal affairs was included in most Anglo-Portuguese treaties, Mackintosh argued that British help in releasing Portugal from tyranny would be both justifiable and desirable. Mackintosh thought the British government was partly to blame for Miguel's usurpation, insisting that it was now Britain's duty 'to place Portugal as it was before Miguel left Vienna, were it only by the encouragements and hopes which we gave and created in the minds of the people of Portugal'.[32]

Virtually all the opposition speakers claimed that the principle of non-intervention – upon which the ministers based their case – was fraudulent in that it actually favoured Miguel. Brougham, who had acted as legal adviser to Palmela, had studied the issues closely and now declared that 'His objection to the measures of the government was, not that they evinced too little disposition to interference, but that there had been interference'.[33] Thus there had been interference in the negotiations leading to Portuguese recognition of Brazilian independence in 1825, as well as in the granting of Pedro's Charter one year later. In respect of the present case,

> We had interfered, however, and interfered in favour of Don Miguel's policy instead of against him; and he still desiderated an answer to the question which had been asked by his hon. friend [Mackintosh], by what right or title we interfered with the expedition to Terceira.[34]

After a neutral speech from Huskisson, who was reluctant to give an opinion since the papers were still not before the House, and some inaudible observations from Hudson

28. *Lady Holland to Her Son*, 104 (1 June [1829]).
29. Peel, Speech on 'Portugal', in *Parl. Deb.*, 21 (1 June 1829), c. 1624.
30. Mackintosh, Speech on 'Portugal', in *Parl. Deb.*, 21 (1 June 1829): c. 1603.
31. Mackintosh, Speech on 'Portugal', *The Times*, 2 June 1829, 2; also *Parl. Deb.*, 21 (1 June 1829): c. 1622.
32. Ibid., ibid.
33. Brougham, Speech on 'Portugal', in *Parl. Deb.*, 21 (1 June 1829): c. 1636; *The Times*, 2 June 1829, 2.
34. Ibid., c. 1638; ibid., 2.

Gurney,[35] Palmerston made what was probably the best speech in the debate. The fact that Palmerston was taking up the Portuguese Liberal cause had major implications both for Portugal and for Britain, in that it marked an important step in the transformation of Palmerston from Tory to Whig – or rather in the emergence of a Whig/Tory synthesis. In the past Tory ideas on foreign policy had tended to focus on considerations of national interest whereas Whigs focused on questions of principle, in this instance exemplified in Mackintosh's speech on Portugal. But Palmerston was developing an ability to mingle the two by arguing that what was right in principle was also in Britain's national interest – a facility that was to pay political dividends in the future. Thus, while not disagreeing with Mackintosh or Brougham, Palmertson introduced an element of pragmatism when he insisted that 'the Tagus should be in the hands of a friendly power'[36] and that 'the best security for Portuguese independence was to be found in the selfish interests of England'.[37] If Wellington had nothing to fear from 'the old Opposition, the Whigs',[38] the same could not be said about the representatives of the new generation of politicians. Men like Palmerston and Russell were less predictable and reliable than the old Foxite school. Of course Palmerston was still regarded as a Huskinssonian – that is to say, a Canningite – but the amalgamation of his line of approach with that of Whigs after 1830 brought a new breadth to the old 'Party' while, at the same time, representing what John Clarke calls 'the swan song of eighteenth-century enlightened aristocratic internationalism'.[39]

Instead of focussing on the mistreatment of the refugees by the British government, Palmerston concentrated on the mistreatment of British subjects by the Miguelite regime 'their long imprisonment without trial, sometimes in loathsome dungeons, sometimes in prisons crowded to suffocation; the seizure of their property; the visits, and searches, of their houses, books, and papers'.[40] They included Mr Young, Mr O'Brien, Sir John Doyle,[41] Mr Askoly and Mr Noble,[42] all languishing in Miguel's dungeons while the

35. Debates in the Commons on the Affairs of 'Portugal', *The Times*, 2 June 1829, 2.

36. Palmerston, *Speech of Viscount Palmerston in the House of Commons, Wednesday, the Tenth of March, 1830 on Moving for Papers, Respecting the Relations of England with Portugal* (Londres: James Ridgway, [1830]), 7; *Parl. Deb.*, 21 (1 June 1829), c. 1646.

37. Ibid., 8; ibid.

38. Croker, *The Croker Papers*, 2: 10 (Tuesday, 10 February 1829).

39. John Clarke, *British Diplomacy and Foreign Policy 1782–1865* (London: Unwin Hyman, 1989), 186.

40. Palmerston, *Speech*, 26; *Parl. Deb.*, 21 (1 June 1829), c. 1658.

41. Sir John Doyle (1756–1834), 1st Baronet, Knight of the Portuguese Order of Tower and Sword, British officer, served with distinction in the American War of Independence and in the Peninsular War. In 1828, on Miguel's orders, Doyle was arrested on a charge of treason, though he was saved through the influence of a powerful friend in Lisbon.

42. Charles Henry Noble was arrested at Oporto in September 1828 during Miguel's dictatorship and his property confiscated. Charles was the son of John Hatt Noble, a member of the British Factory of Oporto from 1806 who met the Hollands at Oporto in 1808, and with whom Holland maintained a regular correspondence for many years. In a dispatch to the Visconde de Santarém dated 19 November 1828, Asseca warned of the danger of keeping Noble in prison; he believed that Noble should be released and pardoned as soon as possible in order to put an

British government did nothing to help them. Palmerston wondered what could justify or even explain such supine behaviour, concluding that 'It must then be that Miguel was the *Pet* of the English Government'.[43]

In the face of this onslaught, the government adopted a defensive posture, shielding itself behind technical issues and arguing that it had acted in the national interest. Since Wellington and Aberdeen were in the House of Lords, the home secretary, Robert Peel, had to lead for the Ministry in the Commons. Peel insisted that the government had pursued 'the line of policy better calculated to promote and maintain our tranquillity and national faith',[44] justifying the British action at Terceira on the grounds that the Portuguese troops had sailed from Plymouth after obtaining false clearances from the Customhouse.[45] Predictably, Peel argued that the Anglo-Portuguese treaties 'did not contain, either expressly or implied, a single article to warrant England's interfering in the present intestine dissensions of Portugal'.[46] While admitting that 'the King of Great Britain and the Emperor of Austria took certain measures to induce Don Miguel to comply with the engagements, and conceding that the engagements Miguel had contracted with Don Pedro were not fulfilled',[47] Peel insisted that Britain had no obligation to act in respect of 'the vices and the crimes of this individual [Miguel]' which were properly 'a matter of consideration for the inhabitants of Portugal'.[48] The ultimate question was whether Britain should invade Portugal to install Maria as queen. Although deploring 'Don Miguel's non-observance of those stipulations [at Vienna], and his want of faith',[49] Peel 'could not think it prudent on the part of England to undertake to displace him and to dictate to the Portuguese who should be their ruler'.[50]

On 19 June, the issue was taken to the House of Lords, with Aberdeen laying on the table papers on relations with Portugal. The debate was inaugurated by the Marquess of Clanricarde,[51] who accused the government of systematically disregarding 'our councils', in contrast with the respect always demonstrated in Canning's time.[52] In the vein adopted by the Opposition in the Commons a few days earlier, Clanricarde examined the doctrine of non-interference allegedly pursued by the Cabinet, concluding that, although wise, 'there were exceptions to its general observance'.[53] Clanricarde also accused the

end to the uproar in the British press (The Visconde de Asseca 'Para o Visconde de Santarem', in *Correspondencia*, 1: 474).

43. Palmerston, Speech on 'Portugal', *The Times*, 2 June 1829, 3.
44. Peel, Speech on 'Portugal', *The Times*, 2 June 1829, 2.
45. Peel, Speech on 'Portugal', in *Parl. Deb.*, 21 (1 June 1829), c. 1635.
46. Peel, Speech on 'Portugal', *The Times*, 2 June 1829, 2; *Parl. Deb.*, 21 (1 June 1829), c. 1625.
47. Ibid.; ibid., c. 1629.
48. Ibid.; ibid., c. 1630.
49. Ibid.; ibid., c. 1631.
50. Ibid., 2, E; ibid., c. 1632.
51. Ulick de Burgh (1802–1874), 1st Marquess of Clanricarde, styled Lord Dunkellin until 1808, British Whig politician, son of John de Burgh, 13th Earl of Clanricarde, and Elizabeth, daughter of Sir Thomas Burke.
52. The Marquis of Clanricarde on 'Foreign Relations', in *Parl. Deb.*, 21 (19 June 1829), c. 1795.
53. Ibid.

Cabinet of having, ' adhered to this doctrine in favour of the usurper', yet 'departed from it by firing on the subjects of Donna Maria of Terceira',[54] an accusation Aberdeen dismissed as a surmise.[55]

Lord Holland's speech was effective in exposing the weaknesses of the Cabinet's case. Like his colleague, Holland concentrated on the exposition of ideological principles and on demonstrating the hypocrisy behind the alleged doctrine of non-intervention. Portugal, he declared, 'was a subject on which he did not mean to enter into detail though it was one on which he felt deeply. No man who regarded the safety and honour of this country but must regret the course adopted with respect to Portugal'.[56] Holland began by criticizing Aberdeen for 'so meagre and jejune a communication as that which he had made to parliament', when the Cabinet 'had allowed the session to pass over without communicating to Parliament any thing with respect to the foreign relations'.[57] Effectively accusing the government of intentionally withholding information, he warned Aberdeen that Parliament did not 'place such confidence in ministers, that every thing was to be allowed to go on without examination or enquiry'.[58]

Holland dismissed the alleged 'rigid system of neutrality' as false: 'Away with all the nonsense as to non-interference in the internal affairs of Portugal'. Rather, 'The whole history of the transactions of this country with Portugal was one of interference', a conclusion that the meanest clerk could reach after searching the archives of the office.[59] There had been 'interference heretofore with regard to the succession, to a change of ministry, and as to other internal arrangements connected with the kingdom of Portugal'.[60] And if it had not been 'for England and Austria, Don Miguel would not have been able to effect his usurpation'.[61] As Holland also observed, 'The language always held by our diplomatists was "As to Portugal, that is an English affair".'[62] Holland considered the Terceira affair as a 'heartbreaking transaction' and 'a gross violation of the law of nations',[63] arguing that 'the offence even against Don Miguel was not so great as the offence against the law of nations in that transaction'.[64] The feeble argument that the British government could treat Portuguese refugees upon the high seas as if they were in Britain was the same as plunging 'them deeper in the mire'.[65] Holland adopted the same line in a protest entered in the Journals of the House of Lords on 23 March 1830, as a response to the eventual rejection of the

54. Ibid., c. 1796.
55. The Earl of Aberdeen on 'Foreign Relations', in *Parl. Deb.*, 21 (19 June 1829), c. 1796.
56. Holland on 'Foreign Relations', in *Parl. Deb.*, 21 (19 June 1829), c. 1802.
57. Ibid., c. 1800.
58. Ibid.
59. Ibid., c. 1802.
60. Ibid.
61. Ibid., c. 1805.
62. Ibid., c. 1800.
63. Ibid., c. 1803.
64. Ibid., c. 1804.
65. Ibid.

resolutions condemning the government's conduct at Terceira, which he described as 'odious and ungenerous'.[66]

In his reply to Holland, Wellington repeated the claims made earlier by Aberdeen and Peel, although perhaps more magisterially. Regarding the alleged concealment of information from Parliament, Wellington argued that, despite his anxiety to inform Parliament about the Terceira affair, he had patiently awaited from the beginning of the session

> that the noble baron would have brought forward this subject. For this reason he had abstained from noticing the subject to their lordships, though he knew that the motives of his majesty's government had been calumniated abroad; but calumny did not afford ground for a minister to come down to parliament with information on the subject [...].[67]

In other words, Wellington was attempting to blame Holland for any delay. The prime minister was equally dismissive of accusations of lack of neutrality. There had been not 'a single instance, at any time within the last century, of interference on the part of this country with the internal affairs of Portugal by arms'.[68] Of course recent events at Terceira hardly supported such a claim but Wellington proceeded to get round the inconvenience by declaring that 'these persons had violated the laws of nations by organizing in this country an attack against the dominions of a power with which we were not only in peace, but which we were at the very time engaged by a treaty'.[69] To put it mildly, Wellington's argument was thin because Terceira was *de facto et de jure* a dominion of Maria II. Yet Wellington's position was not entirely wrongheaded. Whatever Portuguese or British Liberals wanted to believe, the fact was that, in 1828 and 1829, Portugal was largely in favour of Miguel. Perhaps the most telling point in Wellington's speech was when he observed 'Those gentlemen who were in favour of Donna Maria, quitted Portugal when they found the country against them',[70] a fact that not even Holland could contradict.[71]

On the whole, the Opposition had the better of the debate, 'The papers were then ordered to be printed' and, even more important, public opinion had been won over.[72] An anonymous tract, actually quite favourable to Wellington and published in 1830, acknowledged 'No government, whatever be its strength, can long resist the force of public opinion in such a country as Great Britain'.[73] In fact, despite the initial negative impression of *The Times*, declaring that Mackintosh's arguments failed to 'create that interest, we observe, which their importance in a moral, if not in a national point

66. Holland, 'Dissent: 23rd March, 1830 (Terceira)', in *The Opinions*, 188–90.
67. Wellington on 'Foreign Relations', in *Parl. Deb.*, 21 (19 June 1829), c. 1806.
68. Ibid.
69. Ibid., c. 1808.
70. Ibid., c. 1807.
71. The affairs of Portugal were also discussed in France, at the *Chambre des Députés*, on 9 July 1829, with Lafayette doing an energetic speech against the British Cabinet (Lafayette, *Mémoires*, 2: 424–26).
72. Debates in the House of Lords on 'Foreign Relations', in *Parl. Deb.*, 21 (19 June 1829), c. 1813.
73. *The Duke of Wellington and the Whigs* (London: J. Hatchard, 1830), [1].

of view, might seem to impart to them',[74] the Parliamentary debates had a significant impact on public opinion, as several tracts, representing a variety of standpoints, were to reveal.[75]

Yet, when their prospects seemed to be improving, the Portuguese Liberals experienced a new setback. Barbacena, commissioned by Pedro to negotiate the terms of his second marriage to Amélie of Leuchtenberg, had concluded his mission in the spring 1829.[76] On 30 August, the future empress and Maria, escorted by Barbacena, left Falmouth on the Brazilian frigate *Imperatriz* for Rio de Janeiro, where they landed on 16 October. The young queen's presence in London had been a major factor in maintaining the hopes of the refugees but her departure, together with Pedro's decision to reduce funding for diplomatic activities in Britain, left Palmela in a desperate situation. In a letter to Grey dated 7 December 1829, Lieven reported that 'He [Aberdeen] had a long interview with Palmella, with whom, as I gathered, he was well satisfied; that is to say, he finds him resigned to the worst, and in truth there is nothing else to be expected'.[77]

But even worse things were happening in France. In April 1829, the Martignac[78] ministry had been defeated in the Chamber and, after some delay, was replaced by a government headed by the Prince de Polignac.[79] Martignac's ministry, in which Ferronays and Hyde de Neuville were prominent members, had achieved the classic Liberal goal of

74. *The Times*, 3 June 1829, 3. In a review of Mackintosh's *History of the Revolution in England in 1688* in the *Edinburgh Review*, Macaulay declared, perhaps correctly, that 'Mr Fox with a pen in his hand, and Sir James on his legs in the House of Commons, were, we think, each out of his proper element'. Mackintosh was more of an historian than a speaker and, as Macaulay also observed, 'we could never read a page of Mr Fox's writing, we could never listen for a quarter of an hour to the speaking of Sir James, without feeling that there was a constant effort, a tug up hill'. ('History of the Revolution in England in 1688… by the late Right Honourable Sir James Mackintosh', *The Edinburgh Review* 124 [July 1835]: 266). Mackintosh himself told Macvey Napier on 18 June 1829, 'I am alive, that I have recovered from my speech [on Portugal] of two hours and a half'. (*Memoirs of the Life of the Right Honourable Sir James Mackintosh.* 2 vols [London: Edward Moxon, 1835], 2: 445).
75. The printed material included Portuguese translations of the speeches by Mackintosh and Palmerston, as well as of the debates in both houses, published anonymously in England by R. Greenlaw, as *Indicação e discurso do muito honrado Sir James Mackintosh na camara dos communs na sessão de segunda-feira, 1 de Junho de 1829, sobre negocios de Portugal* (Londres: 1829), *Falla do Visconde de Palmerston sôbre as relações de Inglaterra com Portugal* (Londres: 1829) and *Debates no Parlamento Britanico sôbre os negocios de Portugal, em sessão do 1.° de Junho na camara dos communs, e de 19 do mesmo mes na camara dos pares. Com a historia e annalyse d'esta discussão e das circumstancias que a motivaram* (Londres: 1829). These translations, later attributed to Almeida Garrett, were probably commissioned and paid for by Palmela.
76. Amélie Auguste of Leuchtenberg (1812–1873), Duchess of Leuchtenberg and Empress of Brazil, daughter of Eugène de Beauharnais, only son of Empress Josephine and her first husband Alexandre de Beauharnais, by Princess Augusta Amélia, daughter of Maximilian I of Bavaria.
77. Lieven 'To Earl Grey', *Correspondence*, 1: 376 (7 December 1829).
78. Jean-Baptiste Silvère Gay (1778–1832), vicomte de Martignac.
79. Auguste Jules Armand Marie de Polignac (1780–1847), comte de Polignac and prince du Saint-Empire, afterwards 3rd duc de Polignac.

abolishing press censorship – so ardently desired by Lord Holland in his time in Spain. It was clear that Polignac would be far more absolutist-inclined. Liberals throughout Europe were alarmed and the implications for the constitutional cause in Portugal appeared especially worrying. As we have seen, when faced with the ill-concealed hostility of Wellington, the Portuguese had turned to France, but now this option seemed likely to be closing.

Without the benefit of hindsight, at the close of the 1820s, it must have seemed that the prevailing wind in Europe was blowing in an anti-Liberal direction. Perhaps the Miguelite usurpation would be the more secure because it was part of a general 'swing to the Right', with Polignac replacing Martignac and Wellington replacing Canning – perhaps even Cumberland replacing Wellington. Polignac, described by Rev. Bright as 'a friend of Wellington and a strong royalist', appeared to be adopting a policy similar to the Duke's.[80] Polignac, who had served as French minister to Britain since 1823, left London for Paris on 24 November 1828 to conspire against Martignac. It was not until 8 August 1829, however, that Charles X committed what Lady Morgan described as an 'act of royal violation (or rather of royal insanity)', by placing him at the head of his Cabinet.[81]

Although a government grounded on Polignac's principles could not endure, for the time being European Legitimists professed pleasure. As Metternich observed a few days later in a dispatch to Emperor Francis, 'The change of ministry in France is an event of the highest importance. [...] Polignac, Minister of Foreign Affairs, holds our opinions thoroughly. This appointment will act very favourably on the English Cabinet and be a thunderclap for the Russians'.[82] On 16 September 1829, Palmela's triumvirate informed Pedro that

> the new French Ministry, following the example of the British Government, has now communicated their intention to separate the officers from the soldiers, and spread them through a greater number of depots. This communication forced us to arrange for them to leave France without further delay, at least the soldiers, whose discipline would be lost as soon as they were separated from their officers.[83]

In his speech at the opening of the French Parliament on 2 March 1830, Charles X declared, 'I pursue, at this moment, in agreement with my allies, negotiations with the

---

80. James Frank Bright, *A History of England*. 9th Impr. 5 vols (London: Longmans, Green, 1900–5), 3: 1413.
81. Sydney Morgan, *France in 1829–30*. 2 vols (London: Saunders and Otley, 1830), 2: 524.
82. 'Metternich to the Emperor Francis', in *Memoirs*, 4: 625 (Königswart, 13 August 1829).
83. 'O Marquez de Palmella, Marquez de Valença e José Antonio Guerreiro a S. M. o Imperador do Brazil', in *Despachos*, 4: 578–79 (16 September 1829); 'o novo ministerio francez, adoptando o exemplo do gabinete de Londres, acaba de nos significar a determinação em que está de separar os officiaes dos soldados, e de os disseminar n'um maior numero de depositos. Esta communicação obrigou-nos a tratar sem perda de tempo de fazer sair de França ao menos os soldados, cuja disciplina ficaria perdida logoque os separassem dos seus officiaes.' (My translation).

objective of promoting reconciliation between the two princes of the House of Bragança, necessary to the peace of the Peninsula'.[84] Charles was clearly referring to Wellington and Metternich, while by 'reconciliation' he meant recognition of Miguel as legitimate sovereign of Portugal. A few months earlier, Palmerston had written from Paris to the Countess Cowper,

> I believe it is quite true that the Polignac Govt, is as much for Miguel as ours; The 400 Men that are gone to Terceira did not go straight from hence. They were told they must not stay in France, & must not go from thence to Terceira; They went to Ostend where they had some difficulty in landing & from thence on to Terceira. Miguel has just Confiscated the Property of Villa Real & the other absentees.[85]

The Portuguese Liberal cause seemed now more desperate than ever. But Palmela was not a man to give up, nor was Holland. On 23 March 1830, Clanricarde tabled a number of motions in the House of Lords. Clanricarde claimed that Saldanha's protest against the British attack on the vessels sailing to Terceira – which ministers had kept from the House – constituted a new piece of evidence, which justified the reopening of the debate on the affair. According to Clanricarde, the attack on the Portuguese ships constituted a 'a violent breach of that neutrality which was avowed, and also an infraction of the law of nations, greatly aggravated by the previous declaration of neutrality'.[86] Finally, Clanricarde warned of the risks of letting France 'regain her influence in Portugal, while our own, which was already shaken, would be entirely lost'.[87]

Aberdeen accused Clanricarde of distorting the truth by focusing on one episode without telling the whole story and by 'colouring this transaction'. The foreign secretary maintained that the ministers had adopted a system of 'strict neutrality' in the contest, and had subsequently sought 'to interpret that course according to our opinions, our feelings, or our interests'.[88] It was unfair to say that 'we had followed unarmed men and cruelly fired upon them' when 'they ought to have expected what would follow, if, in the face of them, they should attempt a landing at Terceira'.[89] While Clanricarde's version of events was correct in some respects, Aberdeen had a duty to oppose it because it implied censure on the government, which he considered unfair and unacceptable.[90]

---

84. 'Séance royale pour l'ouverture de la session des deux chambres en 1830', in *Journal des débats*, mars 3, 1830, [2]; 'Je poursuis, en ce moment, de concert avec mes alliés, des négociations dont le but est d'amener, entre les princes de la maison de Bragance, une réconciliation nécessaire au repos de la Péninsule.' (My translation).
85. 'To the Countess Cowper from Lord Palmerston' (Paris, 14 December 1829), in *Lady Palmerston and Her Times*. 2 vols (London: Hodder and Stoughton, 1922), 1: 168.
86. Clanricarde, Motion Submitted to the House of Lords on the 'Affair at Terceira', in *Parl. Deb.*, 23 (23 March 1830), c. 739.
87. Ibid., c. 744.
88. Aberdeen, Speech in the House of Lords on the 'Affair at Terceira', in *Parl. Deb.*, 23 (23 March 1830), c. 745.
89. Ibid.
90. Ibid., c. 751.

In a wide-ranging and passionate speech – one of the longest in the debate – Holland insisted that both Clanricarde and Aberdeen had missed the crucial point; recent actions had called into question the 'strict and austere adherence to the terms of our conventions with other countries, and a most unbounded respect for the opinion of the people in them'.[91] Rather than promoting peace, as they should have done, the ministers had promoted 'a pusillanimous war' and engaged in 'a violent outrage on the people of a country most nearly and dearly connected with Great Britain'.[92] When the affairs of Portugal had been debated in 1829, Holland had not challenged the ministers' claim that a majority of the people of Portugal were in favour of Miguel. This time, however, Holland was better prepared, asking Aberdeen 'by what magic the noble Earl had taken the exact poll of the people of Portugal'.[93] The statement that 'the Government of Don Miguel was preferred to the charter accorded by Don Pedro', was a mere assumption that ministers could not substantiate.[94] As for the government's alleged impartiality and adherence to the principle of non-intervention, Holland declared, 'We acted for our enemy, and against our friend'.[95] Despite his reputation as a Francophile, Holland described himself as 'so much of the John Bull Englishman'[96] that he could not avoid worrying about the prospect of giving France 'a chance of acquiring an ascendancy over Portugal, which, if the opportunity were afforded, he would not say that it was not its duty to secure'.[97] Of course, the fall of Martignac, only a few days later, substantially diminished that danger. Holland concluded by hoping that

> a light might have broken in on the noble Duke from some quarter or other within the last two months (he hoped it had) which might perhaps show him that it would be better, he did not say to prepare for war, but to support the interests of Donna Maria with more energy, sincerity, and decision than before.[98]

Wellington's reply took the same line as Aberdeen and followed his earlier speeches on the Portuguese question. Thus the 'whole kingdom of Portugal, civil as well as military, was adverse to the party which wished to interfere with the then existing state of things',[99] while the Opposition had pronounced 'the most violent invectives against Ministers'.[100] Like Aberdeen, the prime minister insisted that 'the party in Portugal which supported the government of Don Miguel consisted of the decided friends to this country'.[101] This

91. Holland, Speech in the House of Lords on the 'Affair at Terceira', in *Parl. Deb.*, 23 (23 March 1830), c. 753.
92. Ibid., c. 754.
93. Ibid., c. 753.
94. Ibid.
95. Ibid., c. 756.
96. Ibid., c. 765.
97. Ibid.
98. Ibid., c. 766.
99. Wellington, Speech in the House of Lords on the 'Affair at Terceira', in *Parl. Deb.*, 23 (23 March 1830), c. 766.
100. Ibid., c. 766.
101. Ibid.

was the fourth time the matter had been debated, which was surely sufficient. Hence Clanicarde's motion had not been 'calculated to produce public benefit; and on this, as on former occasions, he would meet the Motion with a negative'.[102]

During the debates Clanricarde had threatened to enter a protest in the Journals of the House should his motion be rejected – in fact a predicable outcome.[103] The motion was eventually lost by 95 votes but, in any event, it was Holland rather than Clanicarde who wrote the protest, condemning the minister's conduct in forthright terms. Holland had declared in his speech that

> he had in his pocket a list of the names of four-and-twenty or thirty of these brave and noble men, and there were individuals not less distinguished for rank, wealth, and talent, than for the unflinching manner in which they had adhered to their principles.[104]

The list included Palmela, described in flattering terms, including the 'splendor of his talents', 'his conciliatory character', 'his address', 'his zeal in the service of his country', and 'the disposition which he manifested to cement the union between England and Portugal', which ' placed himself upon a level with the first diplomatists of the day, and entitled himself to our lasting gratitude'.[105] Holland also spoke favourably of Funchal and Vila Real; these men were 'the real friends of England!' and not Miguel's supporters, as Wellington pretended'.[106] When he learned of Holland's speech, Palmela's eldest son, Alexandre, hastened to write to his father: 'There was a debate in the House of Lords upon the affairs of Terceira last Tuesday; as Your Excellency will see in the newspapers Lord Holland has shown his friendship for you'.[107]

It was now believed that the British government intended to recognize Miguel as the legitimate sovereign of Portugal. On 29 March 1830, Lieven told Grey: 'The recognition of Don Miguel will take place after the Session of Parliament is over'.[108] British recognition would encourage France and Austria to follow suit. Metternich had already advised the Marquês de Maceió, the Brazilian minister at Vienna, that Austria was ready to recognize Miguel as soon as Britain did so. The United States had already recognized Miguel at the beginning of 1830, and Russia, which had previously given some tentative support to the Liberal cause, now moved towards Miguel. But now that Maria's possible marriage to Miguel had become less likely after her move to Rio de Janeiro, Aberdeen

---

102. Ibid., c. 772.
103. Clanricarde, Speech in the House of Lords on the 'Affair at Terceira', in *Parl. Deb.*, 23 (23 March 1830), cc. 752–53.
104. Holland, Speech in the House of Lords on the 'Affair at Terceira', in *Parl. Deb.*, 23 (23 March 1830), c. 756.
105. Ibid.
106. Ibid.
107. PALM, MSS Cx. 169, Mç. 3 (MIC. 5744), Alexandre de Sousa e Hosltein to his father, f. 1128 (Londres: 26 March 1830); 'Terça feira passada houve um debate na Camara dos Pares sobre os negocios da Terceira; V. Ex.ª vera pelas gazetas que Lord Holland mostrou bem a amizade que lhe tem.' (My translation).
108. Lieven 'To Earl Grey', in *Correspondence*, 1: 473 (29 March 1830).

had to find some other pretext to justify recognition of the usurper. As Lieven explained to Grey, Aberdeen decided that the essential condition for the recognition of Miguel would be 'the restitution of the confiscated property and the titles of the refugees'.[109]

The idea of persuading Miguel to proclaim a general amnesty in return for his recognition as King of Portugal had been raised in October 1829. In a dispatch to Santarém dated 16 December, Asseca alluded to Aberdeen's insistence that Miguel must grant an amnesty, adding that the broader the pardon, the better.[110] But the prince was unwilling to grant a 'broad pardon', one broad enough to include Palmela. According to the Portuguese government, Miguel's refusal to grant a general amnesty was justified in that the beneficiaries of the proposed amnesty – especially Palmela – could endanger the safety of the Kingdom and bring new 'catastrophes even more regrettable than those of the last revolution'.[111] While the Portuguese ministers honestly feared Palmela, their refusal was probably motivated by a desire for revenge. Although recent historians like Joel Serrão attribute the evils of Miguel's regime to the ministers rather than to the infante himself, he was never a generous or kindly man.

On 28 January 1830, while Miguel still hesitated, Aberdeen declared: 'if you don't want to grant it, then don't do it, but, we repeat, that would be a way to hasten recognition'.[112] Negotiations proceeded throughout the following months though little progress was made. Aberdeen was forced to declare emphatically that 'the proposed Amnesty is absolutely essential so that the King may be Recognised'.[113] Spain and France also pressed for a general amnesty but achieved no more. After six months of fruitless discussions, the Spanish proposal, conveyed to the Portuguese government by the Conde de Montalegre, was rejected for containing 'shameful terms and strange to all of the niceties of diplomatic transactions'.[114] Through the marquis de Ballune, France presented a similar request as late as 21 July 1830 – but with no better result.

As negotiations with Miguel were still ongoing when the British Parliament was opened on 2 November 1830, the government could not announce the reestablishment of diplomatic relations with Portugal – as Wellington had wished. Hence, the king's speech was vague though perhaps naïvely optimistic or even misleading about relations with Portugal:

109. Ibid., 1: 376 (7 December 1829).

110. The Visconde de Asseca 'Para o Visconde de Santarem', in *Correspondencia*, 3: 57(16 December 1829); the same to the same, ibid., 3: 82 (2 January 1829).

111. The Visconde de Santarém 'Para o Conde da Figueira', ibid., 3:164 (15 April 1830); 'catástrofes ainda mais lamentáveis do que as da ultima revolução.' (My translation).

112. Aberdeen, quoted by Asseca in Santarém's *Correspondencia*, 3: 102 (28 January 1830); 'se não a quiserem dar a não dêem, mas, repetimos, que seria hum meio de adiantar o Reconhecimento'. (My translation).

113. 'Do Visconde d'Asseca para o Visconde de Santarem', in *Correspondencia*, 3: 152 (25 March 1830); 'que era absolutamente precisa a medida da Amnistia como se tinha proposto, para que El-Rey podesse ser Reconhecido'. (My translation).

114. 'Do Visconde de Santarem para El-Rei D. Miguel I', ibid., 3: 121 (16 February 1830); 'termos tão indecorosos, e alheios de todas as formas mais treviaes das transacções diplomáticas'. (My translation).

> I have not yet accredited my Ambassador to the Court of Lisbon; but the Portuguese Government having determined to perform a great act of justice and humanity by the grant of a general amnesty, I think that the time may shortly arrive when the interests of my subjects will demand a renewal of those relations which had so long existed between the countries.[115]

Of course the whole point was that the Portuguese government had not granted a general amnesty and was interested only in a more limited measure, which did not go anywhere near as far as the British government wished. Grey, who had awakened from his long melancholy after his 66th birthday to adopt a more active attitude in British politics, regretted His Majesty's – that is, Wellington's – declaration about the likely recognition of Miguel, which he did not think 'consistent with a statesmanlike view of our relations with that country'.[116] Grey could not understand how the government could announce a recognition based on a hypothetical amnesty promised by a prince of whose private character he did not wish to speak there. Predictably, Grey seized the opportunity to accuse the government of systematically violating the principle of non-interference so earnestly advocated by the ministers.

Despite Roebuck's assertion that Grey was still undecided on the issue – based on the rhetorical admission that he was 'not now prepared to say whether the Government that has been for some time established in Portugal be or not a proper one, or whether the period may not now be arrived for recognizing it'[117] – a letter to Lieven dated 10 December 1829, clearly shows otherwise:

> What right have we to interfere with respect to the conduct of the King of Portugal towards his own subjects? Do we mean not only to stipulate for, but to guarantee the restoration of, the rights and titles of the exiles? If not, what do we prepare for ourselves but fresh insult? Such an interference would not be less objectionable in principle than an interference to support the title of Donna Maria; and I certainly should have preferred that which would have been at once more honourable and more effectual.[118]

Wellington's answer to Grey was an upgraded version of the doctrine of non-interference, which had now evolved into a wider perception of the proper nature of British neutrality towards Portugal:

> I do not, however, mean to say that we shall not be obliged to interfere by remonstrance – by advice – by our influence – by every means in our power short of war, in order to prevent a recurrence of such transactions as have before taken place, or any violation of that amnesty.[119]

This argument still pointed to the recognition of Miguel's sovereignty in a near future, whatever the nature of the promised amnesty. According to Magalhães, based

115. 'Parliamentary Intelligence: House of Lords, Tuesday, Nov. 2. The King's Speech at the Opening of the Session', *The Times*, 3 November 1830, 3.
116. Ibid.
117. Grey, Address upon 'His Majesty's Speech' (2 November 1830), *The Mirror of Parliament*, 15.
118. Earl Grey to Princess Leaven, in *Correspondence*, 1: 385 (10 December 1829).
119. Grey, Address upon 'His Majesty's Speech' (2 November 1830), *The Mirror of Parliament*, 15.

on a dispatch from José Balbino de Araújo,[120] Chargé d'Affaires to London, dated 24 November 1830, Miguel's recognition by the British government had already been on its way to Lisbon but providential strong winds prevented the dispatch from reaching its destination, and it had returned to Plymouth after Wellington's resignation.[121] Although Araújo did not give a date for the packet's departure from England, it is possible that the British government really had intended to announce its recognition of Miguel at the opening of the Parliament, a plan frustrated only by adverse weather conditions. If Wellington had remained prime minister a while longer, Portuguese history might have been entirely different. In the event, a change of ministry as to mark the beginning of a new and in some respects happier phase in Anglo-Portuguese relations.

120. José Balbino de Barbosa Araújo (1787–1846), later 1st Visconde de Telheiras.

121. José Balbino Barbosa de Araújo, quoted in Félix Magalhães, *Apontamentos para a historia diplomatica de Portugal: desde 1826 em que falleceu o Imperador e Rei D. João VI até 1834 em que se completou a restauração da Coroa da Rainha D. Maria II usurpada em 1828 por seu tio o Infante D. Miguel* (Lisboa: Imprensa de J. G. de Sousa Neves, 1871), 73.

Chapter Nine

THE RETURN OF THE WHIGS

Beginning reform is beginning revolution.[*]

The British government's clumsy handling of the Portuguese question and its unconvincing and ineffective attempts to justify its conduct certainly led to a decline in the reputation of Wellington's ministry, especially in Liberal circles on the Continent. Henry Knight, a frequent visitor to Paris, regretted that 'England was no longer the object of universal approbation. She was no longer considered as the enlightened advocate of liberal principles abroad'.[1] This negative image was due, in a great measure, to Palmela's manipulation of press treatment of the Terceira affair. Internally, however, Wellington still enjoyed the support of a substantial number of British politicians. Apart from occasional outbursts of radicalism – for example on 30 June 1830 when Brougham denounced the ministers as Wellington's 'flatterers, his mean, fawning parasites', the duke encountered more criticism abroad than at home.[2] This probably explains why Lord Holland, although critical of the ministry's foreign policies, was less hostile in matters of domestic policies.

Another political mistake generally attributed to Wellington was the alleged interference of the British government in French internal affairs. According to some versions, Wellington was involved in an intrigue whereby Charles X was persuaded to replace Martignac by Polignac as President of Ministers. Charles's speech at the opening of the French Chambers on 2 March 1830 seemed like a declaration of war on the opposition, when he warned that any attempt to obstruct his government would be defeated by his strong commitment to the maintenance of public order. Charles's threats materialized a few days later, when, on 19 March, the Chamber of Deputies was summarily prorogued to 1 September. This measure was followed by its dissolution on 16 May and the electoral colleges summoned for 23 June and 5 July to elect a new Parliament. But the French Liberals were determined to thwart the king and Polignac. As Morgan observed, 'The guard of resistance was simultaneously mounted; and the press, the free press, took the initiative, and formed the videttes of the great force of public opinion.'[3] As a consequence,

---

* Wellington, quoted in *The Journals of Mrs. Arbuthnot, 1820–1832.* 2 vols (London: Macmillan, 1950), 2: 399.

1. Henry Gally Knight, *A Letter Addressed to the Earl of Aberdeen, Secretary of State for Foreign Affairs.* 2nd edn (London: James Ridgway, 1829), 7.
2. 'House of Commons, Wednesday, June 30', *The Times*, 1 July 1820, 3.
3. Morgan, *France in 1829–30*, 2: 525.

while the opposition obtained a comfortable majority of more than a hundred votes, the government faced an acute dilemma.

Rather than accept the nation's verdict, Charles, imagining that his life was endangered by some impending coup, decided on extreme measures and effectively tore up the Charter granted by Louis XVIII in 1814. On 25 July, the king summoned his ministers to St Cloud to decree the indefinite suspension of freedom of the press, the dissolution of the Chamber of Deputies, the restriction of the franchise and the convocation of new elections for 6 and 18 September. Charles's Ordinances were published the next day in the *Moniteur* and left France in a state of shock. When journalists protested, the printing presses of several newspapers were seized, including the *Journal des débats*, which did not appear for the next two days. About 600 barricades were raised in Paris and the protesters were soon joined by increasing numbers of the National Guard and other troops. In the early hours of 31 July, when the rioters threatened to attack the royal palace, Charles left for Versailles with his family and from thence to Rambouillet. On 2 August, he abdicated in favour of his nine-year-old grandson, Henri, duc de Bordeaux, but Parliament refused to accept Bordeaux and proclaimed Louis Philippe, Charles's second cousin, King of France on 9 August. On 16 August, accompanied by his family, Charles embarked for England from Cherbourg on the American vessels *Great Britain* and *Charles Carroll*, arriving off Portsmouth on the following day.

While France changed its kings, England was preparing for an almost equally dramatic change, one based on the reform of Parliament and in sum perhaps amounting to a 'Whig revolution'.[4] As early as 5 June 1830, Metternich observed to Apponyi: 'What a confusion at Paris and London! Looking on from a distance, one would say they were a couple of mad-houses.'[5] The English public received news of developments in France with mixed feelings while the response of leading figures was equally varied and sometimes unexpected. Memories of the early 1790s were still fresh, and there were fears that terror and war would return. Concerns rose when, early in October 1830, a wave of riots similar to those that had terrorized the English countryside 20 years earlier, broke out in Kent with an 'organised system of stack-burning and machine-breaking'.[6] The 'Captain Swing Riots', as they were known, were ostensibly directed against the introduction of threshing machines with the resulting loss of employment for agricultural labourers but probably reflected more widespread discontent in rural areas at a time of economic difficulty. Despite the author's denials, it seems likely that some of the rioters drew inspiration from William Cobbett's *Rural Rides*. The riots subsequently spread to other parts of England, including Sussex, Hampshire, Wiltshire, Berkshire, Oxfordshire, Buckinghamshire, Huntingdon and Northamptonshire. During the riots Holland's own Wiltshire properties were so badly damaged that, according to Mitchell, he found it hard to give his son any allowance in 1832.[7] Yet, even these developments were not sufficient

4. Clarke, *British Diplomacy*, [184].
5. Metternich to Apponyi, *Memoirs*, 5: 4–5 (5 June 1820).
6. William Carpenter, 'A Monitory Letter to Sir Robert Peel: Outrages in Kent', in *Political Letters and Pamphlets*… (London: William Carpenter, 1830–31), 9–10 (15 October 1830).
7. Mitchell, *Holland House*, 90.

to shaken Holland's strong convictions; in a letter to Palmela, his eldest son Alexandre explained that 'at Holland House they gave the triumph of the Liberals for certain and think that it will have a great influence in our affairs'.[8]

An exhausting Parliamentary session marked by a number of political blunders had left Wellington increasingly isolated and, as Roebuck observed, when 'He looked wistfully to his former friends [...] they were no longer friendly or confiding'.[9] But if Wellington's ministry still had any chances of survival, these vanished after George IV's death on 26 June 1830. George IV was succeeded by William IV – clearly more sympathetic to the Whigs and related to the Hollands.[10] Wellington's unrealistic hopes that 'things would wear a new face in the new Parliament', were disappointed after the loss of the clear majority he had hitherto enjoyed in Parliament.[11] In a desperate attempt to improve matters, Wellington tried overtures to the Canningites and invited Palmerston to take office. But Palmerston replied he would not enter the Cabinet unless Grey and Lansdowne joined him, a condition the duke considered unacceptable.

Earlier hopes that Wellington might be persuaded to introduce a moderate electoral reform vanished on 2 November at the opening of the new Parliament. While promising strong measures to deal with the rural riots, the king's speech (Wellington's) said nothing about Parliamentary reform. During the subsequent debates, Wellington committed his last and greatest political error as prime minister, when he dismissed all notion of reform, stating that 'the legislature and the system of representation possessed the full and entire confidence of the country'.[12] Although the Whigs would have been glad to leave Wellington to deal with the complicated business of drawing up and passing a reform bill, they could not simply pretend that the issue did not exist. But Parliamentary reform did not provide the *coup de grâce* to Wellington's premiership – as might have been expected – but rather the end came with Sir Henry Parnell's motion on the Civil List. The motion was debated on 15 November and the government was defeated by a majority of 29. The next morning Wellington used this defeat as a pretext to tender his resignation, thus avoiding discussion on the Parliamentary reform he so much detested and scheduled for that day.

William IV gave Grey carte-blanche to form a cabinet. Grey constructed a predominantly Whig ministry, somewhat reminiscent of 'All the Talents' of 1806.[13] Holland was

8. PALM, MSS Cx. 169, Mç. 3 (MIC. 5744), Alexandre de Sousa e Holstein to his father, f. 1171 (London: 2 August 1830); 'em Holland House davão por certo o triumpho dos liberaes e julgão que hade ter grande influencia nos nossos negocios.' (My translation).
9. Arthur Roebuck, *History of the Whig Ministry of 1830, to the Passing of the Reform Bill.* 2 vols (London: J. W. Parker, 1852), 1: 130.
10. Charles Richard Fox, Lady and Lord Holland's natural son born before their marriage, married in 1824 to Lady Mary Fitz Clarence, a daughter of William IV by his mistress Dorothy Jordan. This relation may explain why William was more sympathetic to the Whigs.
11. Henry Brougham, *The Result of the General Election: or, What Has the Duke of Wellington Gained by the Dissolution?* 4th edn (London: James Ridgway, 1830), 5.
12. Wellington, Speech upon 'Parliamentary Intelligence: House of Lords, Tuesday, Nov. 2. Speech upon the King's Speech at the Opening of the Session', *The Times*, 3 November 1830, 4.
13. Grey's Cabinet included Lansdowne, Holland's archrival (Lord President of Council), Althorp, an old Aristocratic Whig (Chancellor of the Exchequer and Leader of the Commons), the

offered the Duchy Lancaster, on the face of it a relatively insignificant post for Grey's closest friend and supporter, who was also the nephew of Charles James Fox. Had it not been for Holland's frequent attacks of gout, which left him incapacitated for long periods – 'eleven months out of twelve', according to Durham – he would probably have been Grey's first choice for the foreign office.[14] The issue was certainly discussed in private between the two friends and it was probably Holland who requested a comparatively lowly position on account of his poor health. But the fact that Holland did not go to the foreign office does not mean that he was inactive in foreign policy matters. There were times when it seemed there were two rival foreign secretaries, Holland and Palmerston, a rivalry especially sharp in virtually everything that concerned Portugal.

In the early days of February 1830, Tomás Assis de Mascarenhas had arrived in England with fresh instructions from Pedro about Portugal.[15] Mascarenhas left Rio de Janeiro on 20 December 1829 invested with full powers to act on behalf of Queen D. Maria II. In particular, he brought instructions to Palmela to transfer the triumvirate to Terceira as quickly as possible, together with funds to effect this. Palmela and Guerreiro left London for Plymouth on 27 February 1830 and on 3 March embarked for the Azores on *The Jack of the Lantern*. Every effort was made to keep these plans secret – mainly in order to avoid the attentions of British creditors, especially John Maberly, a London banker who had advanced considerable sums to Palmela against monies due from Brazil. Palmela entrusted his son, Alexandre, with the sale of his house, furniture, cutlery and his wife's jewellery to pay his private debts, but the loans taken to support the refugees and the government of Terceira remained unpaid.[16] On 15 March, after successfully avoiding Miguel's fleet, the two men landed safely at Angra and, on the following day, reinstated the regency.[17] In the absence of the Marquês de Valença, the third member of the triumvirate, Vila Flor occupied the post in an interim capacity, while Luís Mouzinho de Albuquerque was appointed secretary.[18]

The Whigs' accession to government was warmly welcomed by the Portuguese Liberals. On 24 November, Abreu Lima triumphantly informed Palmela of the fall

moderate Whigs, Graham (Admiralty) and Morpeth (Minister without Portfolio), the progressive Whigs, Brougham (Lord Chancellor) and Durham, also known as 'Radical Jack' (Lord Privy Seal), the Huskissonians or Canningites, Melbourne (Home Secretary), Palmerston (Foreign Secretary), Goderich (War and Colonies) and Charles Grant (President of the Board of Control), and the ultra-Tory Duke of Richmond (Postmaster-General).

14. Lord Durham to his wife, in *Life and Letters of the First Earl of Durham*. 2 vols (London: Longmans, Green, 1906), 1: 216.
15. Tomás de Assis de Mascarenhas (1771–1833), Portuguese officer and diplomat. Supported Miguel in 1828, but when the infante adhered to Absolutism emigrated to Brazil to serve under Pedro.
16. PALM, MSS Cx. 169, Mç. 3 (MIC. 5744), Alexandre de Sousa e Holstein to his father, ff. 1115–22 (London: 15 March 1830); Palmela, *Memórias*, p. 220.
17. *Chronica da Terceira*, 14 April 1830, 1–2.
18. Luís da Silva Mouzinho de Albuquerque (1792–1846), Portuguese army officer, engineer, poet, scientist and politician, son of João Pedro Mouzinho de Albuquerque (1736–1802) and Luísa da Silva Gutiérrez de Ataíde.

of Wellington's ministry and its replacement by a cabinet 'in which many of Your Excellency's private friends and supporters of our cause are included'.[19] In his reply, dated 22 December, Mouzinho de Albuquerque acknowledged that the membership of the new Ministry was 'more favourable than we could possibly expect [...] and Lord Palmerston and Lord Holland must be considered as our most valuable supporters'.[20] But the initial hopes were dashed when José Balbino de Araújo – the Chargé d'Affaires left by Palmela – had his first meeting with Palmerston. The new foreign secretary declined to include any acknowledgement of the regency in the King's Speech at the opening of Parliament, and insisted that Britain would have to recognize Miguel if he agreed to grant an amnesty. In December 1830, however, Luís de Abreu Lima, the regency's diplomatic agent at The Hague, arrived in London to replace José Balbino de Araújo as minister plenipotentiary. Lima was more successful than his predecessor, obtaining from Palmerston a promise that Miguel would not be recognized, at least not in the immediate future, and an assurance that all members of the Cabinet were sympathetic to Maria's cause. Yet, as Palmerston noted, swift action was required, since the passage of time would confer a degree of legitimacy on the usurpation. The most pressing task was to capture the other islands of the Azores, particularly São Miguel – which had the largest population and was eventually taken by Liberal forces on 2 August 1831.

In Paris, despite the apparently liberal character of the new regime, Francisco de Almeida was at first no more successful than Araújo in London. In an interview with Molé, Louis Philippe's foreign minister, Almeida was told that France could only recognize de facto governments.[21] At least, Molé's argument was consistent with the way his master had become king – that is by revolutionary means. Following the appointment of Laffitte's ministry on 2 November 1830 and Molé's replacement by Sébastiani, French policy towards the Portuguese Liberals changed, with Sébastiani declaring that Portugal was a British affair and that France would follow whatever line the British government decided to take.

Meanwhile, on the night of 7 April 1831, in a replica of the July revolution, Pedro had been forced to abdicate the Brazilian throne in favour of his son, D. Pedro II. The emperor, for whom Portugal was barely more than a memory, seems to have regarded his native country with something approaching contempt. He had left Lisbon for Rio de Janeiro in 1807, aged nine, and had grown up in Brazil, which he obviously loved more than Portugal. The readiness with which he had proclaimed the independence of Brazil in 1822 and abdicated his rights to the Portuguese Crown to his daughter in

19. 'Luiz Antonio de Abreu Lima (Conde da Carreira) ao Marquez de Palmella', in *Despachos*, 4: 673 (24 November 1830); 'em que entram os particulares amigos de V. Ex.ª e os defensores da nossa causa.' (My translation).

20. 'Da Regencia da Terceira para Luiz Antonio d'Abreu Lima', in *Correspondencia official de Luiz António de Abreu e Lima, actualmente Conde da Carreira com o Duque de Palmela: regencia da Terceira e governo do Porto de 1828 a 1835* (Lisboa: Imprensa Nacional, 1871), 264 (22 December 1830); 'mais favoravel que podiamos esperar [...] e devendo especialmente Lord Palmerston e Lord Holland ser classificados como os nossos mais vailosos defensores.' (My translation).

21. Louis-Mathieu Molé (1781–1855), comte Molé, French statesman, prime minister (6 September 1836–31 March 1839).

1826 suggests a lack of interest in Portugal. But the Brazilians had now rejected Pedro. Though regarded as a Liberal in Europe, in Brazil he was seen as an absolutist-inclined authoritarian and this reputation gradually undermined the popularity he gained at the time of independence. As Palmela later admitted, Pedro 'revealed from time to time reminiscences or inclination for absolute power, contrasting with his Liberal principles and pretensions'.[22]

Rejected in Brazil, the ex-emperor determined to leave for Europe to assist his daughter's cause, or – according to some versions – to recover the crown of Portugal for himself. Following his abdication, Pedro 'voluntarily' embarked with his wife and daughter aboard H.M.S. *Warspite*, where they remained until 12 April. Fearing that the vessel might be attacked by the mob, Admiral Baker transferred Pedro and his entourage to H.M.S. *Volage* frigate under Lord Colchester. The next morning the *Volage* sailed for Europe, followed by the French frigate *Le Seine* carrying Maria da Glória and the Loulés. On 30 May, Pedro arrived off the Faial, Azores, and from thence sailed to Falmouth, where the *Volage* put in for a few hours on 7 June before resuming its journey to France. Although the ex-emperor had at first planned to live in England he changed his mind 'from a consideration of the great expense of living in this country compared with the continent'.[23] On 12 June, Pedro and his wife landed at Cherbourg, where they were welcomed with the 21-gun salute due to reigning monarchs.

According to *The Times*, 'Ever since the Emperor Don Pedro arrived in France, Louis Philip and his Government have omitted no opportunity of showing him the most delicate attentions', a kindness later extended to Maria da Glória.[24] The French king had prepared the Château of Saint-Germain-en-Laye – ironically the residence of James II of England in his final years – to receive Pedro and his family, but the ex-emperor preferred to remain at Cherbourg. Liberato claimed that Louis Philippe planned to marry one of his sons to the young queen and proposed to recognize her rights if Pedro agreed to let her live in Paris. Louis Philippe's plan was obviously to gain influence over Portugal by placing Prince Louis Charles on the Portuguese throne.[25] On 30 July 1831, the king's sister, Adélaïde d'Orléans, admitted to Prince Talleyrand, once more French minister in London, that 'I should have liked him [Pedro] to leave his wife, and his daughter, the Queen, here with us; and if he consulted his real interests, after paying his visit to England, he would return here with her; but I fear that he has no settled plans'.[26] Pedro, accused by Liberato of seeking to regain the Portuguese throne for

22. Palmela, *Memórias*, 248; 'apresentava de quando em quando reminiscências ou veleidades de poder absoluto, que formavam contraste com os seus princípios e pretensões liberais.' (My translation).
23. 'Money Market and City Intelligence', *The Times*, 13 June 1831, 4.
24. 'The Queen of Portugal in France', *The Times*, 23 July 1831, 5.
25. Louis Charles Philippe Raphaël d'Orléans (1814–1896), duc de Nemours, Louis Philippe's second son.
26. 'Madame Adélaïde d'Orléans to the Prince de Talleyrand', in *Memoirs of the Prince de Talleyrand*, edited by The Duc de Broglie. 5 vols (London: Griffith Farran Okeden and Welsh, 1891–92) 4: 167 (Paris, 30 July 1831).

himself, ignored Louis Philippe's offer.[27] But although Liberato's memoirs are a valuable source, his claims must be treated with caution. Soriano, more scrupulous, believed that some of Liberato's assertions were simply products of his own imagination or cheap anti-Palmela propaganda.[28]

Despite all the honours and proofs of friendship received while in France, Pedro appreciated that really decisive support could be procured only on the other side of the Channel. Leaving his wife at Cherbourg, the ex-emperor paid a short visit to England to seek British assistance for his daughter's cause. Pedro travelled on 21 June 1831 accompanied by his old friends Francisco Gomes da Silva and the Marquês de Resende, who had joined him at Cherbourg. When he arrived in London on 26 June, Pedro took up residence at the Clarendon Hotel under the name of Duque de Bragança. Pedro was fascinated by the sparkling life he found in London, certainly very different from that of his former court in Rio. On 30 June, he was invited to a musical party and a magnificent ball at St James and, on 1 July, William IV gave a state dinner in his honour. Guests included ambassadors and Cabinet members, among them Earl Grey and Lord Holland. On 2 July, Pedro went to *Othello* at the Italian Opera House with Resende, Gomes da Silva, João da Rocha Pinto and Major Henry Webster, Lady Holland's second son, who had been commissioned by the government to escort the ex-emperor.[29] Two days later, Pedro was invited to a grand entertainment given by Prince Leopold at Marlborough House, attended by the royal family and 'a very numerous musical party'.[30] On 9 July, Pedro was at the Guildhall when the Lord Mayor presented the freedom of the city to Lord John Russell and was loudly cheered when he attended the subsequent reception at the Mansion House.

Yet compared to his enthusiastic reception in France, there were times in England when Pedro might have felt neglected, although it is well to remember that the Reform Crisis was engrossing the attention of both court and ministry at this time. Pedro was cordially received by Palmerston on 27 but rather indifferently by the king on the afternoon of 29 June 1831. Grey, who had scheduled an interview with Pedro for the 20th, admitted in a letter to Princess Lieven on 27 June that 'I have not seen Don Pedro',[31] and again, two days later, that 'Don Pedro had his audience [with the king], but I did not see him'.[32] Finally, on 1 July, Grey told the princess, 'I am going, notwithstanding, to dine at St James's, at a dinner given to Don Pedro.'[33] Webster, effectively Pedro's 'minder', went

27. Carvalho, *Memorias da Vida de José Liberato Freire de Carvalho* (Lisboa: Typografia de José Baptista Morando, 1855), 336.
28. Soriano, *HGC*, 3.ª época, t. III, pt. 2 [15]: 95.
29. Sir Henry Vassall Webster (1793–1847), British officer, second son of Sir Godfrey Webster and his wife Elizabeth Vassall (afterwards Lady Holland). Henry Webster entered the army in 1810 to serve in the Peninsular War. In 1831, he was promoted to lieutenant-colonel and commissioned to escort D. Pedro during his stay in England. His service earned him the Portuguese Knighthood of Tower and Sword and, in 1838, on Palmela's recommendation, the Military Order of São Bento de Avis.
30. 'Court Circular', *The Times*, 6 July 1831, 5.
31. Grey to Lieven, in *Correspondence*, 2: 250 (27 June 1831).
32. Ibid., 2: 251 (29 June 1831).
33. Ibid., 2: 255 (1 July 1831).

so far as to protest to Lord Holland 'with truth, but perhaps with more asperity than is prudent or justified, that our indifference to Pedro forms a strong contrast to the cordiality of the French Govt'.[34]

This somewhat unsatisfactory story and the undoubted fact that Pedro left without securing financial support has led some historians to see the mission as a failure. However, analysis of Abreu Lima's dispatches to the Terceira Regency and of Holland's diaries suggests that more had been achieved than was immediately apparent. Thus Lima reported to Terceira on 6 July, 'The Emperor was very happy with the declarations and hints of the two ministers [Holland and Palmerston], and the good reception and excellent support he has found at Court'.[35] Holland's efforts certainly contributed to Pedro's perception of success. In the face of the initial coldness of the British ministers, Holland did much to break the ice and to facilitate discussion and communication. In his political diaries, Holland observed that 'Grey as well as Palmerston spoke handsomely of Don Pedro and more favorably of his character and conduct than from previous representation they had apprehended he deserved'.[36]

During his meeting with William IV on 29 June, Pedro listed the requests he hoped His Britannic Majesty would not deny. In a most informal way, Pedro declared that

> he did not require direct and material support to overthrow the usurper from the throne, but only moral support; and that England had now a good opportunity to offer such a mighty help, bringing the Queen from Cherbourg to London aboard British war vessels and taking her to the Palace of His Britannic Majesty, to the very room of the Queen Adelaide, where she would stay only while the Emperor was on his way to Munich to leave the Empress, who will have a better stay there. In short, His Imperial Majesty declared that he asked or wanted nothing for himself, but that in the quality of Father and Tutor he would do all the efforts to place his August Daughter in the throne belonging to her.[37]

A final request, which Pedro decided to leave to advisers to deal with, was for a cash advance on the security of his jewels. The subject was privately and separately discussed

34. Henry Richard Vassall, 3rd Baron of Holland, *The Holland House Diaries 1831–1840: The Diary of Henry Richard Vassall Fox, Third Lord Holland, with Extracts from the Diary of Dr. John Allen* (London: Routledge & Kegan Paul, 1977), 23 (Wednesday, 3 August [1831]).
35. 'De Luiz Antonio d'Abreu Lima para a Regencia da Terceira', in *Correspondencia official*, 446 (London: 6 July 1831); 'O Imperador ficou contentissimo com as declarações e insinuações dos dois ministros britanicos, e a boa recepção, e o optimo acolhimento que encontra n'esta corte'. (My translation).
36. Holland, *The Holland House Diaries*, 4 (15 July [1831]).
37. 'De Luiz Antonio d'Abreu Lima para a Regencia da Terceira', in *Correspondencia official*, 435 (London: 2 July 1831); 'que não precisava de apoio directo e material para derribar o usurpador do throno, mas sómente de apoio moral, e que a Inglaterra tinha agora boa occasião de prestar esse poderoso auxilio, mandando-se vir a Rainha de Cherburgo para Londres em vasos de guerra inglezes, e indo Sua Magestade hospedar-se no Palacio de Sua Magestade Britanica, e no quarto mesmo da Rainha Adelaide, onde ficaria sómente emquanto o Imperador fosse a Munich levar a Imperatriz, que ali deve ter o seu bom successo. Em fim Sua Magestade Imperial declarou que já agora nada queria nem pretendia para si, mas que na sua qualidade

between Resende and Lords Holland and Palmerston, but the request fell through because the required guarantee could not be obtained. According to Holland,

> He [Pedro] was tolerably well satisfied with the answers to his requests, and understood or affected to understand the difficulty, arising from the strict administration of our finnances and the controul of the House of Commons, of our advancing him so small a sum as £15,000 on his jewels.[38]

Alternatively, Holland suggested that Resende write an official letter listing Pedro's needs, including a request for a loan to support the queen. Holland further advised Resende that the letter be written with great care so that the Tories would have no excuse to attack the arrangement in Parliament. Resende then suggested that Mackintosh should write a draft of the letter, a suggestion that seemed to please Holland. In Holland's view the eventual official response to Pedro's request was 'in the main favorable and civil', in that it asserted that the British government wished Maria's cause well.[39] However, the request to lodge the young queen in the royal palace could not be granted owing to the fact that Catholic services were prohibited there. As for the cash advance, nothing could be done without the approval of Parliament – and that made the request impolitic and even unwise. According to Magalhães, refusal to grant Pedro's requests had been due to the opposition of both Brougham and Althorp.[40]

Pedro was particularly distressed with the fact that the ministers were 'styling his daughter La Reine Donna Maria, instead of La Reine de Portugal', which as he explained to Holland seemed puzzling since Wellington himself had allowed the title.[41] Indeed, on the face of it, the Whigs' accession to office had not helped Maria's cause. Holland believed that Pedro should immediately request British recognition of the Terceira Regency as a de facto government. Such a recognition would not mean that the British government would have to break off all contact with Miguel – for the simple reason that Britain could recognize any government she pleased. Resende agreed to take Holland's advice though seeking an assurance that Britain would not use this recognition as a pretext to recognize Miguel. After Palmela's negative experience with Wellington and Aberdeen, the Portuguese agents were understandably suspicious about the real intentions of the British Cabinet. However, as Abreu Lima observed: 'The English Ministry has given us – especially after the Emperor's arrival – enough proofs of their good intentions and good will in our favour, so that we may not suspect that Lord Holland wants to deceive us with his referred to suggestion.'[42]

---

de Pae e Tutor, faria todos os esforços para collocar sua Augusta Filha no throno que lhe pertencia.' (My translation).

38. Holland, *The Holland House Diaries*, 8 (20 July [1831]).
39. Ibid., 4 (15 July [1831]).
40. Magalhães, *Apontamentos*, 79.
41. Holland, *The Holland House Diaries*, 8 (20 July [1831]).
42. 'De Luiz Antonio d'Abreu Lima para a Regencia da Terceira', in *Correspondencia official*, 445 (London: 6 July 1831); 'O Ministerio Inglez tem-nos dado, sobre tudo depois da chagada do Imperador, sobejas provas da sua boa fé, e dos seus bons desejos a nosso favour, para podermos

Palmerston advised Granville, British Ambassador in Paris: 'As to Don Pedro, we have rather chosen to know nothing of his plans; but he makes no secret of his determination to use every effort to reinstate Donna Maria on the throne of Portugal.'[43] Holland was also particularly worried about any suggestion of a 'hostile aggression from our coasts', arguing that the official knowledge of such a plan 'might be embarrassing and impose upon us the necessity of interference in a direction very different from our natural interests and wishes'.[44] On 15 July, while Grey was discussing 'foolish and malevolent questions about Belgium and Prince Leopold', with Lord Londonderry, Holland had a meeting with the ex-emperor in an adjoining room. According to Holland, Pedro

> was in the first instance anxious to have a speedy answer to the requests he had made on the manner of receiving his daughter on her arrival here and, secondly, disposed to communicate to me more of his views and schemes against Don Miguel's government than I deemed it prudent to hear, especially as he was about to consult me on the propriety of asking the Government how far they would assist, sanction, prompte, or connive at them. [...] Lord P[almerston] communicated to me the letters of our King on the project of the answer to be given to Don Pedro 5 requests, which were in the main favorable and civil.[45]

Holland was so concerned that on his return home after his meeting with the Duque de Bragança that he hastened to write to Pedro (in French)' dissuading him from the consultation he had projected'.[46] It is not certain whether Holland gave a full, abbreviated or indeed any account of these conversations to Palmerston. Lima's assertion that 'Lord Palmerston expressed himself in the same direction of Lord Holland, but did not mention the recognition of the Regency', implies that Holland was conducting his own Portuguese policy.[47] It was perhaps this kind of behaviour that Mitchell had in mind when suggesting that 'Palmerston, as Foreign Secretary, was endlessly forced to battle with a Holland House mafia both within the Cabinet and in Europe at large'.[48]

Now that things seem to be going in the right direction with the British government, Pedro left for the Continent to meet his wife and daughter and to try to obtain support from Louis Philippe. Maria had landed at Brest on 14 July, where she had been enthusiastically received by the authorities and the local population. Pedro called at Holland House in the morning of 20 July, to invite Lord Holland to dinner on the following

suspeitar que elle nos queira enganar com a insinuação referida de Lord Holland.' (My translation).

43. Palmerston, 'To the Right Hon. Viscount Granville', in *The Life of Henry John Temple, Viscount Palmerston: with Selections from his Diaries and Correspondence*. 3 vols (London: Richard Bentley, 1870–74), 2: 94 (25 July 1831).
44. Holland, *The Holland House Diaries*, 4 (15 July [1831]).
45. Ibid.
46. Ibid.
47. 'De Luiz Antonio d'Abreu Lima para a Regencia da Terceira', in *Correspondencia official*, 445 (London: 6 July 1831); 'Lord Palmerston exprimiu-se no mesmo sentido que Lord Holland, mas não tocou no reconhecimento da Regencia.' (My translation).
48. Mitchell, *Holland House*, [269].

Sunday (24 July), just before his departure. Holland was, however, obliged to decline the honour 'being invited or rather commanded with all my *Etonian* colleagues to Windsor on that day'.[49] Holland found Pedro

> good humoured and easy, but his countenance was clouded and he spoke with some bitterness when Lady Holland inadvertently asked what become of the Marquis de Barbacena, who formerly conducted the little Queen here. Il est a Rio et c'est pour cela que je suis ici.[50]

On 22 July, Pedro dined at the French Embassy with Holland and Grey, the ministers of Austria, Prussia, and Bavaria, several Ladies and the Chancellor. According to Holland, 'Don Pedro highly satisfied with his reception at Windsor, not a little gratified at his daughter being treated as a Queen in France.'[51] At dinner, Talleyrand advised Pedro to take advantage of Louis Philippe's good will and suggested that the first anniversary of the July revolution would be a good occasion to address the king. According to the French minister, 'Dom Pedro had the greatest wish to go to Paris. But he finds in his wife's name a drawback to doing so, and he does not want to cause any trouble.'[52]

Pedro left for France on 24 July 1831, accompanied by Henry Webster, and arrived just in time for the celebrations marking the first anniversary of 'the glorious week', which had raised the duc d'Orléans to the French throne. According to Holland, Pedro planned to stay in France just for a few days and 'expects to return by Wednesday next'.[53] Pedro embarked at Portsmouth on the *Lightning* steamer to land at Cherbourg on 25 July, and then hurried to Paris. By 26 July, he was sitting at table with Louis Philippe and his queen, Maria Amalia of Naples and Sicily, who received him graciously. Harriet Granville wrote to Lady Carlisle: 'There we found the Dom [Pedro], the Empress and French music; very hot, but amusing from the circumstances, very much so to see the Emperor and Lafayette in a confab.'[54] The next morning, during the celebrations, Harriet Granville observed from the '*balcon* of the Hotêl Bristol *chez* Monsieur Motteux [...] Pedro with all his green feathers rode up to the Queen's *balcon*, like a tourney'.[55]

After dining with Louis Philippe on 27 July, Pedro was taken to a private chamber with Resende, Casimir Périer and Sébastiani to discuss the affairs of Portugal. After reaffirming his wish to see Pedro and his family in Paris, Louis Philippe handed over to

49. Holland, *The Holland House Diaries*, 8 (20 July [1831]); see also Palmerston, 'To the Right Hon. Viscount Granville', in *The Life of Henry John Temple*, 2: 93 (25 July 1831).
50. Holland, *The Holland House Diaries*, 8 (20 July [1831]).
51. Ibid., 12 (22 July 1831).
52. 'Le Prince de Talleyrand a Madame Adélaïde d'Orléans', in *Memoirs*, 4: 165 (London: 20 July 1831). Talleyrand is probably alluding to the fact that Amélie was a daughter of Eugène de Beauharnais and a granddaughter of Empress Josephine, wife of Napoleon Bonaparte. Although not herself a Bonaparte, Amélie might have been regarded as too close to that family to be entirely persona grata in France in the 1830s.
53. Holland, *The Holland House Diaries*, 12 (22 July 1831).
54. Harriet Granville, 'To Lady Carlisle', in *Letters of Harriet Countess Granville1810–1845*. 2 vols (London: Longmans, Green, 1894), 2: 104 (Paris, 29 July 1831).
55. Ibid., 2: 104 (Paris, 29 July 1831).

Sébastiani, who spoke for more than one hour. While arguing that the Portuguese Liberals should not expect any generosity from Britain, Sébastiani insisted that Pedro could trust France to give him all necessary support – provided only that he and his family came to live in Paris. The meeting was abruptly interrupted when, without explanation, Louis Philippe rose and left the room. The next day, the king visited Pedro's apartments accompanied by several ministers, though not Sébastiani. Louis Philippe began by insisting that Pedro should not move back to England – as he seemed inclined – but then changed the subject to the possible election of Prince August to the Belgium throne. On 29 July, after accompanying the king in the review of soldiers who had been decorated with the Grand Cross of the Legion of Honour, Pedro dined with Louis Philippe, who again tried to persuade him to stay in Paris. Despite the king's efforts, Pedro was unmoved and, the next day, took his leave of the royal family and returned to Cherbourg.

On 1 August, Pedro embarked for England with his wife, daughter and entourage aboard the *Lightning*, landing in Falmouth that night to the salute of the warships and batteries. On the next morning, the party proceeded to London and again took a suite in the Clarendon Hotel. One week later, Maria received an invitation from Queen Adelaide to visit her at St James's Palace. But rather than sending his daughter alone to the Royal Palace, as the invitation appeared to suggest, Pedro decided to accompany her and take his wife with him. To make matters worse, rather than conveying the royal visitors through the palace's main door, by some mistake or intentionally, Henry Webster led them directly to the queen's chamber, where she received the intruders with obvious coldness. William IV joined them soon afterwards, but rather than inviting the party to one of the main saloons, as it might have been expected, the king remained with his unwanted guests in the Queen's chamber. Pedro was so distressed and irritated with the episode that he now informed the king that had decided to take up Louis Philippe's kind offer of a suitable residence in Paris.

The story seems so incredible that it is tempting to suspect that something lies behind it. Although etiquette was broadly the same in all courts, there were always differences of detail. It was Webster's job to advise Pedro on these matters, but he does not seem to have been very competent. Taking Pedro directly to the queen's apartments was extremely foolish and Webster should have known better. Despite his complaints on Pedro's behalf, it almost looks as if Webster did not want him to be well received. But what was Webster's role and why did Lima describe him as 'Palmerston's spy' in a letter to the regency?[56] And who had suggested his name to escort Pedro during his stay in England? It seems likely that Webster was recommended by Holland, on Lady Holland's insistence, as on several other occasions. In 1838, probably at Holland's request, Palmela wrote to Sá da Bandeira, then the chief minister of D. Maria II, successfully requesting the military order of São Bento de Avis for Henry Webster.[57] Yet, there are hints that Webster was never fond of the Hollands or grateful to them despite everything they had done for him. After Lady

56. 'De Luiz Antonio d'Abreu Lima para a Regencia da Terceira', in *Correspondencia official*, 454 (London: 10 August 1831).

57. Palmela to Sá da Bandeira, in *Vida do Duque de Palmella D. Pedro de Souza e Holstein*, edited by Maria Amália Vaz de Carvalho. 3 vols (Lisboa: Imprensa Nacional, 1898–1903), 3: 526.

Webster's divorce and subsequent marriage to Lord Holland in 1797, Henry and his elder brother, Godfrey, went to live with their father, who constantly told them of their mother's iniquities. Hence, Henry may have developed a resentment against his mother, and indeed against Holland and his own half-brother Charles. According to Ilchester, Webster was so jealous of Charles Fox that the Hollands had to keep them apart.[58] In 1817, Holland lent Henry Webster two pistols belonging to Charles, which he intentionally left behind in some hackney coach.[59] Hence, it is possible that, knowing Holland was particularly fond of Pedro, Webster may have done all he could to sabotage Pedro's cause, thus irritating and damaging the Hollands. Although Pedro, never a subtle man, was probably unaware of these complexities, Abreu Lima hints that there was something odd about Webster.

Yet not everyone blamed Webster. Liberato claimed that the apparent lack of courtesy towards the Duque de Bragança and his family was really Pedro's fault. As soon as he arrived in London he should have immediately informed the government of his arrival, which he simply omitted to do. Pedro's lack of etiquette was considered an outrage, leading Palmerston to officially ignore his presence.[60] In a dispatch to the Terceira Regency, Abreu Lima contradicted Liberato's version, declaring that Palmerston had been notified of Pedro's arrival on 3 July 1831. According to Lima, Palmerston had also been informed of everything that had passed in the discussions with Louis Philippe – which if true was rather a waste of time since Palmerston had already been given a full report by his 'spy', Major Webster. Although Liberato's statements are not always reliable, on this occasion he was probably not far from the truth.[61] The fact that Lima felt obliged to inform Palmela that Palmerston had been notified of Pedro's arrival makes the whole story seem highly suspicious.

While Holland deplored 'the contrast of their reception here and in France must strike them in a way far from advantageous to this Country',[62] Webster, who accompanied Pedro everywhere, complained that 'Even the Royal carriages, he says, are now withdrawn, and he and his Empress are left to lodge in a tavern and fumble about in a Glass Coach'.[63] Palmerston himself later admitted to Lima, though as a pro-forma, that he strongly regretted that it had been impossible to find a royal residence to receive the Braganças, but none were available. Palmerston further confessed his embarrassment at the tight-fisted behaviour of the government in not paying Pedro's expenses while he was

58. Ilchester, *Chronicles of Holland House 1820–1900* (New York: E. P. Dutton, 1938), 55–56.
59. Keppel, *The Sovereign Lady*, 260–61.
60. George Lloyd Hodges, a British officer who later joined Pedro's expedition to liberate Portugal, alluded to the Duque de Bragança's 'coldness and a too perceptible absence of courtesy'. (*Narrative of the Expedition to Portugal in 1832: under the Orders of His Imperial Majesty, Dom Pedro, Duke of Braganza*. 2 vols (London: James Fraser, 1833), 1: 43).
61. Liberato also accused Pedro of having occupied the entire noble floor of the hotel, while the young Queen of Portugal was left with a small apartment between the ground and first floors, with the door right to the stairs, and forbidden from speaking with Portuguese people (*Memorias da Vida*, 336–37).
62. Holland, *The Holland House Diaries*, 31 (Monday, 15 August [1831]).
63. Major Henry Vassall Webster, quoted in *The Holland House Diaries*, 23 (Wednesday, 3 August [1831]).

in Britain, although this would have been impossible without first submitting the issue to Parliament. Eventually, however, protocol difficulties were overcome and, according to Lima, the Braganças were invited to spend three days at Windsor, an invitation Pedro initially declined on the grounds that his wife was pregnant. Yet, after an affectionate farewell letter from Queen Adelaide to the young queen Maria on 13 August, Pedro reconsidered and accepted the invitation. According to Holland,

> Pedro and the Queen Donna Maria of Portugal went down to Windsor, were received with due honors and much cordiality, and have returned to night to set off for France tomorrow, apparently in better humor with the King, Court, and Country than they were a few days ago.[64]

On 15 August, after taking leave of Lord Holland, Pedro departed with his wife and daughter and spent the night in Dover. The next morning, the party embarked on the *Lightening* to Calais, where they landed later the same day. By 20 August, the Braganças were already established at the Château de Meudon, which had been especially prepared to receive them. On the same day, Pedro left for Paris to meet Louis Philippe, who again received him graciously in the Royal Palace and praised his decision to head an expedition to Portugal. On the following day, the king and queen visited the Braganças and, the day after, Pedro and his wife and daughter returned the courtesy by calling on the French royal family. Holland's response to the news of Pedro's reception in France reveals a mixture of gratification and disappointment. He wrote in his journal on 19 August:

> A glorious piece of news of Don Pedro and his daughter, whom it is unlucky that we should have neglected and the French so warmly and generously received and cultivated. I urged these considerations when he was here, but œconomy, multiplicity of business, silly and over-scrupulous fear of interference, and I am afraid some little prejudice in our King's mind prevailed, and he was allowed to depart with his Empress and Daughter to Paris.[65]

This statement reveals that Holland's views on the policy to be adopted with Pedro were already diverging from those of his colleagues – especially from Palmerston's. It is true that Holland was a staunch Francophile, but that does not fully explain either his differences with Palmerston or his views on what ought to happen 'should his [Pedro's] projects in Portugal ultimately succeed as they ought'.[66] Holland's attitude is probably best explained in terms of the old Whig maxim of principles above everything. As Mitchell observes, Holland always regarded politics in terms of black and white, of good and evil, and 'in each crisis, simply supported the least bad or most good'.[67] Throughout his long years in opposition, Holland had never allowed national interests to prevail over his own principles, a pattern of behaviour that often irritated professional diplomats. Now at the age of 57, he had no intention of changing his ways merely because his party had finally taken office and he was a minister.

---

64. Holland, *The Holland House Diaries*, 31 (Monday, 15 August [1831]).
65. Ibid., 34 (19 August [1831]).
66. Ibid., 31 (Monday, 15 August [1831]).
67. Mitchell, *Holland House*, 48.

Pedro was invited to attend William IV's coronation on 8 September 1831, but after some hesitation – and probably unwisely – decided to decline the honour, a decision much deplored by Abreu Lima.[68] Even Louis Philippe had 'been persuading Dom Pedro to take a journey to London, in order to assist at the coronation of the English king', but, true to form, he remained stubborn.[69] Pedro's apparent irresponsibility and poor judgement, which Canning had noted a few years earlier, was perhaps one of the reasons why Palmerston was reluctant to grant him the support he asked for. The foreign secretary told Abreu Lima on 2 July 1831, 'The Emperor says he is animated with the best of intentions and that he wants to act; however we do not yet know what he wants or what he can do'.[70] On 4 August Lord Londonderry raised the question of Pedro in the House of Lords. Grey explained that 'it was agreed that Royal honours should be paid to Don Pedro and his daughter Donna Maria' but went on to stress

> these honours are paid in the same way to all individuals connected by relationship with the Royal houses of Europe – they are not paid to them in their political character of crowned heads – they are paid to them as a mark of respect to their Royal rank.[71]

The real issue was whether Pedro could be induced to change his mind and agree to attend William IV's coronation. Three weeks later, Holland noted that it had been agreed that Pedro be 'accommodated with carriages [...] and every attention shewn that may induce him to attend it'.[72] On 26 August, Lady Holland wrote to her son that 'Don Pedro is to return for the Coronation at his *own* request, & will be lodged & conducted about in Royal carriages, etc., all free of expense. This is very right. [...] Henry Webster is again appointed to attend him.'[73] Yet, as Lord Holland observed, 'It is rather too late now, but the impolicy of neglecting him begins to be felt as the prospect of Miguel's overthrow becomes more certain.'[74]

Holland seems to have sensed that the tide of affairs in Portugal was about to turn in favour of the Liberals. Holland certainly had 'blind spots' but his long experience of politics and personal acquaintance with countries such as Portugal sometimes allowed him to see below the surface of day to day events to identify a broader pattern – something that Palmerston probably lacked. At least in retrospect, however, there were too many signs of impending change to be ignored.

68. 'De Luiz Antonio d'Abreu Lima para a Regencia da Terceira', in *Correspondencia official*, 482 (London: 7 September 1831).
69. 'King Louis Philippe to the Prince de Talleyrand', *Memoirs*, 4: 194 (Paris, Saturday, 3 September 1831).
70. 'De Luiz Antonio d'Abreu Lima para a Regencia da Terceira', in *Correspondencia official*, 438 (London: 2 July 1831); 'L'Empereur dit être animé des meilleures intentions, et qu'il veut agir; cependant nous ne savons encore ni ce qu'il veut, ni ce qu'il peut.' (My translation).
71. Grey, Speech of 4 August 1831 on the 'Queen of Portugal', *The Times*, 5 August 1831, 3.
72. Holland, *The Holland House Diaries*, 38 (Wednesday, 24 [August] [1831]).
73. *Lady Holland to Her Son*, 113 (26 August 1831).
74. Holland, *The Holland House Diaries*, 38 (Wednesday, 24 [August] [1831]).

Chapter Ten

PEDRO'S 'ARGONAUTS'

Less than nine thousand men to make their way, opposed by upwards of eighty thousand troops well organised and completely armed; never was so quixotic an expedition planned.[*]

Miguel was becoming isolated and, worse still, he was losing control over his ruffians – if indeed he ever had any. The situation had become worse after the death of Carlota Joaquina on 7 January 1830. Despite her many faults, the Dowager Queen had had an enormous influence over her wayward son, not all of it bad. Her death was followed, two months later, by that of the Marquês de Chaves, one of Miguel's most effective supporters. Worst of all, on 1 July 1831, during the French blockade of the Tagus as a response to the mistreatments imposed by the Portuguese authorities to several French citizens, Miguel had been forced to sign a *Carta Régia* accepting the resignation of his chief minister, the Duque de Cadaval – on the questionable grounds of ill health. The next day, the old ultra-royalist and sanguinary Conde de Basto was appointed acting chief minister.[1] Under the administration of Basto, whose cruelty was equalled only by his incompetence, Portugal descended into an orgy of violence.

Palmerston's tardiness in committing himself unequivocally to the Portuguese Liberals stemmed from his doubts about Pedro, especially his unstable character and incapacity to give serious or sustained commitment to any business – a characteristic inherited from his father. Talleyrand expressed similar reservations about Pedro in a conversation with Resende in August 1831, arguing that it was essential that Pedro clarify his plans.[2] Yet, given to the increasing violence of Miguel's regime, Palmerston was coming to the conclusion that the Liberals were the only acceptable solution for Portugal, especially after Pedro's declaration that the English predominance would be fully respected after her daughter's restoration to the throne. In mid-September, Palmerston told Asseca that his government was not trustworthy and that Miguel could not count on British aid. Perhaps as a result of this conversation, Asseca decided that it was useless to remain in London and on 20 September, after selling all his furniture, left for Falmouth to embark for Lisbon.[3] He had submitted his resignation on 10 August,

---

* Owen, *The Civil War in Portugal*, 85.

1. José António de Oliveira Leite de Barros (1749–1833), 1st Conde de Basto.
2. 'De Luiz Antonio d'Abreu Lima para a Regencia da Terceira', in *Correspondencia official*, 455–56 (London: 10 August 1831).
3. Ibid., 484 (London: 20 September 1831); *The Times*, September 23, 1831, 2.

insisting in a letter to Santarém that there was no point in hoping that the present British government would work towards the reestablishment of the diplomatic relations between the two countries.[4]

Asseca's assessment was probably correct; after the obvious sympathy of Wellington's ministry for Miguel and the equivocal attitude of the Whigs in their first months in office, the British government was finally moving towards support for the Liberals. This development owed much to Palmela's standing and his continued efforts, backed up by Holland, to persuade the Cabinet that the Liberals had a coherent plan for Portugal. Palmela returned to London from the Azores on 19 September 1831 at Pedro's request, but immediately discovered that Pedro was in France. Before leaving for the Continent, however, Palmela called upon Palmerston and 'those of his colleagues who had been friendly with me for a long time, and held sound views about the affairs of Portugal'.[5] These colleagues included Holland, with whom Palmela dined on 20 September.[6] Palmela understood that any solution favourable to the Portuguese Liberals would have to pass through the Holland House circle, where the true friends of D. Maria were to be found.

Holland welcomed Palmela back to Holland House, as something of a hero, 'who has thriven on his hard fare and poverty and subsequent success in the Azores'.[7] Holland also explained in his diary that Palmela was anxious to learn his opinion about a number of questions concerning Portugal, especially 'whether there existed any jealousy between the two Countries [Britain and France] on that subject'.[8] Holland advised Palmela to 'see Lords Grey and Palmerston without loss of time, to speak openly and consult with them unreservedly as he would with me'.[9] Palmela followed Holland's advice and arranged meetings with Palmerston and Grey, but while Palmerston still insisted on the doctrine of non-interference, Grey admitted in a letter to Lieven on 23 September: 'I saw Palmella the other day. You may easily imagine the object of his interview. If my hands were free, I might, perhaps, have answered him more satisfactorily'.[10] At least, as Holland remarked in his diary, 'Palmela's interview with Grey and Palmerston had inspired the first with confidence in him and revived in the latter some of his old and just indignation against Miguel'.[11]

4. Visconde de Asseca to Visconde de Santarém, in *Documentos para a historia das Cortes Geraes*, 8: 500 (10 August 1831).
5. 'O Marquez de Palmella a S. M. I. o Duque de Bragança', in *Despachos*, 4: 675 (23 September 1831); 'com aquelles de entre os seus collegas no gabinete que têem commigo ha mais tempo relações de amizade, a fim de sondar as suas idéas ácerca dos negocios de Portugal'. (My translation).
6. BL, HHP, MSS Add. 51954, Dinner Books: 1825–31, f. 185^r (20 September 1831).
7. Holland, *The Holland House Diaries*, 57 (Monday, 19 September [1831]).
8. Ibid.
9. Ibid.
10. The Earl Grey to Princess Lieven, in *Correspondence*, 2: 282 (23 September 1831).
11. Holland, *The Holland House Diaries*, 59 (Friday, 23 September [1831]).

Hitherto, apart from lack of funds, the main obstacle to the organization of an expedition to liberate Portugal had been the British government's failure to adopt a clear position. The issue was discussed by the Ministers on 22 September, with Holland arguing that 'we have a cause of war against Miguel and we should declare it', while warning his colleagues of the 'danger of leaving to the French exclusively the credit and advantage of restoring a good government in Portugal, and not taking the lead in so righteous a cause which France very handsomely and fairly was disposed to allow us'.[12] While a majority of ministers – including Grey, Palmerston, Stanley, Russell, Graham and Althorp – agreed with Holland, many had already left the Cabinet room by the time the issue was discussed and thus 'nothing consequently was settled'.[13] There was opposition from Lord Goderich and the duke of Richmond – the first questioning the right, the second the wisdom of going to open war with Miguel. Yet, on the evening of 25 September, Palmela seemed satisfied when he called at Holland House to tell Holland about the meeting he had had with Grey. Mackintosh, who was also at Kensington, promised to write a letter, to be shown to the Cabinet, on the affairs of Portugal: the letter was ready on 1 November.[14]

Although there are no further records of the conversation between Holland and Palmela on 20 September, probably because Palmela was the only guest (a sign of his importance to Holland), it seems likely that it covered matters discussed in a lengthy letter, dated 27 September, from Palmela to Holland. The letter makes it clear that Palmela had asked Holland to intercede on his behalf in the Cabinet, and that Holland had agreed. Palmela's assurance that, despite its confidential character, Holland was free to 'use this letter in the way you think more convenient', may suggest that it was Holland who had asked Palmela to write the letter a week earlier.[15] It seems unlikely that Holland needed any further persuasion and, indeed, Holland may have had a hand in composing the letter. In any event, the real objective was almost certainly to put together a document that Holland could use to commend Palmela's ideas to 'the political conscience and generosity' of his colleagues.[16] After a few introductory remarks, the letter of 27 September insisted:

> The British Government will have no other option but *to accept the role that its own relations will impose* and to openly take the party of the Infante or of the Emperor D. Pedro and his August Daughter! And in this case I hope there will be no doubt in England's choice.[17]

12. Ibid.
13. Ibid.
14. Ibid., 61 (25 September [1831]).
15. BL, HHP, MSS Add. 51632, Papers Relative to Portugal: Palmela (27 September 1831); 'votre bienveillance pour moi vous engagera, à faire de cette lettre l'usage qui vous saurez le plus convainable'. (My translation).
16. Ibid.; 'Enfin permettez-moi, mon cher Lord Holland, de vous presénter encore une dernière consideration et de l'adresser non seulement au jugement mais aussi à la conscience politique et à la generosité de vous et de votre collégues'. (My translation).
17. Ibid.; 'il ne resterai pour le Gouvt. Brit.[e] d'autre parti à prendre que *de se charger lui méme du rôle que ses relations le mettent dans le cas d'exercer* et de prendre ouvertement parti ou pour l'Infant D. Miguel ou pour l'Empereur D. Pedro et son August Fille! Et dans cette alternative j'ose esperer que le choix de l'Angletêrre ne peut être douteux'. (My translation).

Palmela argued that the principle of non-intervention, so used as a convenient fall-back by British ministers, was not applicable to Portugal in present circumstances. While it appeared obvious 'that no power needs to interfere in the internal affairs of another country *provided that its own interests are not compromised*', it was also evident that it had 'the right of so doing if the duration and nature of these disputes *undermines its political and commercial interests*'.[18] The question now was how to work out a basis upon which the British government could persuade the European powers that military intervention in Portugal was justified. Palmela proposed a simple solution, suggesting that it was

> indispensable that His Britannic Majesty should simply say that the interests of his subjects compels him to hasten the reestablishment of the discontinued relations between the two Crowns; given that the Portuguese territory is divided between two parties which are at war, England is forced to choose between them and to declare for the one that appears to her the most just and, in this case, the more humane and more inspiring more interest in all Foreign Nations.[19]

As Palmela further reminded his readers, the frequent insults and maltreatments inflicted on British subjects by Miguel's ruffians provided another 'motive to add to those I have just identified to fully justify the English resolution' to intervene.[20] Palmela concluded with an emotional appeal to 'a Cabinet so happily formed like yours' to abandon indecision and 'cold indifference which seems so contrary to a healthy policy and to the immutable principle of the sentiments of humanity!'[21]

When Palmela left London for Paris on 27 September 1831, he already knew, probably through Holland, that he could count, at least, 'on the moral support of the English Government, as well as its good offices with the French Cabinet, and on the

---

18. Ibid.; 'Le principe de mon intervention, qui pourrait être allégué pour empêcher le Gouvernement Britannique de se mêler des affaires Portugaises, ne me parait pas applicable au cas présent. Il est clair qu'aucune puissance n'a besoin de se mêler des querelles internes d'un autre Pays, *si ses propres intérêts ne s'y trouvent pas compromis* mais il est également évident qu'elle en a le droit si la durée on la nature de ces querelles *compromet ses intérêts politiques et commerciaux* et il serait facile d'énumérer une longue liste de précédents pour prouver ce que je viens de dire'. (My translation).
19. Ibid.; 'Je crois donc, que pour motiver son intervention désormais indispensable dans les affaires Portugaises, Sa Majesté Britannique n'aurait qu'à dire que l'intérêt de ses sujets l'oblige à hâter le moment du rétablissement des relations qui se trouvent interrompues car les deux Couronnes et que le territoire Portugais se trouvant partagé entre deux parties qui se font la guerre, l'Angleterre est forcée de choisir entre les deux et qu'elle se déclare pour celui qui lui parait le plus juste et qui en ce cas est le plus humain et celui qui inspire le plus d'intérêt à toutes les Nations Etrangères'. (My translation).
20. Ibid.; 'Les insultes et les provocations frequents qui ont eu lieu de la part de D. Miguel et de ses employés contre les sujets Britanniques ajouteraient encore un motif de plus a ceux que je viens d'indiquer pour justifier pleinement la resolution de l'Angletêrre'. (My translation).
21. Ibid.; 'Vous permettez-moi de le dire, je ne sçaurais croire qu'en envisageant avec candeur toute cette question un Cabinêt composé comme l'est heureusement le votre en appelle, encore au temps et s'enveloppe dans une froide indifference qui me parait aussi contraire à une saine politique qu'au principe immuable des sentiments d'humanité!' (My translation).

necessary tolerance in providing us with an indirect support in the preparation of any intended expedition'.[22] But instead of giving Palmela clear answers to his pleas for assistance, both the English and French governments seemed to expect the other to be the first to make a decisive commitment. According to Abreu Lima, Palmerston had declared on 6 August that although the British government could not openly support the Portuguese Liberals, it would not oppose to any discreet aid that France might offer them, provided that Portugal remained in Britain's sphere of influence. By mid-September 1831, Holland alluded in his diary to some reluctance in the Cabinet to 'inviting Pedro here, winking at his preparations and half encouraging his expedition from our coasts and against our laws, yet not openly espousing his cause'.[23] Similarly, Sébastiani formally announced in a meeting with Palmela on 21 October that although France could not support or promote a civil war between Portugal and the Azores, his government was ready to favour Maria II. Yet, France was ready to follow any measures that Britain would think advisable to favour Maria's cause. This apparent diplomatic 'ping-pong' – whether previously arranged or not – probably sprang from a fear of doing anything precipitate before things became clearer, especially if this might damage their own national interests or prejudice the success of the Liberal cause. Another possible explanation is that both countries were waiting for the other to take the initiative and thus save themselves a lot of unnecessary trouble and expense. On 1 November, Holland told Grey that

> as the French had proposed to us to espouse the cause of Donna Maria and there were so many reasons to justify and so many motives to induce us to do it, we should without delay acknowledge Donna Maria's Regency, accredit Ministers to it, and offer jointly with France a mediation for the pacification of Portugal.[24]

The matters discussed in the meeting between Palmela and Sébastiani were transcribed into a memorandum, a copy of which Palmela attached to a dispatch to Palmerston on 27 October. The fact that several ideas mentioned in both the dispatch and the memorandum were virtually identical – both in content and in language – to parts of Palmela's letter of 27 September, suggests that Holland himself was behind the scheme. Their strategy was starting to bear fruits as, on 1 November, Palmela wrote enthusiastically to Palmerston:

> I cannot write in the margin of your memorandum but *amen, amen, amen*! I sincerely thank you for the proof of confidence that you kindly gave me. You have revealed a perfect lucidity – analogous to the whole affair – by showing us the only thread that can get us out of the labyrinth.[25]

---

22. Palmela, *Memórias*, 232; 'com o apoio moral do Governo inglês, assim como com os seus bons ofícios junto do Gabinete francês, e com a tolerância necessária para nos prestar um auxílio indirecto nos aprestos da expedição que se quisesse empreender'. (My translation).
23. Holland, *The Holland House Diaries*, 59 (Friday, 23 September [1831]).
24. Ibid., 72–73 (1 November [1831]).
25. 'Le Marquis de Palmella a Lord Palmerston', in *Despachos*, 4: 693 (1 November 1831); 'Je ne saurais écrire à la marge de votre mémoire, qu'amen, amen, amen. Je vous le rends avec les

The reason for such an excitement was Palmerston's decision that, henceforth, he would deal with Pedro in all matters relating to Portugal, amounting to tacit recognition of D. Maria II as the legitimate sovereign of Portugal and her father as a regent. In the same letter, Palmela confidentially informed the foreign secretary that Pedro's expedition was due to leave France on 20 November.[26] Palmela further explained that although he was leaving for Brighton that morning, he would be back in London the next day to request Lord Holland's support.[27] In fact, on the evening of 2 November, Palmela was already dining at Kensington and consulting Lord Holland 'on the practicability of prevailing on our government to act in concert with France in recognising the party of Donna Maria'.[28] On 15 November, Palmela commented in a despatch to Cândido Xavier: 'Lord Holland arrives in London this evening and we will have his mighty power in the Council'.[29] The following day, when Holland returned to Kensington he found Palmela waiting to enquire about any decision on the affairs of Portugal. But Holland had nothing conclusive to report as yet.

By this time, as Palmela later admitted in his memoirs, 'we wished and still entertained the hope that the English Government would openly and ostensibly embrace the cause of the Queen'.[30] But again, Palmela's hopes were disappointed when, on 17 November, and despite Hollands efforts, a few members of the Cabinet voted against open intervention in the conflict. In Holland's words,

> We came to the worst of all decisions, namely none at all, when the golden opportunity of reclaiming Spain from her ultra Miguelite policy in Portugal, of cementing our union with France, and restoring English ascendency in Portugal had offered itself.[31]

That evening, Palmela dined at Holland House, where the issue was discussed at length.[32] According to Holland, Palmela was depressed and

> disappointed at our want of decision and broken hearted at the dismal consequences to himself and his countrymen. He is overwhelmed with the responsibility of having engaged so many Portuguese in an enterprize now nearly hopeless, and confesses that the reproaches which will follow, however unmerited, will overwhelm him.[33]

---

remerciements les plus sincères de la preuve de confiance que vous avez bien voulu m'accorder. Vous me paraissez avoir présenté avec une lucidité parfaite l'analogue de toute cette affaire, et indiqué le seul fil qui peut nous faire sortir du labyrinthe'. (My translation).

26. 'Le Marquis de Palmella a Lord Palmerston', ibid., 4: 693–94 (1 November 1831).
27. Ibid., 4: 693 (1 November 1831).
28. Holland, *The Holland House Diaries*, 73 (Wednesday, 2 November [1831]); BL, HHP, MSS Add. 51955, Dinner Books: 1831–38, f. 2^v (2 November 1831).
29. 'Le Marquis de Palmella a Lord Palmerston', in *Despachos*, 4: 706 (15 October 1831); 'Esta noite chega lord Holland a Londres, e teremos o seu apoio poderoso no conselho'. (My translation).
30. Palmela, *Memórias*, 238; 'desejávamos mais, e concebíamos ainda a esperança de que o governo inglês aberta e ostensivamente abraçasse a causa da Rainha'. (My translation).
31. Holland, *The Holland House Diaries*, 80 (17 November 1831).
32. BL, HHP, MSS Add. 51955, Dinner Books: 1831–38, f. 4^r (Thursday, 17 November 1831).
33. Holland, *The Holland House Diaries*, 80–81 (17 November 1831).

The next day, still recovering from the setback, Palmela wrote to Holland: 'Is it too much to ask him [Palmerston] to request from Britain at least peaceful and moral support for Queen Maria II; and does he want to do less than Spain who openly acts as a mediator on behalf of D. Miguel?'[34] Palmela concluded his note by requesting Holland do one more thing for Maria's cause. Palmela had an interview with Grey on 3 December at the Treasury but, for the time being, the Portuguese Liberals had to content themselves with only the tacit support of Great Britain. The limited extent of British aid – viz. a 'most vigilant attention to events' – was defined in the king's speech at the opening of the parliamentary session on 6 December:

> The conduct of the Portuguese Government, and the repeated injuries to which my subjects have been exposed, have prevented a renewal of my diplomatic relations with that kingdom. The state of a country, so long united with this by the ties of the most intimate alliance, must necessarily be to me an object of the deepest interest. The return to Europe of the elder branch of the illustrious house of Braganza, and the dangers of a disputed succession will require my most vigilant attention to events, by which not only the safety of Portugal but the general interests of Europe, may be effected.[35]

Although Palmela would have preferred it if 'the sentiments of the Cabinet were more openly expressed', occasionally, British support was more explicit – as when Palmerston promised to give Palmela a copy of a map, sent to London by Richard Hoppner, the British consul at Lisbon, giving details of Miguel's military and naval forces.[36]

Under pressure from Palmela, Palmerston agreed to issue a written declaration explaining Britain's position. Although ruling out direct intervention, as contrary to the spirit of the existing Anglo-Portuguese treaties, the government was ready to guarantee the safety of Portugal if any other power, especially Spain, intervened in favour of Miguel. Holland found Palmerston's letter 'more favourable to Donna Maria than I expected, though it does not expressly say we will not allow of Spanish interference in Portugal'.[37] Fearing that the reestablishment of a Constitutional government in Portugal would encourage the Spanish Liberals to do the same thing, Spain was threatening to assist Miguel in case of an invasion. Pedro was particularly anxious to obtain a guarantee against Spanish intervention. If he could obtain that, then 'I will march and you may count that the expedition will definitely be held'.[38] France was more ready than Britain

---

34. BL, HHP, MSS Add. 51632, Papers Relative to Portugal: Palmela (18 November 1831); 'Serait-ce trop demander à Angletêrre que le lui demand au moins *l'appui pacifique et moral en faveur de la Reine Marie 2.ª* et voudra t'elle faire moins que l'Espagne qui agit ouvertement comme mediatrice en faveur de l'Infant D. Miguel?' (My translation).
35. William IV, Speech in the House of Lords at the Opening of the Parliamentary Session on 6 December 1831, *The Times*, 7 December 1830, 1.
36. 'O Marquez de Palmella a Candido José Xavier', in *Despachos*, 4: 721 (6 December 1831); 'os sentimentos do gabinete de Londres fossem mais claramente manifestados'. (My translation).
37. Holland, *The Holland House Diaries*, 99 (Monday, 19 December [1831]).
38. 'O Duque de Bragança ao Marquês de Palmella', in *Despachos*, 4: 683 (27 October 1831); 'eu marcho, e contem que a expedição se ha de fazer infallivelmente'. (My translation).

to make serious commitments, declaring that if Spain gave military assistance to Miguel, France would treat it as a declaration of war. After securing Palmerston's half-guarantee, Palmela decided that his work in London was complete and hence left for France to join Pedro, arriving in Paris on 26 December.

Even after the problem of political recognition had been solved, there still remained the major challenge of how to finance an expedition that would have a reasonable chance of liberating Portugal from the usurper. As Palmerston observed in a conversation with Abreu Lima on 2 July 1831, 'war cannot be made without money'.[39] In fact, while Miguel had about 80,000 regular troops, the Liberals could raise a force of barely 4,000 men, many of them untrained volunteers, plus any additional foreign mercenaries they could afford. The only way the Liberals could hope to raise a serious force would be by means of a loan – but that would be difficult to obtain. The Portuguese properties of the Liberal aristocrats and merchants had been confiscated and they were thus unable to make a significant contribution, while bankers in England or France were understandably reluctant to risk their money on an enterprise whose chances of success appeared extremely remote. The only 'security' that Pedro could now offer to prospective investors was the recovery of the Portuguese throne for his daughter, but the odds against that happening were high. It is true that British political recognition somewhat improved prospects of obtaining a loan. Further, if Britain and France gave clear backing to an expedition, it would be more likely to succeed and hence investors would have a better chance of seeing their money again.

Yet the only foreign capitalist who seemed interested was Juan Mendizábal,[40] a Spanish visionary businessman of Jewish origin described by Palmela as 'the soul of the whole business'.[41] Mendizábal's role proved crucial in attracting other investors, including the French banker A. Ardoin. Unlike the majority of financers who thought that lending money to the Portuguese Liberals would be like throwing it into the sea, Mendizábal supported the project as a matter of faith. He believed that if the Liberals succeeded in Portugal, their victory could be replicated in Spain. Through Mendizábal's efforts a sum of £100,000 was raised 'for the preparations for the projected expedition, and for its progress to the coast of Portugal'.[42] Mendizábal, who had been commissioned to acquire ships and equip them, bought two frigates, the *Congress* and the *Asia*, and the *Juno* corvette, and chartered the *Fairlie* frigate, three old steamers and the transports *Edward*, *Tyrian* and *Fileria*.

Another major difficulty involved trying to get around the Foreign Enlistment Act without seriously compromising the Cabinet. This act, prohibiting the enlistment of

39. 'De Luiz Antonio d'Abreu Lima para a Regencia da Terceira', in *Correspondencia official*, 438 (London: 2 July 1831); 'la guerre ne se fait pas sans argent'. (My translation).

40. Juan Álvarez Mendizábal, *née* Juan Álvarez Méndez (1790–1853), Spanish economist, politician and Freemason, the son of Rafael Álvarez Montañés, a cloth merchant, by Margarita Méndez.

41. 'O Marquês de Palmella a Candido Jose Xavier', in *Despachos*, 4: 695 (4 November 1831).

42. *Reports, Transmitted to the Portuguese Government, of the Proceedings of the Commission, Appointed to Conduct the Arrangements for the Expeditions to Portugal in Favour of Her Most Faithful Majesty Donna Maria, in the Years 1831, 1832, and 1833…* (London: Whittaker, 1835), 2.

men or the equipment of vessels for foreign service in British harbours, had passed the Commons after a third reading on 21 June 1819 – in the face of strong opposition from the Whigs. Thereafter the Whigs had made a number of unsuccessful attempts to amend or even repeal the measure. Although Palmerston now tried to close his eyes to what was happening in the way of preparing and fitting out the expedition, it was clear that he could not go too far – especially after Miguel's agent, Consul-General Sampaio, officially complained about these activities. Palmerston's connivance – and his concerns – are revealed in a note to Palmela on 26 November:

> My Dear Marquis,
>
> I strongly advise you to send your vessels away without further delay to avoid new difficulties that D. Miguel's agents may create. I have received this morning another series of complaints from Sampaio which I will return to him. But as your vessels have not left yet, there is the risk of further obstacles. Yours. Palmerston.[43]

Eventually, on 6 November, Sampaio succeeded in obtaining a temporary embargo on the *Congress* and the *Asia*, which were enlisting troops at Gravesend. Although this manoeuvre caused a slight delay to the preparations, the embargo was lifted a few days later and the ships allowed to sail for France. However, as there remained the possibility of further obstruction in England, the only way forward was to persuade the French authorities to allow the main base of the expedition to move to France. Eventually Pedro was allowed to use Belle-Île, a small island off the south coast of Brittany, as a military base, although with the proviso that the expedition would sail soon. In addition, the French government gave instructions to the local governor, Colonel Martin, to receive Pedro as a foreign prince and to provide the expedition with all the assistance it might need.

The command of the expeditionary fleet was entrusted to George Sartorius, a Royal Navy officer who had served in the *Tonnant* at Trafalgar.[44] Sartorius was created vice admiral of the Portuguese Royal Navy and given carte-blanche to hire whatever crew he considered necessary. According to Colonel George Hodges,[45] one of the British volunteers who joined Sartorius in the autumn of 1831, 'the prospects of the intended Expedition had begun

43. 'Lord Palmerston au Marquis de Palmella', in *Despachos*, 4: 720 (26 November 1831); 'Mon Cher Marquis, Je vous conseille fortement de faire partir vos vaisseaux sans le moindre délai, afin d'éviter de nouvelles difficultés, que les agents de D. Miguel pourraient vous susciter. Je viens de recevoir une autre série d'affidavits ce matin de la part de Sampayo que je vais lui rendre. Mais tant que vos vaisseaux ne sont pas partis il y a risque de quelques autres embarras. Tout à vous. Palmerston'. (My translation).
44. Sir George Rose Sartorius (1790–1885), British Admiral of the Fleet, eldest son of Colonel John Conrad Sartorius (†1801), and officer of the East India Company, and his wife, Annabella, a granddaughter of Admiral Harvey.
45. George Lloyd Hodges (1792–1862), British officer and diplomat, served with gallantry in Pedro's army in 1832. Hodges was appointed commander of a battalion of marines, the so-called *Auxiliares Ingleses*. According to Soriano, however, Hodges disappeared from Oporto on 2 December, taking with him money belonging to the English battalion under his command.

to assume in England a more flattering appearance'.[46] The British officers who agreed to serve under Sartorius included Captains Shaw, Staunton, Rose and Crosby, the latter having served under Lord Cochrane in the Brazilian Navy.[47] Learning that Sartorius had entered Pedro's service, Sampaio protested to the king with the assistance of Aberdeen, Beresford and other Tories. William IV, who took offence at the alleged violation of the Foreign Enlistment Act, urged Graham to warn Sartorius that, if he persisted, he would lose his rank and commission in the Royal Navy. As Holland noted, this was an empty threat because it disregarded the 'distinction between the law and the Prerogative' – however, if it were to be taken seriously it would not only work to Pedro's disadvantage, but would also affect many British officers then engaged in foreign service.[48] Probably at Holland's suggestion, Sartorius applied for leave of absence but 'somewhat incorrectly affirmed that he wished to pass the winter at Palermo, when it was notorious he was about to take command of Don Pedro's fleet'.[49] One way or another, the situation seems to have been satisfactorily resolved and Sartorius retained command of the expeditionary fleet.

Pedro and Palmela left Paris on 25 January for Orleans and embarked at Nantes on the *Superb* steamer, arriving at Belle-Île on 2 February. Even though many seamen considered it bad luck to commence a voyage on a Friday, it was at daybreak on Friday, 10 February 1832, that the main expeditionary force set sail for the Azores. The first vessel to reach the Azores was the *Edward*, which arrived at Terceira on 22 February. This was followed by the *Dona Maria*, which anchored there two days later. The *Ilha Terceira* arrived off Angra on 25 but adverse weather conditions delayed a landing. The *Tyrian* arrived at Terceira on the following day, carrying Loulé, Conde de Ficalho, Captain Crosby and Hodges – who had changed ship in São Miguel – and other 150 foreign volunteers. The flagship *Rainha de Portugal*, which had been diverted to São Miguel by a strong gale, reached Ponta Delgada on 22 February. There Pedro was greeted by a huge crowd shouting 'vivas' – coincidently four years after Miguel's landing in Lisbon. On 2 March, Pedro and his suite re-embarked on the *Rainha de Portugal* to arrive on the following day at Terceira, where they were enthusiastically received.

Intrigues against Palmela led Pedro to treat him with scarcely disguised contempt from the moment they left Belle-Île. According to Hodges, during the first dinner aboard the *Rainha de Portugal*, 'the Emperor's coldness and indifference to him were visible to everyone. He was seated opposite his Majesty at dinner, yet hardly a word passed between them'.[50] Hodges suggested that while Palmela's gout had confined him to the *Superb*, Xavier and his party had been poisoning Pedro's 'too credulous mind' against Palmela. Cândido Xavier, whom Hodges described as 'a wily, intriguing courtier, and therefore no favourable specimen of the Portuguese or any other national character',[51] had gained the

46. Hodges, *Narrative*, 1: 2.
47. Thomas Sackville Crosby (†1847), British Navy officer, awarded the Portuguese Order of Tower and Sword.
48. Holland, *The Holland House Diaries*, 103 (Tuesday, 27 [December 1831]).
49. Ibid., 133 (Sunday, 19 February [1832]).
50. Hodges, *Narrative*, 1: 91.
51. Ibid., 1: 34.

emperor's confidence and became his private secretary'.[52] But it was only at the time of the landing at Angra on 3 March 1831 that Palmela 'had the first proof (hitherto I had only hints) of the change in the *Senhor* D. Pedro's mind about me', when instead of calling upon him to form the new Cabinet, as expected, Pedro appointed Xavier as his chief minister.[53] Palmela was offered the foreign and home ministries, an invitation he did not immediately accept, requesting 24 hours to think. Patriotism prevailed over his pride and he agreed to accept the appointment.

The following months were employed in the final preparations of the expedition to the mainland, in which Pedro was actively involved. According to Hodges, 'Transports and other vessels were daily arriving from England and France', bringing equipment and new levies, including foreign mercenaries.[54] Two alternatives were now on the table: the one, proposed by Cochrane and Talleyrand, identified the capture of Madeira as the first objective, to be followed by a series of attacks on different points on the coast of the mainland; the other, suggested by Marshal Soult, involved a massive and concentrated attack on a specific point, preferably in the north, which would then be turned into a focus of resistance. Although the first option seemed safer, it required more time and would, sooner or later, lead to British intervention; the second was more risky since the outcome of a single attack would determine the success or failure of the whole enterprise. After much discussion, however, the second option was chosen and on 27 June 1832 the fleet left São Miguel for Portugal.

Strangely, it was not until 8 July, when the fleet was already off the northern coast of Portugal, that a meeting held aboard the corvette *Juno* (renamed *Amélia*) decided on the precise spot where the landing should be attempted. A wide range of options were considered. While some proposed to force the entrance of the Tagus and go straight to the capital, others suggested doing the same in the Douro; some preferred a landing in Peniche or Ericeira, northwards of Lisbon, while a few wanted to land on the northern coast. In any event, it was the last option that prevailed and, after consulting Sartorius, it was decided to land on the *Praia dos Ladrões* (Beach of the Thieves), at Arnosa de Pampelido, one league south of Vila do Conde. For some unknown reason – probably owing to the proximity of the two spots – it passed into history that the landing had been made in Mindelo rather than in Pampelido, and this is why the episode is known as the 'The Landing at Mindelo'. By the end of the day (8 July), the whole force had already safely disembarked on the beach. From thence, the 'Bravos do Mindelo', as they were later known, marched southwards to Oporto, which they reached the next morning. Learning of the approach of the enemy, the Absolutist general Visconde de Santa Marta, despite possessing superior forces, retreated to the southern bank of the Douro without offering resistance.[55]

52. During the French invasions Xavier had fought under Massena against his own countrymen, which led to his condemnation to death in absentia in 1810 and the public burning of his effigy.

53. Palmela, *Memórias*, 247; 'tive a primeira prova (até então só tinha tido indícios) da mudança que a meu respeito se havia operado no ânimo do Sr. D. Pedro'. (My translation).

54. Hodges, *Narrative*, 1: 220.

55. Manuel Gregório de Sousa Pereira de Sampaio (1766–1844), 1st Visconde de Santa Marta.

While the total number of Pedro's 'Liberation Army' – as it was pompously called – rose to 7,500 troops, Santa Marta, the commander in chief of the Northern Army, had 14,000. According to Hodges, although a young man, Santa Marta 'has none of the energy of youth: slow in perception, feeble in execution, and timid where any degree of responsibility is to be incurred'.[56] To be fair to Santa Marta, it is possible that he overestimated his enemy's strength, supposing that others would follow behind Pedro's force or even that there had been direct British intervention. Another plausible explanation is that Santa Marta may have feared a massive popular uprising in favour of the 'Liberation Army', although perhaps without reason. Fearing a repetition of the events of 1828, several important people in Oporto, who had formerly declared for the Constitution, had abandoned the town at the approach of the Liberals. Although the official gazette declared that the 'Father of the Nation' was 'always followed by an immense crowd of people shouting *vivas* and acclamations to the *Senhora* Dona Maria II',[57] this version was contradicted by Hodges, who argued that Pedro's entry into Oporto 'was anything but enthusiastic on the part of the inhabitants generally'.[58] Besides, Santa Marta was probably aware that while the Absolutists were merely following their orders, the Liberals were fighting for an ideal and, more importantly, after four years in exile, they were anxious to recover their homes and families, in short, their lives. Before the landing, Pedro had proclaimed: 'Soldiers! – These beaches belong to the unfortunate Portugal; there, your fathers, mothers, children, wives, relatives and friends yearn for your return and trust in your sentiments, merit and generosity'.[59]

On 10 July, threatened by a few corps of *chasseurs* under Schwalbach, a German officer in Pedro's service who managed to cross the Douro under the protection of friendly fire, Santa Marta withdrew from Vila Nova de Gaia and repositioned his troops further south in Oliveira de Azemeis. After this action, the Liberals gained control of both banks of the Douro. The new defensive line occupied by the Absolutists effectively became those of the Siege of Oporto, which lasted until 18 August 1833, when the comte d'Almer, a French general in Miguel's service, was defeated by Saldanha. Hence, Pedro and his 'Bravos' had still a long way to go before they could claim victory. Yet, as Serrão suggested, the 'Landing at Mindelo' was the decisive event in the long process that eventually led to the complete defeat of Miguel; in other words, it may be taken as marking the beginning of the restoration of representative government in Portugal.

56. Hodges, *Narrative*, 1: 300–301.

57. *Chronica constitucional do Porto*, 11 July 1831, 3; 'seguido sempre por um immenso concurso de povo, e acompanhado de vivas e acclamações á Senhora D. Maria II'. (My translation).

58. Hodges, *Narrative*, 1: 310; see also Owen, *The Civil War in Portugal*, 85–86; cf. Palmela, *Memórias*, p. 265); Soriano, *HGC*, 3.ª época, t. III, pt. 2 [15]: 286–87.

59. Pedro, Duque de Bragança, Proclaim to the Troops, *Chronica constitucional do Porto*, 11 July 1832, 3; 'Soldados! – Aquellas praias são as do malfadado Portugal: ali, vossos pais, mãis, filhos, esposas, parentes e amigos suspirão pela vossa vinda, e confião nos vossos sentimentos, valor e generosidade'. (My translation).

Chapter Eleven

BOULEVARD OF FREEDOM

D. Pedro est decidé à se deffendre et la Ville de Porto j'espere será le boulevard de la liberté Portugaise.[*]

Pedro was convinced – somewhat narcissistically – that his mere presence and charisma would have a magical effect and bring thousands flocking to his cause. The folly of these expectations was revealed when Oporto responded to Pedro's entry with marked lack of enthusiasm and many notable people proved reluctant to trust him or serve under him. The truth of Aberdeen's 'magic poll', to borrow Holland's words, had been now confirmed.[1] This caution or reluctance – probably due more to fear of Miguel's agents than to genuine rejection of the Liberal cause – was strengthened by the attitude of the Church. Priests consistently warned their congregations of the spiritual dangers of adherence to the Liberal cause, which they equated with Freemasonry and heresy. Ironically, Pedro's first act as regent on the behalf of his daughter was to order the temporary suspension of the civil liberties, under the terms of the Constitutional Charter. Pedro's decree, which also carried Palmela's signature, was intended to prevent the spread of anti-Liberal propaganda, especially by the clergy.[2]

In the absence of a specific plan to liberate the rest of Portugal and without enough resources to mount such a campaign, the Liberals applied themselves to strengthening the defences of Oporto against attack by the Absolutists. As Palmela noted, even if a plan for offensive operations had existed, nothing of significance could be attempted until the cavalrymen had been provided with suitable horses.[3] In a letter to Lord William Russell, who had been sent to Lisbon on a special mission, Palmela explained that a number of things were needed to give the enterprise any chance of success.[4] The requirements included horses for the senior officers, artillery and fifty guides.[5] Palmela was accordingly ordered to London to 'press for the remittance of money and assistance of all kinds which

---

* BL, HHP, MSS Add. 51632, Papers relative to Portugal: Palmella (Le 13 Septembre 1832).

1. See Chapter Eight.
2. Pedro, Duque de Bragança, Decree of 10 July 1832 Suspending Civil Liberties, *Chronica constitucional do Porto*, Julho 11, 1832, 4–5.
3. Palmela, *Memórias*, 266.
4. Lord George William Russell (1790–1846), British officer and diplomat, was sent on a special mission to Lisbon, where he arrived early in June 1832. He remained in Lisbon unaccredited until 15 August 1833, when his credentials were acknowledged by the regent D. Pedro.
5. 'O Marquez de Palmella a Lord William Russell', in *Despachos*, 4: 748 (Porto: 20 July 1832).

are urgently needed to continue the operations that have been undertaken'.[6] Palmela was instructed 'to collect a few clever senior officers and, if possible, some levies'.[7] There can be little doubt that these were genuine requirements and that, given his contacts and experience, Palmela was the right man for the job.

Palmela embarked for England on 29 July and landed at Plymouth on 4 August. As soon as he arrived at London on 6 August, Palmela sent a confidential dispatch to Palmerston, announcing his arrival and explaining the reasons for his visit.[8] Pedro had given him full powers – also assigned to Funchal and Abreu Lima – to 'request the intervention of H. B. M. in favour of the interests of the Queen his Daughter, and to acquire the formal commitments that such intervention may require'.[9] Palmerston agreed to meet Palmela at the Foreign Office on 9 August, but appeared unenthusiastic. As Palmela observed in his memoirs, 'Ministers and even the public had begun to doubt the result of our expedition and to realize that the earlier claims as to the general disaffection towards Miguel in Portugal had been exaggerated'.[10] Even Holland seemed doubtful, writing in his diary that 'Palmela arrived from Oporto with accounts not quite so desperate as his arrival seemed at first to imply, but yet far from encouraging'.[11] A few days earlier, in the absence of favourable news from Portugal, Holland had admitted in his journal: 'In truth we have been guilty of a great error in policy in not espousing Don Pedro's cause or at least shewing more openly and ostentatiously our countenance and good wishes'.[12]

On 7 August, the Liberals had been forced to withdraw from Souto Redondo after losing 200 men in an action against the Absolutists. One week later, Vila Flor wrote to Palmela: 'Here we are much worse since you left us, because the enemy has been receiving reinforcements and continues receiving them'.[13] As Wellington remarked in the House of Lords on 15 August, 'notwithstanding the Prince [Pedro] who had recently gone to Portugal, went under most advantageous circumstances, yet, though a month

6. 'Le Marquis de Palmella a Lord Palmerston', ibid., 4: 749 (London: ce 2 Août de 1832); 'presser la remise d'argent et les secours de toute espèce dont il a le plus urgent besoin pour continuer les opérations qu'il a entreprises'. (My translation).
7. Pedro, Duque de Bragança, 'Instrucções', ibid., 4: 750–51 (28 July 1832); 'para buscar alguns officiaes superiors intelligentes, e alguma tropa, sendo possível'. (My translation).
8. 'Le Marquis de Palmella a Lord Palmerston', ibid., 4: 749 (London: ce 2 Août de 1832). Although the deipatch is dated 2 August, it was probably written while Palmela was still aboard, thus pre-dated.
9. 'Le Marquis de Palmella a Lord Palmerston', ibid., 4: 749 (London: ce 2 Août de 1832); 'solliciter l'intervention du gouvernement de S. M. B. en faveur des intérêts de la Reine sa Fille, et à contracter les engagements formels que cette intervention pouvait exiger'. (My translation).
10. Palmela, *Memórias*, 269; 'os Ministros e até o público principiavam já a considerar como duvidoso o resultado da nossa expedição, e a desenganar-se de que haviam sido exageradas as ideias, anteriormente concebidas, da desafeição geral existente em Portugal contra D. Miguel'. (My translation).
11. Holland, *The Holland House Diaries*, 202 (6 [August 1832]).
12. Ibid., 199 (31 July 1832]).
13. 'O Conde de Villa Flor ao Marquez de Palmella', in *Despachos*, 4: 762 (Porto: 14 August 1832); 'Nós aqui estamos muito peior do que nos deixaste, porque o inimigo tem recebido forças e continua a receber'. (My translation).

had elapsed, he had yet made no progress, further than the town in which he landed'.[14] In any event, Pedro warned Palmela that the Liberals were considering requesting an armistice that would allow them to withdraw from Oporto unmolested. Palmela was instructed to communicate this intention to Palmerston and to request the assistance of the Royal Navy should a general evacuation be required. According to Palmela:

> Lord Palmerston was very distressed with this communication; and declared that, if the predicted event came to pass, the captains of the British vessels would be ordered to protect our embarkation and to guarantee the safety of individuals; however, the British Government would then consider the affair closed and would recognise the Government of Lisbon, while opposing any new attempt against Portugal. These details are entirely true and known to very few people, as this is the first time I have trusted them to paper.[15]

Palmela was so devastated that, at a dinner at Palmerston's on 23 August, Villiers described him as 'evidently very much depressed by the state of Pedro's affairs at Oporto'.[16] But, once the initial shock had passed, the Liberals' defeat at Souto Redondo had the unexpected effect of forcing Pedro to give more commitment to the cause. Seized with new enthusiasm, Pedro took on the supervision of Oporto's defences – previously somewhat neglected. A few days later, Pedro informed Palmela that he had decided to stay in Portugal and asked him to promise – on his word of honour – never to reveal the contents of his previous letter, the result of a moment of depression. Hence, on 13 September, just before his return to Portugal, Palmela could write enthusiastically to Lady Holland: 'D. Pedro is determined to defend himself and I hope the town of Oporto will be the boulevard to the freedom of Portugal. I have done all I could to organise assistance and I think with little money I did a lot'.[17] In fact, on the same day, *The Times* announced 'that a British officer of high rank had made an offer of his services, with a large body of men, to the Marquis de Palmella, for the reinforcement of the constitutional Portuguese army'.[18] During his stay in London, Palmela had also engaged

---

14. Wellington, Speech in the House of Lords upon the Third Reading of the 'West India Relief Bill', *The Times*, 16 August 1832, 1.
15. Palmela, *Memórias*, 269; 'Lord Palmerston mostrou-se muito sentido desta comunicação; e declarou-me que se o caso previsto acontecesse, os comandantes das embarcações britânicas teriam ordens para proteger o nosso embarque e garantir a segurança dos indivíduos; mas que o Governo britânico consideraria então a questão como decidida, e trataria de reconhecer o Governo de Lisboa, opondo-se a qualquer nova tentativa contra Portugal. Estes detalhes são escrupulosamente verídicos, e conhecidos de mui pouca gente, porque pela primeira vez os confio ao papel'. (My translation).
16. Thomas Raikes, *A Portion of the Journal Kept by Thomas Raikes, Esq., from 1831 to 1847*… 4 vols (London: Longman, Brown, Green and Longmans, 1856–57), 1: 77 (28 September 1832).
17. BL, HHP, MSS Add. 51632, Papers Relative to Portugal: Palmela (13 September 1832); 'D. Pedro est decidé à se deffendre et la Ville de Porto j'espere será le boulevard de la liberté Portugaise. J'ai fait tout ce que j'ai pu ici pour preparer des supportes et je crois avec peu d'argent avoir fait beaucoup'. (My translation).
18. *The Times*, 13 September 1832, 2.

in discussions with diplomats, especially with the Russian and Prussian ministers, who joined him at dinner with Palmerston on 23 August. Villiers found them conversing 'on very intimate terms with him'.[19]

Palmela embarked from Falmouth on 16 September and arrived in Oporto just in time to attend the celebrations for a Liberal victory on 29 September, when an attack had been successfully repulsed. As Palmela observed, this victory was crucial because it enabled the Liberals to regain the self-esteem lost at Souto Redondo. Learning of this and subsequent successes, Palmerston addressed a private note to Palmela, congratulating him on the favourable course of events yet complaining about the constant pressure from Funchal to persuade the Cabinet to recognize D. Maria II. Palmerston insisted that although Britain had already acknowledged Maria as de jure Queen of Portugal, she could not be recognized as the de facto sovereign, simply because she did not rule over most of Portugal. Palmerston had already told William Russell:

> Whether we ought or ought not six months ago to have boldly and openly espoused the cause of Donna Maria and declared her to be Queen and made her so de facto as well as de jure, is a question on which two opinions may fairly be entertained, and my own personal opinion was, and is, that it would have been wiser for us to have taken her decidedly by the hand and have aided her as an ally; but the English Govt. having taken the other course and having proclaimed its resolution to preserve strict neutrality between the rival candidates we are bound to stick to our promises [...]. You will, therefore, be very careful to avoid anything that may be inconsistent with our neutral position.[20]

On 16 November 1832, Pedro again ordered Palmela to London to request the material and political intervention of Britain, even if this involved the sacrifice of part or even the whole of the Constitutional Charter. Given the delicate nature of the mission, which if known would have provoked a major rebellion in the Liberal ranks, Pedro asked Palmela to keep his mission secret. Palmela went so far as to explain his unexpected departure as the result of intrigues against him. Palmela left for England on 20 November on the *London Merchant*, accompanied by his son Domingos, Barbosa de Araújo, Mouzinho de Albuquerque and Almeida Garrett, who had been appointed assistant to both the Secretary of the Kingdom and to the Minister of Foreign Affairs on 22 August.

The party arrived in London on 29 November and, on the following evening Palmela dined at Holland House in the company of Miss Fox, Lady Mary Fox, Lady Lilford, Frederick Byng and Mr Woobrych.[21] Unfortunately, Holland did not keep his diary from mid-August 1832 – when the king himself dined at Holland House – to 19 May 1833, and his recollections of this period are confined to a summary of the main events. This hiatus was the result of a serious attack of gout, which left Holland incapacitated 'for

19. Raikes, *A Portion of the Journal*, 1: 77 (28 September 1832).
20. Palmerston to William Russell, in *The Foreign Policy of Palmerston*, 1: 249 (23 May–10 August 1832).
21. Palmela to His Wife, in *Vida do Duque de Palmella*, 2: 491 (London: 30 November 1832); BL, HHP, MSS Add. 51955, Dinner Books: 1831–38, f. 31v (Friday, 30 November 1832).

weeks and months'.[22] Hence, not only were most of the facts relating Pedro's progress in Portugal and Palmela's activities in London not recorded, but the Portuguese Liberals were temporarily deprived of their main ally in Britain. Holland's illness had unfortunate consequences for the Liberal cause, not least because it resulted in a deterioration of relations with the British Cabinet. The suggestion, advanced earlier, that Grey's government had two different policies on Portuguese matters – the official line represented by Palmerston and the unofficial one by Holland – actually becomes more persuasive when the period of Holland's virtual absence is examined.

In November 1832, as in August, Palmela found British public opinion sceptical about a Liberal victory. Palmerston was showing signs of tiring of the affairs of Portugal, while Grey thought Pedro's situation hopeless. It was now anticipated that sooner or later the conflict would be resolved by removing both Pedro and Miguel from the scene and then placing D. Maria on the throne – without real guarantee that her government would be a Liberal one. Palmerston seemed to favour this solution, provided that Spain would cooperate in it, while Grey went as far as to suggest to Neumann that Maria might marry an Austrian Archduke. While Palmela generally disliked the idea, describing it as an 'intrigue', he thought it could be the only way to involve Britain in the search for a settlement. On 21 December, Palmela sent a note to Holland, attaching a long dispatch addressed to Grey. In order to prevent disaster in Portugal, Palmela requested a loan of £32,000 to pay creditors and to finance the government of Oporto. He warned

> that the material interests of the subjects of H. B. M. established in Oporto will suffer considerably, and even the security of a large number of those individuals would be seriously compromised; I am also convinced that, regardless of any such calculation, the Government of H. B. M. would not hesitate to do whatever possible to prevent the city of Oporto from the risk of becoming the theatre of scenes of confusion and horror.[23]

Palmela further requested 'the immediate intervention of H. B. M. to stop the bloodshed in Portugal and promote a national reconciliation', which he believed was essential now that negotiations for a general armistice had begun.[24] As Palmela noted, the British government had already sent Stratford Canning to Madrid to open negotiations for a peaceful Anglo-Spanish intervention in Portugal. Grey's refusal to accept Palmela's request was

22. Holland, *The Holland House Diaries*, 203 (Summer and Autumn 1732 [1832]).
23. BL, HHP, MSS Add. 51632, Papers Relative to Portugal: Palmela: the Marquis de Palmela to Earl Grey (21 December 1832); 'mais j'aurai assurer que des interêts materiéls des sujets de S. M. B. établis à Oporto en souffriraient considerabelement, et que la securité même d'un grande nombre de ces individus serait gravement compromise je suis bien convaincu d'ailleurs, qu'independament de tout semblable calcul le Gouvt. de S. M. B. n'hesiterait pas à faire tout ce qu'il jugerait praticable pour éviter que la ville d'Oporto ne courre le risque de devenir le théatre de scenes de désordre et d'horreur'. (My translation).
24. BL, HHP, MSS Add. 51632, Papers Relative to Portugal: Palmella: the Marquis de Palmela to Earl Grey (21 December 1832); 'l'immediate intervention de S. M. B. pour arreter l'effusion du sang en Portugal et amener une reconciliation national'. (My translation).

communicated in a dispatch of 23 December. Talleyrand had also raised the issue with his government on Palmela's behalf, but with no more success.

This was Palmela's last action as Pedro's envoy, since, on the same day, anticipating his master's reaction, he offered his resignation. On 25 December, understandably irritated with the signs that his own interests were being ignored, Pedro reprimanded Palmela for exceeding his instructions. Pedro had been particularly irritated with the contents of a letter sent by Palmela to Palmerston on 8 December, stating that 'H. M. the Duque de Bragança declares, in requesting the support of England, he is ready in advance and unconditionally to accept all conditions that the judgement of H. B. M. will think most appropriate to ask from him'.[25] Hence, on 21 January 1833, Pedro accepted Palmela's resignation, stating that 'it would be neither fair nor reasonable to refuse the resignation from the ministry as requested and Senhor Marquês will receive my decision in this respect at the relevant department'.[26] Pedro further explained that while resignation from the ministry did not necessarily entail the end of Palmela's diplomatic mission, given the letter to Palmerston, the Regent had little choice but to withdraw his confidence. Thereafter, negotiations with the British Cabinet were conducted by Funchal and Abreu Lima, but little progress was made.

Soriano suggested that Palmela may also have discussed a marriage between Maria and the Spanish prince Don Carlos[27] with Palmerston as a means of pacifying Fernando

---

25. 'O Duque de Bragança ao Marquez de Palmela', in *Despachos*, 4: 860 (Porto: 11 January 1833); 'S. M. le Duc de Bragança déclare, en invoquant l'appui de l'Angleterre, qu'il est prêt à accéder d'avance et sans bornes à toutes les conditions que la sagesse de S. M. B. jugera convenable de lui demander'. (My translation).
26. 'O Duque de Bragança ao Marquez de Palmela', ibid., 4: 859 (Porto: 11 January 1833); 'nem seria justo nem rasoavel recusar-lhe a demissão que me pede do ministerio, e pela repartição competente receberá o sr. marquez a minha decisão a esse respeito'. (My translation).
27. Don Carlos (1788–1855), Infante of Spain, second surviving son of Carlos IV and María Luisa de Parma. In 1830, Fernando VII, Carlos's eldest brother, issued the Pragmatic Sanction abolishing the Salic Law, which had excluded women from the Spanish throne. Although Fernando's decree had been originally approved by *Cortes* in 1789, it had never been promulgated. Carlos, hitherto the heir to the throne, was displaced from the line of succession by his niece, Isabel, afterwards Isabel II of Spain. Refusing to renounce his claim to the Spanish throne, Carlos decided to fight for his rights and to conspire against his brother. In the meanwhile, the Infanta Maria Teresa de Bragança (1793–1874), D. João VI's eldest daughter, and her son, Don Sebastián de Borbón y Bragança, both ardent Legitimists, decided to support Carlos's claims. As a result, Queen María Cristina de Borbón, regent during the king's illness, advised them to leave Spain for Portugal, an order also extending to Carlos. The party arrived in Aldeia Galega on 26 March and, in the same day, moved into the Palace of Ajuda, later transferring to the Ramalhão. As Holland observed in his diary, 'The Infant Don Carlos, for whom his brother's Government had sent a frigate to the Tagus to convey him to Civita Vecchia, decamped with all his family the eve of the day he was expected to sail and proceeded to Don Miguel at Coimbra, with whom he had manifestly concerted this flight'. (*The Holland House Diaries*, 220 (14 [June] Friday [1834]). Following the death of Fernando VII, while María Cristina assumed the regency during Isabel II's minority, Don Carlos proclaimed himself King of Spain.

VII.[28] Given Palmerston's commitment in finding a proper match for the young queen a few years later, Soriano's suggestion is not entirely absurd. Whatever really passed between Palmerston and Palmela, stories of the envoy's 'achievement' in London were regarded with suspicion in Oporto. The *Crónica constitucional* tried to minimize the issue, arguing that 'It is credible that the bases of the negotiations were the acknowledgement of the Queen, the reestablishment of the Constitutional Charter and the departure of the Infante from the Kingdom', while, at the same time, implicitly censuring Palmela for agreeing to things that only the national parliament could determine.[29]

Palmela's enemies had finally managed to get rid of their main foe. On 20 February 1833, the editor of *The Times* regretted: 'The Movement party now rules his [Pedro's] general policy, and Palmella is displaced to make way for less able and experienced Ministers'.[30] However, Palmela himself does not appear to have been either surprised or distressed to learn that his services were no longer required. As we have seen, his relationship with Pedro had often been strained and he had been very disappointed when Pedro did not call upon him to lead the government when they landed in Terceira. Palmela seemed relieved that he could finally meet his wife and children in Paris. On 28 December, he informed his wife that he had resigned adding that he hoped that Pedro would agree that he should cease to be both minister and plenipotentiary: 'As far as I am concerned, I would appreciate that and would immediately go to Oporto in a private capacity'.[31] Before leaving for the Continent, however, Palmela and his son, Domingos, paid a last visit to Holland House, where they dined on 28 December in the company of Charles Fox, Dr Holland and Woobrych.[32] Palmela had also the opportunity of visiting Talleyrand, with whom he dined twice or three times a week, sometimes at Lieven's.[33] On 5 February, when Palmela was ready to leave his beloved Britain, he admitted to his wife that it was 'very uncertain that I will ever return to London'.[34] Palmela left for France on 17 February.

Palmela was in Paris when, in April 1833, a few days before his return to Oporto, he received Pedro's decree of 4 April creating him Duque do Faial, while Funchal was elevated to Marquês.[35] As he admitted in his memoirs, after all his misunderstandings with Pedro, he was far from expecting such recognition.[36] On 1 May, when Palmela was already in London on his way to Oporto, he wrote to Pedro to thank him. Now that Palmela was a free man, at his own expense, he decided to use his own contacts and influence to recruit additional reinforcements to assist in the defence of Oporto. While in London, Palmela and Mendizábal had contacted several bankers, hoping to obtain

---

28. Soriano, *HGC*, 3.ª época, t. IV [16]: 168–69.
29. *Chronica constitucional do Porto*, 4 January, 1833, 646.
30. *The Times*, 20 February 1833, 5.
31. Palmela to His Wife, in *Vida do Duque de Palmella*, 2: 495 (28 December 1832); 'Pelo que me toca estima-lo-ia, e voltava logo para o Porto como simples particular'. (My translation).
32. BL, HHP, MSS Add. 51955, Dinner Books: 1831–38, f. 33ᵛ (28 December 1832).
33. Palmela to His Wife, in *Vida do Duque de Palmella*, 2: 497 (11 January [1833]).
34. Ibid., 2: 499 (5 February [1833]).
35. *Chronica constitucional do Porto*, 9 April 1833, 1059.
36. Palmela, *Memórias*, 275.

funding for the Liberal cause. Eventually, assisted by Abreu Lima and Mendizabál, Palmela secured a loan of £40,000, which allowed him to purchase a merchant ship, later transformed into a fine frigate, and to charter five steamers, as well as to enlist new levies, including an English battalion under Colonel Dudgeon. He had also managed to persuade Charles Napier, a talented Scottish Navy officer, to accompany him on his return to Portugal. Napier agreed on condition that he was appointed admiral of the fleet. Palmela had approached Napier in August 1832, but he had refused to serve under Sartorius, who was his junior in the service. On 8 January, Napier had written to Palmela declaring that, although he was ready to accept any assignment the queen considered appropriate, he could not serve under a less senior officer.

In parallel with the diplomatic activities undertaken by Funchal and Lima in London, Palmela decided to maintain his own connections with Palmerston and Grey, although without much success. Palmela called at Holland House on 5 May, where he dined with the Duke of Bedford, Lords Melbourne, Granville and Duncannon,[37] and 20 May, 'on the point of sailing with reinforcements to Oporto'.[38] As Holland observed:

> he goes with heavy heart at finding that the English Government will not define the contingency which would induce them to espouse more openly the cause of Donna Maria, nor even suggest the advice which they would be best pleased Don Pedro should follow, whom Palmella thinks he could persuade to abandon the Regency, or take any other step we might deem proper, provided he could hold out to him with any certainty the prospect of England's countenance or interference in behalf of his daughter.[39]

Once more, Holland insisted that 'we lose an opportunity, and throw the Liberal party if successful into the arms of France', who, despite her reluctance to give any financial support to the Liberal cause, had permitted Pedro to equip a fleet and to recruit French and Polish levies on her territory.[40] Holland's long period of illness meant that he had lost ground to Palmerston who had effectively seen off the challenge of an alternative foreign policy. At least, Palmela could assure Holland 'that the money he has unexpectedly raised does not come from France'.[41]

Solignac, a 62-year-old French veteran who had served under Napoleon, had been commissioned to command Pedro's soldiers.[42] Solignac, who travelled from Ostend on the *London Merchant*, landed in Oporto on 1 January 1833, accompanied by several fresh Belgian levies. But Solignac also carried a terrible unseen passenger, more dangerous to the Liberals than the Absolutists themselves: the *cholera morbus*.[43] The shortage of food

37. BL, HHP, MSS Add. 51955, Dinner Books: 1831–38, f. 43^{v} (5 May 1833).
38. Holland, *The Holland House Diaries*, 210 (20 Holland House [May 1833]).
39. Ibid., 210–11.
40. Ibid., 211.
41. Ibid., p. 211 (20 Holland House [May 1833]).
42. Jean-Baptiste Solignac (1773–1850), French general, the brother-in-law of Jean-Baptiste Jourdan (1762–1833), 1st comte Jourdan.
43. This infection, a form of non-epidemic cholera currently known as gastroenteritis, is believed to have first appeared in the Ganges Valley in 1817 and from thence spread to the whole world,

and fuel during autumn and winter 1832–33, together with inadequate hygiene, made the population of Oporto vulnerable to disease. Although Dr João Tavares, the health inspector of the army, had inspected the *London Merchant* before its passengers were allowed ashore, he misdiagnosed the symptoms of several recruits and did not enforce the quarantine.[44] The epidemic spread rapidly among the population, reaching its peak during February and early March and resulting in 3,621 deaths. The winter was dark and humid, and the church bells never seemed to stop ringing for funerals. By mid-February the conditions were so bad that a general withdraw was again contemplated. Fortunately, either in an act of heroism or in an attempt to redeem his alleged cowardice during the *Belfastada* episode, Saldanha opposed the idea of a retreat. Saldanha arrived in Oporto on 28 January 1833 and was appointed field marshal on 2 February.[45]

At first the Liberals contemplated an advance to Lisbon over land but, in the face of the overwhelmingly numerical superiority of Miguel's army, were forced to explore alternative strategies. Further, initial expectations as to Solignac's military capabilities were disappointed when the marshal, probably due to his advanced age, proved unwilling to engage in operations involving significant risk. Even the limited actions Solignac did undertake – those against the Fortress of Queijo and stronghold of Crasto on 24 January – were unsuccessful. Soldiers began to lose respect for Solignac, calling him 'General Batata' ('General Potato'),[46] while Raimundo Cunha Matos, a Luso-Brazilian officer in Pedro's service, described him as a 'weak, coward and charlatan who promised much and did nothing'.[47] The Liberals' only chance of success – if they had any – was to attack Lisbon from the sea, and even then they had to appreciate that the Absolutists possessed a considerable naval force. Hence, in the spring of 1833, the appearance of Palmela and Napier with more ships and soldiers was regarded as a very good omen.

Palmela had left London for Falmouth on 23 May to join what was later known as his Steamer Expedition, due to the large number of steam vessels. The expedition sailed on 28 May and on 1 June Palmela, Mendizábal and Napier landed at a small beach near Oporto, where Saldanha was expecting them with open arms. Palmela, Mendizábal and Napier went directly to see Pedro, who was surprised when given sufficient funds to cover arrears of pay owed to his soldiers. Under these circumstances, Pedro had little choice but to accept Palmela's insistence that Napier must replace Sartorius. Once again, Palmela had redeemed himself for his apparent irresponsibility during the *Belfastada* episode, although there was still the matter of the allegations of exceeding his authority and of betraying Pedro's confidence. As Napier observed, 'It is clear the Emperor did not like the Duke of Palmella, whom he fancied had lent himself to an intrigue to displace

---

taking the lives of 40–45 million people. It reached Moscow and St Petersburg in 1823 and from then spread to Western Europe, reaching Paris and London in 1832.

44. João Fernandes Tavares (1795–1874), Visconde de Ponte Ferreira, Brazilian physician.

45. Saldanha arrived in Oporto on 28 January 1833 accompanied by his radical followers, including Stubbs, Cabreira, Rodrigo Pinto Pizarro, later Barão da Ribeira de Sabrosa, and Liberato, who had been allowed to move to Oporto by a decree of 3 November.

46. Saldanha and Athelstane, *Memoirs*, 1: 257.

47. Raimundo José Cunha Matos, quoted in *HGC*, 3.ª época, t. IV [16]: 199; 'fraco, cobarde, ignorante e charlatão, que prometteu muito e nada fez'. (My translation).

him'.[48] Napier added: 'I believed nothing but fear kept his ministers from either sending Palmella away or to prison'.[49] After all, Pedro had been forced to accept Palmela's virtual order to appoint Napier, a humiliation which did not improve their relations.

The most pressing question now was to decide on a plan that would result in the overthrow of Miguel, but opinions were deeply divided. The initial plan had been to send the whole army – now amounting to about 18,000 men – south to meet the enemy. However, as noted earlier, given the Absolutists' clear superiority this would have been suicidal. A second plan, initially supported by Napier and Saldanha, involved a direct attack on Lisbon by sea, in other words an assault on the very heart of Absolutism. Napier had already outlined his plan in a letter to Palmela written on 8 January 1833. If Napier had command of the fleet, he would force the entry of the Tagus and disembark in Lisbon, even if only with the steamers. In his own words: 'The passage to Lisbon is short and I give you my word that they [the vessels] would be between the Bugio and São Julião before dawn'.[50] This plan was, however, also considered impracticable and thus abandoned. Miguel had a considerable number of warships stationed in the Tagus and the people of Lisbon seemed in no mood to rebel against him. A variation of the second plan was to embark about one third of the Liberal army and then make a landing somewhere near the capital, perhaps in Peniche or Ericeira, and from there march on Lisbon. A third plan involved the dispatch of a naval expedition to capture the Algarve and from then march north to the capital. After some hesitation, the last option was preferred despite the opposition of Solignac, who, according to Palmela, 'wished to butt against the enemy lines'.[51] If the Algarve scheme worked, the Liberals would have secured control of both north and south of the kingdom, and would become the besiegers instead of the besieged. The French marshal offered his resignation, which was immediately accepted while Saldanha became Supreme Chief of the General Staff.

Early on the morning of 11 June, Sartorius relinquished command of the squadron to Napier, who had adopted the pseudonym of 'Carlos de Ponza' to avoid problems connected with the Foreign Enlistment Act. The crews, including the officers, consisted of about 1,300 men.[52] The command of the military expedition, a force of 2,500 men, was given to Vila Flor, now Duque da Terceira, by *Carta Régia* of 13 June. The expedition embarked between 12 and 14 June.

Palmela, whose title of Duque de Faial had been changed, at his own request, to that of Duque de Palmela by Decree of 14 June 1833, accompanied the expedition in the capacity of civil governor ad interim over the towns and provinces that declared

48. Charles Napier, *An Account of the War in Portugal between Don Pedro and Don Miguel*. 2 vols (London: T. & W. Boone, 1836), 1: 163.
49. Ibid., 2: 227.
50. Charles Napier to Palmela, in *HGC*, 3.ª época, t. IV [16]: 237 (8 January 1833); 'A passagem para Lisboa é curta, e dou a minha palavra, que elles se achariam entre o Bugio e S. Juião antes do romper do dia'. (My translation).
51. Palmela, *Memórias*, 278; 'que desejava ir marrar contra as linhas inimigas'. (My translation).
52. BL, HHP, MSS Add. 51634, Papers Relative to Portugal: 1831–1845: Description of the Battle of Algarve (5 July 1833).

for D. Maria.[53] On 15 June, Palmela and Terceira embarked on the flagship *Rainha de Portugal* 'with a numerous and brilliant staff', and, on the early morning of 21 the fleet finally lifted anchor and sailed southwards with a fair wind.[54] On 23, the fleet rounded the Cape of São Vicente and sailed along the Algarve coastline towards the Guadiana. The next day, they reached Alagoa beach, Monte Gordo, two leagues from the Spanish southeastern border, where the troops were landed. Palmela landed in Tavira to read a proclamation in favour of Maria II, but the local population did not receive him well. On the following day, Palmela moved to Faro, where they 'were tolerably received', and established his headquarters at the Bishop's Palace.[55] In a matter of six days, all the important towns of Algarve fell under Liberal control.

Meanwhile, a few days after Napier had passed Lisbon, Miguel ordered his whole fleet to pursue the enemy squadron. After leaving Palmela in Faro, the Liberal fleet had sailed westwards to Lagos where it anchored on 30 June. On the night of 2 July, leaving the steamers in the Bay of Lagos, they sailed towards Lisbon and, on the next morning, the officers of the watch reported six sails, to Napier's great delight. Acting against all common sense, the Absolutists had made the mistake of going out to meet the enemy, thus putting themselves in a highly vulnerable position. According to Napier, 'During the night the hostile squadrons kept within a musket-shot, – the Miguelite fleet in a compact line, my squadron in two, ready to take advantage of any favourable opportunity'.[56] The strong wind and rough sea that prevented Napier from taking any action during the whole of 4 July, gave place to a fine day and, on the afternoon of 5 July, a decisive battle took place off Cape St Vicente, in which Napier achieved a remarkable victory and captured the whole Absolutist fleet.

The news of Napier's remarkable victory reached Holland House on Sunday 14 July. Lord Holland, visibly satisfied, commented in his diary:

> It gladdened every enemy of tyranny and oppression, depressed the abbetors of all Ultra opinions, and should have induced our Government to send a Mission to the Regency forthwith and to recall by proclamation all our subjects from the service of Don Miguel.[57]

Palmela was in Faro when, on the morning of 6 July, he was surprised by a note from Napier announcing victory over the enemy squadron, which he had now under in his power in Lagos. Palmela and Mendizábal hastened to Lagos where they found the ships of both fleets anchored side by side. Excited with such a remarkable, if unexpected success – which gave the Liberals complete supremacy at sea – Palmela suggested something even bolder. If the army marched towards the capital backed by the fleet sailing

53. *Chronica constitucional do Porto*, 17 June 1833, [1291].
54. Napier, *An Account*, 1: 178.
55. Ibid., 1: 188.
56. Ibid., 1: 193–94.
57. Holland, *The Holland House Diaries*, 230 (Monday, 15 July [1834]). Although the entry is dated 15 July, it comprised a larger period of time, as inferred by the first sentence: 'Went to London and staid till Saturday the 20th'.

along the Atlantic coast, perhaps they would have a chance of capturing Lisbon. The idea was certainly daring but worthwhile trying. Hence, on 13 July, while Napier lifted anchor and sailed towards the Tagus, the Duque da Terceira marched with his 'Bravos' through Algarve and Alentejo. Encountering few obstacles, the Liberals crossed the Sado on 19 July and marched towards Setúbal, where they arrived on the night of 22. After a light skirmish with the local garrison, who withdraw to Azeitão without offering much resistance, Terceira made his triumphant entry into the town. As Soriano remarked, after the defeat at São Vicente, the Absolutists seemed to lose all their former enthusiasm. On 23 July, learning of the approach of the Liberals to the capital, Cadaval ordered about 2,500 men to Cacilhas under Field Marshal Teles Jordão to intercept the enemy.[58] Terceira, who had left Setúbal on that night of 23 on his way to Cacilhas, met Jordão's forces near Almada. There the Absolutists were defeated and the general killed by Romão José Soares, commander of the second Battalion of *Chasseurs*, when trying to escape incognito.

On that night, Cadaval gathered his military council where, given the impossibility of defending Lisbon from a Liberal attack – despite the inferiority of the advancing forces (barely 1,500 men) – it was decided to evacuate the town immediately. Hence, the Absolutist forces, amounting to about 10,000 troops, gathered in Campo Grande and began to retreat northwards to Leiria and Coimbra. As Napier noted, 'Thus by the cowardice and imbecility of Don Miguel's ministers was Lisbon lost to Miguel and the Duke of Terceira saved'.[59] Yet, to be fair to Cadaval, despite the numerical superiority of the Absolutists, his men were now totally demoralized and the population of Lisbon was finally showing signs of rebellion, which, if it had occurred, could easily have resulted in a general massacre. Besides, Cadaval knew that Napier was on his way to the Tagus with the entire Portuguese fleet. However, as Soriano observed, after this episode the Absolutists could no longer mock the Liberals about their shameful retreat from Oporto during the *Belfastada*.[60]

The sight of the blue and white Constitutional flag flying on the Castle of São Jorge on the morning of 24 July, at first interpreted on the opposite bank as a possible trap, turned out to be a sign that the Absolutists had already withdrawn.[61] Hence, between two and three o'clock in the afternoon, Terceira and his 'Bravos' made their triumphal entry in Terreiro de Paço (Praça do Comércio), where an enthusiastic crowd of people was expecting them. After five years of tyranny, Lisbon had been finally liberated. The following note in the dinner books for 2 August 1833, 'Lisbon declared for Doña Maria', the only one of its kind in the whole set of manuscript books, reveals the Hollands' delight when the news arrived in England.[62] There must have been great excitement at

58. Joaquim Teles Jordão (1777–1833), Portuguese army officer, one of the infante's most loyal servants. Jordão was appointed Governor of the Tower of S. Julião da Barra in the mouth of the Tagus and later Field Marshal. He was killed by the Liberals at Cacilhas on 23 July 1833, when he was trying to escape incognito among the crowd.
59. Napier, *An Account,* 1: 217–18.
60. Soriano, *HGC,* 3.ª época, t. IV [16]: 387, 393–94.
61. The blue and white bipartite flag of the constitutionalists was established by decree of the Terceira Regency of 18 October 1830 (*Chronica da Terceira,* 21 October 1830, [1]).
62. BL, HHP, MSS Add. 51955, Dinner Books: 1831–38, f. 51ᵛ (2 August 1833).

the dinner attended by Lord Essex and Mr Tierney, where the tumblers of port much favoured by the Whigs were accompanied by 'vivas'!

When Napier's squadron entered the Tagus on 25 July, Lisbon had already declared for D. Maria. Once he had landed in Lisbon, in accordance with his orders, Palmela took charge of the provisional government of the town and hastened to take the measures necessary for the reestablishment of the Liberal order. On the following day, learning of Terceira's successes, Pedro sailed for Lisbon aboard the *William IV* steamer, leaving Saldanha behind to defend Oporto. On the afternoon of 28 August 1833, a quarter of a century after his departure to Rio de Janeiro, Pedro finally returned to Lisbon, where a huge crowd shouting 'vivas' were expecting him. On 29 July, Pedro visited the Bragança Pantheon at São Vicente de Fora, and affixed the following lines to his father's coffin: 'One son assassinated thee; another son will revenge thee, 29 July 1833. D. Pedro'. Of course, as Soriano remarked, Miguel could well have said the same thing about his brother.[63]

While these events were taking place in Lisbon, Miguel was watching the defeat of his army on the south bank of the Douro opposite to Oporto. While the Liberals were landing in the Algarve, Miguel had sent reinforcements to Oporto, believing that Pedro had not defended it properly. On 25 July, General Bourmont, a French veteran who had been commissioned to command the Absolutist army, launched a massive attack on Oporto – the biggest since the siege had commenced. Saldanha, who had been appointed Pedro's lieutenant-general, defeated the enemy after a fierce battle, thus fully restoring his reputation from the shameful episode of his extraordinary behaviour during the *Belfastada*. Miguel, who was witnessing the battle from the heights of São Gens, was so furious with Bourmont's defeat that he threw his telescope on the ground. On 9 August, leaving the French general Comte d'Almer in command of the Siege of Oporto, Miguel rode southwards to meet Cadaval in Coimbra, where he also found his sisters, including Isabel Maria, and the Spanish prince Don Carlos, who had come from Spain to support his relation and to seek support for his own bid for the Spanish throne. With the approach of the Liberals from Lisbon, the members of the Portuguese and Spanish royal families had accompanied Cadaval in his flight to Coimbra. A British frigate was offered Carlos to convey him to Italy, but he declined. On 18 August, Saldanha defeated d'Almer and forced him to withdraw from Oporto. Two days later, Saldanha entered the city in triumph. After more than a year of siege, Portugal's second city was finally liberated.

Although in formal terms, the Civil War ended only with the conclusion of the armistice of Evoramonte on 26 May 1834, the capture of Lisbon by the Liberals on 24 July 1833 had already brought a reversal of roles. Hitherto, the Liberals had been an army of rebels and foreign mercenaries threatening a de facto regime; after the capture of the capital, the very heart of that regime, it was the Absolutists who were relegated to the role of rebels. This change in the status quo was important not only in Portugal,

63. Soriano, *HGC*, 3.ª época, t. IV [16]: 413; 'Um filho te assassinou, outro filho te vingará, 20 July 1833. D. Pedro'. (My translation).

but had major implications for the achievement of credibility in the courts of Europe, especially in Britain. Pedro could finally claim that his daughter was not only the de jure, but also the de facto, Sovereign of Portugal. Thus on 15 August, William Russell presented Pedro with his credentials as minister plenipotentiary to Lisbon, a document despatched from London one week earlier. Palmerston had finally kept his promise that if Pedro achieved a major victory in Portugal, the British government would recognize his daughter as the legitimate ruler. At the same time, Abreu Lima's credentials as Portuguese ambassador to London were accepted by William IV and diplomatic relations between the two countries were finally re-established. France followed suit on 20 October, when the baron de Mortier received his credentials as Louis Philippe's minister at Lisbon.

On 13 August 1833, Broumont ordered the Absolutist troops at Coimbra to march on the capital. On 3 September, the first Absolutist troops began to arrive in Lumiar and Campo Grande, on the northern outskirts of Lisbon, thus giving the Liberals enough time to organize basic defensive arrangements. Early in the morning of 5 September, the Absolutists attacked the Liberal lines near the Lisbon Aqueduct with a strong column of light troops. Despite the fierce combat that lasted throughout the day and resulted in several casualties on both sides, Broumont failed to break the Liberal lines. Consequently, on 21 September, the French Marshal resigned his command. Broumont was replaced by the British McDonnell, a veteran of the Peninsular War probably hired through Beresford or even Wellington, who, according to Holland, 'is active in directing the employment of the money sent from the Continent by Don Miguel's supporters in equipments, recruiting, &c'.[64] But McDonnell was no more successful than his French predecessor.

The subsequent actions of Miguel's army, mainly in the province of Ribatejo, were essentially a series of desperate attempts to recover what had been already lost. The high morale, characteristic of the Absolutists in the early days, was vanishing and there was a corresponding increase in desertions to the other side – the usual pattern in such situations. The following months were marked by Liberal victories in different parts of country, including that of Asseiceira on 16 May, which forced the Absolutists to abandon Santarém and retreat to Évora, where they arrived on 21 May. Realizing the impossibility of continuing a war against an army now clearly more powerful, the Absolutists had little choice but to seek an armistice from the Liberal generals. Saldanha and Terceira, the victors of Asseiceira, informed the Absolutist general Lemos that Pedro would accept nothing less than Miguel's unconditional surrender.[65] Given the desperate situation of his army – or of what was left of it after thousands of desertions and casualties – Miguel agreed. Hence, on 26 May 1834, an armistice was concluded in Evoramonte between Saldanha, Terceira and Lemos, with John Grant, secretary of the British Legation at Lisbon, as a witness.[66] The Convention – alias Concession – of Evoramonte defined the

64. Holland, *The Holland House Diaries*, 229 ([*c.* 10 July 1834]).
65. José António de Azevedo Lemos (1786–1870), Portuguese officer and Latinist.
66. John McPherson Grant (1804–1850), the son of Sir George McPherson Grant.

terms of a general amnesty and decided the future of Miguel and his closest collaborators. Miguel was also forced to sign the following proclamation:

> To satisfy the supervening exigency made by the Marshals Duque da Terceira and Conde de Saldanha, on the behalf of their government: I declare that I will never again, directly or indirectly, interfere in the political affairs of these Kingdoms or its dominions. Court of Evora, 29 May 1834. Miguel.[67]

On Miguel's acceptance of the concession and in accordance with his own wishes, it was decided that he should embark at Sines, Alentejo, on 30 May. As stipulated in the additional articles, 'He shall be accompanied on his journey thither by the Persons in his personal Suite, by 20 Horse Soldiers, selected from those who previously served in his Army, and by 2 squadrons of the Cavalry of the Queen'.[68] A third agreement also signed at Evoramonte between John Grant, Saldanha and Terceira, concerned the future of Don Carlos of Spain, who had accompanied Miguel to Évora. The first article stipulated that 'His Royal Highness the Infante Don Carlos will leave Évora with his Family and Suite to pass to Aldeia Galega on 30 Inst., and to embark there'.[69] Carlos embarked on 1 June aboard the British man-of-war *Donegal*, which sailed two days later for Portsmouth where he arrived on 12.

The 'Acies fraterna et ineluctabile bellum', as Holland called it, had finally reached its end.[70] Early in the morning of 1 June Miguel left Évora and travelled to Sines, where he embarked on H.M.S. *Stag*, which was to take him to Italy and from thence, to quote Webster, 'into merited oblivion'.[71] As soon as he landed in Genoa on 20 June, Miguel

67. Miguel, Proclaim of Évora of 29 May 1834, in *HGC*, 3.ª época, t. V [17]: 322–23.
68. 'Articles Offered to Dom Miguel by the Portuguese Government; and Articles of Execution Concluded on Their Acceptance by Dom Miguel at Evora Monte. – 26 May 1834. (Translation)', in *British and Foreign State Papers: 1833–34*, 1344.
69. 'Articles of Agreement Concluded between Mr. Grant, His Britannic Majesty's Secretary of Legation at Lisbon, and the Duke of Terceira and Marshal Saldanha, for the Retirement of Don Carlos from Portugal. – Evora Monte, 26 May 1834', in *British and Foreign State Papers: 1833–34*, 1345; 'Art. I. Son Altesse Royale l'Infant Don Carlos quitera Evora, avec sa Famille et sa Suite, pour passer à Aldea Gallega, le 30 Courant, et pour s'y embarquer'. (My translation).
70. Holland, *The Holland House Diaries*, 232 (Wednesday, 17, Thursday, 18 and Friday, 19 [1834]).
71. Webster, *The Foreign Policy of Palmerston*, 1: 399. For several years, Miguel lived in either Italy or in England. He moved to Germany in 1851, to marry Princess Adelaide of Löwenstein-Wertheim-Rosenberg on 19 September. The couple settled in a former Cistercian monastery at Bronnbach, Grand Duchy of Baden, where they raised six daughters and one son, Miguel (1853–1927), who, after his father's death, proclaimed himself D. Miguel II. On 18 June 1852, Miguel had issued a declaration stating that he had never given up his rights to the Portuguese throne, which he was now pleased to transmit to his son who was yet to be born or to others that he would father. On 19 November 1866, *The Times* announced the 'death of a person who once made a great noise in the world, but whose very existence has been for the last 20 years utterly forgotten'. (*The Times*, 19 November 1866, 7). Miguel died on 14 November 1866 after a stroke of apoplexy while hunting. He was buried in the Franciscan Convent of Engelberg, in Großheubach, Miltenberg, and his remains translated to the Braganças Pantheon on 5 April 1967.

issued a declaration protesting that the capitulation was null and void because he had been compelled to sign under duress:

> My acquiescence in all stipulations imposed upon me by the preponderating forces confided to the generals of the two governments now existing in Madrid and Lisbon, in accord with two great powers, was a mere provisional action on my part, for the purpose of saving my subjects in Portugal from misfortunes, which the just resistance I might have made would not have spared them, having been surprised by an unexpected and unwarranted attack from a friendly and allied power.[72]

In other words, Miguel attributed his ultimate downfall to the Quadruple Alliance concluded on 22 April 1834 between Great Britain, France, Spain and Portugal, to decide the latter's future. However, as Napier remarked, Miguel's claim was nonsense because the real outcome of the Portuguese Civil War had been decided in the summer of 1833, when Lisbon fell to the Liberals. In Napier's words, 'When the Emperor was in distress, neither France nor England would give him assistance. What then, was the use of a treaty when we had the ball at our feet and were driving it before us?'[73]

All in all, it is difficult to follow the story of the Portuguese Civil War of 1832–34 without recognizing that the Liberals' achievements were truly remarkable and, indeed, almost incredible. How could a small army of barely 7,500 men, mostly ill-clad volunteers, defeat a mighty conventional army of 80,000? While the stupidity and cowardice of the Absolutist leaders certainly contributed to this unlikely outcome, such a feat would have been made impossible without a great deal of heroism and sacrifice on the part of the Liberals. And how could Miguel, who had the whole nation at his feet in 1828, squander this capital in a matter of two months? Had Miguel surrounded himself with wise and moderate men like Palmela or Vila Real, who were at first eager to support him, rather than with bloodthirsty extremists such as Cadaval or Basto, the result might have been totally different. Perhaps the crucial moment came when Wellington asked Miguel to issue a general amnesty, in effect to provide Britain with a pretext to recognize the Absolutist regime. If Vila Real or Palmela had been ministers, they would surely have agreed to Wellington's proposal. With British and probable French recognition, Miguel's position would have been infinitely more secure. As Napier observed,

---

72. D. Miguel de Bragança, Proclaim in Genoa, 20 August 1834, quoted in *Annual Register*, 76 (1834), 435. Miguel's repudiation of the Concession of Evoramonte cost him the pension of 60,000 reis from the Portuguese state, but left him free to renew his claim to the Portuguese throne, especially after the Banishment Law of 19 December 1834. This act not only excluded Miguel and all his descendants from the line of succession to the throne, but also deprived him of Portuguese nationality. The Banishment Law was replaced by Article 90 of the Constitution of 1838 that lasted until 1842. It was reinstated after the establishment of the Republic in 1910 and extended to apply to all members of the House of Bragança. On 27 May 1950, during the Salazar regime, the Banishment Law was revoked by an act of Parliament.
73. Napier, *An Account*, 2: 210.

'His refusal to grant an amnesty, notwithstanding the frequent warnings he had from the Tory administration, was also another cause of his fall'.[74] But Miguel was never really free to choose his own ministers, because it was really they who controlled him. While Miguel appeared to have a firm character, in reality he was as weak as his father. He may have been less fearful, though even this may have been indicative of a streak of irresponsibility rather than of genuine valour. He had always been dominated by Queen Dowager, who, despite her many faults, was certainly a tough and remarkable woman. But when Carlota Joaquina died early in 1830, Miguel was left in the hands of her supporters, who although equally bloodthirsty, were not as clever as she had been. Pedro, on the other hand, had inherited his father's generosity and hesitant character, though he did have some of his mother's audacity and impetuosity. These mixed and often contradictory qualities made him a remarkable, though sometimes perplexing character.

In the late 1820s and early 1830s Pedro and Miguel became the archetypes – if not the victims – of two opposing views of the future. While Miguel was adopted by the legitimists as the symbol of a traditional and unchanging world, Pedro was turned into a symbol of liberty and progress. Hence, it is not surprising that Holland was fascinated by Pedro, 'the ardent and spirited Prince' whom he identified as the hero of the hour.[75] In his own words, 'In sober truth Pedro may be a Madman and perhaps is, but as Allen well and justly observes, he has done more for the recovery of a legitimate throne than any Prince since Henry IV of France'.[76] In the eyes of the public, Pedro and Miguel became what the opinion makers wanted them to be, which, ultimately, conditioned their lives forever. The figure on the cover, a caricature by Daumier representing Pedro and Miguel as two fighting dogs – the first fanned by Louis Philippe of France and the second pushed forward by Czar Nicholas representing the Holy Alliance – speaks louder than any words.

But in reality, Pedro and Miguel were more like two sides of the same coin. Miguel was not the *bête noire* of the Liberal imagination, nor was Pedro the white knight of liberty that Liberal historians have described. They were simply the children of the old good and fearful João VI and his heartless and ambitious queen, Carlota Joaquina. Both Pedro and Miguel were trapped in a web of international intrigues in a rapidly changing world and were used by European leaders to advance their own agendas.[77] To paraphrase Hegel, like so many 'heroes of an epoch', Pedro and Miguel fell off the world stage 'like empty hulls from the kernel' once their tasks were complete.[78] Like Caesar or

---

74. Ibid., 2: 220.
75. Holland, *The Holland House Diaries*, 267 ([Nov. 1834]).
76. Ibid., 250 (22 June 1834).
77. According to Webster, Lord William Russell compared the attitude of the European powers towards the Portuguese Civil War to Romans watching a show of gladiators (*The Foreign Policy of Palmerston*, 1: 248).
78. Georg Friedrich Hegel, *Philosophy of History*. Revised edn (New York: The Colonial Press, 1899), 31.

Napoleon before them, Pedro and Miguel simply disappeared from the scene as soon as their roles in the historical process were accomplished. Not long after Miguel had been banished to Vienna in 1834, his brother succumbed to tuberculosis in Quixote's room at the Palace of Queluz. In the end, as Britain and Austria had always wished, Brazil had finally cut the chains with her former metropolis, while Portugal became weaker and more dependent on her ancient ally.

Part 3

AFTERMATH

Chapter Twelve

REVOLUTION

*The Duke of Richmond, though in his usual good humoured way, was full of taunts at my predilection for foreigners, and Portuguese in particular [...].**

Miguel's departure into exile on 2 June 1834 marks the final disintegration of the *Ancien Régime*. Although several historians associate the beginning of the Portuguese contemporaneity with the French invasions (when the old eighteenth-century Portugal collapsed), it was only with the establishment of the Terceira Regency – or perhaps after the 'Landing at Mindelo' and even more clearly following the capture of Lisbon – that the Liberal regime finally began to settle down. The period between 1807 and 1834, so often marked by violence, corresponds to the time that Portuguese society needed to prepare itself for a new age and a new order: the epoch of Liberalism.

But there was still a long way to go before Portugal could even remotely be described as a liberal society. In other words, once the 'political revolution' had been achieved, further revolutions would be needed. These included economic and social revolutions, but most of all a revolution in outlook and in ways of thinking. As Pulido Valente notes, Portugal still lacked the essential foundation needed to sustain the 'Liberal edifice', a strong and self-confident 'middle-class'.[1] Without such a class, the Liberal regime would have a poor chance of survival. The question, therefore, was should the Liberals just wait for the middle class to develop – which was likely to take a long time – or should they try to 'force the pace' by taking steps to promote or even invent this vital ingredient? The second option, inevitably involving an element of artificiality, was the one adopted. Thus Liberal institutions based on Liberal values were imposed by decree, in much the same way as in Napoleonic France. Portuguese Liberalism began by committing crime against its own doctrine – that is, it sought to impose liberty by force.

However, the imposition of liberty by decree was inherently so unnatural that it could not be achieved without a temporary suppression of freedom, that is to say, without a virtual dictatorship. Perhaps things were not really so different to the days of Pombal. Taking advantage of the exceptional circumstances offered by civil war, Pedro and his collaborators decided to launch their own 'revolution'. Despite his intellectual sympathy for Liberalism, he could never rid himself of his subconscious tendency to despotism

---

* Holland, *The Holland House Diaries*, 248 ([after] 22 June [1834]).

1. Vasco Pulido Valente, *Os «devoristas»: a revolução liberal (1834–1836)*. 2nd edn (Lisboa: Quetzal Editores, 1993), 15.

or, as Napier put it, Pedro 'was very fond of having his own way'.[2] Arguably, Pedro's somewhat hesitant character was the product of a mixture of his father's moderation and his mother's tyrannical impetuosity. While in Brazil, Pedro had already shown that, while playing the champion of liberties, he was by no means averse to the role of the enlightened despot. According to Holland:

> The station he [Pedro] was born in necessarily and the education he received purposely were formed to corrupt a nature, by constitution susceptible and irascible to a high degree; it is then a slight panegyrick to say that he personally did more, he grew both wiser and better every year he lived, that he displayed more personal vigor and spirit on recovering a crown and more political honesty and zeal in extending the freedom of his people, than any legitimate Prince for a century?[3]

One of the reasons for the failure of previous attempts at a Parliamentary regime – in 1820–23 and again in 1826–28 – was that while there were deep divisions between the Constitutionalists, their main foe, the Absolutists, were relatively united. It is tempting to argue that the main enemies of Constitutionalism were the Constitutionalists themselves. The old problems re-emerged once the Liberals had captured Lisbon. With the defeat of a common enemy, tensions became internal to the Constitutionalists. As we have seen, divisions within the Liberal party had become apparent during and after the *Belfastada* episode which, not surprisingly, produced a plethora of recriminations. While Palmela emerged as the undisputed head of the aristocratic or moderate party, a Portuguese version of English Whiggism, the flamboyant Saldanha was adopted as the leader of the left-wing radicals. Beneath their personal rivalry, there was an undercurrent of a long-standing quarrel between the two families. Saldanha was the grandson of Pombal, while Palmela's grandfather, D. Manuel de Sousa, had been a victim of Pombal and had died in prison.

Yet, Pedro had not appointed either Palmela or Saldanha as his chief advisors during the Civil War, but turned to 'recycled' progressive Liberals of 1820, such as Silva Carvalho[4] and Agostinho José Freire.[5] As Valente observes, Pedro's choice represented something of a halfway position between Palmela's 'Whiggism' – in this context associated with conservativism – and Saldanha's radicalism. While Holland described Carvalho as 'a popular and virtuous Minister',[6] Napier considered Freire 'a man much too incapable and indolent'[7] who 'had the art of disgusting every person he had to treat with, whether

2. Napier, *An Account*, 2: 24.
3. Holland, *The Holland House Diaries*, 268 ([After] 22 June [1834]).
4. José da Silva Carvalho (1782–1856), a hardworking and skilful magistrate of humble origin, son of José da Silva Carvalho, a farmer, and his wife Ana de Carvalho. Associated with the Liberal Revolution of 1820, Silva Carvalho became a member of the regency and Minister of Justice during the first constitutional regime.
5. Agostinho José Freire (1780–1836), army officer and statesman, originated from a noble family of Évora.
6. Holland, *The Holland House Diaries*, 312 (Wednesday, 24 June 1835).
7. Napier, *An Account*, 2: 24.

native or foreigner'.[8] 'His [Freire's] office', he added, 'was filled by twenty or thirty clerks lounging over their desks; the two principal ones as great intriguers as were to be found in Lisbon'.[9] Ironically, these self-proclaimed champions of liberty proved more like 'little Robespierres' and, as Napier noted, 'they were not liked by the Queen's party, and hated, feared, and detested by the Miguelites'.[10] As Oliveira Martins observed:

> The Regency, they said, is a collective Quixote. In the name of law they do what Miguel did tyrannically. They promulgate doctrines, but do not reform abuses. Their policy is less motivated by their hate of tyranny and Miguel, than by the hate they profess for a great citizen (Saldanha).[11]

Although Palmela had taken the government of Lisbon after its capture by the Liberal forces, when Pedro arrived in the capital on 28 August 1833 he was immediately superseded by the Oporto ministers and relegated to the role of leader of the opposition. Pedro and his ministers tried to induce Palmela to leave by offering him either the London or Paris embassy. But Palmela refused, arguing that he wished to stay at Pedro's side in a private capacity until the Civil War was over and insisting that he could serve his country better by his presence than by his absence. On 19 September 1833, Palmela was chosen as a member of the restored Council of State – last been summoned on 30 May 1823 by João VI during the *Vilafrancada*. In the council, Palmela opposed many of the measures proposed by Pedro's ministers.[12]

In August 1834, learning of these difficulties, Lord Holland regretted that 'They [are] said to be nearly as irreconcilable with the spirit, temper, or form of any regular or constitutional Government'.[13] Two months later, Grey told Princess Lieven:

> In Portugal I consider the contest decided, though there may be yet a good deal to do to bring a country from such a state of disorganization to a permanent settlement; and this work is not in the best hands, being committed to Pedro and his Ministers.[14]

Hopes of a change following the death of Cândido Xavier on 18 October 1833 were frustrated. Pedro not only confirmed the appointments of Silva Carvalho and Freire but chose Joaquim António de Aguiar as Minister of Home Affairs and, later, Minister of

8. Ibid., 2: 230.
9. Ibid., 2: 24.
10. Ibid., 1: 276.
11. Martins, *Portugal contemporaneo*, 1: 226; 'A Regência, diziam, é um quixote collectivo. Faz em nome do direito o mesmo que D. Miguel faz tyrannicamente. Promulga doutrinas, não reforma os abusos. A sua politica é menos dirigida por ódio á tyrannia e a D. Miguel, do que pelo ódio que professa a um grande cidadão (Saldanha)'. (My translation).
12. ANTT, Conselho de Estado: 1821–1910, MSS Actas do Conselho de Estado, Acta n. 1 (1821–44) [Decree of D. Pedro, Duque de Bragança, restoring the Council of State, 19 September 1833], ff. 94r–94v; [Acta] 1.ª Sessão, f. 95r (15 November 1833); Palmela, *Memórias*, 289.
13. Holland, *The Holland House Diaries*, 240 (16–24 August [1833]).
14. Grey to Princess Lieven, in *Correspondence*, 2: 486 (27 October 1833).

Justice.[15] Although an honest man, Aguiar was a fanatic who brought excessive zeal to the suppression of religious orders and the persecution of the Absolutists. Dorothée Dino, a guest at Holland House, wrote in her memoirs:

> Dom Pedro is hardly relieved of his brother's presence and free of the supervision of the Cortes, and he has already begun to destroy convents, monks, and nuns. I do not know whether this, too, will excite the admiration at Holland House, but to me it seems a piece of impious folly which may well bring speedy repentance in its train.[16]

The wounds of the Civil War were still too fresh to allow any effective reconciliation. After five years of tyranny and persecution, it would have been surprising, if after the fall of Lisbon, the Liberals had not settled old scores by taking their revenge on the Absolutists. A few days after he landed in Oporto in July 1832, Pedro had decreed a general amnesty for supporters of his brother's regime. There were, however, a substantial number of exclusions, notably ministers and secretaries of state, the Duque de Lafões, for having promoted a petition in favour of the usurpation, the Marquês de Olhão, who did the same in the Municipal Assembly of Lisbon, the Bishop of Viseu and Acúrcio das Neves, for their conduct during the so-called Assembly of the Three Estates of the Kingdom, as well as any magistrate who had sanctioned the punishment of political prisoners. Pedro's decree stipulated that those exempted from the amnesty were to be brought to justice, although not put to death.

Although Pedro's decree was reissued following the capture of Lisbon, this did not prevent revenge against those associated with the Absolutist regime. Furthermore, since the amnesty did not cover professional positions, all civil officers who had served in Miguel's administration were replaced by those Liberals who had been removed from their former positions in 1828 and their wages paid in arrears. Similarly, officers who had been promoted by Miguel were now 'degraded, and in the most ungracious way'.[17] Properties confiscated by Miguel's government, as well as noble titles that had been suppressed, were restored to their owners, while those who had escaped from Lisbon when the Liberals approached, saw theirs confiscated. The Viscondessa de Juromenha, Beresford's mistress in Lisbon, was sent to a convent, though shortly after released, while the English marshal's correspondence with Broumont was published in the Portuguese

---

15. Joaquim António de Aguiar (1792–1884), Portuguese magistrate, professor of law at the University of Coimbra and politician, son of Xavier António de Aguiar, a surgeon, by Teresa Angélica de Aguiar. Joaquim António de Aguiar held several political posts during the Portuguese Constitutional Monarchy, and was Chief Minister three times: 1841–42, 1860 and 1865–68. As Minister of Justice during Pedro's regency, Aguiar was responsible for the dissolution of convents, monasteries, colleges, hospices and other houses of the religious orders, transferring their vast patrimony to the Portuguese state. These actions together with his anti-ecclesiastical spirit earned Aguiar the nickname *O Mata-Frades* ('The Friar-Killer').
16. Dorothée Dino, *Memoirs of the Duchesse de Dino: (afterwards Duchesse de Talleyrand et de Sagan), 1831–1835* (London: W. Heinemann, 1909), 89.
17. Napier, *An Account*, 1: 257–58.

and British press.[18] Jesuits, who had been allowed to return to Portugal in 1829, after 68 years of banishment, were again expelled. Monastic orders were also suppressed and their properties confiscated. The Papal Nuncio, who had supported Miguel, was required to leave without delay, and a ship was offered to convey him.

Given the widespread thirst for revenge, the measures were generally popular, but a few, including Palmela, expressed concern. As Napier observed:

> In fact one species of tyranny was substituted for another; there was a change of men, but none of measures; they were rulers of a party, not of a Kingdom. One half of Portugal had been confiscated by Don Miguel's ministers, and the other half by Don Pedro's.[19]

Yet, as Soriano remarked, the relative mildness with which previous constitutional regimes had treated their enemies, had only made those enemies stronger and more dangerous. As Valente notes, 'the program of the aristocrats, a *Whig* program of gradual and pacific reform, made no sense after the slaughter of the last two years (if it had ever made any) [...] and of the legislative revolution of the dictators, now irreversible'.[20] The question is: should liberal or democratic regimes use despotic means to preserve themselves and secure liberty? Palmela thought not. In his memoirs, he regretted Pedro's weakness in allowing the persecution of the Absolutists, which too often extended to the innocent as well as the guilty.[21]

Lord Holland never really answered this question directly, probably for the same reason that he could never make up his mind about Pombal or Napoleon. However, Holland could not avoid regretting 'The conduct of Pedro on his arrival at Lisbon', which he considered 'very injudicious and offensive'.[22] He was especially disappointed that his friend, 'The Duke of Palmela and the Moderate party' had been passed over in favour of 'inefficient and violent Men, and he [Pedro] has had recourse to arbitrary illegal and precipitate measures of a revolutionary and vindictive character'.[23] Yet, in a marginal note written after receiving further intelligence, Holland questioned his previous judgement:

> Such were the first impressions given us by the official reports from Lisbon, and Hoppner, our Consul, was in truth recalled (I suspect against Palmerston's wishes) because his accounts were at variance with these reports and chiefly because he expressed his conviction of the necessity of revolutionary measures to secure the success of a revolution in somewhat uncourtly and violent terms.[24]

---

18. D. Maria da Luz Willoughby da Silveira (1787–1861), the wife of António de Lemos Pereira de Lacerda (1761–1828), 1st Visconde de Juromenha, who served under Beresford in the Peninsular War.
19. Napier, *An Account*, 1: 277.
20. Valente, *Os «devoristas»*, 14; 'o programa dos aristocratas, um programa whig de reforma paulatina e pacífica, não fazia sentido (se alguma vez o fizera) depois da matança dos últimos dois anos [...] e da revolução legislativa dos *ditadores*, agora irreversível'. (My translation).
21. See *Memórias*, 286–87.
22. Holland, *The Holland House Diaries*, 240 (16–24 August [1833]).
23. Ibid.
24. Ibid.

Thereafter differences began to develop between Holland and Palmela. In a marginal note commenting on Pedro's acknowledgement of the 'necessity of establishing the constitution', Holland criticized his old friend:

> Palmela, satisfied in his own mind that the Constitution was unpopular, fondly imagining that Royalty and Nobility still commanded favor in Portugal, and perhaps not overfond of a free government, uniformly deprecated all declaration of a Constitution; and this was the reason that Pedro served under his daughter's colours and never raised his own, and he did so with the reservation of being at liberty to convoke Cortes and proclaim the constitution the moment the Usurper was restored [*sic*]. The Fidalgo party there and perhaps many Carlists and Tories elsewhere soon had an inkling of his sincerity and determination on these points – they hated him for his honesty more than for his views – and soon betook themselves to denying and calumniating the first and very grossly exaggerating the latter.[25]

Holland's criticism is unfair. Although Palmela was probably more conservative than Holland, there is no evidence, either in his memoirs or in the main histories, to suggest that Palmela was hostile to the Charter. Furthermore, Holland admitted that Palmela had recommended a 'conciliatory policy and Cabinet', which is obviously not the same as a non-representative regime.[26] It is true that Palmela was accused of being a secret Absolutist, but this accusation came from the extreme Radicals such as Liberato. Holland's comments suggest either that he had been in contact with the anti-*Palmelista* clique or, more likely, that at least subconsciously, he was trying to burnish the image of Pedro, his new hero.

Holland admitted that he had received several letters from Portugal at this time including those from 'Admiral Parker, Lord William Russell, Mr. Hoppner, Mr. Sorrell,[27] Palmela and Admiral Napier'.[28] One or more of these correspondents were probably hostile to Palmela. The most likely is Hoppner, who, despite his former alleged connivance with Miguel's party, now adopted a pro-Radical attitude. In a marginal note to his diary, Holland admitted that Hoppner was later 'recalled for too much partiality to that party [Pedro's]'.[29] Russell and Napier had always supported Palmela, and were thus unlikely to make hostile comments about him. As Holland admitted, 'On Pedro's arrival at Lisbon he [Russell] implied in contradiction to Hoppner that the appointment of a Moderate and Palmela Ministry should be a sinequânon condition of recognition and assistance'.[30] The favourable way Holland describes Hoppner in his journal gives weight to this theory.

On 15 August 1833, Pedro issued a summons for an extraordinary *Cortes* to decide on urgent matters, including the marriage of his daughter.[31] Elections were due to begin on 1 October and the Chambers would assemble as soon as the stipulated minimum

25. Ibid., 242 (Tuesday, 27 [August 1833]).
26. Ibid.
27. Thomas S. Sorrell, British Consul at Oporto.
28. Holland, *The Holland House Diaries*, 241 (Tuesday, 27 [August 1833]).
29. Ibid., 249 (22 June 1834).
30. Ibid.
31. *Chronica constitucional de Lisboa*, 15 August 1833, 85.

number of deputies was reached.[32] On 27 September, however, Pedro was forced to issue a new decree proroguing the elections *sine die* as a result of the insufficient quorum achieved. It was not until 28 May 1834 that the *Cortes* was finally called to meet on 15 August. In the meantime, pressing matters had to be decided as hitherto, that is to say, by ministerial decree, now upon the advice of the Council of State, which first assembled at the Palace of Bemposta on 15 November 1833.

Maria, who had been living in France with her stepmother since Pedro's departure to Terceira, was called to Lisbon as soon as the situation was considered safe. Maria embarked at Le Havre on the *Soho* steamer to Portsmouth, where she landed on 8 September 1833. While in England, where she remained one week, Maria was warmly received, not least by members of the royal family, who, according to Holland, 'express satisfaction at the arrival of Donna Maria'.[33] On 17 September, Maria embarked again on the *Soho* at Portsmouth, arriving in Lisbon on 22 September.[34]

Pedro was determined that his daughter should marry his brother-in-law, the duc de Leuchtenberg, a grandson of Josephine, who had accompanied his sister to Rio de Janeiro in 1829.[35] This projected marriage was not to the taste of Louis Philippe, who, as earlier noted, hoped that Maria would marry one of his sons. Aware of French opposition, Pedro had decided to act in secrecy, but he was never noted for discretion and his plan soon became public knowledge. In a letter to Talleyrand dated 16 August 1833 the duc de Broglie had commented: 'It is clear that Dom Pedro and his wife intend to endeavour, at once and openly, to bring about a marriage between Dona Maria and the Duc de Leuchtenberg'.[36] As a result, Louis Philippe ordered Leuchtenberg to leave France immediately, even breaking protocol by forbidding the authorities to afford the duke any formal mark of respect on his departure. Leuchtenberg, whom Holland described as 'full of high spirit and vivacity', planned to accompany his future bride to Portugal, but the French authorities forced him to go to Munich.[37] As Holland observed, 'Not only were the Queen Donna Maria and her Step Mother coldly received at Havre, but the Sous Prefet took upon him to admonish Leuchtenberg that his appearance on French soil was an infraction of the Law'.[38] Earlier, fearing that Britain would lose another opportunity to exert her 'beneficial' influence over the affairs of Portugal if she failed to support a

32. Ibid.
33. Holland, *The Holland House Diaries*, 247 ([After] 5 September [August 1833]).
34. *Chronica constitucional de Lisboa*, 23–24 September 1833, 267, 273.
35. August Charles Eugène de Beauharnais Napoléon de Beauharnais (1810–1835), duc de Leuchtenberg, Prince Consort of D. Maria II of Portugal, the eldest son of Eugène de Beauharnais, Napoleon's stepson, and Princess Augusta of Bavaria.
36. 'The Duc de Broglie to the Prince de Talleyrand', in *Memoirs*, trans. Mrs. Angus Hall, 5: 154 (Paris: 15 August 1833).
37. Holland, *The Holland House Diaries*, 246 ([After] 5 September [August 1833]).
38. Ibid.

marriage 'infinitely preferable to any with a Neapolitan, Spanish or French prince of the Bourbon branches',[39] Holland had already

> urged but in vain the policy of taking such steps before Lisbon was in possession of Queen Maria's party, that we might have the grace of serving her cause in its adversity and have some right to assume authority in advising the settlement of the Government and the marriage of the Young Queen.[40]

On 28 September 1833 George Villiers arrived in Madrid with instructions to press the Spanish government to exert influence in favour of Maria.[41] In November, after some hesitation, Zea Bermudéz, the Spanish chief minister, described by Holland as being 'no doubt directed in his view of Portuguese or of all foreign politicks by the Holy Alliance', agreed to mediate between the conflicting parties in Portugal in conjunction with Great Britain.[42] Fernando VII had died on 23 September and his wife, María Cristina de Borbón, was appointed regent during Isabel II's minority, while in Portugal the Spanish prince Don Carlos had proclaimed himself Carlos V of Spain. Pedro accepted the Spanish proposal – provided that Miguel left the country – and reaffirmed his confidence in Lord William Russell as a mediator on behalf of Britain. After some procrastination, Miguel formally rejected the proposed terms, while declaring his willingness to consider any other concession consistent with his dignity. It was the beginning of the Quadruple Alliance of 22 April 1834, in which Palmerston was proud to have played a crucial part.

Pedro ordered Cristovão de Morais Sarmento to London on 21 December 1833 to enquire about the British government's readiness to send an expedition to Portugal under the terms of the Anglo-Portuguese Alliance. Sarmento, later Barão da Torre de Moncorvo, had his first audience with William IV on 5 January 1834, to whom he was introduced by Palmerston. He had already served as Chargé d'Affaires to London in 1822 in succession to Oliveira – and was thus an 1820 Radical and, most probably, a Freemason. A letter of 2 February 1834 suggests that Sarmento maintained a regular correspondence with Holland, who was well informed about the activities of Pedro's ministers, Silva Carvalho and Freire. Sarmento wrote:

> I have the great satisfaction informing your Lordship that your suggestion which I so thoroughly recommended in my letters to Lisbon, have been acted upon and attended with the consideration they deserved. I received with my dispatches *private* letters from Mr. Carvalho & from Mr. Freire. Both these Ministers assure me that notwithstanding the great disappointment felt at Lisbon by the decision of the British Cabinet with respect to the interference in our affairs; the Duke of Braganza & the Ministers would not be influenced by it in the welcome & friendly reception that Lord Howard de Walden was to have. I will copy here

39. Ibid., 240 (16–24 August [1833]).
40. Ibid., 230 (Monday, 15 July–Saturday, 20 July [1833]).
41. George William Frederick Villiers (1800–1870), 4th Earl of Clarendon, English diplomat and statesman.
42. Holland, *The Holland House Diaries*, 250 ([After] 22 June [1834]).

> Mr. Carvalho's own expressions; "*We will receive and treat him with sincerity and loyalty, despite the great grief and sorrow caused by the decision of the British Government; we thus hope that Lord Howard will do us justice and will retribute with the same sincerity and confidence that he will find here.*"[43] – Mr. Freire's expressions are about the same, and in a postscriptum he adds that he had already seen Lord Howard and that as far as appearances could go, he was much pleased with Lord H. – "Would be good (add Mr. Freire) that the British Government played some attention to his reports, and that he only confirmed what Lord William Russell has probably said over and over again."[44]

In the early days of 1834, Sarmento had formally requested a British intervention in Portugal in terms identical those used in 1827, alleging the arrival of a *casus fœderis*. In his own words:

> Dom Pedro earnestly requests the assistance of Great Britain to effect the pacification of Portugal; and he considers that such pacification may be summed up in the following conditions: the expulsion of Dom Miguel, the establishment of Doña Maria and the execution of the Charter; that with respect to an amnesty, Dom Pedro is prepared to grant the fullest and most complete amnesty for all political offences, with the single exception of excluding some of the strong adherents of Dom Miguel from the House of Peers.[45]

Palmerston hastened to forward Sarmento's proposal to William IV, arguing

> that Dom Pedro does not wish to have British troops marched into the interior of Portugal to carry on a warfare against the Miguelites. That what he asks is that a British force should be sent to occupy Lisbon and Oporto, to hold those places in safe custody and to set free the whole of the Portuguese troops for operations in the interior.[46]

According to Webster, 'The Prime Minister was especially eager for action at the end of the year [1833] and Palmerston was in full agreement with him'.[47] On 1 January Grey seemed reasonably good humoured and even satisfied with the course of the events in Portugal, telling Lieven: 'In Spain things appear to be going on very well. In Portugal *les freres enemis* appear to be vying with each other, which shall entitle himself to the greatest share of the general abhorrence'.[48] Both Grey and Palmerston thought Sarmento's proposal reasonable and were prepared to give it their full support. According to Holland, 'The bare moral effect of British succour would secure the

43. 'Havemos de recebelo tratalo com franqueza e lealdade, apesar do grande desgosto e magoa que nos cauza a decisão do Gabinete Britannico; esperamos pois que Lord Howard nos fará justiça e nos retribuirá a mesma franqueza e confiança que encontrará em nós'. (My translation).
44. BL, HHP, MSS Add. 51634, Papers Relative to Portugal: 1831–45: Letter from C.[ristovão] P.[edro] de Moræs Sarmento to Lord Holland (67 Baker Street, 28 February 1834).
45. Morais Sarmento to Agostinho Freire, in *The Foreign Policy of Palmerston*, 1: 387 (10 January 1834).
46. Palmerston to William IV, ibid., 1: 387 (8 January 1834).
47. Webster, ibid., 1: 384.
48. Grey to Lieven, in *Correspondence*, 2: 494 (1 January 1834).

rapid success and permanent establishment of Donna Maria's Government, and by such a step we might recover all our pristine ascendancy in Portugal'.[49] Moreover, by sending a force to Portugal they would assist the Liberal cause in Spain and indirectly 'secured and established by our ascendancy [one] in Portugal'.[50] Grey went as far as to suggest to Sarmento that the Duque de Bragança should try to form a more balanced Cabinet which included persons respected in the European courts – viz. code for Palmela. Although the instructions of the Portuguese minister did not run to such matters, Sarmento felt able to assure Grey that he was certain that Pedro would not oppose this development.

All seemed settled when, on 13 January, William IV gave his provisional assent to the scheme. However, the project was abandoned in the face of unexpectedly strong opposition in Cabinet – including the Duke of Richmond, Stanley, Melbourne, one of the Grants and Althorp. The latter even threatened to resign if the ministers agreed to the plan. Grey retreated but also threatened to resign. As Holland observed in a marginal note to his diary, there was in the Cabinet a complete 'concurrence of opinion in all matters excepting Portugal, or at least in all such as regarded the domestick affairs of the country'.[51] As he further noted:

> There had been throughout, in the mind of many of my Colleagues, in some from fear of war, in others from dislike of foreigners, in some one or two from a dread of democracy, and in Lord Grey from some private and very prejudiced sources of information,[52] and unwarrantable repugnance and suspicion of Pedro, but Lord Palmerston was always more just to him and I was at a very early period satisfied from the admission of those who complained of him, and of Palmela in particular, that tho' ungovernable in his temper and yet more in his language, and tho' occasionally swayed by most unwarrantable affections and resentments, he was yet full of good and even great qualities and true to his word, zealous in the cause of his daughter and the people, incapable of disguise or dissimulation even to a fault, affectionate to his family and his friends, and, though intemperately violent in language and sometimes hasty even to brutality in his actions, by no means implacable or unforgiving.[53]

On 14 January, the issue was discussed at a dinner at Althorp's, when it appeared that Grey had decided to offer his resignation to the king the next morning. The situation seemed so desperate that Althorp begged Holland and Grey's closest friends to press him 'to remain, insisting, with his usual vehemence and exaggeration, that the question relating to Portugal was as nothing'.[54] Holland and Grey's friends signed a paper urging the prime minister to reconsider and this, together with the king's sincere wish to keep him, led Grey to stay on for a while.

49. Holland, *The Holland House Diaries*, 247 ([After] 22 June [1834]).
50. Ibid.
51. Ibid., 249 ([After] 22 June [1834]).
52. Obviously sources opposite to Pedro's ministers, probably close to Palmela.
53. Holland, *The Holland House Diaries*, 250 ([After] 22 June [1834]).
54. Ibid., 248.

On 25 January, Martínez de la Rosa, a Liberal recently appointed Spain's chief minister, proposed to Villiers that Britain, Spain and Portugal conclude an alliance whose purpose would be to eject the two rebellious princes – Miguel and Carlos – from the Peninsula.[55] When it became clear that Britain was reluctant to intervene openly in the affairs of Portugal, Pedro decided to explore an alternative approach. On 17 February 1834, Alexandre de Morais Sarmento, an elder brother of Cristovão de Morais Sarmento, was ordered to Madrid to negotiate a defensive and offensive alliance.[56] Although favouring the scheme, Martínez de la Rosa was reluctant to interfere in the affairs of Portugal without the express consent of Britain and the support of France. As soon as Rosa took office, he wrote to Lord Holland, urging

> with much warmth and apparent sincerity his sense of the advantages of an early and open concert with England on all foreign matters, and especially on those of Portugal, where he hoped for our assistance in expelling Don Carlos, and expressed a willingness to acknowledge Donna Maria *after* such a measure had been accomplished and the Portugueze Cortes called.[57]

Rosa obviously feared that neither the British nor the French governments would accept a bilateral alliance between the Liberal regimes in Spain and Portugal. It is true that on 19 March, pressed by Cristovão de Morais Sarmento, Palmerston declared that the British government would not oppose such an alliance. Yet, when on 15 March Villiers informed Howard de Walden – who had arrived in Lisbon on 14 February to replace William Russell – that the Spanish were ready to send troops to Portugal.[58] Walden warned Pedro that no foreign troops could be allowed on Portuguese soil without previous British consent and urged the Portuguese ministers to take the steps necessary to obtain Miguel's capitulation on acceptable terms. Stung by what he considered Walden's arrogance, Pedro instructed Alexandre de Morais Sarmento to inform the Spanish government that the troops of Her Catholic Majesty could enter Portugal without reference to the wishes of any foreign power. Again Martínez de la Rosa vacillated.

In March 1834, the duc de Broglie, always reluctant to support the Portuguese Liberal cause, ceased to be foreign minister of France and was replaced by the more sympathetic comte de Rigny, thus giving Rosa sufficient confidence to declare open support for Maria.[59]

55. Francisco de Paula Martínez de la Rosa y Berdejo (1787–1862), Spanish statesman and dramatist, was appointed First Minister after Fernando VII's death.
56. Alexandre Tomás de Morais Sarmento (1786–1840), 1st Visconde do Banho, Portuguese politician and diplomat, son of Tomás Inácio de Morais Sarmento (b. 1750) and elder brother of Cristóvão Pedro de Morais Sarmento (1788–1851), 1st Barão da Torre de Moncorvo.
57. Holland, *The Holland House Diaries*, 250–51 ([After] 22 June [1834]).
58. Charles Augustus Ellis (1799–1868), 6th Baron Howard de Walden, British diplomat, Extraordinary Minister Plenipotentiary to Lisbon from 1833 to 1846. Howard de Walden was appointed on 26 November 1833 and arrived in the Portuguese capital on 14 February 1834. He was absent on leave between 23 May to 17 November 1838 and again on 12 October 1846, when, on the pretext of taking leave, he embarked on the *Cyclops* never to return to Portugal.
59. Marie Henry Daniel Gauthier (1782–1835), comte de Rigny, French admiral and statesman.

A convention was concluded in Madrid between Alexandre de Morais Sarmento and Rosa, but this was never ratified. Once Palmerston learned of the bilateral negotiations, he hastened to prepare his own draft of a quadruple alliance to be signed between Britain, France, Spain and Portugal. When he first saw the text proposed by Palmerston, Cristovão de Morais Sarmento claimed that he did not have the power to enter into such an agreement and, in any case, references to Miguel as prince precluded his acceptance. Palmerston suggested that Sarmento could use the general instructions from his government to justify signing and the question of Miguel's status could be circumvented by preparing a separate codicil to the treaty, a device frequently employed in the treaties making up the Vienna settlement. Sarmento consented.

The treaty establishing the Quadruple Alliance was signed in London on 22 April 1834 by Palmerston, Sarmento, Talleyrand and the Marqués de Miraflores, the Spanish minister.[60] Under the terms of the treaty, the Regent of Portugal agreed 'to use all the means in His power, to compel Infante Don Carlos to withdraw from the Portuguese Dominions' (Art. I), while Spain promised to send an unspecified number of troops into 'the Portuguese territory, in order to cooperate with the troops of Her Most Faithful Majesty, for the purpose of compelling infantes Don Carlos and Don Miguel of Portugal to withdraw from the Portuguese Dominions' (Art. II). Britain agreed 'to cooperate, by the employment of a naval force, in aid of operations to be undertaken, in conformity with the engagements of this Treaty, by the troops of Portugal and Spain' (Art. III), while France agreed to offer any cooperation 'deemed necessary by the High Contracting Parties for the complete attainment of the object of this Treaty' (Art. IV).[61] Britain was the first party to ratify the treaty (29 April), followed by France and Spain (5 May) and Portugal (10 May). Following the Evoramonte conventions, four additional articles to the Treaty of Quadruple Alliance were signed in London on 18 August 1834. This additional act, however, only concerned hypothetical aid to be afforded to Her Catholic Majesty if the need arose.[62]

60. Manuel Pando Fernández de Pinedo (1792–1872), Marqués de Miraflores y de Pontejos, Spanish Minister to London. He was at Holland House on 12 June 1834 (BL, HHP, MSS Add. 51955, Dinner Books: 1831–38, f. 74^v (Thursday, 12 June 1834)).

61. 'Tratado da quadrupla alliança celebrado entre Sua Magestade Imperial o Duque de Bragança, Regente do Reino em nome da Rainha a Senhora Dona Maria II, a Senhora Dona Maria Christina, Regente de Hespanha durante a menoridade da Senhora Dona Izabel II, Rainha de Espanha, Luiz Filippe Rei dos Francezes, e Jorge IV [*sic*] Rei da Gran-Bretanha, para a expulsão da Peninsula dos Ex-Infantes Dom Miguel de Portugal e Dom Carlos de Hespanha, assignado em Londres a 22 de Abril de 1834, e ratificado por parte de Portugal em 10 de Maio, pela de França em 5 do mesmo mez, pela da Gran-Bretanha em 29 de Abril, e pela de Hespanha em 5 de Maio do mencionado anno', in *Collecção dos tratados*, 6: 120–37.

62. 'Artigos addicionais ao tratado da quadrupla alliança de 22 de Abril de 1834, assignados em Londres a 18 de Agosto de 1834, e ratificados por parte de Portugal em 8 de Setembro, pela França em 21 de Agosto, pela da Gran-Bretanha em 27 e pela Hespanha em 22 do dito mez e anno', in *Collecção dos tratados*, 6: 142–49.

With this alliance, Palmerston claimed '*a capital hit, and all my own doing*', he could actually kill three birds with one stone: France, Spain and Portugal.[63] Although his original scheme had contemplated a treaty only with Spain and Portugal, he later extended it to include France. France had been pressing Britain for sometime for a general treaty of alliance to pacify Europe, but Palmerston had been unenthusiastic. On 14 April, a few days before the conclusion of the Quadruple Alliance, Talleyrand reported to Paris: 'They [the British Government] persist in their scheme of a treaty between the Courts of England, Spain, and Portugal, to which we shall be asked to assent'.[64] Palmerston had worked on the draft between 4 and 11 April and, on the following day, even before obtaining the Cabinet's consent or the king's approval, he submitted it to Miraflores. Only after that, on 13 April, did he show it to both Sarmento and Talleyrand. But while the first consented to sign it after some hesitation, others proved more difficult 'with old Talley and the French Government, for they have made objections in plenty'.[65] Meantime, Holland declared in his diary:

> I believe before it [the treaty] was signed and certainly before it was ratified, the Duke de Broglie had retired from the French Ministry and the Duke of Richmond, Sir James Graham, Lord Ripon, and Mr Stanley had resigned their seats in the British Cabinet. The loss of the Duke of Broglie seemed to us irreparable.[66]

Holland's comment is enigmatic, not only because it seems unlikely that he did not know of the treaty in advance, but also because it suggests that he did not totally approve of it. Holland's reaction is probably another instance of disagreements with Palmerston, hinted in a memorandum on foreign policy by Silva Carvalho when arguing that while Holland is 'more sincere than his colleagues', Palmerston is rather dissimulating, insisting in his system of threats and accusations against Pedro's ministers.[67]

Magalhães sought to explain the apparent discomfort of some British Ministers in respect of the Quadruple Alliance treaty by claiming that Palmerston had also prepared a draft for a general amnesty extending to all Miguel's supporters – and which he expected Pedro to ratify alongside the treaty. Yet, although Pedro signed the main agreement on 10 May, he refused to ratify the amnesty, perhaps anticipating the end of hostilities. In fact, the Evoramonte concessions, concluded a few days later, did contain a general amnesty. Nevertheless, Palmerston was furious when he learned that Pedro had not ratified the amnesty, declaring: 'He [Pedro] and his camarilla, soi disant Ministers, will perhaps be the persons who after the Holy Alliance will be the most discomposed at the transaction,

63. Palmerston, 'To the Hon. Wm. Temple, Naples', in *The Life of Henry John Temple*, 2: 186 (Foreign Office, 12 May 1834).
64. 'The Prince de Talleyrand to the Comte de Rigny', in: *Memoirs*, trans. Angus Hall, 5: 242–43 (14 April [1834]).
65. Palmerston, 'To the Hon. Wm. Temple, Naples', in *The Life of Henry John Temple*, 2: 180 (Stanhope Street, 21 April 1834).
66. Holland, *The Holland House Diaries*, 251 ([After] 22 June [1834]).
67. 'Politica externa', in *Documentos para a historia contemporanea: José da Silva Carvalho e o seu tempo*, ed. António Viana. 3 vols (Lisboa: Imprensa Nacional, 1891–94), 2: 11–12.

and Sarmento has neither powers nor instructions for such a treaty'.[68] Grey, also visibly irritated with Pedro's apparent obduracy, commented to Sarmento: 'Make no mistake, the British Government had no preference for any foreign government or regnant family; their resolution has for ultimate goal the promotion of the national interests'.[69]

Whatever really happened behind the scenes, on 4 June, Grey wrote to Lieven with evident relief: 'Well, there is, at last, one affair brought to a conclusion – the war in Portugal is over. It is now to be seen how Don Pedro conducts himself after his victory. Here, also, is matter for doubt as well as congratulation'.[70] Little more than one month later, Grey retired from public life. After accomplishing the two great tasks of his political career, Parliamentary reform and the re-establishment of Liberalism in Portugal, Grey could finally rest in the arms of his preferred mistress, melancholy.[71] Although his colleagues had caustically remarked on his habit of threatening resignation after every setback, this time, Grey kept his promise and for good. On 9 July, just before informing the House of Lords of his impending departure, 'Lord Grey laid upon the table a copy of the treaty between France, Spain, Portugal, and England, relative to the affairs of the Peninsula'.[72] Palmerston did the same in the Commons.

William IV sent for Melbourne, who formed a Cabinet not very different from Grey's and with Holland continuing as Chancellor of the Duchy of Lancaster. Melbourne had been a regular visitor to Holland House since 1828 and, as Ilchester noted, could be regarded as one of Lady Holland's protégés.[73] Melbourne's first ministry, however, was not to last for long, falling after only a few months. Unable to accept Melbourne's wish to appoint John Russell as Leader of the Commons after Althorp moved to the Lords, William IV dismissed the Cabinet on 14 November 1834 and called upon Peel. Holland immediately offered his resignation, which, although at first refused, was eventually accepted. Peel led a minority government for a while but then called a general election in an attempt to secure a majority. Although the Tories, now calling themselves Conservatives, gained some seats from the Whigs, they were still short of a majority and hence the king had no choice but to recall Melbourne in April 1835 and to agree to Russell's appointment as Leader of the House and Home Secretary. Holland resumed the Chancellery of the Duchy of Lancaster on 23 April 1835, a position he held until his death in 1840.

In the meantime, while 'Portugal and Europe were about to derive the full advantages of the gallant resistance to Tyranny, the ultimate expulsion of Don Miguel, the establishment of representative government in the Peninsula'[74] to quote Lord Holland, 'the

68. Palmerston, quoted in *The Foreign Policy of Palmerston*, 1: 397.

69. Grey, quoted in *Apontamentos*, 142; 'Desenganem-se todos que o Governo inglez não tem predilecção por governo algum estrangeiro, nem por alguma familia reinante; as suas resoluções teem sómente por fim promover os interesses nacionaes'. (My translation).

70. Grey to Lieven, in *Correspondence*, 2: 504 (4 June 1834).

71. Ilchester, *Chronicles of Holland House*, 169.

72. *The Times*, July 10, 1834, 2.

73. Ilchester, *Chronicles of Holland House*, 170.

74. Holland, *The Holland House Diaries*, 267 ([After] 22 June [1834]).

ardent and spirited Prince Dom Pedro, to whom they were mainly indebted for these blessings, was languishing under a Mortal disease'.[75] A cold caught in November 1833 together with the exhausting effects of almost four years of fighting and an ill-advised visit to the baths at Caldas da Rainha in August 1834 hastened the inevitable end. Pedro died on 24 September 1834 at the Palace of Queluz, in the 'Quixote Chamber', a small square bedroom adorned with scenes from Cervantes where he had also been born.[76] He died peacefully, according to Palmela with 'courage and Christian firmness', his conscience tranquil, knowing that he had accomplished his duty.[77] He had recovered the throne for his daughter against the odds, and, above all, he had restored constitutional government to Portugal. Pedro's last hours were described by Holland at length in a most dramatic and touching way:

> She [Maria] as well as the Empress spent many hours at the side of the dying Emperor's bed and received from his lips many earnest injunctions to preserve the privileges granted to the people, as well as assurances of affection and devotion. His touching interview with the Officers and his farewell message to his troops are faithfully recorded in publications of the day, and I have been assured by persons present at that interesting scene that there was not a rugged face of all the veterans but was bedewed with tears at the interview. As the fatal moment approached he made signs for the Uniform of that Regiment which had first declared for his daughter in Terceira and which he had adopted and served with as peculiarly His own. It was put on with some difficulty, and himself once more in a Soldier's dress, he surveyed with complacency [and] He seemed soothed with the scenes of glory it recalled and then, sinking on his bed as on the field of victory, closed his singular and adventurous life in the very room in which he was born.[78]

On 28 September, Pedro's remains were moved by torchlight from Queluz to the Bragança Pantheon at the Church of São Vicente de Fora. Saldanha, Terceira and Napier were his chief mourners. Pedro's heart was offered to the City of Oporto – as he had stipulated in his will – where it is preserved at the Church of Lapa. In 1972, as part of the celebrations marking the 150th anniversary of the Independence of Brazil, Pedro's remains were moved to Ipiranga, São Paulo.[79] When Miguel's remains were translated to São Vicente de Fora in 1967, they were placed alongside the grave of Pedro's wife, the empress Amélia, whose remains, in their turn, were translated to Brazil in 1982.

75. Ibid.
76. Ibid.
77. Palmela, *Memórias*, 295; 'coragem e firmeza cristã'. (My translation).
78. Holland, *The Holland House Diaries*, 268 ([After] 22 June [1834]).
79. ANTT, MSS Gav. 16, Mç. 4, n. 1326, Auto da exumação dos restos mortais D. Pedro IV ['Act of exhumation of Pedro's remains']: [copy] (September 1972).

Chapter Thirteen

LIBERALISM AND ITS PROBLEMS

*Pedro wants to form his Govt. on the support of the middle and lower classes. This might do if they were virtuous and well educated as they are in England but here they are very little less corrupt than the noble [. . .].**

In the last days of his life, Pedro had been busy making arrangements for the future. He had always been a lively man, full of energy, according to Hodges 'systematically an early riser',[1] and he was not going to stop now that 'He was fully aware of his approaching death'.[2] On 15 September 1834, Pedro made his will and dictated a letter to his future son-in-law, to whom he left his sword.[3] On the following day, he was occupied with his ministers dealing with urgent matters of the state. On 17 September, Pedro received the last sacrament and, on the day after, informed the *Cortes* that he could no longer continue as regent. A few hours later, D. Maria was called to take the regency herself. Finally, on 19 September, Pedro received his friends and closest collaborators in his bedroom for a last farewell.

As Lord Holland observed, Pedro's death had snatched him 'from the scene of his glory and triumph before it was entirely crowned and completed by the marriage of his daughter'.[4] On 18 September, while sick with fever, Pedro had sent Ildefonso Bayard to Munich to negotiate the terms of his daughter's marriage.[5] Bayard had successfully

---

* William Russell to Palmerston, in *The Foreign Policy of Palmerston*, 1: 378 (August–September 1833).

1. Hodges, *Narrative*, 1: 80.
2. Holland, *The Holland House Diaries*, 267 ([After] 22 June [1834]).
3. Pedro's sword was entrusted to Bayard, who had been commissioned the day before to go to Munich to negotiate the terms of Maria's marriage to Leuchtenberg.
4. Holland, *The Holland House Diaries*, 267 ([After] 22 June [1834]).
5. Ildefonso Leopoldo Bayard (1785–1856), Portuguese diplomat, was appointed officer of the Secretary of State of Marine and Overseas Affairs in 1816 and Chargé d'Affaires to Copenhagen in 1822, where he remained until 1824, when he was transferred to Berlin. In July 1828, after Miguel's usurpation, Bayard resigned his post. Learning that D. Maria was on her way from Rio de Janeiro to Europe, Resende and Itabaiana sent him to Gibraltar to warn Barbacena not to take the young queen to Vienna, as initially planned, but rather to England. It was also Bayard who was commissioned to go to Munich to negotiate the terms of Pedro's marriage to Amélie de Leuchtenberg. In January 1829, Bayard emigrated to Brazil, where he remained until the end of 1833, when he moved back to Portugal. On 13 August 1834, Bayard was appointed Senior Officer of the Secretary of State of Foreign Affairs and, on 14 September, commissioned to negotiate the terms of Maria's marriage to the duc de Leuchtenberg. He was appointed Foreign Minister in 1847, a position occupied for only a few days. Bayard was murdered by a servant on 25 January 1856.

conducted the negotiations for Pedro's own marriage to Amélie de Leuchtenberg in 1829. Bearing Pedro's instructions and sword, Bayard left Lisbon for London to meet Sarmento before going on to Bavaria. In the evening of 16 November, Sarmento paid a visit to Kensington accompanied by Bayard who, according to Holland, 'is returning with [the] "procuration" of the Duke of Leuchtenberg to enable the Duke of Terceira to marry the Young Queen of Portugal by proxy'.[6] As Holland observed, some intriguing courtiers at Lisbon, namely Terceira and Vila Real, had tried to prevent the marriage:

> They hinted that the Gentleman named by Pedro and the Queen was not of sufficient rank to undertake the mission to Munich, but the Queen's better judgement or advisers suspected an intrigue and, on the same ground of adhering religiously to Pedro's injunction, dispatch Mr Bayard, who is to bring back the procuration and then to be followed by the Duke.[7]

The pre-nuptial contract was signed in Munich on 8 November and the marriage celebrated by proxy in Lisbon on 1 December. The religious ceremony was held on 26 January 1835, the day after Leuchtenberg's arrival. However, the Prince Consort of Portugal did not live long to enjoy his position, dying on 28 March 1835 from crupal angina.

The premature death of Leuchtenberg only two months after the royal wedding meant that it was urgent to find another suitable husband for the young queen in order to guarantee the succession. Since the prince was expected to be a Catholic, there appeared to be only two suitable candidates – one from Austria, the other the duc de Nemours, son of Louis Philippe. But while the Austrian candidate carried associations with Absolutism, the prospect of a French marriage was likely to encounter objections from Britain. Hence, the Conde de Lavradio was sent to London with instructions to discuss Maria's marriage with Palmerston. A few names were considered, including those of the son of the Archduke Charles, Albrecht, and the Neapolitan prince of Carignan, but there was no agreement. Lavradio was inclined to the Austrian match, while Palmerston objected, not just due to Albrecht's aversion to Liberalism but also because 'The Austrian family are neither healthy nor handsome. Big lips and epilepsy are greatly abundant therein'.[8] On 22 July 1835, during a meeting between Palmerston, Lavradio, Mendizábal and Sarmento, the name of Ferdinand August Saxe-Coburg Gotha emerged as the perfect match. Not only was Ferdinand a Catholic, but he was also a cousin of Princess Victoria. Negotiations were held, in which the Duchess of Kent, the princess's mother and Ferdinand's aunt, was personally involved. Apart from Lavradio who was not present, almost the same party had assembled at Holland House on 1 March 1835, although there had been additional guests including the Duke of Devonshire, John Russell and the Granvilles.[9] Both Sarmento and Lavradio were at Kensington on 16 June, where the

6. Holland, *The Holland House Diaries*, 276 (Sunday, 16 November [1834]).
7. Ibid., 267 ([After] 22 June [1834]).
8. Palmerston, quoted in *The Foreign Policy of Palmerston*, 1: 483.
9. BL, HHP, MSS Add. 51955, Dinner Books: 1831–38, f. 95^{r} (Sunday, 1 March 1835).

subject was certainly discussed.[10] In December 1835, Sarmento informed Holland that 'the treaty for Marriage with Ferd[inand] of Coburgh is advancing and that Lavradio hopes to complete it before the 2d. of Jany. when Cortes meet'.[11] Lavradio's instructions to conclude the contract of marriage were issued on 11 December. The royal marriage was celebrated by proxy in the Cathedral of Lisbon on 1 January 1836, with Terceira acting on Ferdinand's behalf. Ferdinand arrived in Lisbon on 8 April and, unlike his predecessor, he had a long and worthy life.

The establishment of a new constitutional order in Portugal required new interpreters and Palmela seemed the right man to lead the transition to Liberalism. His time in England meant that he had acquired a good understanding of operations and subtleties of the representative system. He knew how to obtain votes, how to manipulate the press and how to turn public opinion to his advantage. In short, Palmela's hour had finally arrived. Ironically, now that Palmela was enjoying so much success, Holland began to resent him for his apparent appetite for power. Yet, the fact that the period between Maria's accession in 1834 and the progressive coup of 9 September 1836 became known as *Devorismo* ('Devourism') and its leaders *Devoristas* – in short, a regime in which some prominent people lined their pockets at the expense of the public – suggests that Holland may have had a point. In his own words, while Pedro had been breathing his last: 'the Fidalgo party headed by Palmela and Terceira, and too much supported by England and France, were urging, if not a change, an extension of the Ministry in a manner harsh, indelicate, and offensive to the dying Prince'.[12] On 17 September, while Pedro was receiving the Last Rites, the Council of State agreed that, since the Duque de Bragança was no longer capable of running the kingdom, the regency should pass directly to the queen. Maria would be assisted by the senior state counsellors, namely Palmela, Fernando Luís de Sousa Barradas, Silva Carvalho and Freire.[13] As Holland should have known, in politics things are not always very 'polite'. Palmela acted before his enemies – Pedro's protégés – had time to regain their ascendancy.

Palmela had hoped to work with some of the members of the aristocracy who had supported Miguel. The refusal of Pedro's ministers to agree to the rehabilitation of this group meant that Palmela had little choice but to form a coalition with Pedro's friends, known as *dictators* or *chamorros*, under his own leadership.[14] In the general election held from 13 to 27 July 1834, the performance of Palmela's coalition was unimpressive. Forty-three of its candidates were returned, as compared to 32 Progressives and 44 Independents. The coalition did however rule the country until the Progressive coup d'état of 9 September 1836, although its ministers soon became known as *estacionários* or *retrogrados* (*stationaries* or *retrogrades*), as opposed to those who aimed at movement.

10. Holland, *The Holland House Diaries*, 308 (16 [June 1835]).
11. Ibid., 336 (1 December 1835).
12. Ibid., 267 ([After] 22 June [1834]).
13. ANTT, Conselho de Estado: 1821–1910, MSS Actas do Conselho de Estado: Acta n. 1 (1821–44), Session n. 20, f. 109r (17 September 1834).
14. *Chamorro* (Port. slang; from the Castilian), pejorative term given by the Spaniards to the Portuguese and later adopted by the *Miguelistas* when referring to the liberals.

As noted earlier, on 28 May 1834 – two days after the conclusion of the Concession of Evoramonte – Pedro had announced that a new *Cortes* would meet on 15 August. The regent indicated that major issues for resolution included 'Whether the Regency ought or ought not to be continued during the remainder of the Queen's minority', the young queen's marriage to a foreign prince, the liberty of press, the responsibility of ministers, the inviolability of private property, etc.[15] Regarding the Upper Chamber, it had been decided that only those peers who had remained loyal to the Constitutional Charter should be admitted. Since a high proportion of the Portuguese nobility had supported Miguel, only eleven existing peers were eligible and so, on 1 September, using the prerogatives of the Charter, Pedro created 24 new peers, all of them favourable to the ministry. Palmela was appointed president for life on 14 August.

On 15 August, Pedro opened the *Cortes Gerais e Extraordinárias da Nação Portuguesa* with a long speech, which he read with visible difficulty.[16] According to Napier,

> He now suffered so much from a difficulty of breathing, that it was with evident pain and inconvenience that he got through the ceremony, and after remaining a short time in the Ajuda, during which he got rapidly worse, he retired to Queluz.[17]

Pedro's speech, probably written by Freire or Silva Carvalho, was intended to promote calm and hence said little about the conflicts between the various factions, preferring to concentrate on the 'patriotism and love of liberty' of the Portuguese nation, 'and the efforts of civilization incombating servitude, barbarism, and tyranny, and continually gaining signal victories over those monsters'.[18] Pedro's speech concluded with an expression of total indifference to power, sentiments which, coming from a dying man who had fulfilled his mission in life, could only be interpreted as sincere and genuine.

On 20 September 1834, Palmela became the chief minister in the queen's first Cabinet, apparently against Pedro's own wishes. Yet, Palmela had been unable to get rid of Silva Carvalho and Agostinho Freire, now his main political foes, and whose names he proposed to the queen 'although with great repugnance'.[19] In Napier's words, 'the Duke was obliged to consign himself again into the hands of the men who had before put him out of the ministry'.[20] Mendizábal, who had contributed significantly to the reestablishment of the Liberal regime, was appointed Minister without Portfolio, even though he was technically a foreigner.[21] This Cabinet, which Pulido

15. Pedro, Duque de Bragança, 'Speech from the Throne, in the Royal Session of the Extraordinary Cortes of the Portuguese Nation in 1834', in *An Account*, 2: App. XXXIV, 330.
16. Holland, *The Holland House Diaries*, 267 ([After] 22 June [1834]); Palmela, *Memórias*, 293.
17. Napier, *An Account*, 2: 333.
18. Pedro, Duque de Bragança, 'Speech from the Throne, in the Royal Session of the Extraordinary Cortes of the Portuguese Nation in 1834', ibid., 2: App. XXXIV, 324.
19. Palmela, *Memórias* 298; 'ainda que com bastante repugnância'. (My translation).
20. Napier, *An Account*, 2: 235.
21. Carvalho was appointed Finance Minister, while Freire became Minister of the Marine and Overseas Affairs. Terceira was created Minister of War, while his protégé, Vila Real, against whom Pedro had strongly objected, was appointed Foreign Minister. Francisco de São Luís

Valente described as a 'pie without stuffing', represented an artificial attempt to combine all factions in the same Cabinet – except for the radicals who rejected the ministerial melting pot.[22] Refusing to serve with Carvalho and Freire, Saldanha became the undisputed leader of the progressive opposition, although not for long, as he was soon persuaded to adhere to the ministry. As soon as the new Cabinet was formed, Napier submitted a plan for the reorganization of the navy; the plan was rejected and Napier resigned.

As Palmela observed, this Cabinet was the first in Portugal formed according to the methods used in the other constitutional countries – that is to say, the ministers were chosen by the prime minister and expected to take collective responsibility for all the actions of the government. Of course, although Palmela referred to other countries in general, he was obviously thinking about the English system, which he knew better and admired above any other system.[23] However, as Palmela later admitted, acceptance of the premiership without any specific ministerial portfolio proved a big mistake in the long run. While Freire and Palmela were moving further and further apart, the public finances, under Silva Carvalho, were getting out of control. It was precisely the bad management of the public finances and the systematic disposal of state assets as a means of meeting increased expenditure – seldom wisely employed – that earned the regime the name of *Devorismo*.

Relations between Palmela and Freire became so strained that Vila Real was forced tell the queen that she must choose between them. Maria eventually decided in favour of Freire, and so Palmela was dismissed on 28 April 1835 and replaced by his brother-in-law, Vitório de Sousa Coutinho.[24] According to Webster, Palmela's dismissal had been brought about 'largely by means of an intrigue of Mendizebel with whom he had quarrelled over stock jobbing operations'.[25] Although Palmela's memoirs do not mention these problems, the fact that Webster's account was based on Howard de Walden's despatches from Lisbon and on Palmerston's private correspondence suggests that there is some truth in the story: according to Holland,

> The Queen, Saldanha, and Palmela writes most earnest and even fulsome letters to Mendizabal, entreating him to continue their agent in finance matters, but he with great truth

---

Saraiva, formerly Bishop of Coimbra, was created Minister of Interior and António Barreto Ferraz e Vasconcelos (1779–1861), 1st Visconde da Granja, was entrusted with justice and ecclesiastical affairs.

22. Valente, *Os «devoristas»*, 20–21.
23. Palmela, *Memórias*, 298.
24. D. Vitório Maria Francisco de Sousa Coutinho Teixeira de Andrada de Barbosa (1790–1857), 2nd Conde de Linhares, Portuguese diplomat and statesman. The eldest son of D. Rodrigo de Sousa Coutinho Teixeira de Andrade Barbosa (1755–1812), 1st Conde de Linhares and his wife, Gabriella Maria Ignazia Asinari dei Marchesi di San Marzano (1770–1821), and nephew of Funchal. On 16 February 1835, Vitório was appointed Minister of Naval and Overseas Affairs in the Cabinet of his brother-in-law Palmela – who he replaced as Acting Chief Minister on 28 April 1835. He married on 4 September 1820 D. Catarina Juliana de Sousa Holstein (1791–1871), a sister of Palmela.
25. Webster, *The Foreign Policy of Palmerston*, 1: 481.

and disinterestedness, though he complies with the request, remarks both to Palmerston *and to them* that such solicitations to an individual are proofs of weakness and want of real system and plan rather than of confidence.[26]

However, according to a letter from Sir William Cage, the British admiral on the Tagus, quoted by Holland, it appears that Maria soon regretted her choice:

the young Queen in the late transactions has shewn great levity and caprice, some duplicity and much intrepidity, not to say violence of character. When Freire was admitted to her presence one day, she greeted him by expressing a hope that he was come to 'tender his resignation'; he hesitated, and said he was not prepared to do so. She replied, you had better, for 'if not I will dismiss your directly'.[27]

Linhares's ministry was short lived. According to Palmela, Linhares's fall on 27 May, after less than one month in office, was the result of intrigues. Although Palmela did not specify the names of those responsible, it is possible that Freire may have been involved. Maria then sent for Saldanha who offered the foreign ministry to Palmela. Palmela hesitated, but accepted when Saldanha insisted – a weakness he later regretted.[28] Howard de Walden, quoted by Holland, reported from Lisbon 'that the Cortes and publick opinion will compel the Queen to recall the Ministry of Palmela, Saldanha, and Carvalho'.[29] But Saldanha's Ministry lasted only until 18 November 1835 when the premier resigned.[30] Morais Sarmento, now Barão de Torre de Moncorvo, who had been a frequent guest at Holland House in 1834–35, was critical of all involved but especially of the queen:

though he equally laments the interference of the Army and the hasty and precipitate conduct of the Queen, so indicative of a hasty and despotick disposition, criticises the policy and property of the late Ministry, and especially Carvalho, in forcing the Queen to retract her conduct in a letter to be published. It was, he says, crying peccary in a way derogatory to her dignity; and the moment she was apprized of the nature of the step she had been advised and, in a way compelled to take, her objections to the policy of her advisers, which

26. Holland, *The Holland House Diaries*, 307 (10–16 June [1835]).
27. Ibid.
28. Palmela, *Memórias*, 308–9.
29. Holland, *The Holland House Diaries*, 336 (1 December 1835).
30. In the terms of the Quadruple Alliance, Spain had requested foreign aid to suppress a rebellion in Navarre headed by the Don Carlos. While France seemed to hesitate, Britain agreed to provide the Spanish government with naval support. The Portuguese ministers, deciding that the *casus fœderis* had arrived, proposed to the queen that an expeditionary force of 6,000 men should be sent to Spain to assist Her Catholic Majesty. Unexpectedly, Maria indicated her opposition although she seemed to back down when the ministers threatened to resign. In the meanwhile, the decision to send troops to Spain caused uproar in the army. Several officers associated with the progressive party, who regarded Saldanha as a turncoat – perhaps with reason – begun to demonstrate against the ministers. As a result, Saldanha and Palmela offered their resignations – which the queen accepted at once.

> had hitherto been ignorance, levity, and childishness, became resentment. She wished before to govern or rather misgovern them and have her way, she is now bent on dismissing, mortifying, and punishing them.[31]

Maria had now only two options: either to call upon the Radicals, or to form a government of her own. She decided on the second course and sent for José Jorge Loureiro, an army officer who had served as Archibald Campbell's aid-de-champs in the Peninsular War.[32] But although Loureiro was appointed President of the Council of Ministers, formally the head of Cabinet, the real leader was actually Maria's uncle, Loulé, whom she appointed to the foreign ministry. Loureiro's government also included Sá da Bandeira, Minister of Marine and Colonies, the Barão do Sobral,[33] a guest at Holland House on 3 July 1814,[34] who took the Ministry of Internal Affairs briefly before being replaced by Mouzinho de Albuquerque. Loureiro's Cabinet represented a broad range of opinions and was designed to please everyone yet it ended by pleasing no one. As a veteran of war, Loureiro was supposed to appeal to the army, while Mouzinho de Albuquerque, described by Pulido Valente as 'Palmela's client', was meant to satisfy England; Loulé and Sá da Bandeira, the only nobles in the Cabinet, represented the aristocracy, while Francisco António de Campos, Minister of Finance, was expected to please the radicals.

According to Holland, the new ministers 'excepting Loulé and perhaps Campos, are he [Sarmento] contends not ill selected'.[35] However, as Palmela observed in his memoirs, Loureiro's government was in the main leftist. Loureiro remained in the office until April 1836, when he was replaced by Terceira. In the early days of April, Francisco António de Campos, the only leftist figure in the Cabinet, offered his resignation – which was accepted by a decree of 6 April. Failing to find a suitable replacement for Campos, Loureiro offered his own resignation one week later. The queen sent for Terceira, who formed an essentially conservative Cabinet similar to the first *Devorista* administration. It included Joaquim António de Aguiar, Agostinho Freire and Silva Carvalho – that is to say, it was controlled by Freemasons. Terceira remained in the Cabinet until 11 September 1836, when he was dismissed after a successful leftist coup d'état in Lisbon.

---

31. Holland, *The Holland House Diaries*, 336 (1 December 1835).
32. José Jorge Loureiro (1791–1860), Portuguese army officer and statesman.
33. Hermano José Braamcamp de Almeida Castelo Branco (1775–1846), 2nd Barão do Sobral, 1st Visconde and 1st Conde do Sobral, Portuguese politician and statesman, son of Geraldo Vensceslau Braamcamp de Almeida Castelo Branco (1752–1828), 1st Barão do Sobral, and his wife D. Joana Maria da Cruz Sobral (1760–1812). On 17 February 1806 Hermano married Louise-Amable-Françoise Riom de Narbonne-Lara (1786–1849), daughter of the comte de Narbonne-Lara (1755–1813), Minister of Louis XVI, Napoleon's aid-de-champs and ambassador to Vienna in 1813. Hermano was a member of the *Junta Provisional do Supremo Governo do Reino*, established in September 1820, Minister of Finance in 1826 during the Regency of Isabel Maria, and Minister of Internal Affairs in 1835.
34. BL, HHP, MSS Add. 51952, Dinner Books: 1813–19, f. 50v (Sunday, 3 July 1814).
35. Holland, *The Holland House Diaries*, 336 (1 December 1835).

Despite changes of ministers and cabinets, the *Devorista* regime proved unable to avert social and economic crisis, particularly the growing problem of public finances. As Oliveira Marques observed, between November/December 1832 and September 1836, Portugal had seven ministries, corresponding to an average of one government every six months. Although the government achieved a majority in the general elections of 17 July 1836, the opposition obtained important victories in the circles of Oporto, Viseu and Faro, giving it effective control of the provinces of Douro, Beira Alta and Algarve. On 9 September, the steamer *Napier* arrived in the Tagus conveying several of the new deputies from Douro and Beira Alta, including the famous Passos brothers, José and Manuel, both from Oporto, who were to play an important role in national politics. At Lisbon they were greeted enthusiastically by thousands of people shouting 'vivas' to the Constitution of 1822 and 'morras' to the ministers.[36] That evening, when the demonstrators had already dispersed, the National Guard begun to assemble at the Príncipe Real Square and from thence marched over to Rossio. Meanwhile, in the early hours of 10 September, a few troops of the line under Baltasar Pimentel were sent to Terreiro do Paço and from thence to Rossio to deal with the rebel guards.[37] While Pimentel was approaching Rossio, his own troops began to shout 'vivas' to the Constitution of 1822 and proceeded to join the rebels. The 'Revolução de Setembro', as it was later known, broke out almost spontaneously and was virtually bloodless. According to Liberato, 'No one reacted [...]. No one dared to defend the Charter, which fell without noise or fight, like a building ruined by time that falls when no one expects it'.[38]

The next morning, the leaders of the progressive party agreed to form a commission which would go to the queen and demand the dismissal of the existing ministers and the re-establishment of the Constitution of 1822. Sá da Bandeira was invited to head the commissioners, but when he refused, the Conde de Lumiares accepted the mission.[39] The queen had peremptorily and wisely rejected suggestions from her husband and some advisors that she should seek refuge aboard an English vessel in the Tagus, arguing that would be tantamount to abdication. Interestingly, Holland had a totally different opinion:

> Read the dispatches from Lisbon. Lord Howard seems to me to have given the Queen bad advice and She to have followed it in making and communicating to the diplomacy a declaration that in accepting the Constitution she was *not* a free agent. If she could have resisted doing so, or could have escaped, it might possibly have been wiser and more justifiable to have done so; but if she yielded, though it were in fear of life, she had much better have

36. *Morra* (Port.), imperative of the verb *morrer* (to die).

37. Baltasar de Almeida Pimentel (1771–1876), 1st Barão, Visconde and Conde de Campanhã.

38. José Liberato Freire de Carvalho, *A Carta e os seus vinte e dois annos de idade* (Lisboa: Typographia da Revolução de Septembro, 1848), quoted in *Luctas caseiras de 1834 a 1851*, by João Augusto Marques Gomes (Lisboa: Imprensa Nacional, 1894), 1: 199; 'Ninguem reagiu [...]. Ninguem se atraveu a defender a Carta, que caiu sem ruido nem bulha, como edificio arruinado pelo tempo, que desaba quando menos se espera'. (My translation).

39. José Manuel Inácio da Cunha e Meneses da Gama e Vasconcelos Carneiro de Sousa Portugal e Faro (1788–1849), 4th Conde de Lumiares.

> assumed the appearance of being a free agent and striven to make the best of a bad bargain. She has acted as persons of her Class almost always in a way to satisfy no one of any thing but her weakness and insincerity – Charles I and Lewis XVI, over again to the end of the Chapter.[40]

Maria received the commissioners at the Royal Palace of Necessidades and promised to consider the matter. The ministers advised the queen to accept the commissioners' demands to avoid civil war. On 11 September, irritated with the apparent cowardice of her ministers, Maria dismissed both Cabinet and renounced the Charter and, according to a report from a British officer stationed in the Tagus, was 'compelled by force of arms to sign the Constitution of 1822 under which at this moment Lisbon is Governed'. Chief Commissioner Lumiares was called to form a Cabinet, which included Sá da Bandeira, António Manuel Vieira de Castro and Manuel Passos, one of the Oporto Radicals.[41] Sá da Bandeira had at first refused to serve, telling Maria II that he had always been loyal to the Charter. However, under pressure from several persons, including Prince Ferdinand and the British and Belgian ministers, Howard de Walden and Van der Weyer, Bandeira agreed.

On 24 September, upon receiving further details of the 'revolution' in Portugal, Holland concluded rather precipitately:

> Bad news from Lisbon and Madrid. At the former the Queen seems to have provoked the revolution by misgovernment, favouritism, and intrigue, to have met it without courage or dignity, and finally to have submitted to it with duplicity and insincerity. She lodged with the Diplomats a paper protesting against the act she communicated to them as invalid and extorted from her by force! – and they had the folly not to say more, to accept and conceal it! It is by such practices Ch[arle]s I and Lewis XVI arrived at the Scaffold, and surely a Stern Moralist might say ὡς ἀπόλοιτο καὶ ἄλλος, ὅτις τοιαῦτά γε ῥέζοι.[42] Forced or not, the moment a Sovereign yields, the thing yielded becomes his own and, if he has common sense or common honesty, he will abide by it.[43]

The September Revolution put an end to the *Devorismo* and inaugurated a new period termed *Setembrismo* (1836–42). The rebellion, which has been compared to the *juste milieu* of the Orleanist monarchy due to the fraternization of the National Guard with the people, was a replica of the Spanish uprising of La Granja of 12 August 1836, which forced the regent María Cristina to re-establish the Cadiz Constitution of 1812. In early October Sarmento confessed to Holland his 'disgust with the late revolution and appalled at the consequences'.[44] When listening to Sarmento's version and interpretation

40. Holland, *The Holland House Diaries*, 350–51 (20 September [1836]).
41. BL, HHP, MSS Add. 51634, Papers Relative to Portugal: 1831–45 (18 September 1836).
42. Homer, *Odyssey*. 2nd edn (Oxford: Clarendon Press, 1886), 1.1.47: 6; 'So perish likewise all who work such deeds'. Passage quoted by Scipio Africanus on the death of Tiberius Gracchus.
43. Holland, *The Holland House Diaries*, 351 (24–27 September [1836]).
44. Ibid., 352 (October 1836).

of the facts, Holland could not be persuaded that the queen had been wiser than he had supposed:

> He [Sarmento] wishes to resign, seems to think all true Pedroites will do the same, attributes the discontent and revolution more to secret societies and desorganizing principles propagated throughout France, Spain, and Portugal, and less to the mismanagement and corruption of the Queen's government than I believe the real truth would exhibit.[45]

As time passed, however, Holland became more apprehensive about the situation in Portugal and more sympathetic to Maria:

> Whatever might be the defects or offences of the Queen's government, and I suspect there were both in it, the Method of repressing it was as bad as possible, and the persons who conducted the Revolution, to all appearance men of no honesty, no honour, no sense, and little popularity.[46]

Unlike earlier rebellions in the nineteenth century – which had been essentially elitist, the September Revolution had a more popular character and enjoyed strong support from the middle and lower classes. In a way, the rebellion of 1836 was a result of the reforms of 1832–34, in that it revealed the presence of a growing 'middle class' with its own political values and agenda. Traces of democracy and republicanism are also recognisable in this movement as well as in the speeches and intentions of the leading *Setembristas*. As Howard de Walden observed in a report to Palmerston, 'What I fear now is the savage joy of the Red Republicans and the language of their press'.[47] Holland's comments about the opinions about the whole affair reveals his defence of 'liberties' and 'revolutions' had limits.

An extraordinary *Cortes* was summoned on 8 October to draw up a brand new Constitution, the *Constituição política da Monarquia Portuguesa*, which the queen swore to abide by on 4 April 1838 and which lasted until February 1842 – when a rightist coup led by Costa Cabral restored the Constitutional Charter. The Constitution of 1838 reflected aspects of the progressive Constitution of 1822, the Charter and the Belgian and Spanish Constitutions of 1831 and 1837. But despite the apparently more progressive character of *Setembrismo*, the new arrangement was less favourable to the lower classes than the Constitution of 1822 had been and strengthened the position of the bourgeoisie. As Oliveira Marques observed, the Constitution of 1838 'tended to emphasise order and to lapse into authoritarianism'.[48]

The September Revolution provoked great anxiety in Britain, with the Princess Victoria describing it as 'horrid transactions',[49] while Eugène Goblet d'Alviella, the

45. Ibid.
46. Ibid., 352 (1–20 October 1836).
47. Howard de Walden, in *The Foreign Policy of Palmerston*, 1: 485 (4, 7 November 1836).
48. A. H. de Oliveira Marques, *History of Portugal*. 2 vols (London: Columbia University Press, 1972), 2: 66.
49. Queen Victoria, Journal, in *The Girlhood of Queen Victoria: a Selection of Her Majesty's Diaries between the Years 1832 and 1840*. 2 vols (London: John Murray, 1912), 1: 166.

Belgian minister at London, wrote to his colleague in Lisbon that the events in Portugal were 'a plague' which 'exceeded His [Britannic] Majesty's expectations'.[50] Howard de Walden was at Sintra on the morning of 10 September, when he received letters from both Van der Weyer and Vila Real informing him of what had happened in Lisbon. Walden was probably staying with Palmela, whose memoirs explain that he was at Sintra at the time and remained there despite the disturbances in the capital. Walden hastened to Lisbon, accompanied by Count Reventhow, the Danish Chargé d'Affaires.[51] As Webster observed, while the *Devoristas* or *Cartistas* (Chartists) were generally sympathetic to England, especially while Palmela was their main figure, the left-wing *Setembristas* 'were, for a time, at any rate pro-French. Under their principal leaders, Sá da Bandeira, Manuel Passos and Vieira de Castro, they made themselves objectionable as possible to Britain'.[52] Yet, although Webster bracketed Sá da Bandeira with Passos and Castro, as noted earlier, it was pressure from Ferdinand and from the Belgian and British ambassadors that induced Sá da Bandeira to join the Cabinet. In other words, Sá da Bandeira was placed in the government as a pro-British element to counterbalance the increasing French influence.

Under these circumstances, it is hardly surprising that the English party, including Palmela, did not make any attempt to regain their former influence. In his own words, the repudiation of the Charter had been an unexpected consequence of a rising whose real objective had been to remove an incompetent Cabinet. The Portuguese had never wanted the Constitution of 1822 back and were even suspicious about the agenda of the new ministers, who seemed inclined to democracy. As Holland observed in his diary,

> it is clear that the Country does not approve of the late transactions and there is reason to apprehend that they will pave the way for a Miguelite insurrection in the Algarves, which the Anarchists or lovers of confusion are said to [prefer] to the Constitutional system established by Pedro.[53]

A counter-revolutionary movement was set up by Terceira and Saldanha on 2 November 1836, with connivance of the queen and the English and Belgian ministers. Movements of the British fleet were observed in the Tagus, which seemed to presage an imminent landing of troops. A few days earlier, Howard de Walden had warned Sá da Bandeira that, if the queen were in any danger, British troops would be landed at once. As the situation became critical, Manuel Passos hastened to the Royal Palace to meet the queen. While Passos assured Maria that there was no intention to move against the monarchy, he also warned Maria that if she sought refuge on an English vessel – as

50. Eugène Goblet d'Alviella to M. Van der Weyer, in *L'établissement des Cobourg en Portugal*, 71–72 (London: 19 September 1836); 'mais la grandeur de la plaie a dépassé toutes les prévisions de Sa Majésté'. (My translation).
51. BL, HHP, MSS Add. 51634, Papers Relative to Portugal: 1831–45: Narrative of Occurrences at Lisbon between the 10th of September and 5th of November, 1836; Drawn up from Lord Howard de Walden's Despatches, No. 204 (10 September 1836).
52. Webster, *The Foreign Policy of Palmerston*, 1: 485.
53. Holland, *The Holland House Diaries*, 352 (October 1836).

her late grandfather had done in 1824 – this would be considered an act of abdication. Passos concluded his speech by putting his office at Maria's disposal, which she neither accepted nor refused. While crossing the corridors of the palace, the minister met Terceira and told him: 'We are on the eve of the civil war; tomorrow Your Excellency will command the Queen's troops; and I those of the Republic'.[54] A few years later, on 18 October 1844, Passos admitted in the Parliament that he had used the word 'republic' but only metaphorically.

On 3 November, with the National Guard assembling at Campo de Ourique, the royal family moved from the Palace of Necessidades to Belém, where they would be under the protection of British guns. This earned the plot the name of *Belenzada*. The queen then summoned her ministers to dismiss them and, if necessary, to arrest them. Vieira de Castro, who anticipated the plot, ordered Sá da Bandeira to organize a popular resistance, while he went to Belém to meet the queen. At his arrival, Maria immediately confirmed the dismissal of all members of the Cabinet and the appointment of a new ministry headed by the Marquês de Valença. This administration was known as 'Gabinete dos Finados' (Cabinet of the Dead) owing to its short life. On the morning of 4 November, one of the alleged plotters, the former minister Agostinho Freire was murdered by the mob on his way to Belém. Manuel Passos, now at the head of the National Guard in Campo de Ourique, was called to the royal palace. There he found Maria and Ferdinand accompanied by Palmela, Saldanha, Francisco Trigoso, Walden and Weyer.[55] Passos and his followers, later known as the 'Belém Commissioners', presented the queen with a number of demands and, after a difficult negotiation, an agreement was eventually reached, consisting of a compromise between the Constitution of 1822 and the Constitutional Charter. During the discussions, when Ferdinand commented that Passos and his followers had refused to obey their queen, he replied: 'Because Her Majesty orders what she cannot – and what she should not!'[56] According to Webster, in a conversation with Palmerston, Palmela admitted:

> he always believed that the left wing parties would acquire a sense of responsibility with power. Much as he regretted that the 'Chartists' could not prevail, he advised the Queen to work with their rivals and Howard de Walden to keep in touch with them and try to get them to cooperate with their opponents. This policy he constantly urged throughout the troublous year 1837. Sometimes he thought that the best policy was just to wait.[57]

54. Passos Manuel, Speech to the Chamber of Deputies on 18 October 1844, in *Diario da Camara dos Senhores Deputados da Nacao Portugueza* (Lisboa: Na Impressão Regia, 1827–10), 196; 'Estamos em vespera da guerra civil; amanhã V. Ex.ª vae commandar os exercitos da rainha; e eu – os da Republica'. (My translation).
55. Francisco Manuel Trigoso de Aragão Morato (1777–1838), better known as Francisco Trigoso, Portugal Liberal politician and statesman, son of Francisco Mendo Trigoso Pereira Homem de Magalhães and Antónia Joaquina Teresa de Sousa Morato.
56. Martins, *Portugal contemporaneo*, 2: 82; 'Porque S. M. manda o que não póde – e o que não deve!' (My translation).
57. Webster, *The Foreign Policy of Palmerston*, 1: 487.

While Sá da Bandeira was appointed president of the Council of Ministers (chief minister) in a Cabinet including Passos and Vieira de Castro, Palmela was again forced to leave for England and later moved to France, where he remained until early 1839.[58] Palmela and several leading Chartists, including Silva Carvalho, Joaquim de Aguiar and Rendufe, were later accused of the crime of *lesa patria*. Among the prosecution witnesses, there was Almeida Garrett, Palmela's former protégé. The formal accusation was entered by José Calazans da Fonseca e Castro, sub-delegate of the royal procurator, but the case was dismissed.[59] Palmela, who should have learned from the *Belfastada* episode that 'revolutions' cannot be successfully effectuated in a rush and before the right time, was forced into exile once more and removed from political circles for many years. He was again chief minister for two days from 7 to 9 February 1842, in the so-called 'Governo do Entrudo' (Carnival Cabinet), and from 20 May to 6 October 1846, when he also held the Ministry of Home Affairs.[60] Fearing for his life after the *Belenzada*, Palmela and his son Domingos had sought refuge aboard the *Malabar*, an English ship anchored in the Tagus. He was accompanied by Silva Carvalho, Vila Real and many other Chartists. While still at the Tagus, Palmela and his son, Vila Real and Rendufe transferred to *The Liverpool*, which sailed for England on 15 November to arrive off Falmouth on 21. Silva Carvalho went aboard the steamer *Iberia*, sailing on 10 November to land in Falmouth on 15.

Although historians like Oliveira Martins claimed that Walden and Weyer –especially Weyer – were heavily implicated in the plot,[61] Webster argued: 'The British Ambassador had no responsibility for the attempted counter-revolution though he certainly knew all about it'.[62] Obviously the same can be said about Palmela, as his escape aboard an English vessel seems to suggest. As Webster also noted, sometime before the plot, Napier offered to go to Portugal and repeat the feat of 1832. His plan was to take the queen to his own ship and reduce the rebels, while declaring: 'All that would be necessary was to take the tompions out of the guns and that the people would all run away or give in'.[63] Palmerston, well acquainted with Napier's capacities, was for a moment, tempted to agree.

Palmela and his friends lodged at the Coburg Hotel, Charles St, Grosvenor Sq. Vila Real and Rendufe checked out on 17 December and left for Paris, while Palmela and his son remained in Britain a little longer before also leaving for France. As soon as Palmela arrived in London, he tried to persuade Palmerston to intervene 'in our affairs and settle them, for without your interference they never will be settled'. But Palmerston refused,

58. Sá da Bandeira remained in the Cabinet until 18 April 1839, when he was superseded by Rodrigo Pinto Pizarro, Barão da Ribeira de Sabrosa.
59. Victor de Sá, *A Revolução de Setembro de 1836* (Lisboa: Livros Horizonte, 1969), 140; Gomes, *Luctas caseiras*, 1: 266–67; Carvalho, *Vida do Duque de Palmella*, 3: 137.
60. PALM, MSS Cx. 203 (MIC. 5792), Nota pela ordem chronologica dos títulos e condecorações concedidas a Sua Ex.ª o Duque de Palmela, D. Pedro, e bem das diferentes Comissões de que foi encarregado, f. 79.
61. Martins, *Portugal contemporaneo*, 2: 74.
62. Webster, *The Foreign Policy of Palmerston*, 1: 485.
63. Napier quoted in a despatch from Palmerston to Howard de Walden, in *The Foreign Policy of Palmerston*, 1: 487 (15 October 1836).

declaring 'you may depend upon it, we shall not interfere'.[64] In a letter to his wife, Palmela complained of Napier, who came especially from Portsmouth to see him. He 'Tormented me with questions, with rubbish, with grog and cigarettes, but what is worse is that he made me promise, either by force or by will, to see him in Portsmouth, where I will have another two days of tedium'.[65] It is possible that the two old friends may have discussed some wild plan to reduce the rebels, but if they did, it was never put into action.

While in London, Palmela could not miss the opportunity to visit his old acquaintances and friends, including Colonel Hare, Admiral Parker, Polignac, Esterhazy and, especially, Lord and Lady Holland. Palmela and his son dined several times at Kensington, on 27 November,[66] 4 December[67] and on Christmas, when they also spent the night.[68] On 31 December, Palmela wrote to his wife, 'We spent a very pleasant day and a night at Holland House. Lady Holland asked me to send her *manjar branco*'.[69] Lady Holland had first tried this typical Portuguese dessert made with chicken in Coimbra on 27 December 1808. Unfortunately, Lord Holland's journal was interrupted between 20 October 1836 and 26 March 1837, thus omitting the *Belenzada* episode and Palmela's last exile in Britain.[70] In fact, Holland's last reference to Palmela in his diary dates back to 1 December 1835, when alluding to his appointment to the Cabinet headed by Saldanha.[71]

On 14 March, *The Times* announced that 'The Duke of Palmella, accompanied by his two sons, the Marquis de Fayal and Don Rodrigo de Sousa, are making a tour in the manufacturing districts'.[72] According to correspondence with his wife, Palmela had been busy from February 1837 finding a place at Hinckley College for Rodrigo. As he had left Lisbon with only one child, the eldest surviving son Domingos, it is possible that one of the younger children, Rodrigo, later came to England for his education. Unfortunately, Rodrigo died in 1844, aged 14, from tuberculosis, the same disease that had killed his brothers Alexandre, in 1832, and Manuel, who died on 3 February 1837, aged 17, while his father was in Britain. Palmela remained in England until the end of March, when he left for Paris to await the arrival of his wife and children from Portugal. Palmela remained in France for more than one year, until his old friend Sá da Bandeira, then still the chief and foreign minister, suggested that he should represent Portugal at Queen

64. Palmerston to Howard de Walden, in *The Foreign Policy of Palmerston*, 1: 487.
65. Palmela to His Wife, in *Vida do Duque de Palmella*, 3: 138 [December 1836]; 'Atormentou-me com perguntas, com porcarias, com *grogs* e cigarros, e o pior é que me fez prometter por força ou pro vontade de o ir vêr a Portsmouth, onde vou têr outros dois dias de sécca'. (My translation).
66. BL, HHP, MSS Add. 51955, Dinner Books: 1831–38, f. 140r (27 November 1836).
67. Ibid., f. 140v (4 December 1836).
68. Ibid., f. 142r (25 December 1836).
69. Palmela to His Wife, in *Vida do Duque de Palmella*, 3, 141 (31 December 1836); 'Passámos um dia e uma noite em Holland House muito agradavelmente. Lady Holland pediu-me que lhe mandasse vir *manjar branco*'. (My translation).
70. Holland, *The Holland House Diaries*, 354.
71. Ibid., 336 (1 December 1835).
72. *The Times*, 21 April 1837, 4.

Victoria's Coronation. Palmela accepted the honour and refused to be paid for his work. The credentials as Envoy Extraordinary were issued on 26 May 1838.

Palmela arrived in London towards the end of June 1838 and on 1 July made his last appearance at Holland House, where he dined in the company of Prince von Putbus,[73] the Prussian ambassador, and the Baron de Bulon.[74] On 26 June, Lady Holland, clearly excited, announced to her son: 'On Sunday we shall have the Palmellas & Brignollés'.[75] Lady Holland, apparently indifferent to her husband's reservations about Palmela's later political conduct, had never lost her affection for her Portuguese friend. In a letter to her son written many years earlier, when Palmela was taking part in Napier's expedition to the Algarve, she admitted she was: 'very much founded upon poor Palmella's safety & prospect of well doing; as, poor fellow, these last two years my heart has ached at the sight of his deep grief & despair'.[76] In fact, one of Palmela's greatest achievements – apart from his political and diplomatic feats – was his capacity to conquer Lady Holland's heart, a conquest few other men on earth could boast of.

While in England, Palmela was received with the deference due to an ambassador. On 22 July, Palmela invited his friends to a grand dinner at his residence, attended by a large party including Lord Holland, Lord and Lady Jersey, Lord and Lady Stuart de Rothesay, Count Flahaut and Lady Keith, Lord Seaforth, Lord John Russell, the Barão de Torre de Moncorvo and several other members of the Portuguese Embassy. Lord Broughton, one of the guests, later recounted an amusing conversation he had held with Lord Stuart de Rothesay, the famous bearer of Pedro's Constitutional Charter to Europe in 1826. Stuart de Rothesay criticized all ambassadors except Soult and Palmela, but the latter joined the conversation 'for his share of criticism'.[77] In fact, this dinner seems more like a gathering of old friends meeting for last time to recall the days gone by than an ordinary social occasion.

On 30 July, Palmela took his leave of several members of the Cabinet. On 4 August, the Palmelas left England for France, arriving in Paris the next day.[78] They returned briefly to England to take the steamer *Iberia* from Portsmouth to Lisbon, arriving on 23 February 1839. Palmela visited London at least once in May and June 1847, but did not call at Holland House. Of course, by then, Lord Holland was already gone, and with his death on 22 October 1840, to quote Greville, 'the curtain suddenly fall upon a scene so brilliant and apparently prosperous, and the light which for nearly half a century has adorned and cheered the world, thus suddenly and for ever extinguished'.[79] As

73. Wilhelm Malte I (1783–1854), Prince of Putbus, was a German prince from the old Slavic Rügen noble family.
74. BL. HHP, MSS Add. 51955, Dinner Books: 1831–38, f. 185r (Sunday, 1 July 1838).
75. *Lady Holland to Her Son*, 168 (26 June [1838]). Brignollés, the Sardinian Envoy-Extraordinary.
76. Ibid., 142 (16 July 1833).
77. John Cam Hobhouse, Lord Broughton, *Recollections of a Long Life*. 6 vols (London: John Murray, 1910–11), 5: 156.
78. *The Times*, 9 August 1838, 4.
79. Charles Greville, *Memoirs (Second Part): A Journal of the Reign of Queen Victoria from 1837 to 1852*. 3 vols (London: Longmans, Green, 1885), 1: 341 (23 October 1840).

earlier noted, Henry Edward Fox, fourth Lord Holland, never showed any particular interest in Portugal or the Portuguese, though he had taken first steps at Lisbon in 1805. Holland's death marked more than the end of a brilliant period in the social, intellectual and political life of England; it also marked the conclusion of the remarkable relationship between Holland House and Portugal.

REFERENCES

Manuscripts

1. Arquivo Nacional-Torre do Tombo (ANTT) [National Archives, Portugal]
   - Auto da exumação dos restos mortais D. Pedro IV [Act of exhumation of Pedro's remains: [copy] (September 1972) (Gav. 16, Mç. 4, n. 1326).
   - *Conselho de Estado* [Council of Estate]: 1821–1910: Actas do Conselho de Estado, Acta No. 1 (1821–44).
   - Ministério dos Negócios Estrangeiros (MNE) [Foreign Ministry]: Arquivo da Legação Portuguesa em Londres: Emigração [Archive of the Portuguese Legation in London: Emigration]:
     Cx. 161, Mç. 33: *Ordens do Dia* [Daily Orders], Plymouth Depot (1828–29).
     Cx. 161, Mç. 34: Correspondence from the Exiles to the Portuguese Legation in London; Despatches from the Commanders of the Plymouth Depot; Lists of Troops and Refugees (1828–34).
2. British Library, Department of Manuscripts: Holland House Papers (BL, HHP)
   - Add. 51618: Papers Relative to Spain: G. M. Jovellanos: 1808–9.
   - Add. 51632–51634: Papers Relative to Portugal: 1801–45.
   - Add. 51737–51738: Lord Holland with Caroline Fox: 1804–8.
   - Add. 51860–51862: Lord Holland's Travel Journals: 1802–9.
   - Add. 51933–51937: Lady Holland's Journals: 1806–9.
   - Add. 51950–51955: Dinner Books: 1799–1838.
   - Add. 52199: John Allen's Account Books & Journal Spain-Portugal.
   - Add. 52200: John Allen's Journal of a Tour to Spain in 1808–9.
3. Casa Palmela (PALM): [Papers Relative to Dom Pedro de Sousa Holstein, 1st Conde, Marquês and Duque de Palmela] (Cxs. 169, 203). NB: Accessed at the National Archives Torre do Tombo.

Primary Printed Sources

Alcala-Galiano, Antonio. *An Introductory Lecture Delivered in the University of London, on Saturday, November 15, 1828*. 2nd edn. London: Printed for John Taylor, 1829.

Alighieri, Dante. *Della commedia di Dante Alighieri: transportata in verso latino Eroico da Carlo d'Aquino.* 3 vols. Napoli: per Felice Mosca, 1728.

Allen, John. *Suggestions on the Cortes*. London: [Printed for the author by] E. Blackader, 1809.

Anonymous. *A Brief Exposition of the Foreign Policy of Mr. Canning: As Contrasted with that of the Existing Administration*. London: J. Hatchard, 1830.

———. *The Duke of Wellington and the Whigs*. London: J. Hatchard, 1830.

———. Descripsam das trez cidades unidas [Poem]: Plymouth, Ston Hause, e Devenport. Mostra-se a sua grandeza, Industria, Religião, Commercio, Policia, e Costumes, &c. Angra: Impressam do Governo, 1829.

Arbuthnot, Harriet (Fane). *The Journals of Mrs. Arbuthnot, 1820–1832*. 2 vols. London: Macmillan, 1950.

Assento dos Três Estados do Reino juntos em cortes na cidade de Lisboa, feito a onze de Julho de mil oitocentos e vinte e oito. Lisboa: Na Impressão Regia, 1828.

British and Foreign State Papers. 170 vols. London: James Ridgway, 1812–1968.

Brougham, Henry. *The Life and Times of Henry Brougham Written by Himself*. 2nd edn. 3 vols. Edinburgh; London: William Blackwood, 1871.

———. *The Result of the General Election: or, What Has the Duke of Wellington Gained by the Dissolution?* 4th edn. London: James Ridgway, 1830.

Broughton, John Cam Hobhouse, Baron. *Recollections of a Long Life*. 6 vols. London: John Murray, 1910–11.

Carpenter, William. *Political Letters and Pamphlets*... London: William Carpenter, 1830–31.

Carvalho, José Liberato Freire de. *Memorias com o titulo de annaes, para a historia do tempo que durou a usurpação de D. Miguel*. 4 vols. Lisboa: Na Imprensa Nevesiana, 1841.

———. *Memorias da Vida de José Liberato Freire de Carvalho*. Lisboa: Typografia de José Baptista Morando, 1855.

Carvalhosa, Manuel Francisco de Barros e Sousa de Mesquita de Macedo Leitão e, 2nd Viscount of Santarém. *Correspondência do 2.° Visconde de Santarém*. 8 vols. Lisboa: Alfredo Lamas, Motta & C.ª L.da, 1918–1919.

Cervantes, Miguel de. *The History and Adventures of the Renowned Don Quixote*, translated by T. Smollett. 2 vols. London: A. Millar, 1755.

Collecção dos tratados, convenções, contratos e actos publicos celebrados entre a Corôa de Portugal e as mais potencias desde 1640 até ao presente, edited by José Ferreira Borges de Castro. 8 vols. Lisboa: Imprensa Nacional, 1856–58.

Constitucion política de la Monarquia Española: Promulgada en Cádiz á 19 de Marzo de 1812. Cadiz: en la Imprenta Real, dicho año [1812].

Corneille, Pierre. *Oeuvres de P. Corneille*. Nouvelle ed. Paris: L. Hachette, 1862.

Crespo, José Maria Blanco y (after Joseph Blanco White). *The Life of the Rev. Joseph Blanco White: Written by Himself; with Portions of His Correspondence*, edited by John Hamilton Thom. London: John Chapman, 1845.

Crocker, John Wilson. *The Croker Papers: the Correspondence and Diaries of the Late Right Honourable John Wilson Croker, LL.D, F.R.S., Secretary to the Admiralty from 1809 to 1830*, edited by Louis J. Jennings. 3 vols. London: John Murray, 1884.

Dalrymple, Hew. 'Proclamação do General Dalrymple aos Portuguezes (Praias, 11 Sept. 1808)'. In *Supplemento á collecção dos tratados, convenções, contratos e actos publicos celebrados entre a Corôa de Portugal e as mais potencias desde 1640 até ao presente*, 16: [105]–07. Lisboa: Imprensa Nacional, 1872–80.

Daun, João Carlos Gregório Domingos Vicente Francisco de Saldanha Oliveira e, 1st Duke of Saldanha. *Observations of Count de Saldanha to a Letter which the Members of the Oporto Junta Addressed to His Imperial Majesty the Emperor of Brazil... Translated from the Portuguese*. London: A. Redford and W. Robins, 1830.

———. *A perfidia desmascarada: ou a carta da Junta do Porto a sua Magestade o Imperador do Brazil... pelo Conde de Saldanha e por outro emigrado*. Paris: [n. pub.], 1830.

Daun, João Carlos Gregório Domingos Vicente Francisco de Saldanha Oliveira e, 1st Duke of Saldanha, and Athelstane, John Smith, 1st Count of Carnota. *Memoirs of Field-Marshal The Duke de Saldanha with Selections from His Correspondence*. 2 vols. London: John Murray, 1880.

———. *Memórias do Duque de Palmela*. Lisboa: Dom Quixote, 2010.

Debates no Parlamento Britanico sôbre os negocios de Portugal, em sessão do 1.° de Junho na Camara dos Communs, e de 19 do mesmo mez na Camara dos Pares. Com a historia e annalyse d'esta discussão e das circumstancias que a motivaram [translated by Almeida Garrett]. London: Impresso por R. Greenlaw, 1829.

Dino, Dorothée. *Memoirs of the Duchesse de Dino: (afterwards Duchesse de Talleyrand et de Sagan), 1831–1835*. London: W. Heinemann, 1909.

Documentos para a historia das Cortes Geraes da Nação Portugueza. 8 vols. Lisboa: Imprensa Nacional, 1883–1891.

Figueiredo, Bernardo de Sá Nogueira de, 1st Marquis of Sá da Bandeira. *Diário da Guerra Civil (1826–1832)*. 2 vols. Lisboa: Seara Nova, 1975.

Fox, Charles James. *Memorials and Correspondence of Charles James Fox*. 4 vols London: Richard Bentley, 1853–57.

Francis, Philip. *A Letter Missive from Sir Philip Francis, K. B. to Lord Holland*. London: Printed for Ridgways, 1816.

Garrett, João Baptista de Almeida. 'Parte politica: introdução, ou razão d'ordem da chronica da primeira semana'. *O chronista: semanario de politica, litteratura, sciências e artes* 1 (March 1827): [1].

Gower, Henrietta Elizabeth Leveson, Countess Granville. *Letters of Harriet Countess Granville 1810–1845*. 2 vols. London: Longmans, Green, 1894.

Gower, Lord Granville Leveson, 1st Earl Granville. *Lord Granville Leveson Gower (First Earl Granville): Private Correspondence 1781–1821*. 2 vols. London: John Murray, 1916.

Greville, Charles Cavendish Fulke. *The Greville Memoirs (Second Part): A Journal of the Reign of Queen Victoria from 1837 to 1852* [edited by Henry Reeves]. 3 vols. London: Longmans, Green, 1885.

———. *The Greville Memoirs: A Journal of the Reigns of King George IV and King William IV*, edited by Henry Reeves… 3 vols. London: Longmans, Green, 1874.

Hegel, Georg Friedrich. *Philosophy of History*. Revised edn. New York: The Colonial Press, 1899.

Herbert, Henry George, 2nd Earl of Carnarvon, Lord Porchester. *The Last Days of the Portuguese Constitution*. London: Henry Colburn and Richard Bentley, 1830.

Hodges, George Lloyd. *Narrative of the Expedition to Portugal in 1832: under the Orders of His Imperial Majesty, Dom Pedro, Duke of Braganza*. 2 vols. London: James Fraser, 1833.

Holstein, Pedro de Sousa e, 1st Duke of Palmela. *Despachos e Correspondencia do Duque de Palmella*. 4 vols. Lisboa: Imprensa Nacional, 1851.

Homer. *Odyssey*. 2nd edn. Oxford: At the Clarendon Press, 1886.

Hope, John. 'Proclamação do Tenente General Hope, e Commandante das tropas Britanicas, para a immediata segurança de Lisboa'. *Gazeta de Lisboa*, 16 Setembro 1808, [3].

Jung, Carl Gustav. *Memories, Dreams, Reflections*. New York, Vintage Books, 1965.

Junot, Jean-Andoche. 'Habitantes de Portugal'. *Gazeta de Lisboa*, 5 Fevereiro 1808, [1].

Knight, Henry Gally. *A Letter Addressed to the Earl of Aberdeen, Secretary of State for Foreign Affairs*. 2nd edn. London: James Ridgway, 1829.

Lafayette, Marquis de. *Mémoires, correspondance et manuscrits du général Lafayette*. 6 vols. Bruxelles: Société Belge de Librairie, 1837–38.

Lamb, Frederick James, 3rd Viscount Melbourne. *Observations on the Papers Lately Submitted to Parliament upon the Subject of the Affairs of Portugal*. London: Edward Bull, 1830.

Lambton, John George, 1st Earl of Durham. *Life and Letters of the First Earl of Durham*, edited by Stuart J. Reid. 2 vols. London: Longmans, Green, 1906.

Law, Edward, Earl of Ellenborough. *A Political Diary 1828–1830*. 2 vols. London: Richard Bentley, 1881.

Lieven, Dorothea Christorovna Benckendorff, Princess Lieven, and Grey, Charles, 2nd Earl Grey. *Correspondence of Princess Lieven and Earl Grey*. 3 vols. London: Richard Bentley, 1890.

Lima, Luís António de Abreu e, Conde da Carreira. *Correspondencia official de Luiz António de Abreu e Lima, actualmente Conde da Carreira com o Duque de Palmella: regencia da Terceira e governo do Porto de 1828 a 1835*. Lisboa: Imprensa Nacional, 1871.

Lobo, Francisco Alexandre. *Rezumida noticia da vida de D. Nuno Caetano Alvares Pereira de Mello, sexto Duque de Cadaval*. Paris: Na Typographia de Casimir, 1837.

Lothar, Klemens Wenzel, Fürst von Metternich. *Memoirs of Prince Metternich*. 4 vols. London: Richard Bentley, 1880–81.

Mackintosh, James. *Indicação e discurso do muito honrado Sir James Mackintosh na camara dos communs na sessão de segunda-feira, 1 de Junho de 1829, sobre negocios de Portugal* [translated by Almeida Garrett]. London: R. Greenlaw, 1829.

———. *Memoirs of the Life of the Right Honourable Sir James Mackintosh*. 2 vols. London: Edward Moxon, 1835.

Magalhães, Félix. *Apontamentos para a historia diplomatica de Portugal: desde 1826 em que falleceu o Imperador e Rei D. João VI até 1834 em que se completou a restauração da Coroa da Rainha D. Maria II usurpada em 1828 por seu tio o Infante D. Miguel.* Lisboa: Imprensa de J. G. de Sousa Neves, 1871.

Maia, Joaquim José da Silva. *Memorias historicas, politicas e filosoficas da Revolução do Porto em Maio de 1828, e dos emigrados portuguezes pela Hespanha, Inglaterra, França e Belgica.* Rio de Janeiro: Typographia de Laemmert, 1841.

Marx, Karl. 'Revolutionary Spain'. In *Collected works*, 13: 389–446. Moscow: Progress Publishers, 1975–2004. Originally published in *The New York Daily Tribune*, 9 September–2 December 1854.

Meneses, Antonio Teles da Silva Caminha e, 1st Marquis of Resende. *Éclaircissements historiques sur mes négociations relatives aux affaires du Portugal, depuis le mort du roi Don Jean VI. jusqu'à mon arrivée en France comme ministre près de cette cour.* Paris: Éverat, 1832.

———. *Elogio historico do Senhor Rei D. Pedro IV: recitado na Academia Real das Sciencias de Lisboa em sessão ordinaria de 13 de Julho de 1836.* Lisboa: Typographia da Academia, 1867.

Morgan, Sydney. *France in 1829–30.* 2 vols. London: Saunders and Otley, 1830.

Napier, Charles. *An Account of the War in Portugal between Don Pedro and Don Miguel.* 2 vols. London: T. & W. Boone, 1836.

Owen, Hugh. *The Civil War in Portugal and the Siege of Oporto.* London: Edward Moxon, 1836.

Papers Respecting the Relations between Great Britain and Portugal. London: J. Harrison, 1829.

Pecchio, Giuseppe. *Anecdotes of the Spanish and Portuguese Revolutions.* London: G. and W. B. Whittaker, 1823.

Queipo de Llano Ruiz de Saravia, Jose Maria, 7th Count of Toreno. *Historia del Levantamiento, Guerra y Revolucion de España.* 5 vols. Madrid: Imprenta de Don Tomas de Jordán, 1835–37.

Raikes, Thomas. *A Portion of the Journal Kept by Thomas Raikes, Esq., from 1831 to 1847…* 4 vols. London: Longman, Brown, Green and Longmans, 1856–57.

Reports, Transmitted to the Portuguese Government, of the Proceedings of the Commission, Appointed to Conduct the Arrangements for the Expeditions to Portugal in Favour of Her Most Faithful Majesty Donna Maria, in the Years 1831, 1832, and 1833… London: Whittaker and Co., 1835.

Russell, John, 1st Earl Russell. *A Letter to Lord Holland on Foreign Politics.* London: James Ridgway. 1819.

———. Preface to *Memorials and Correspondence of Charles James Fox*, 1: viii–ix. London: Richard Bentley, 1853–57.

Silveira, Jose Xavier Mouzinho da. *Obras de Mouzinho da Silveira.* 2 vols. Lisboa: Fundação Calouste Gulbenkian, 1989.

Soriano, Simão José da Luz. *Historia da Guerra Civil e do estabelecimento do governo parlamentar em Portugal comprehendendo a historia diplomatica militar e política d'este reino desde 1777 até 1834.* 19 vols. Lisboa: Imprensa Nacional, 1866–90.

———. *Revelações da minha vida e memorias de alguns factos e homens meus contemporaneos.* Lisboa: Typographia Universal, 1860.

Supplemento á collecção dos tratados, convenções, contratos e actos publicos celebrados entre a Corôa de Portugal e as mais potencias desde 1640 até ao presente, edited by José Ferreira Borges de Castro. 22 vols. Lisboa: Imprensa Nacional, 1872–80.

Talleyrand, Charles-Maurice de, Prince of Talleyrand-Périgord. *Memoirs of the Prince de Talleyrand*, edited by The Duc de Broglie. 5 vols. London: Griffith Farran Okeden and Welsh, 1891–92.

Temple, Henry John, 3rd Viscount Palmerston. *Falla do Visconde Palmerston sôbre as relações de Inglaterra com Portugal* [translated by Almeida Garrett]. Londres: R. Greenlaw, 1829.

———. *Speech of Viscount Palmerston in the House of Commons, Wednesday, the Tenth of March, 1830 on Moving for Papers, Respecting the Relations of England with Portugal.* London: James Ridgway, [1830].

———. *The Life of Henry John Temple, Viscount Palmerston: with Selections from his Diaries and Correspondence*, edited by the Right Hon. Sir Henry Lytton Bulwer. 3 vols. London: Richard Bentley, 1870–74.

Varnhagen, Francisco Adolfo de. *História da independência do Brasil.* Rio de Janeiro: Imprensa Nacional, 1917.

Vassall, Elizabeth, 3rd Baroness of Holland. *Lady Holland to Her Son 1821–1845.* London: John Murray, 1946.

———. *The Journal of Elizabeth Lady Holland (1791–1811).* 2 vols. London: Longmans, Green, 1908.

———. *The Spanish Journal of Elizabeth Lady Holland.* London: Longmans, Green, 1910.

Vassall Fox, Henry Richard, 3rd Baron of Holland, 'Carta ou memoria de lord Holland dirigida ao conde do Funchal relativamente á saida da côrte portugueza para o Brazil'. In *Historia da Guerra Civil e do estabelecimento do governo parlamentar em Portugal comprehendendo a historia diplomatica militar e política d'este reino desde 1777 até 1834*, by Simão José da Luz Soriano, 2.ª época, t. V, pt. 1 [9]: 249–56. Lisboa: Imprensa Nacional, 1866–90.

———. 'Dedication to Don Manuel Josef Quintana'. In *Some Account of the Life and Writings of Lope Felix de Vega Carpio.* London: Longman, Hurst, Rees, and Orme, 1806, [v]–vii.

———. *Foreign Reminiscences.* London: Longman, Brown, Green, and Longmans, 1850.

———. *Further Memoirs of the Whig Party 1807–1821: with some miscellaneous reminiscences.* London: John Murray, 1905.

———. *Letter to a Neapolitan from an Englishman, 1815.* London: Thomas Davison, 1818.

———. 'Lord Holland's Portuguese Journal (1805): Extract', edited by José Baptista de Sousa and John Clarke. *Revista de estudos anglo-portugueses* 23 (2014): 260–63.

———. *Memoirs of the Whig Party during My Time.* 2 vols. London: Longman, Brown, Green and Longmans, 1852–54.

———. 'Negotiations for Peace between England and France'. *Annual Register for the Year 1806* 47 (1806): 172–86.

———. *The Holland House Diaries 1831–1840: The Diary of Henry Richard Vassall Fox, Third Lord Holland, with Extracts from the Diary of Dr. John Allen.* London: Routledge & Kegan Paul, 1977.

———. *The Opinions of Lord Holland, as Recorded in the Journals of the House of Lords, from 1797 to 1841.* London: J. Ridgway, 1841.

Vassall Fox, Henry Richard, 3rd Baron of Holland, and de Jovellanos, Gaspar Melchor. *Cartas de Jovellanos y Lord Vassall Holland sobre la guerra de la independencia (1801–1811).* 2 vols. Madrid: Imprenta de los Hijos de Gómez Fuentenebro, 1911.

Vassall Fox, Henry Richard, 3rd Baron of Holland, Elizabeth Vassall, 3rd Lady Holland, and Allen, John. *Três diários de viagem em Portugal em 1808–1809*, invest., transcr., trans. and notes by José Baptista de Sousa. Lisboa: Caleidoscópio / CETAPS, 2011.

Victoria, Queen of the United Kingdom of Great Britain and Ireland. *The Girlhood of Queen Victoria: a Selection of Her Majesty's Diaries between the Years 1832 and 1840.* 2 vols. London: John Murray, 1912.

Walton, William. *Dom Pedro's Expedition: or Neutrality in Disguise.* London: Hatchard, J. Richardson, and Booth, 1832.

Wellesley, Arthur, 1st Duke of Wellington. *Despatches, Correspondence, and Memoranda of Field Marshal Arthur Duke of Wellington, K.G.*, edited by his son [A. R. Wellesley] the Duke of Wellington, K.G. 8 vols. London: John Murray, 1867–80.

———. *Supplementary Despatches, Correspondence, and Memoranda of Field Marshal Arthur Duke of Wellington, K.G.* 15 vols. London: John Murray, 1858–72.

Wordsworth, William. *Concerning the Relations of Great Britain, Spain and Portugal to Catch Other and to the Common Enemy, at the Crisis and Specifically as Affected by the Convention of Cintra.* London: Longman, Hurst, Rees, and Orme, 1809.

Newspapers and Serials

Chronica constitucional de Lisboa. N. 1 (25 Julho 1833)–n. 152 (30 Junho 1834). Lisboa: Impressão Regia, 1833–34.

Chronica constitucional do Porto, edited by António Pereira dos Reis. N. 1 (11 Julho 1832)–n. 308 (31 Dezembro 1833). Porto: Na Typographia de Viuva Alvarez Ribeiro & Filhos, 1832–33.

Chronica da Terceira [edited by Simão José da Luz Soriano, et al.]. N. 1 (1830)–n. 44 (1831). Angra: Impressão do Governo, 1830–31.

Chronista (O): semanário de política, litteratura, sciências e artes [edited by Almeida Garrett]. V. 1, n. 1 (Março 1827)–v. 2, n. 24/26 (Agosto 1827). Lisboa: Na Imprensa do Portuguez, 1827.

Diario da Camara dos Senhores Deputados da Nação Portugueza. Lisboa: Na Impressão Regia, 1827–1910.

Diario das Cortes Geraes e Extraordinarias da Nação Portugueza. 10 vols. Lisboa: Imprensa Nacional, 1821–23.

European Magazine and London Review: Containing the Literature, History, Politics, Arts, Manners & Amusements of the Age, by the Philological Society of London. V. 1 (January 1782)–v. 89 (1826). London: J. Sewell, 1782–1826.

Gazeta de Lisboa, edited by José Freyre Monterroyo Mascarenhas. N. 1 (10 Agosto 1715)–n. 173 (24 Julho 1833). Lisboa: Na Regia Officina Typografica, 1715–1833.

Gazeta do Rio de Janeiro. N. 1 (10 Setembro 1808)–n. 157 (31 Dezembro 1822). Rio de Janeiro: Na Impressão Regia, 1808–22.

Journal des débats politiques et littéraires. (1 avril 1814)–a. 156, n. 1410 (19 août 1944). Paris: [n. pub.], 1814–1944.

Mirror of Parliament, edited by John Henry Barrow. V. 1 (1828)–(1843). London: The Proprietors, 1828–43.

New Monthly Magazine and Literary Journal. V. 1, n. 1 (1821)–v. 47, n. 188 (1836). London: Henry Colburn and Co., 1821–36.

Parliamentary Debates: from the Year 1803 to the Present Time. [1st ser.], v. 1 (1803–4)–. Continuation of Cobbett's *The Parliamentary History of England: from the Earliest Period to the Year 1803*, v. 1 (1072–1624)–v. 36 (1801–3).

Portuguez emigrado (O): ou realista constitucional = The Portuguese Emigrant: or Constitutional Royalist [edited by Marcos Pinto Soares Vaz Preto]. N. 1 (7 Outubro 1828). Plymouth: W. W. Arliss, 1828.

Royal Devonport Telegraph & Plymouth Chronicle (The). N.? (1824)–n. 1320 (29 June 1833). Plymouth: 1824–33 (continues *Plymouth and Dock Telegraph and Chronicle or Naval and Commercial Register*; continued as *Devonport Telegraph & Plymouth Chronicle*).

Times. N. 1 (1 January 1785)–. London: James Fleming, 1785–.

Secondary Printed Sources

A Hand-Book for Travellers in Devon & Cornwall. London: John Murray, 1851.

Alonso, Manuel Moreno. 'Principios políticos y razones personales para la reforma del estado en España (1805–1840): (De la correspondencia inédita de M. J. Quintana con Lord Holland)'. *Revista de estudios políticos* 70 (October–December 1990): 289–338.

———. *La forja del liberalismo en España: (Los amigos españoles de Lord Holland 1793–1840).* Madrid: Congreso de los Diputados, 1997.

Alviella, Eugene Goblet d'. *L'établissement des Cobourg en Portugal: études sur les débuts d'une monarchie constitutionnelle.* Paris: Librairie Internationale, 1869.

Amorim, Francisco Gomes de. *Garrett: memorias biographicas.* 3 vols. Lisboa: Imprensa Nacional, 1881–84.

Aristotle. *Politics*, edited by Henry William Carless Davis. Oxford: Clarendon Press, 1916.

Arnould, Joseph. *Memoir of Thomas, First Lord Denman: Formerly Lord Chief Justice of England.* 2 vols. London: Longmans, Green, 1873.

Bright, James Frank. *A History of England.* 9th Impr. 5 vols. London: Longmans, Green, 1900–5.

Carvalho, Maria Amália Vaz de. *Vida do Duque de Palmella D. Pedro de Souza e Holstein.* 3 vols. Lisboa: Imprensa Nacional, 1898–1903.

Clarke, John. *British Diplomacy and Foreign Policy 1782–1865.* London: Unwin Hyman, 1989.

———. Preface to *Três diários de viagem em Portugal em 1808–1809*, 9–16. Lisboa: Caleidoscópio / CETAPS, 2011.

Gomes, João Augusto Marques. *Luctas caseiras de 1834 a 1851.* Lisboa: Imprensa Nacional, 1894.

Hamilton, Cynthia Parks. 'Caroline Fox, 1767–1845: An Aristocratic Woman of Her Time'. PhD diss., University of Iowa, 1995.

Holland Fox-Strangways, Giles Stephen, 6th Earl of Ilchester. *Chronicles of Holland House 1820–1900*. New York: E. P. Dutton, 1938.

Keppel, Sonia. *The Sovereign Lady: a Life of Elizabeth Vassall, Third Lady Holland, with Her Family*. London: Hamish Hamilton, 1974.

Leslie, Shane. *George the Fourth*. London: E. Benn, 1926.

Liechtenstein, Marie. *Holland House*. 2 vols. London: Macmillan and Co., 1874.

Mabell, Countess of Airlie. *Lady Palmerston and Her Times*. 2 vols. London: Hodder and Stoughton, 1822.

Macaulay, Thomas Babington. 'History of the Revolution in England in 1688… by the Late Right Honourable Sir James Mackintosh'. *The Edinburgh Review: or Critical Journal* 124 (July 1835): [261]–322.

———. 'The Late Lord Holland'. *The Edinburgh Review: or Critical Journal* 148 (July 1841): 560–68.

Marques, A. H. de Oliveira. *History of Portugal*. 2 vols. London: Columbia University Press, 1972.

Martins, Joaquim Pedro de Oliveira. *Portugal contemporaneo*. 3rd edn. 2 vols. Lisboa: Livraria de Antonio Maria Pereira, 1895.

Mitchell, Leslie. *Holland House*. London: Duckworth, 1980.

Monteiro, Ofélia Paiva. *A formação de Almeida Garrett: experiência e criação*. 2 vols. Coimbra: Centro de Estudos Românicos, 1972.

Nemésio, Vitorino. *Exilados, 1828–1832: história sentimental e política do liberalismo na emigração*. Lisboa: Livraria Bertrand [n.d.].

Newitt, Malyn, and Robson, Martin. *Lord Beresford and British Intervention in Portugal 1807–1820*. Lisboa: Imprensa de Ciências Sociais, 2004.

Quental, Antero de. *Conferencias democraticas: Causas da decadencia dos povos peninsulares nos ultimos tres seculos. Discurso pronunciado na noite de 27 de Maio, na sala do Casino Lisbonense*. Porto: Na Typographia Commercial, 1871.

Quintana, Manuel José. 'Necrologia: Lord Holland'. *Gaceta de Madrid*, 23 enero 1841, 3–4.

Roebuck, Arthur. *History of the Whig Ministry of 1830, to the Passing of the Reform Bill*. 2 vols. London: J. W. Parker, 1852.

Silva, João Manuel Pereira da. *História da fundação do imperio brazileiro*. 7 vols. Rio de Janeiro: B. L. Garnier, 1864–68.

Sá, Victor de. *A crise do liberalismo e as primeiras manifestações das ideias socialistas em Portugal 1820–1852*. Lisboa: Seara Nova, 1969.

———. *A Revolução de Setembro de 1836*. Lisboa: Livros Horizonte, 1969.

Sousa, José Baptista de. *Almeida Garrett (1799–1854) the Founder of Portuguese Romanticism: A Study in Anglo-Portuguese Cultural Interaction* (Lewiston: Edwin Mellen, 2011).

———. '*Catão* em Plymouth'. *Revista de estudos anglo-portugueses* 10 (2001): 23–41.

Sousa, José Baptista de, and Clarke, John. 'Critics to Enthusiasts: The Hollands Discover Portugal'. *Portuguese Studies* 21 (2005): 70–89.

Southey, Robert. *History of the Peninsular War*. 3 vols. London: John Murray, 1823–32.

Tanguy, Jean-François. 'Les réfugiés portugais dans l'Ouest de 1829 à 1834: l'émigration politique d'une élite'. *Annales de Bretagne et des Pays de l'Ouest* 109: 4 (2002): 59–78.

Temperley, Harold William Vazeille. *Life of Canning*. London: James Finch, 1905.

Valente, Vasco Pulido. *Os «devoristas»: a revolução liberal (1834–1836)*. 2nd edn. Lisboa: Quetzal Editores, 1993.

Vassall Fox, Henry Richard, 3rd Baron of Holland. *Some Account of the Life and Writings of Lope Felix de Vega Carpio*. London: Longman, Hurst, Rees, and Orme, 1806.

Viana, António. *Documentos para a historia contemporanea: José da Silva Carvalho e o seu tempo*. 3 vols. Lisboa: Imprensa Nacional, 1891–94.

Webster, Charles. *The Foreign Policy of Palmerston 1830–1841: Britain, the Liberal Movement and the Eastern Question*. 2 vols. London: G. Bell, 1951.

INDEX

Lightning Source UK Ltd.
Milton Keynes UK
UKHW02n0634090318
319166UK00010B/507/P

9 781783 087563